T0355533

Named in remembrance of

the onetime *Antioch Review* editor

and longtime Bay Area resident,

the Lawrence Grauman, Jr. Fund

supports books that address

a wide range of human rights,

free speech, and social justice issues.

The publisher and the University of California Press Foundation gratefully acknowledge the generous support of the Lawrence Grauman, Jr. Fund.

The publisher and the University of California Press Foundation also gratefully acknowledge the generous support of the Anne G. Lipow Endowment Fund in Social Justice and Human Rights.

The War in Court

The War in Court

INSIDE THE LONG FIGHT AGAINST TORTURE

Lisa Hajjar

UNIVERSITY OF CALIFORNIA PRESS

University of California Press
Oakland, California

© 2022 by Lisa Hajjar

Library of Congress Cataloging-in-Publication Data
First Paperback Printing 2024
Names: Hajjar, Lisa, author.
Title: The war in court : inside the long fight against torture / Lisa Hajjar.
Description: Oakland, California : University of California Press, [2023] |
    Includes bibliographical references and index.
Identifiers: LCCN 2022007220 (print) | LCCN 2022007221 (ebook) |
    ISBN 9780520409675 (pbk) | ISBN 9780520976443 (ebook) Subjects:
LCSH: Guantánamo Bay Detention Camp. | Torture—Government
    policy—United States. | Torture—Law and legislation—United States. |
    Torture—Moral and ethical aspects—United States. | Human rights—
    United States.
Classification: LCC HV8599.U6 H46 2023 (print) | LCC HV8599.U6 (ebook) |
    DDC 364.6/75—dc23/eng/20220613
LC record available at https://lccn.loc.gov/2022007220
LC ebook record available at https://lccn.loc.gov/2022007221

Manufactured in the United States of America

31 30 29 28 27 26 25 24
10 9 8 7 6 5 4 3 2 1

This book is dedicated to the people who stepped up, spoke out, and took action to fight torture, and to my late father, Victor Hajjar, who always hoped that I would write a book without footnotes.

CONTENTS

ILLUSTRATIONS

ABBREVIATIONS

ACLU	American Civil Liberties Union
AEI	American Enterprise Institute
ARB	Administrative Review Board
ATS	Alien Tort Statute
AU	The American University (Washington, DC)
CAT	Convention against Torture and Other Cruel, Inhuman, or Degrading Treatment or Punishment
CCR	Center for Constitutional Rights
CENTCOM	US Central Command
CIA	Central Intelligence Agency
CIDT	cruel, inhuman or degrading treatment
CMCR	Court of Military Commission Review
CSRT	Combatant Status Review Tribunal
DAB	Detainee Assessment Brief
DoD	Department of Defense
DoJ	Department of Justice
DTA	Detainee Treatment Act
ECCHR	European Center for Constitutional and Human Rights
ECHR	European Court of Human Rights
EITs	enhanced interrogation techniques
FBI	Federal Bureau of Investigation
FOIA	Freedom of Information Act

HCJ	High Court of Justice (Israel)
HRF	Human Rights First
HRW	Human Rights Watch
IACHR	Inter-American Commission on Human Rights
ICRC	International Committee of the Red Cross
IEDs	improvised explosive devices
IHL	international humanitarian law
INS	Immigration and Naturalization Service
IRF	Immediate Response Force (Guantánamo)
JAG	judge advocate general
JTF-GTMO	Joint Task Force Guantánamo
LHM	letterhead memorandum
MCA	Military Commissions Act
MCDO	Military Commissions Defense Office
MOC	Media Operations Center (Guantánamo)
MOU	memorandum of understanding
MP	military police
MRI	magnetic resonance imaging
NACDL	National Association of Criminal Defense Lawyers
NGO	nongovernmental organization
OAS	Organization of American States
OGA	other government agency
OLC	Office of Legal Counsel
OPR	Office of Professional Responsibility
OSF	Open Society Foundation
POW	prisoner of war
PTSD	post-traumatic stress disorder
PUC	person under custody
RCMP	Royal Canadian Mounted Police
RDI	rendition, detention, and interrogation

SASC	Senate Armed Services Committee
SERE	Survival, Evasion, Resistance, Escape program
SOUTHCOM	United States Southern Command
SSCI	Senate Select Committee on Intelligence
TVPA	Torture Victim Protection Act
UCMJ	Uniform Code of Military Justice
UFI	unique functional identifier
VFM	9/11 victim family members
WMD	weapons of mass destruction

A few minutes before midnight on May 1, 2011, President Barack Obama appeared on television to announce that the nation's most wanted and hunted man was dead. Al-Qaeda leader Osama bin Laden, who orchestrated the terrorist attacks of September 11, 2001, that killed almost three thousand people, now lay in a watery grave in an undisclosed location. "Justice has been done," Obama said. "The cause of securing our country is not complete. But tonight, we are once again reminded that America can do whatever we set our mind to."

Justice had been delivered with a couple of bullets.

The bin Laden operation was directed by the CIA from headquarters in Langley, Virginia. The boots on the ground were special forces from Navy SEAL Team 6. The president and members of his cabinet gathered in the White House Situation Room to watch a video feed of unfolding events, narrated by CIA Director Leon Panetta. The stealth helicopters landed in a compound on the outskirts of the Pakistani city of Abbottabad where bin Laden was living in hiding. There was a shoot-out that left several people dead. The SEALs entered a bedroom and visually identified the chief target. Then Panetta, using the code name for bin Laden, said, "Geronimo EKIA." Enemy killed in action.

In his television address, President Obama didn't explain why bin Laden had been killed rather than captured. But at a press conference the next morning, a national security official said, "This was a kill operation." By the afternoon, White House counterterrorism adviser John Brennan sought to smooth the rough edges off that answer by stating that the SEALs would have taken bin Laden alive if they had had the chance. In the initial attempt to craft a riveting narrative for the public, officials claimed that bin Laden was killed in a firefight, and that he had attempted to use one of his wives as a human shield. But at an off-camera briefing later that day, another senior White House official told reporters that bin Laden was not armed when he was shot once in the head and once in the chest ("double-tapped").

According to the laws of war, an enemy who has surrendered, is injured, unarmed, or otherwise out of the fight should be captured rather than killed. On May 3, Brian Williams of NBC Nightly News put the question to Panetta: "Did the president's order read 'capture' or 'kill' or both or just one of those?" Panetta said that the order was to kill bin Laden. "But," he added, "if he suddenly put up his hands and offered to be captured, then—they would have the opportunity, obviously, to capture him. But that opportunity never developed."

What would have happened to bin Laden if he had been taken alive?

That question was discussed in the months before the operation. At a February 16 hearing of the Senate Select Committee on Intelligence, Panetta was asked what the Obama administration would do if bin Laden or al-Qaeda's second-in-command, Ayman al-Zawahiri, were captured. He responded, "We would probably move them quickly into military jurisdiction at Bagram [the main US prison in Afghanistan] for questioning and then eventually move them probably to Guantánamo." At the time, Panetta's comments were interpreted as pure speculation because, as far as the public or even officials beyond a tight inner circle were aware, bin Laden's whereabouts were unknown. Yet even as speculation, Panetta's statement seemed oddly dissonant with the president's goal to close the military detention facility at Guantánamo Bay. At the same hearing and in response to the same question, Secretary of Defense Robert Gates said, "The honest answer to that question is that we don't know."

Those uncertain answers in the spring of 2011 highlighted the lack of a clear detention policy. More than that, they highlighted the lack of a will to detain people at all. Harvard law professor Jack Goldsmith, who served in the Defense and Justice Departments in the George W. Bush administration, summed up the dilemma: "We are all obsessed with Gitmo [Guantánamo], but I don't think that's where the important action is. The important action is who we are not detaining because Gitmo has become this black-eye place where we can't have future detentions."

The Bush administration selected the Guantánamo naval base on the south side of Cuba in December 2001 as the main site for long-term detention of prisoners captured in the "war on terror." Airlifts into the facility began the following month. At its peak, Guantánamo held seven hundred and eighty people. But by the end of President Bush's second term in office, over five hundred had been transferred out, and he had come to accept the idea that this notorious prison should be closed.

President Obama signed an executive order on his second day in office pledging to close Guantánamo within a year. In that political moment, closure seemed to have bipartisan appeal. But that moment passed quickly and demands to keep Guantánamo open became a rallying cry for Obama's political opponents.

The prospect of closure became infinitely harder in 2010 when Congress passed legislation restricting the president's ability to move people out of Guantánamo; they couldn't be brought into the United States for any reason, including trials, and if they were to be transferred elsewhere, the secretary of defense was required to provide burdensome assurances that they wouldn't pose a future threat to national security. These barriers functioned as a deterrent to capturing people. Where would they be held if Guantánamo wasn't an option? According to Goldsmith, "The lack of a detention policy and the inability to detain members of the enemy going forward creates a heightened incentive to kill people."

By the time bin Laden was killed, targeted killing had supplanted capture and detention of suspected enemies as the strategic cornerstone of the "war on terror." In Bush's last year in office, there was a 94 percent increase in drone strikes over the year before. After Obama took office, targeted killing escalated dramatically in terms of the number of lethal strikes per month and the geographic scope of operations. During Obama's two terms in office, a handful of foreign terror suspects were captured alive—none of whom ended up in Guantánamo—while thousands of people died as a result of targeted killing operations.

What explains this strategic shift from capture and detention to targeted killing? In a word, torture.

The "war on terror" began as a war for information because the government needed "actionable intelligence" about unknown individuals and clandestine organizations that carried out the attacks of September 11 or had knowledge about plans for future terrorist attacks. As in other asymmetric wars, when a state is fighting against unconventional enemies, the standard means of getting such information is to capture, detain, and interrogate people. That explains *why* interrogation was the strategic centerpiece in the early years of the war. But *how* interrogations were conducted has a specificity shaped by policy decisions. It is a matter of public record that, at the start of the war, the Bush administration decided to authorize the CIA and the military to utilize coercive interrogation techniques on captured terror suspects. It is also well established that these decisions were driven by Vice President Dick Cheney and other top officials who believed that the use of violence and degradation would be necessary and effective to elicit information that would help the government find and fight terrorists. A wide paper trail proves that these policy choices were supported with legal opinions by government lawyers. There is no serious dispute among people paying attention to the course of the "war on terror," regardless of vast differences in political views, that for five years—from 2001 to 2006—the strategic priority was to capture people in order to detain and interrogate them, and by 2008, the priority had changed to a strategic reliance on targeted killing.

But why and how did this shift occur? It wasn't because officials suddenly concluded that killing was a better national security option than capturing and coercively interrogating suspected enemies. On the contrary, targeted killing became the strategic preference because torture was taken off the table. And torture wasn't taken off the table as the result of some public reckoning that it is illegal and ineffective. Many politicians, including Obama's successor, Donald Trump, regard the cancelation of "enhanced interrogation techniques," the official euphemism for US torture, a mistake. Torture was taken off the table because lawyers decided to fight the government over the treatment of prisoners detained at Guantánamo and other overseas facilities, and they won a few key battles.

Hundreds of lawyers—military and civilian, Democrats and Republicans, corporate and human rights and small-firm private practice lawyers, law professors and their students—felt ethically motivated or professionally obligated to challenge the government's authorization of torture, as well as long-term incommunicado detention, kidnapping, and forced disappearance to secret prisons (black sites). Some saw their roles as defenders of the rule of law and due process norms that are the pillars of American legal traditions, while others saw their roles in more global terms as defenders of human rights. What these lawyers had in common was a willingness to act in the name of the laws that were upended by the torture policy. Their victories—few and far between though they were—helped force an end to the torture program. But these victories had the unintended consequence of triggering the shift to targeted killing, a paradoxical testament to the effectiveness of the fights that lawyers waged on behalf of people detained by the United States. Dead men don't need lawyers. (Actually, they do, but that is another story.)

The War in Court tells the story of the fight against torture and the complicated legacy it has left. The narrative traces what lawyers and their allies did to expose and challenge illegal government policies, why and how they waged this fight, and how their individual and collective actions forced the government to alter the way the "war on terror" was waged. The book has three central contentions. First, if lawyers had not taken up this cause, the US torture policy would have gone unchallenged because the American public, with a few exceptions like Witness against Torture, Code Pink, and the ecumenical National Religious Campaign against Torture, never mobilized to oppose it. Second, this fight *had to be waged by lawyers* because the government based its interrogation and detention operations on novel interpretations of federal and international laws, and therefore, the battles had to be waged on the terrain of law. These challenges brought the "war on terror" *into* courts and developed over time into a war *in* court. Third, the US government's torture policy and the fight against it have had transformative effects on the post-9/11 legal landscape—in the United States and on a global scale—and, therefore, a robust understanding of the present must take account of this war in court.

Beyond the details of the fight against torture, *The War in Court* reflects on questions of monumental, global significance: What is legal in war? And how, if at all, can a superpower be impelled to abide by the law when national security is at risk?

Introduction

ON SEPTEMBER 11, 2001, I woke up in a motel room along a highway in New Mexico. I was on a cross-country trek to a new job at the University of California—Santa Barbara. When I turned on the television to watch the morning news, I saw the footage of the collapse of the World Trade Center, which had been hit by two hijacked commercial airplanes. The scene was unfathomable. Then there was footage of the Pentagon, which had been hit by another plane. A fourth plane crashed in a field near Shanksville, Pennsylvania, and it was later reported that passengers had overpowered their hijackers. The morning anchors were scrambling to cloak their panic and confusion in broadcaster professionalism. They were seeking answers from official spokespeople and national security experts who had been hastily recruited for on-air interviews. Finally, I turned off the television. I had to move on.

Somewhere along the road, I pulled over to call the switchboard of my new university. I asked to be connected to one of my new colleagues, an expert on religiously motivated terrorism. Although he and I had not yet met, I wanted to do *something,* and the only thing I could think of was reaching out to him to offer my services if the university were to organize an event to address these terrible attacks and think together about what it meant for the nation.

The first week of the fall 2001 quarter, the university hosted a teach-in, and I was one of the speakers. The large auditorium was crowded with somber students and faculty.

By then, President George W. Bush had already announced that the response to the attacks of September 11 would be to launch a "war on terror." Congress had already passed legislation authorizing the president to use all necessary and appropriate force against those he determined to be responsible for the attacks, as well as nations that harbored or abetted the perpetrators. And Vice President Dick Cheney had already given an interview on *Meet the Press* in which he stated: "A lot of what needs to be done here will have to be done quietly, without any discussion, using sources and methods that are available to our intelligence agencies—if we are going to be successful . . . [I]t's going to be vital for us to use any means at our disposal . . . to achieve our objectives."

Any means at our disposal? I heard that remark by Cheney as a hint that he wanted the government to resurrect something like the Phoenix program, a Vietnam War counterinsurgency strategy that involved capturing and torturing thousands of people for information about the Viet Cong on the assumption that this would provide a war-winning advantage. With Cheney's comments in mind, I warned my new colleagues and students of the possibility that we—the nation, that is—were likely to respond to terror with torture.

This wasn't the kind of concern that most people were thinking about so soon after 9/11, as the horrific event had already been named. But torture was always on my mind.

I started my academic career in the early 1990s as a graduate student doing research on the Israeli military court system in the West Bank and Gaza. My original plan had been to study how conflicting nationalisms—Israeli and Palestinian—played out in these military courts. But once I got to the field, I learned two things that changed the focus of my research and the trajectory of my career. One was the importance of torture—specifically tortured confessions—to Israel's strategies to control and punish Palestinians in the occupied territories. The other lesson was that law is a battlefield in its own right. I saw law's capacity to function as a double-edged sword: It can be wielded by government lawyers and officials to produce legal justifications for security policies with oppressive and discriminatory consequences, and it also can be wielded by victims and critics to challenge unlawful state policies. As I dug into research on the workings of the Israeli military courts, I came to appreciate the unique role that lawyers play in this conflict because only they are trained to make legal arguments and positioned to use legal processes to combat their adversaries on the terrain of law. Many of the Israeli and Palestinian lawyers who taught me this lesson were, themselves, cynical about the law. But I came to love the law—not as a lawyer, which I am not, but as a sociologist. I became fascinated by fights over what is legal and what isn't, who wins and who doesn't, and why.

The terrain of law and conflict in Israel/Palestine had been dramatically altered in 1987 when Israel became the first government in the world to publicly claim the right to use violent interrogation techniques as a legitimate prerogative to protect national security. This decision followed the recommendation of an official commission of inquiry, headed by Moshe Landau, a retired High Court justice. The Landau Commission had been created to investigate the General Security Services, or Shin Bet, which recently had been implicated in two scandals. One was the revelation that an Israeli Circassian army officer had been court-martialed and convicted of treason on the basis of a tortured confession; the other was the cold-blooded execution of two Palestinian bus hijackers immediately after they were taken into custody. The Landau Commission cast a wide net to examine other possible Shin Bet transgressions and its report confirmed something that had long been alleged, but that the Israeli government had resolutely denied: Shin Bet agents had been using violent interrogation techniques on Palestinians since at least 1971.

What scandalized the Landau Commission was not this abuse, but the fact that Shin Bet agents routinely lied to military court judges when defense lawyers challenged their clients' confessions as coerced. The commissioners could not abide perjury, but they accepted the Shin Bet's contention that abuse, which they euphemized as "moderate amounts of physical pressure," was necessary to fight "hostile terrorist activity," which encompassed not only acts of violence but any expressions of Palestinian nationalism or opposition to the occupation. In their thinking about how to justify this reliance on interrogational violence, the commissioners looked to the first major court case that tested the question of how to draw the line between what was and was not torture: In the 1970s, the Republic of Ireland sued the United Kingdom in the European Court of Human Rights (ECHR) over British interrogators' use of the so-called "five techniques"—prolonged wall standing, hooding, subjection to loud noise, deprivation of sleep, and deprivation of food and drink—on Northern Irish Republicans in the context of "the troubles." Although the ECHR majority decided that none of these techniques, individually, rose to the level of torture, they found that the techniques did constitute cruel, inhuman, and degrading treatment. For the ECHR minority, the British techniques did constitute torture because they were used in combination. The lesson the British government took from the case was to stop using those techniques. The Landau Commission took a different lesson: since the ECHR had decided that Britain's five techniques were not torture, the Shin Bet's methods, which approximated those used by the British, were not torture either. The commission recommended that the Israeli government sanction these abusive interrogation techniques so that Shin Bet agents could stop lying about their use to judges.

The Landau Commission rationalized this recommendation by distorting the concept of the necessity defense. This is a legal defense that an *individual* can claim when she or he has broken the law in order to prevent a grave harm of an immediate kind—for example, if a bystander assaults a kidnapper who is trying to snatch a child. The commissioners contended that this necessity defense could shield systematic abuses by state agents who were acting to protect Israeli security. The Israeli government accepted the Landau Commission's recommendation to own up to coercive interrogation tactics and the distorted necessity defense rationale that came with it. As a result, what had previously been extralegal and deniable torture became publicly acknowledged official policy covered with a patina of legality.

As coincidence would have it, one week after the Israeli government endorsed the Landau Commission's recommendations, Gaza and West Bank Palestinians started an intifada (uprising) to protest the brutalities of military rule and the political stalemate that frustrated their aspirations for national self-determination. To put down this intifada, the Israeli army and the Shin Bet embarked on a program of mass arrests. Palestinians by the thousands—mostly men and teenaged boys, but some women and children as well—were channeled through interrogation, then through the military court system that was working overtime to handle the deluge, and then into prisons. Tortured confessions were at the heart of the strategy to break the intifada with mass incarceration. In the late 1980s, Israel/Palestine had the largest per capita prison population in the world.

At the beginning of the 1990s, while I was doing my fieldwork, Israeli human rights lawyers started challenging the government's interrogation policy in the High Court of Justice (HCJ). This running battle pitted the universal right not to be tortured against official claims of national security prerogatives. In 1999, the HCJ issued a landmark ruling prohibiting the routine use of coercive interrogation tactics. But the court left a crack in the door on the presumption that, in emergencies, torture can save innocent lives.

Torture became a central focus of my research and writing, and a consuming topic of my thoughts. I came to understand that torture is distinct from other forms of violence because of the context in which it occurs and the status of victims and perpetrators: torture involves intentionally harming individuals—physically, psychologically, or both—who are in custody but have not been convicted of a crime. Legally, torture is an extralegal practice because it excludes harms resulting from court-ordered punishments that comport with a country's criminal laws. The use of torture serves different purposes in different contexts. If the objective is to imprison people, as was the case in Israel and the occupied territories, torture may be used to elicit confessions that a court can use to convict them. If the objective is to elicit information from suspected enemies in the context of a war or armed conflict, torture may be used to gather actionable intelligence. If the objective is to quell political dissent and intimidate opponents of a government, then the purpose of torturing some people may be to instill fear in other people or society at large. But under all circumstances, it was well established and universally agreed that torture is illegal. Even the Israeli government acknowledged the illegality of torture by adopting the "moderate physical pressure" euphemism.

I vividly recall a moment in 1997 when I had what felt like an epiphany: Because the prohibition of torture is absolute, everyone everywhere and under all circumstances has the right not to be tortured. This makes the right not to be tortured the most universal right that human beings have, paralleled only by the right not to be enslaved, because there are no exceptions to these prohibitions. The right to life doesn't compare because there are many ways in which people legally can be killed and circumstances when killing is not a crime. Other kinds of political and civil rights can be suspended or even violated temporarily in times of emergency. The unique strength of the right not to be tortured, I realized, gives all people a kind of sovereignty over their bodies. Sovereign bodies, like modern sovereign states, are independent and autonomous and have borders that should not be aggressively invaded. The "problem of torture," therefore, could be understood as sovereign states transgressing sovereign bodies for whatever security or political reasons drive custodial abuse in any given context.

My fascination with this notion of competing sovereignties only deepened when, in 1998, British police, acting on a Spanish warrant, arrested former Chilean dictator Augusto Pinochet while he was in London. The Spanish judge who issued the warrant wanted Britain to extradite Pinochet to Spain to stand trial for his role in the torture and murder of thousands of people during Chile's "dirty war" years. When the British House of Lords evaluated the charges in the warrant, they decided that murder isn't an extraditable offense because killing enemies is a legitimate aspect of war. But to the shock of the champions of unaccountable state power, the law lords decided that, because the prohibition of torture is absolute, Pinochet could not claim sovereign immunity for the legal consequences of this crime, although for political reasons, the British government decided to send him back to Chile rather than extradite him to Spain. Nevertheless, this "Pinochet precedent," which held that even a former head of state is prosecutable for the crime of torture, offered a forceful answer to the question about the limits of state sovereignty. Torture was beyond the limit.

By September 2001, I was primed to hear the dog whistle in Cheney's *Meet the Press* comment about using "any means at our disposal."

Within weeks of 9/11, a full-blown debate about torture erupted in the United States as politicians and commentators fixated on whether it might be justified under exceptional circumstances. A dominating theme in this debate was the hypothetical ticking bomb; in this scenario, a bomb is set to explode, endangering the lives of hundreds, thousands, or even millions of people, depending on its location and destructive force. The person who knows how to defuse the bomb has been captured but is refusing to divulge the information. The debate turns on the question: should the recalcitrant terrorist be tortured to avert a catastrophic attack? Some people argued that certain exceptional circumstances might warrant torture to get lifesaving information. Those who took this position were not suggesting that the government should forsake the principle that torture is wrong, but rather that the principle could be temporarily suspended to keep innocent people safe. On an October 27 segment of CNN's *Crossfire,* for example, commentator Tucker Carlson said: "Torture is bad. [But] some things are worse. And under some circumstances, it may be the lesser of two evils." Alan Dershowitz, a Harvard law professor, became a prolific advocate for exceptions to the prohibition of torture. In an article titled "Let America Take Its Cues from Israel Regarding Torture," he wrote: "I have absolutely no doubt that . . . the vast majority of Americans would expect the officers to engage in that time-tested technique for loosening tongues, notwithstanding our unequivocal treaty obligations never to employ torture, no matter how exigent the circumstances. The real question is not whether torture would be used—it would—but whether it would be used outside of the law or within the law." Dershowitz offered a suggestion reminiscent of England's medieval Star Chamber that torture could be brought within the law by empowering special judges to issue torture warrants.

In order to hold the line at lesser evil and not slide into the terrain of absolute evil, the pro-torture advocates in this public debate insisted on limits to the kinds of techniques that would be acceptable. The terrorist couldn't be put on the rack or burned with a blowtorch. Rather, they advocated what they liked to refer to as "torture lite"—tactics that don't permanently damage or destroy the body. Dershowitz proposed sterilized needles under the fingernails. "I wanted to come up with a tactic that can't possibly cause permanent physical harm but is excruciatingly painful . . . I want maximal pain, minimum lethality."

On the other side of post-9/11 torture debate were human rights practitioners and civil rights advocates who argued that no cause or crisis justifies disregarding the prohibition. They explained that torture is always illegal, desperate, and a patently unreliable means of obtaining accurate information. Variations of the anti-torture position included moral arguments that using torture makes you no better than your enemy, and empirical slippery-slope arguments that there is no such thing as just a little torture, because once you start torturing suspected terrorists, you open the door to torturing anyone in the future.

Those on the pro-torture side of the debate referenced the past death and destruction of 9/11 to rationalize the necessity of future torture, and they tried to shame anyone who opposed torture under all circumstances by arguing that the latter were less concerned about the safety of innocent victims than the sanctity of legal principles and/or the rights of terrorists. But their arguments depended entirely on the belief that torture works. As this belief infused the popular imagination, ginned up by the hypothetical ticking bomb scenario, torturing terrorists came to be imagined as a heroic enterprise. Fox Television tapped this zeitgeist with a new drama series, 24, which aired its first episode on November 1, 2001. The show's lead character, a vigilante named Jack Bauer (played by Kiefer Sutherland), became a national icon as enthralled viewers cheered the ways he brutally tortured bad guys to elicit some lifesaving piece of information.

Meanwhile, unbeknownst to the public, policy decisions were being made about how to wage the "war on terror" that would congeal, by the first anniversary of 9/11, into official authorization for torture. Cheney, who assumed control of the national security portfolio, was driving this decision-making, aided by his legal counsel David Addington. They wanted to unfetter the president's powers from the system of checks and balances designed by the nation's founders and to inoculate those who carried out the president's orders from judicial scrutiny. A tight circle of like-minded lawyers from the White House, the Pentagon, and the Justice Department, who referred to themselves as "the war council," were busy crafting legal arguments and reinterpreting laws to empower the president to authorize anything deemed necessary to combat terrorism and protect national security. The war council rejected the idea that the president's options must comport with the 1949 Geneva Conventions, which they scorned as too quaint to be relevant to this new kind of war. As had been the case when Israel publicly claimed the right to use violent interrogation tactics, these lawyers wanted the US government's prerogative to brutalize terror suspects to have the imprimatur of law.

The public was exposed to very few glimpses of this "new paradigm," as its intellectual authors described the expansion of executive power that they were constructing in the shadows. One glimpse was President Bush's November 13, 2001, military order regarding the treatment of captured enemies. He pronounced that our enemies in this war are "unlawful enemy combatants." This was a radical repudiation of the laws of war because, in any armed conflict, people fall into one of two categories: combatants, meaning soldiers, and civilians, which encompasses everyone else. This new category of unlawful enemy combatants was cut from whole cloth, and it flowed from the earlier decision to classify the terrorist attacks of 9/11 as an act of *war* rather than what they actually were: a crime against humanity. If the attacks were an act of war, this reasoning went, then the perpetrators weren't civilians, because civilians can't start a war and you can't declare war on civilians. If they weren't soldiers either, you wouldn't have to treat those who were captured like prisoners of war. According to President Bush's order, foreigners taken into US custody in the "war on terror" would be barred from challenging their detention or appealing to any court anywhere over how they would be treated. The order threw habeas corpus—Latin for "show us the body," which prohibits secret detention—under the bus. Perhaps because these foreign enemies would be detained overseas, habeas corpus wasn't a right they could claim anyway. But neither would they be put through any kind of military vetting process of the kind available to POWs because, although they were captured in a war, they weren't soldiers. Hence, by order of the president, anyone who was captured, kidnapped, or sold for bounty into US custody *was* an unlawful enemy combatant and had no rights. The other element of the president's military order was that any detainees the government chose to prosecute would be tried in a new military commission system created just for them.

To understand the public reception of the president's military order, we must recall that in November 2001, the World Trade Center was still a disaster site where human remains were being excavated. The month before, al-Qaeda leader Osama bin Laden, who was deemed responsible for the attacks, had evaded capture in Afghanistan and gone into hiding. The hunt was on for terrorist sleeper cells inside the United States who might be planning more attacks, and for terrorist leaders and operatives overseas. The torture debate, going full throttle, had already lubricated public discourse with the idea that the law could be bent or set aside to respond to a national emergency. Public reception of the president's order regarded it as an appropriately muscular response to deal with such nefarious enemies.

The next glimpse of the new paradigm was the release of trophy-shot photos of the first prisoners to arrive at Guantánamo on January 11, 2002. The month before, the US naval base on the south side of Cuba had been selected as the site for long-term interrogation and detention of unlawful enemy combatants. The Pentagon assumed that a vengeful public would celebrate the images of men kneeling on the ground in a barbed wire pen, wearing blackout goggles, earmuffs, and padded mittens. This assumption proved to be a slight miscalculation. For it was one thing to debate torture in the abstract but another to see pictures of actual people bound up in contorted positions in sensory deprivation gear. People who voiced criticisms of what these images depicted were countered with officials' forceful claims that the men in the photos were "the worst of the worst." Nevertheless, as prisoners continued to be airlifted into Guantánamo, it was decided that, from then on, all information about them would be tightly restricted. The public could know almost nothing about them, including their identities or how they were being treated by interrogators and guards.

This is where the story of the fight against torture in the "war on terror" begins.

Michael Ratner, president of the Center for Constitutional Rights (CCR), a progressive legal organization, was alarmed by the president's military order. He was even more alarmed by the selection of Guantánamo as a detention site because he had been there before. In the 1990s, Ratner was part of a team of lawyers who fought the administrations of George H. W. Bush and Bill Clinton for using that naval base to detain Haitian refugees interdicted at sea before they could reach the shores of Florida. When Guantánamo was resurrected as a detention facility, Ratner decided he had to fight the government, again. He and his CCR colleagues joined forces with two death penalty lawyers, Joseph Margulies and Clive Stafford Smith. In February 2002, they took the difficult and politically unpopular decision to file a lawsuit challenging the president's authority to secretly detain people at Guantánamo. This lawsuit, *Rasul v. Bush,* was the first salvo of what would eventually develop into a war in court.

For the first two years of the "war on terror," the public knew almost nothing of the CIA's kill-or-capture mission, which President Bush had authorized six days after 9/11. The exceptions were occasional pronouncements about the capture of individuals touted as top al-Qaeda operatives who were being questioned in undisclosed locations. There were hints, though. On September 26, 2002, Cofer Black, a CIA counterterrorism analyst, testified in Congress that there "was a before 9/11 and an after 9/11, and after 9/11 the gloves came off."

The first major reveal that there might be a torture *policy* occurred on December 26, 2002, when the *Washington Post* published a groundbreaking article by investigative journalists Dana Priest and Barton Gellman. They reported that US agents were using "stress and duress" tactics to interrogate people captured in Afghanistan and elsewhere, and that detainees who couldn't be broken by such methods might be given mind-altering drugs or be "extraordinarily rendered" (extralegally transported) to foreign countries with well-documented records of torture, like Egypt and Morocco. According to Priest and Gellman, "While the US government publicly denounces the use of torture, each of the current national security officials interviewed for this article defended the use of violence against captives as just and necessary. They expressed confidence that the American public would back their view."

I gleaned from this *Washington Post* article that the US government was emulating the Israeli model by euphemizing torture as stress and duress and rationalizing it as a national security necessity. I crafted this idea into a paper which I presented in November 2003 at the annual meeting of the Middle East Studies Association (MESA). That year, the conference was held in Anchorage, Alaska, a rather odd setting for a gathering of Middle East Studies scholars. Not many people had chosen to attend. At my panel, the small audience included five people wearing US military uniforms who sat in the back row. Why, I wondered, was a group of soldiers at MESA, and my panel? They were obviously paying close attention and taking notes. The next day, a couple of friends and I decided to take a walk in the tundra on the outskirts of town. Because the path through the permafrost was narrow, we had to walk single file. On the way back, I was in the lead. Down the path heading toward us was a group of people, and in their lead was a woman wearing a pink parka. She shouted my name and rushed toward me. Who was this hot pink apparition in the Alaska twilight? As it turned out, her name was Sharon Shaffer—*Lieutenant Colonel* Sharon Shaffer. She said that she had come to Alaska to hear my paper. She was one of five JAGs (judge advocates general) recently appointed to be defense lawyers for the first Guantánamo detainees whom the government planned to prosecute in the new military commissions. Although she hadn't been assigned a client yet, she knew that people detained at Guantánamo had been abused, and that the rules of the military commissions would allow prosecutors to use coerced statements in the trials. She was furious. But she was on legally uncharted territory so she wanted to hear my presentation in order to see what she could learn from me. I wanted to see what I could learn from her too, and we exchanged numbers.

Shaffer's shocked frankness about prisoner abuse and her professional gall about the military commissions inspired the research that culminates in this book. Shaffer and her JAG colleagues played an early and important role in the fight against torture when they decided to challenge the Pentagon over the military commissions. Their actions sowed the seeds for an unprecedented military–civilian alliance that mobilized to wage the war in court.

A week after I returned from Alaska, my university invited me to give a public lecture about my research. I picked a title, "Torture and the Future," and a date, May 4, 2004. Over the winter and spring, I worked on the talk. I would tell my audience about the history of torture, from its invention by the ancient Greeks to elicit statements from slaves to be used as evidence in trials, which the Greeks also invented, to its incorporation into the law of the Roman Empire. The twelfth century "rediscovery" of Roman law in continental Europe spurred the vast use of torture by medieval rulers and religious inquisitors to garner confessions—commonly referred to as "the queen of proofs"—that were needed to enforce criminal and ecclesiastical laws. I would tell the audience why torture became a casualty of the Enlightenment because it was scorned as an unenlightened way to govern, and why the prohibition of torture became a cornerstone of the modern rule of law. I would explain why torture, which was abolished from the law by the end of the eighteenth century, made a comeback *outside the law* in the twentieth century with the rise of the national security state. I would discuss the "paradox of torture"—the fact that, in the modern era, it is illegal under all circumstances, yet so pervasive that millions of people are its victims every year. I would explain why, of all the horrors in the world, it was torture that instigated the birth of a human rights movement in the 1960s, and how, after the

FIGURE 1. Abu Ghraib prison in Iraq: two US soldiers with naked, hooded prisoners who were forced to form a human pyramid. Source: Wiki Commons.

end of the Cold War, the work of some lawyers had made it possible, finally, to pursue accountability for government officials responsible for torture—like Pinochet. As I prepared my lecture, I decided to make my maiden voyage into the world of PowerPoint. I wouldn't use it in the boring way that many academics do, loading slides up with words; rather, I would use it to illustrate my talk with images of torture, ancient and modern, so that the audience could visualize the horrors.

On April 28, 2004, six days before my lecture, CBS's *60 Minutes II* broadcast photos of abused, humiliated, bloodied, and dead prisoners from the Abu Ghraib prison in Iraq. There were photos of naked detainees chained to metal bars with women's underwear on their heads, menaced with snarling dogs, and piled up in pyramids with grinning US soldiers behind them. There was a photo of a female soldier holding a leash attached to a collar around the neck of a naked man lying on the ground, one of a hooded man standing precariously on a cardboard box with his arms outstretched and wires attached to his fingers, and one of a dead man on ice with a female soldier giving a thumbs up to the camera.

I hustled to develop an analysis of what these revelations meant, and I incorporated some of the Abu Ghraib photos into my PowerPoint. On May 4, with the scandal dominating the news, seven hundred people crowded into the auditorium to hear about "Torture and the Future." It was a rare kind of experience for an academic to be in front of a breaking story. As my talk wound into the part about Abu Ghraib and some of the images were projected on the large screen, I could hear gasps from the audience. I could see my chancellor sitting in the front row, ashen faced. I concluded the talk by stating that US torture was now an irrefutable reality.

The immediate official response to the Abu Ghraib scandal was to lay all the blame on the soldiers in the photos, who were branded "bad apples." Even as officials were trying to deflect blame for prisoner abuse, there were people who applauded the horrors the photos depicted. Right-wing politicians and commentators insisted that these people—the humiliated, abused, and dead men at Abu Ghraib, along with any other Muslims in the lands where the "war on terror" was being waged—deserved this and worse. A Republican senator from Oklahoma, James Inhofe, said he was "more outraged by the outrage" over the photos than the torture they depicted. "These prisoners," he claimed, "they're murderers, they're terrorists, they're insurgents. Many of them probably have American blood on their hands, and here we're so concerned about the treatment of those individuals." Right-wing radio personality Rush Limbaugh told his millions of "dittohead" fans: "I don't understand what we're so worried about. These are the people that are trying to kill us."

Official excuses that Abu Ghraib was an aberration collapsed in early June. The Bush administration, under pressure from Congress for information about interrogation and detention operations, declassified some policy documents and legal memos. Others were leaked to the press. Although these documents were peppered with redactions, they exposed the fact that violent and degrading interrogation tactics had been sanctioned from the top. The documents were instantly and aptly nicknamed the "torture memos."

The torture memos provided substantive evidence that the Bush administration had authorized military interrogators, CIA agents, and government contractors to strip prisoners naked; short-shackle them to the floor for protracted periods; force them to defecate and urinate on themselves; subject them to days or weeks of sleep deprivation by bombarding them with constant light, excruciatingly loud music or grating sounds, and extremes in temperature; put them in stress positions such as "long time standing"; hang them from hooks on the ceiling; bash them into walls; and waterboarding, which involved strapping people to a board while water was poured on their cloth-covered faces to induce the feeling and fear of death by drowning.

A new wave of torture debating flooded the land in the summer of 2004, this time with a decidedly partisan cast. Because a Republican administration had instituted this torture policy, defending it became a matter of Republican Party pride. Some politicians, echoing statements by officials, insisted that these tactics were necessary, effective, and "not torture," at least not when used by US agents on our enemies. Waterboarding was the hardest to pass off as not torture because it had been used by medieval inquisitors and Nazis, and in the twentieth century, there were cases in which soldiers and police officers were prosecuted for it in US courts. A vocal constituency took up the cause of defending waterboarding (which became the catchphrase for US torture more broadly), and painted critics as unpatriotic or even terrorist sympathizers.

One sociological truism is that members of the general public, when confronted with new issues or complex problems, often adopt ideas and embrace beliefs advocated by figures they trust, including influential politicians and pundits. The shift in official and right-wing discourse in mid-2004 to openly advocate interrogational abuses as necessary, effective, and justifiable caused public support for torture—not hypothetical scenarios or "torture lite," but confirmed, violent, and degrading techniques used on people in US custody—to swell. This made the fight against torture significantly harder and more protracted.

There were, of course, many Americans who were disturbed by the revelations of a torture policy. But one sector, people schooled in the law, were especially appalled by the torture-friendly, outcome-driven, intellectually weak legal interpretations crafted by government lawyers to green-light prisoner abuse. Angry lawyers got the opportunity to translate their rage to action in late June 2004, when the Supreme Court did something that the Bush administration had banked on *not* happening. In a landmark ruling in *Rasul v. Bush,* the Supreme Court decided, contrary to the president's November 2001 military order, that people held at Guantánamo have habeas corpus rights to challenge their detention. CCR had won its case. Over the following months, lawyers by the hundreds started volunteering to represent Guantánamo detainees.

In the autumn of 2004, the first lawyers began traveling to Guantánamo to meet the individuals they were assigned to represent, all of whom, they would learn, had been tortured to some degree. I started collecting these lawyers' names and conducting interviews. As I learned when I spoke with them, most had no prior experience or expertise about torture, but they were gaining that knowledge on the job. The government imposed stringent protective orders that lawyers had to sign to access Guantánamo, so they couldn't discuss details about their clients' treatment with me. But they could speak in general terms about the devastating effects of that treatment, as well as how their own decisions to assume an adversarial position against the government were affecting them professionally and personally. Many also expressed how heartened and moved they were that so many other lawyers— including dyed-in-the-wool conservatives and white-shoe corporate lawyers—had enlisted for this mission.

The Bush administration demonstrated its hostility to legal interventions and judicial oversight with a line in the 2005 National Security Strategy of the United States: "Our strength as a nation-state will continue to be challenged by those who employ a strategy of the weak using international fora, judicial processes and terrorism." But the habeas attorneys as well as the JAGs assigned to defend detainees in the military commissions were unintimidated and undeterred. If the president wanted a fight about prisoner abuse, lawyers were going to give it to him, and many told me that they saw their work in precisely those terms. David Luban, a legal ethicist at Georgetown Law School, coined the term "lawriors" to describe lawyers who decided to do battle with the government. Another term, "lawfare," a neologism of law and warfare (whose coinage predates 9/11), became a popular way to describe fights over the government's war policies on the terrain of law.

Despite a continuing flow of revelations about the torture of people in US custody, the Bush administration insisted that its interrogation and detention operations were legal. Twelve separate investigations were authorized by government agencies to look into prisoner abuse, but none was allowed to follow leads up the chain of command, and as a result none ascribed blame to the nation's top civilian and military leaders who bore responsibility for the torture policy. Compounding these orchestral moves to guarantee officials' impunity for the crime of torture, the fog machines of classification made access to accurate information about the treatment of prisoners an integral part of the fight against torture.

The death knell for the torture policy was the June 2006 Supreme Court ruling in *Hamdan v. Rumsfeld,* a case brought by one of Shaffer's JAG colleagues, Lieutenant Commander Charles Swift. The Court canceled the presidentially created military commissions as unconstitutional and rejected the

Bush administration's claim that the Geneva Conventions don't apply to the "war on terror." The Court decided that Common Article 3, which prohibits torture, cruel treatment, and outrages on personal dignity, applies to everyone detained overseas by the United States, including those in CIA custody.

President Bush responded to the ruling at a press conference on September 6, 2006. He publicly acknowledged, for the first time, the CIA's top-secret rendition, detention, and interrogation (RDI) program. He claimed that "high value" detainees interrogated by CIA agents and contractors had divulged vital information about terrorist plots. By omitting facts and presenting a misleading account of the successes of violent, "alternative" interrogational techniques, Bush was laying the foundation for the grand deception that "this program has saved lives." He added, "I want to be absolutely clear with our people and the world: The United States does not torture. It's against our laws and it's against our values." Bush also announced that he would be sending new legislation to Congress to recreate the military commissions that *Hamdan* had wiped out. We need those commissions, he explained, because fourteen prisoners in CIA custody, including Khalid Sheikh Mohammed, the alleged "mastermind" of 9/11, were about to be transferred to Guantánamo. "As soon as Congress acts to authorize the military commissions I have proposed, the men our intelligence officials believe orchestrated the deaths of nearly 3,000 Americans . . . can face justice."

The following month, Congress passed the Military Commissions Act (MCA). In addition to resurrecting the military commissions, it included a blanket grant of ex post facto immunity for violations of the 1996 War Crimes Act, thereby fulfilling the new paradigm's vision of total unaccountability for torture and other gross crimes, at least in US courts. *Hamdan* may have doomed the torture policy, but rather than bringing government behavior back in line with the law, what ensued in its wake opened new fronts in the war in court.

Lawyers representing victims of US torture started filing civil lawsuits in federal courts against specific officials responsible for the abuse of their clients, and private contractors who abetted it. The Bush administration denounced such litigation and invoked state secrets to persuade courts to dismiss torture-victim lawsuits, which they did in every case. Some American human rights lawyers, including those from CCR, teamed up with some European lawyers to pursue criminal prosecutions of US civilian and military officials in the courts of Germany, Italy, France, and Spain. The Bush administration fought on this front by using diplomatic pressure to persuade these allied governments to clip their own prosecutors' pursuit of cases against Americans, even when the people who had been tortured were their own citizens or residents.

By the last year of Bush's second term, there was growing recognition that coercive interrogations had not only been ineffective, but also had done irreparable damage to national security and other US interests. A 2008 Senate Armed Services Committee report concluded that the use of aggressive techniques and "the redefining of law to create the appearance of their legality damaged our ability to collect accurate intelligence that could save lives, strengthened the hand of our enemies, and compromised our moral authority." Alberto Mora, the top lawyer for the Navy in the early years of the "war on terror," had protested Defense Secretary Donald Rumsfeld's 2002 authorization of torture for military interrogators. In 2008, Mora testified in Congress: "To use so-called 'harsh' interrogation techniques during the war on terror was a mistake of massive proportions. It damaged and continues to damage our nation ... The net effect of this policy of cruelty has been to weaken our defenses, not to strengthen them."

During the 2008 presidential campaign season, the nation was so consumed by the economic meltdown that torture barely registered as an election issue. But to their credit, both candidates—Republican John McCain and Democrat Barack Obama—vaunted their anti-torture credentials on occasion. Obama was the favored choice of most people involved in the war in court because he was more forceful in his condemnation of torture. As a senator, he had voted against the MCA, and he pledged that when he became president, he would restore the rule of law that had been so badly damaged by Bush administration policies.

Those who celebrated Obama's win were cheered that his first official act as president was to sign three executive orders, one shuttering the CIA black sites and essentially taking the spy agency out of the interrogation business, another vowing to close Guantánamo within a year, and a third suspending the military commissions. Many of the lawyers engaged in the war in court assumed that with these executive orders, their mission would soon be accomplished, and they could start demobilizing.

But where torture was concerned, Obama's victory proved to be a pyrrhic victory. While he did keep his promise to end "enhanced interrogation techniques," he refused to pursue any form of accountability for those responsible for the crime of torture and rationalized this refusal with the facile proposition that it was time for the nation to "look forward, not backward."

Despite Obama's willingness to let past crimes be bygones, his acknowledgment that the torture policy was wrong incited former Vice President Cheney to assail the new president for relinquishing methods that, he claimed, work. Cheney's media offensive triggered another round of torture debates, and his assertions about the putative effectiveness of violent and degrading interrogation techniques emboldened pro-torture enthusiasts to take command of the field of public discourse about interrogation policy past, present, and future.

Over Obama's two terms in office, he failed to close Guantánamo. He adopted many of the contra-legal policies instituted during the Bush years, including the use of the military commissions. Since every person put on trial had been tortured, the commissions became the main battleground in the fight against torture.

My research evolved with the shifting terrain of the war in court, but my methods, mainly interviewing people in their offices or by Skype, kept me removed from the action. When I had researched the Israeli military court system, I was able to go into the courts to immerse myself in what I was studying, but I couldn't go to Guantánamo. Or at least that's what I thought. In June 2010, I had lunch with a psychologist friend who was working with defense lawyers in a Guantánamo case. She suggested that I could go to Guantánamo if I went as a journalist. I seized on her advice and applied to join the media delegation for a hearing in July 2010. That was my first trip to Guantánamo. Over the following decade, I went back thirteen more times.

Since 2013, most of my trips were to observe military commission hearings in the 9/11 case against Khalid Sheikh Mohammed and four other defendants who are accused of playing various roles in the attacks. This case was supposed to provide justice for the thousands of people who were killed on that terrible day. As the years passed and the events of 9/11 faded in the public mind, the government hoped this group trial would refocus attention on the terrorist attacks, and that justice would be served by an outcome of guilty verdicts followed by executions.

Yet through four administrations, and more than two decades since 9/11, the case remains mired in the pretrial phase. The main reason is because the defendants were tortured for years by the CIA. The 9/11 case is a perfect illustration of the costs and consequences of government decisions to authorize a torture program, and subsequent efforts to try to keep shameful details secret. Along with many other cases that have been part of the war in court, it shows us that torture and justice are incompatible.

As an educator, I often ponder how these lessons about the high costs of torture will be taught to future generations. The lessons certainly haven't been learned yet. A majority of US citizens have bought into the spurious idea that torture is necessary and effective and, when done or authorized by the US government, is "legal." Some subscribe to the notion that their fellow countrymen and women who have criticized torture and challenged the government in court should be scorned as un-American. Those who assume this position posit torture as some kind of national virtue.

Over the years since 9/11, I have taught numerous courses about torture and the law. Like an itinerant preacher, I have traveled to colleges and universities and community centers across the United States bringing the message about what is wrong with torture. With this book, I offer readers an account of the long and difficult fight against torture in the "war on terror," and the lessons I learned from the hundreds of lawyers I interviewed about their roles in the war in court. I hope that the story I tell in this book will be a small contribution toward the goals that motivated and animated the fight against torture. This war in court is a piece of US history which holds lessons that shouldn't be ignored. It is a history that is still being written.

ONE

Taking the "War on Terror" to Court

IN FEBRUARY 2002, THE CENTER for Constitutional Rights filed a lawsuit against President George W. Bush, which targeted the brand-new policy of secret detention at the Guantánamo naval base. To Bush administration officials, CCR's challenge to the president's wartime authority was an audacious nuisance, but the idea that the government would lose the case, *Rasul v. Bush,* seemed unimaginable. Throughout US history, judicial rulings against the government were exceedingly rare in cases related to war or foreign policy, and in that moment, so soon after the terrorist attacks of 9/11, the country was experiencing an unprecedented national emergency. The prediction that judges would refuse to check executive power held true as CCR lost in the lower courts. But in 2004, the Supreme Court overturned the lower courts' decisions and ruled that Guantánamo detainees have the legal right to challenge their detention.

Rasul rewrote the Bush administration's script on Guantánamo.

I made my first visit to CCR in 2005. I wanted to hear firsthand accounts of how the case had originated. As I approached their building on Broadway in lower Manhattan, I noted the large 666 on the façade. How allegorical, I thought, as I connected the building's street number to the fact that the legal ramifications of CCR's Supreme Court victory were bedeviling the Bush administration. In the Book of Revelations, 666 is the number of the beast, an antagonistic figure who appears during the apocalypse that marks the end of times, and in popular culture, 666 refers to the devil. When the elevator opened on the sixth floor of 666 Broadway, I chuckled at the shabbiness. Surely the devil should have posher headquarters.

The CCR offices are less than a mile as the crow flies from the site where the World Trade Center once stood. In the months after the September 11 attacks, the Twin Towers were a smoking ruin and the city was mourning the dead. The nineteen al-Qaeda terrorists who hijacked four planes to perpetrate the attacks had been living unremarkable lives in the United States before 9/11. That autumn, government policy was driven by fear that more attacks were being plotted by others whose identities and intentions were unknown. Thousands of Muslim immigrants were rounded up by the Immigration and Naturalization Service (INS) and investigated by the FBI for possible terrorist connections. The CCR staff was as scared and mournful as everyone else, but they knew they had to respond to this policy of profiling and detaining Muslims. This type of situation was why the organization existed.

The roots of CCR date back to the 1950s when it began, under a different name, as a nonprofit legal advocacy organization that supported lawyers representing civil rights activists who were fighting against Jim Crow segregation. It became the Center for Constitutional Rights in 1966. Unlike the older, bigger, and more mainstream American Civil Liberties Union (ACLU), whose mandate was to defend people's constitutional rights, left-leaning CCR's mission was to support progressive causes and social-change movements. They developed a strategy of choosing cases that would promote activists' work and using the courts to raise public awareness about injustices.

CCR became part of the first wave of a global human rights movement in the 1970s when the organization started taking cases that involved violations of international law. One such case was *Filártiga v, Peña-Irala*. Dr. Joel Filártiga, a Paraguayan, had been an outspoken critic of the regime of dictator Alfredo Stroessner, and in 1976, as retaliation, Americo Peña-Irala, the inspector general of the police in Asunción, abducted, tortured, and murdered Dr. Filártiga's seventeen-year-old son Joelito. The night of the murder, his daughter, Dolly, was taken to the police station to identify the mutilated body of her brother. In 1978, Dolly Filártiga moved to the United States and was granted asylum. The same year, Peña-Irala came into the country as a tourist and overstayed his visa. When Dolly discovered that her brother's killer was living in New York, she reported him and the INS began deportation proceedings. In 1979, while Peña-Irala was in INS custody in Brooklyn, CCR filed a lawsuit against him seeking a ten-million-dollar judgment for the torture and wrongful death of Joelito. They won.

CCR had sued Peña-Irala under the Alien Tort Statute. This piece of legislation was passed by the First Congress in 1789 to demonstrate the new nation's commitment to the laws of nations, but it had never been used in a lawsuit before. For the first time, a US court agreed to hear a tort claim involving a criminal act committed by one foreigner against another foreigner in a foreign country. By ruling in favor of the Filártigas, the judges recognized that the prohibition of torture is a matter of customary international law that federal courts have the authority and even an obligation to enforce. In their decision, the justices wrote, "The torturer has become—like the pirate and the slave trader before him—*hostis humani generis,* an enemy of all mankind." *Filártiga* was a landmark decision, and it created a precedent for civil cases involving violations of international law perpetrated in other countries.

CCR allied itself with a variety of progressive causes and dissident movements during the tumultuous 1960s and 1970s, years of mass protests against the Vietnam War, nuclear proliferation, and various forms of discrimination. Conservatives regarded the political unrest as the breakdown of law and order and the degradation of respect for authority. Some conservatives resented the gains that Black people had achieved as a result of the Civil Rights Movement and were scornful of the prospect that similar gains might be won by the movements for women's liberation, gay rights, and prisoners' rights. A new-right movement emerged in the 1970s to defend the traditional values that conservatives believed were under threat and to resist and oppose further progressive social changes.

One wing of this new-right movement was composed of lawyers who wanted to counter what they saw as liberals' dominance in law schools and across much of the federal judiciary. They were critical of judges who, in their view, overstepped their roles in the democratic order by "ruling from the bench" when cases were decided in ways that altered the sociopolitical status quo. In 1982, conservatives established the Federalist Society, which soon became one of the most powerful legal organizations in the country. Membership and a record of ideological fealty to right-wing causes became essential criteria for appointments to the bench whenever Republicans were in power, from the Reagan administration onward.

Some Federalist Society luminaries devoted themselves to asserting the legitimacy of an originalist interpretation of the Constitution; they contended that it is not a "living document" that should be interpreted in accordance with the changing times, but rather that courts should preserve the understandings and intentions of its original authors two hundred years earlier. Others dedicated themselves to restoring the full powers and discretion of the presidency that had been clipped in the post-Watergate/post-

Vietnam era by new congressional checks, like the War Powers Act, and the institution of stronger oversight mechanisms. They conceived this power-restoration project as the "unitary executive thesis" by interpreting Article 2 of the Constitution to allow the president to act in the national interest without subjecting decisions to congressional approval or judicial oversight.

Dick Cheney was a Republican representative from Wyoming during the rise of the new right. He was adamantly opposed to the recent restrictions on presidential power, especially in the realms of national security and foreign policy. Because he made it his mission to restore that power, he was attracted to the unitary executive thesis.

Cheney first tried to push this idea of unfettered executive power in January 1987 when Congress launched an investigation into the Iran-Contra scandal. The scandal was triggered by revelations that Reagan administration officials had defied the will of Congress by intervening in the Nicaraguan conflict in support of a right-wing militia, the Contras, who were trying to overthrow the left-wing Sandinista government. Money from clandestine arms sales to Iran had been channeled to the Contras. Congress conducted an Iran-Contra investigation and the resulting report was an indictment of executive branch malfeasance. Cheney authored a minority response protesting what he regarded as congressional overreach.

When Cheney served as George H. W. Bush's secretary of defense, he tried but failed to exclude Congress from having a say in the decision to wage the 1991 Gulf War. He left government when Bush Sr. lost the 1992 election. When Cheney returned to Washington in 2000 as George W. Bush's vice president, he made sure that top positions across the executive branch were filled by people who shared his enthusiasm for strengthening and insulating presidential power. They got their chance to put the unitary executive thesis into practice after 9/11.

The decision to arrest and detain Muslim immigrants without probable cause beyond the suspiciousness of their religious identity was one of the Bush administration's first major moves in the wake of the 9/11 attacks. But this wasn't the first time the country had been down that road. The United States entered World War II in 1941 after the Japanese Imperial Air Force bombed the US naval base at Pearl Harbor. The government feared that people of Japanese heritage might present a danger as fifth columnists, secretly working on behalf of the enemy. President Franklin Roosevelt acted on this fear, ordering the forced displacement and detention of more than one hundred and twenty thousand Japanese Americans in concentration camps located in desolate areas of the country. The Roosevelt administration presented this as a necessary wartime security precaution, but over the decades after the war, the Japanese internment came to be widely regarded as a dark chapter of US history. In 1988, President Ronald Reagan apologized on behalf of the government, and acknowledged that the internment program was motivated by "racial prejudice, wartime hysteria, and a failure of political leadership." Each survivor was paid twenty thousand dollars as civil compensation.

But that historical lesson was lost on the Bush administration after 9/11. If this president wanted to racially profile and detain Muslims for being Muslim, that was his unitary executive prerogative.

Under immigration law, people administratively detained by the INS have fewer rights to due process than criminal suspects. For Muslim immigrants rounded up after 9/11, the government was under no obligation to let them have lawyers, or even to inform their families about where they were or what decisions were being made about their fate.

CCR decided to step into this fray soon after the roundups began. Their first task was to try to find where Muslims were being held and what was happening to them. This task became immensely harder in October when Congress passed the USA PATRIOT Act, an omnibus bill that sanctioned vast new emergency measures. The coordinating agency was the Office of Homeland Security, which President Bush created eleven days after 9/11. The following year, this office was transformed into a new cabinet-level agency, the Department of Homeland Security, which absorbed the functions of the INS and other domestic border and security agencies.

Barbara Olshansky was one of the lawyers I met on my first visit to CCR. She explained that the hunt for detained Muslims in the autumn of 2001 influenced their decision the following February to challenge the president's authority to secretly detain people in Guantánamo. "The disappearing of people inside the country and the horrible abuses in detention facilities were just shocking," she said. "I'd never seen anything like this. It opened my eyes about what the government would do."

Olshansky spoke animatedly about how she was angered by the obstacles thrown in her path while she was trying to find people disappeared into immigration detention facilities, but she acknowledged that her anger was offset by fear that some of the people she was looking for and trying to help might actually be terrorists. Olshansky and her colleagues were New Yorkers whose city had been devastated and who had lost people they knew on 9/11.

By taking the decision to aid detained Muslims, they were swimming against the tide not only of mainstream public opinion but of their own fears. But, Olshansky explained, as they learned that detained Muslims were being subjected to sleep deprivations, beatings, and other abuses, the decision seemed justified.

After my conversation with Olshansky, a paralegal led me to the office of Michael Ratner, the president of CCR. I was excited to meet him because of his reputation as a leader in struggles for human rights and his willingness not just to criticize, but to challenge policies of indefinite detention and torture. When he entered his office, he pumped my hand and asked with a smile what he could do for me. I wanted to hear the origin story of *Rasul*.

Ratner's long career is important background to understand why he brought *Rasul* into the world. He started working at CCR in 1971. His first week on the job, a rebellion broke out at the Attica prison in upstate New York when a thousand inmates demanded better conditions and political rights. They took dozens of prison staff hostage as a bargaining chip. Following several days of negotiations, New York governor Nelson Rockefeller ordered police to raid the prison and take back control. In the process, forty-three people were killed; ten were prison staff and thirty-three were prisoners. Shortly after the rebellion was put down, Ratner went to Attica where he began working with prisoners. Out of this collaboration, he filed his first federal lawsuit, *Inmates of Attica v. Rockefeller,* seeking a ruling that would compel the State of New York to conduct an independent investigation of the events and to order the state's attorney general to prosecute police officers responsible for the willful killing of some inmates and assaults on others after the prison was retaken. By a unanimous decision, Ratner and his clients lost. For the rest of his first decade at CCR, some of his cases targeted the FBI for illegal surveillance of anti-war and anti-racism activists, and agents' role in the killing of two Puerto Rican independence activists.

When Ratner became CCR's legal director in 1984, he expanded the organization's international human rights–oriented work. He brought a case against US officials for supporting and funding Nicaraguan Contras who had committed acts of torture and murder, and two civil suits, based on the *Filártiga* precedent, against Guatemala's defense minister, Héctor Gramajo, for mass murder and persecution of indigenous communities and other gross human rights violations. One of these cases, *Ortiz v. Gramajo,* was brought on behalf of Sister Dianna Ortiz, an American nun who was living in Guatemala teaching literacy and religion to indigenous children when she was kidnapped, gang raped, and tortured. Sister Ortiz and Ratner became life-long friends. In the years after 9/11, she and other members of the Catholic Workers Movement created Witness against Torture, one of the few civil society organizations in the United States to protest Guantánamo and the US torture policy.

Early in his career, Ratner assembled his worldview into Four Key Principles of Being a Radical Lawyer: "1) do not refuse to take a case just because it has long odds of winning in court, 2) use cases to publicize a radical critique of US policy and to promote revolutionary transformation, 3) combine legal work with political advocacy, and 4) love people." These principles became CCR's creed.

Ratner made a career of fighting the government and loving people. In 1991, he sued the George H. W. Bush administration to try to stop the Gulf War. He lost. In 1999, he sued the Bill Clinton administration to try to stop the strategic bombing of Kosovo. He lost again. But one fight he waged and won in the 1990s would come to have a profound resonance with events after 9/11 and the fight he would start with the George W. Bush administration.

After a military coup in September 1991 deposed Haitian President Jean-Bertrand Aristide, there was a campaign of terror against his supporters. Haitians by the thousands fled the country by boats bound for Florida. The US Coast Guard interdicted those boats and transferred their passengers to the naval base at Guantánamo Bay. There they were held in barbed wire cages on hardscrabble ground and put through a screening process to decide who had a legitimate fear of persecution to claim asylum and who should be returned to Haiti. In February 1992, Ratner and Harold Koh, a Yale law professor, decided to bring a case challenging the US government's inhumane treatment of these refugees.

A few days before the first hearing, Ratner and Koh learned that the INS was testing the Haitians detained at Guantánamo for AIDS. Those who were HIV positive were put in a separate camp. The government's HIV exclusion policy meant that their chances for being screened-in for transfer to the United States were much diminished because each one would need a waiver from the attorney general. While the lawyers realized that this situation elevated the importance of their litigation, it also presented a public relations dilemma. This was the height of the AIDS crisis, and Haitians were one of the three widely stigmatized "AIDS-carrying h's," the other two being homosexuals and hemophiliacs. Activists working to change government policy through Congress were trepidatious about any HIV-related issues going to court because, if it resulted in a loss, the fight to protect the rights of people with the disease would be all the harder. Taking these concerns into account, Ratner and the rest of the team decided to frame the case as a violation of the Constitution's Due Process Clause and to argue that the Constitution applies at Guantánamo because the US government has exclusive control over the base. They hoped the court would agree that these Haitians have due process rights, including the right to lawyers who could help them prepare their asylum claims.

The strategy worked, sort of. In the summer of 1992, the Second Circuit Court of Appeals ruled that the government couldn't conduct any further screen-in processing or repatriation without providing the detained Haitians access to attorneys. The government then decided to freeze the screening process; they wanted to un-ring the bell that due process applies to foreigners detained at Guantánamo. Government lawyers made an offer to Ratner's team: agree to vacate the ruling and the processing Haitian detainees will resume with lawyers. But there was nothing on offer about not repatriating them back to Haiti. Nevertheless, the fact that the government was willing to make a deal served as an opening for Ratner and his team to go to Guantánamo to consult with the clients they were representing but had never met.

That first meeting was intense and fraught with emotions all around. Ratner was astounded by the horrific conditions the Haitians were living in, which he compared to the ninth circle of hell in Dante's inferno. As he and his colleagues learned at their first encounter, the Haitians didn't care whether they had lawyers. What they wanted was to get out of that hellscape and go somewhere safe. When the lawyers returned home, they rejected the government's deal and the standoff resumed. This was during the 1992 election season, and the Democratic candidate for president, Bill Clinton, seemed poised to beat George H. W. Bush. Clinton had condemned the policy of interdicting Haitians at sea and repatriating them to Haiti, and he had lauded the Second Circuit decision that due process extends to Guantánamo. He promised a different course of action when he became president. Ratner and his colleagues decided to take Clinton at his word. They put the case on hold until after the election in anticipation that Clinton would free the Haitians.

In the meantime, lawyers continued making trips to Guantánamo. Their top priority was to get the sickest people transferred into the United States, since the government admitted that it was unable to care for them at Guantánamo.

After Clinton was elected, he did an about-face on his campaign promises to stop the high seas interdiction and repatriation of Haitian refugees. Ratner and a few other members of the team met with Michael Cardozo, Clinton's transition person at the Department of Justice, to urge the new administration to bring all the Haitians into the United States. Cardozo told them that Clinton could handle a dead Haitian at Guantánamo better than the negative political fallout that inevitably would result if he transferred HIV-positive people into the country.

Ratner told me that he learned a few lessons from this experience. One was to disregard the promises of politicians. Another was the importance of combining legal work, what he referred to as the "inside strategy," with political advocacy, or the "outside strategy." Ratner and his colleagues needed to mount an aggressive outside strategy to publicize the plight of the Haitians and, hopefully, to win some public sympathy that could be translated into political pressure. The lawyers had allies: AIDS activists—especially those in ACT-UP who hounded President Clinton at every public event, immigration rights activists, civil rights and anti-racist activists, refugee and human rights organizations, and the American Haitian community. They also had their clients who, in frustration and desperation, had started a hunger strike. Jesse Jackson, leader of the Rainbow Coalition, and Cardinal John O'Connor of New York fasted in solidarity with them. This galvanized students across the country to go on hunger strikes in what was named Operation Harriet Tubman, and they were joined by ministers and congregants of Black churches. The hunger strikes were orchestrated to roll from university to university and church to church. At Yale law school, hunger-striking students spent a week in a barbed wire cage they had built to symbolize Guantánamo.

There were strong political headwinds blowing against the efforts to garner sympathy for the Haitians trapped in Guantánamo. Anti-immigration sentiment was pervasive and fierce, and the AIDS panic was at a peak. The fact that these were poor Black foreigners, some of whom were sick, reinforced the animus or indifference of racists and xenophobes. And then there was partisanship. While liberals had been willing to oppose government policy on Haitian refugees when a Republican was president, much of that opposition had dissipated now that a Democrat was in the White House. Among the coalition working on the Haitians' behalf, there were sharp differences of opinion about whether to emphasize the HIV issue. But one thing they all agreed on was that the Guantánamo detention camp must be closed.

The two-pronged inside–outside strategy succeeded. In June 1993, the Washington, DC, District Court ruled that the Haitians had to be released to anywhere but Haiti. Because of the nationwide mobilization to garner publicity for their cause, the Clinton administration decided not to appeal. When the camp was closed and the last of the detained Haitians who had been granted asylum arrived in New York, Ratner wept as he greeted them at the airport. They had been freed, but they had suffered brutal conditions and heartless treatment, and many hadn't survived.

Ratner recalled his shocked reaction when he read the newspaper on the morning of November 14, 2001, and learned that, the previous day, President Bush had issued a new military order classifying anyone taken into US custody overseas as "unlawful enemy combatants" who could be held incommunicado and deprived of all rights. "I couldn't believe what I was reading," he said. "An American president was throwing two hundred years of legal traditions out the window. I took off my glasses and rubbed my eyes. I thought maybe if I looked again, I would see something different." He started calling friends to ask whether they found the order as alarming as he did.

Joseph Margulies, a Minneapolis-based lawyer who had spent much of his career representing clients on death row, was equally alarmed when he read about the president's military order. "Well, this is fucked up," he said to his wife Sandra Babcock, also a lawyer. "What are we going to do?" She urged him to call Ratner, who was a friend of hers. He did. A few days later, a young Scottish lawyer named Steven Watt showed up at CCR with the same concern and offered his services. The three men joined forces.

When Bush issued his military order, US and coalition forces had been fighting in Afghanistan for a month. Although the war involved plenty of killing and bombing, the strategic priority was capture and detention because interrogation was the crucial means to get useful information. Interrogators repeatedly asked the men and boys who were detained at a crude detention facility in Kandahar, "Where is Osama bin Laden?" The fact that no one offered the answer was interpreted as supporting officials' presumptions that they were withholding information because they were trained in the arts of deception. Military interrogators were being commanded by their officers who were being hammered for information from Washington to take the gloves off.

On December 13, the government announced that one of the people now in US custody was an Australian named David Hicks. Several years earlier, Hicks had converted to Islam and moved to Pakistan to study religion. In

2000, he relocated to Afghanistan and became a Taliban foot soldier in the fight against Northern Alliance warlords for control of the country. Shortly after the US-led war in Afghanistan started, he was captured by the Northern Alliance, now a US ally, and turned over to the United States. Officials nicknamed Hicks the "Australian Taliban" and boasted that his capture was a victory in the "war on terror."

In December 2001, the Bush administration decided to reopen the facility that previously had held the Haitians to detain people captured in the "war on terror." Hicks was among the first prisoners airlifted from Afghanistan to Guantánamo in January 2002.

Ratner found the name of the Australian lawyer that Hicks's father had hired and contacted him. They agreed that CCR would file a habeas petition on Hicks's behalf. Margulies's friend Clive Stafford Smith, another death penalty lawyer with dual British and American citizenship, joined the team. Ratner also recruited Eric Freedman, a Hofstra University law professor who is an expert on habeas corpus.

While describing what was going on at CCR as they were deciding what to do about secret detention at Guantánamo, Ratner elaborated on something Olshansky had mentioned: It wasn't an easy decision to challenge government policy so soon after 9/11, although for Ratner, the pictures of prisoners bound and kneeling in the same barbed wire encampment where the Haitians had been held made it imperative. Within CCR they debated for days about the wisdom of coming to the aid of people they didn't know—whose past behavior or intentions they couldn't know and whose politics, if they did know, they might oppose. It felt fundamentally different from CCR's missions to aid civil rights activists or victims of police violence or casualties of US-supported dictatorships in Central America. Ratner described their decision to bring a lawsuit as a leap of faith. But it was so politically unpalatable that none of their political friends or professional allies were willing to make the leap with them.

Information about who was detained at Guantánamo was classified. But the government did inform several allied governments whose citizens were there. A week after the facility opened, the British Foreign Office told the families of three young men from Tipton, England, that their relatives—Shafiq Rasul, Asif Iqbal, and Ruhal Ahmed—were at Guantánamo. CCR seized upon this information and got authorization from the families of Rasul and Iqbal to add them to Hicks as plaintiffs in the lawsuit they were preparing. They filed *Rasul v. Bush* on February 19, 2002.

Around the same time that *Rasul* was filed, the Kuwaiti government retained the tony corporate law firm of Shearman & Sterling to intervene on behalf of twelve Kuwaitis who were in Guantánamo. According to Tom Wilner, a Shearman & Sterling partner, the Kuwaiti government selected his firm because of its oil business connections in the Gulf and because they wanted a well-known, reputable firm, not a legal advocacy organization (like CCR). Wilner and a junior colleague, Kristine Huskey, went to Kuwait to meet the families of the twelve men, who explained that their relatives had gone to Afghanistan or Pakistan to do charitable work. One demonstration of Muslim piety is the duty to help those in need, and Kuwaitis have a strong tradition of spending parts of their vacations abroad—including in conflict zones—doing good deeds. The families showed Wilner and Huskey evidence of the men's previous humanitarian missions overseas. That clinched it for Wilner. "I said 'yes' because I suspected that these men were innocent, picked up by mistake."

One of the twelve Kuwaitis in Guantánamo was Fawzi Al Odah. His father Khalid, a Kuwaiti Air Force pilot, had flown sorties with US fighter pilots during the 1991 Gulf War, and when the Iraqi army was routed from Kuwait City, Fawzi ran to greet and cheer US soldiers waving an America flag. Fawzi Al Odah became the named plaintiff when Wilner filed *Al Odah v. United States Government* on May 1. Some of the Shearman & Sterling partners were not happy, to say the least, about picking a fight with the Bush administration over the treatment of suspected terrorists. To accommodate their concerns, Wilner opted to take a slightly less confrontational route than CCR; instead of a habeas lawsuit, *Al Odah* was a civil complaint, and instead of naming President Bush specifically, the complaint was directed at the government. Nevertheless, *Al Odah* was a legal challenge to arbitrary and secret detention. The Shearman & Sterling lawyers working on the case later teamed up with CCR and *Al Odah* was litigated in tandem and eventually merged with *Rasul*.

When I spoke with Wilner to get his account of these early developments, he made a point of highlighting that he had started this case as "an establishment-type guy" whose comfort zone on the political spectrum was centrist-liberal. Since then, while he hadn't adopted Ratner's vision of radical lawyering, the work had changed him. In addition to losing some hair and gaining some weight, he joked, his shock and anger about what the government was trying to get away with had turned him into a fighter. "The idea that US law can't protect humans at Guantánamo is absurd. Even iguanas are protected there!"

He was referring to the federal Endangered Species Act, which is enforced on the naval base, with high penalties for anyone who kills or harms an iguana. He continued, "Most lawyers—most people—in this country assume all rights come from the Constitution and the Bill of Rights. But habeas is a basic common law right. All human beings have it, regardless of the Constitution. The idea of Americans first, the hell with everyone else is appalling."

The lawyers for *Rasul* and *Al Odah* aimed to convince the DC District Court that people detained at Guantánamo have the right to hearings before an impartial tribunal to determine their status. Their contention was that their clients were neither terrorists nor had they been involved in any conflict with the United States, and therefore they were being imprisoned unjustly. But this couldn't be proven because the president's military order denied them a hearing in any venue. The core legal issue, however, was whether federal courts even had jurisdiction at Guantánamo. Wilner explained, "If you really accept the government's position, you let the government decide when it will submit to judicial review. This is extreme power! This violates a fundamental aspect of separation of powers, which protects *our* liberty. Judicial review is fundamental."

Guantánamo had been selected over other possibilities—like Guam, which has a federal court—because the administration wanted a place that would be the "legal equivalent of outer space." By filing their lawsuits, Teams *Rasul* and *Al Odah* were going where no lawyers had gone before.

From the beginning, Ratner wanted to apply the lessons from his experience with Haitian refugees about the importance of an outside strategy to build political pressure against government policy at Guantánamo. There wasn't much sympathy or concern to be had among the American public, but international opinion about Guantánamo was increasingly critical. CCR wanted to tap that vein. The same month they started their inside strategy by filing *Rasul,* CCR and the Center for Justice and International Law petitioned the Inter-American Commission on Human Rights (IACHR) for an urgent review of Guantánamo; they were seeking a ruling for precautionary measures to protect the rights of people detained there. Steven Watt was CCR's point person for the IACHR petition. He recruited Rick Wilson, a law professor who ran the human rights clinic at The American University (AU), to help with the petition because Wilson had decades of experience working on behalf of victims of Latin American dictatorships. At the time, AU was one of the few US law schools with extensive faculty expertise and clinical training on the intersections of human rights and international humanitarian law.

At my first meeting with Wilson, we talked about Guantánamo and assorted human rights issues. He said, "From the moment we knew that the government was going to use Guantánamo, it resonated with me. I was arrested protesting the Haitian detentions and I met Michael Ratner in jail." At Ratner's suggestion, Wilson had taken on the asylum case of a Haitian woman and her infant child. When Watt asked him for help with the IACHR petition, he immediately said yes. "I love holding the US government's feet to the fire and highlighting its hypocrisy. But on top of that, we're lawyers and we care about how any government treats people in custody, even alleged terrorists."

By going to the IACHR, CCR and its co-petitioners had no illusions that a favorable ruling would persuade or pressure the Bush administration to make a policy retreat. Rather, their objective was to focus international attention on the prison itself. They also hoped that a ruling calling for precautionary measures might have a positive effect on the legal case. At that early juncture, all they had to go on in preparing the IACHR petition was President Bush's military order declaring what could and would happen to people detained by the United States in the "war on terror": any noncitizen suspected of involvement in terrorism could be captured or kidnapped from anywhere and held indefinitely with no access to lawyers or legal proceedings, and those the government chose to prosecute would be tried in military commissions that could rely on coerced statements and hearsay evidence and issue death sentences. As it turned out, that was enough.

Several weeks after the emergency petition was filed, the IACHR issued just the kind of ruling CCR had hoped for: Every human being has status under law and certain inviolable rights, and those who are detained in war have the right to a hearing by a competent court or tribunal to determine their status. According to Wilson, "That decision went whipping through the halls of [the State Department], the Pentagon and the White House. It had some impact. The US government was forced to respond, which they did through an extensive pleading" produced by the State Department.

Rasul and *Al Odah* were argued in the DC District Court on June 26, 2002. According to Watt, one of the few observers in the courtroom that day was John Yoo. At the time, Yoo was a deputy assistant attorney general in the Justice Department's Office of Legal Counsel (OLC). He was working closely with Cheney, and his had been one of the voices advising the administration to select Guantánamo because it would be out of the reach of US courts. Watt speculated that Yoo went to the hearing to see how this argument would hold up. During oral arguments, the judge—in Watt's description—

offended Wilner and "batted him down" a couple of times while he was speaking. For an establishment-type guy, this must have been quite jarring. Margulies leaned over to Wilner and said, "Welcome to civil litigation." When the judge indicated that she would accept the government's motion to dismiss the cases—which she did four days later—Watt overheard Yoo say, "That was the easy one, now on to Hamdi." (Yaser Hamdi was another Guantánamo prisoner. After it was discovered that he was a US citizen, he was relocated to a military brig in South Carolina. His habeas case, *Hamdi v. Rumsfeld,* turned on the question of whether the Bush administration could continue to detain a citizen without due process.)

The *Rasul* and *Al Odah* lawyers appealed the dismissal of their cases to the DC Circuit Court. In their motion, they argued that if the court finds that it has no jurisdiction over US detention facilities overseas, not only would this be a breach of American legal tradition and international law, but it would mean that the US government could act any way it chooses without being subject to any laws. On March 11, 2003, the DC Circuit Court issued a decision upholding the lower court's dismissal. The ruling ignored the fact that the plaintiffs had not been declared enemies of the United States by a competent tribunal. Instead, the court reasoned that these prisoners have no enforceable rights, including habeas corpus, because the courts have no jurisdiction over Guantánamo. The following month, the lawyers filed a motion for a rehearing of the appeal by all the judges on the DC Circuit (which is called a hearing en banc). That motion was denied.

Meanwhile, in May 2002, CCR learned the identity of another person who had been transferred to Guantánamo: Mamdouh Habib was a dual citizen of Australia and Egypt. Unlike Hicks and the Tipton 3 who had been taken into custody in Afghanistan, Habib was arrested in Pakistan in October 2001. Although CCR had no way of knowing at the time, Habib was held and tortured in Pakistan for a month before being extraordinarily rendered (extralegally transferred) by the CIA to his native Egypt. During the almost six months Habib was detained in Egypt, he was tortured with electric prods, had his fingernails pulled out, was injected with drugs, had cigarettes extinguished on his body, and was anally raped with various objects. When he signed a confession, the CIA transferred him to a black site in Afghanistan where his torture continued, this time by CIA agents and contractors. After a month in the black site, he was transferred to Guantánamo. On June 10, 2002, CCR filed *Habib v. Bush.* When that case was also dismissed, Habib was merged with the plaintiffs in *Rasul.*

FIGURE 2. Left to right: Michael Ratner, Tom Wilner, and Joseph Margulies outside the District Court in Washington, DC, December 2, 2002. Stephen Jaffe / AFP via Getty Images.

One of CCR's mottos is "success without victory." Ratner told me there was a silver lining in these losses. After losing in the District Court, support for CCR's legal challenge started building among lawyers who were concerned or offended by a judicially sanctioned policy of secret detention, and this support picked up steam after the DC Circuit Court upheld the dismissal. On top of that, it was becoming less controversial to criticize Guantánamo because reports of prisoner abuse were leaking out of the black hole.

The purpose of detaining people in secret is to facilitate torture and inhumane treatment and to prevent the outside world from knowing about it. Historical examples abound, from the Nazis' Night and Fog decree to transfer suspected resistance movement members "under the cover of night" from occupied countries in Europe to Germany, to the Soviet Union's relegation of enemies of the state to the vast gulag system in the Siberian hinterlands, to the archipelago of torture centers across Latin America during the dirty wars of the 1970s and 1980s where tens of thousands of people were disappeared. In fact, there is no innocent, law-abiding reason to secretly detain people nor any known example where torture was not an underlying purpose.

Guantánamo was designed to function as an interrogation laboratory. Shortly after the first prisoners arrived, White House counsel Alberto Gonzales asked the Defense Department to instruct intelligence officers to fill out a one-page form on each detainee certifying the president's "reason to believe" that this person was involved in terrorism. This demand for self-incriminating statements was the Bush administration's alternative to an impartial vetting process. Within weeks, the officers began reporting that interrogations weren't eliciting the information needed to fill out the form. In August 2002, a senior Arabic-speaking CIA analyst was dispatched to do an assessment. He concluded that at least half and probably more of the people detained at Guantánamo had no ties or useful information about al-Qaeda or the Taliban. He recommended a formal review process and noted that continued imprisonment and interrogation of innocent people could constitute war crimes. John Bellinger, the National Security Agency's top lawyer, scheduled a meeting to discuss the CIA analyst's recommendation to hold hearings. Cheney's counsel, David Addington, intervened, declaring: "No, there will be no review. The President has determined that they are ALL enemy combatants. We are not going to revisit it."

Cheney and other top-tier officials subscribed to the idea that coercive interrogations would be effective in extracting actionable intelligence about terrorist organizations and plots. As a result, people imprisoned at Kandahar or Bagram in Afghanistan, and all of the 780 who were detained at Guantánamo, were subjected to regimens of beatings, sleep deprivation, isolation, forced nakedness and ritual humiliations. The venality of this laboratory of human experimentation was compounded by hubristic ignorance masquerading as "we know all" confidence that everyone in US custody—whether captured in a military roundup, sold for the rich bounty the government was offering, or kidnapped from far afield of Afghanistan—was a terrorist. Anything these prisoners said during their ongoing interrogations came to be treated by the government as "the truth" that could justify their continuing detention and whatever else their captors wanted to do to them. Officials wanted the public to believe that national security depended on incommunicado detention, that every detainee was an enemy "taken off the battlefield," and that interrogation operations were a raging success. From the administration's point of view, the *Rasul* lawsuit was galling because the president had decreed that people captured in the "war on terror" had no legal rights and government lawyers had provided assurances that Guantánamo was beyond the reach of federal courts.

Could the *Rasul* and *Al Odah* lawyers make the case that a legal black hole is inimical to democracy and the rule of law? When they petitioned the Supreme Court for a hearing, which is called a writ of certiorari, their cases were consolidated as *Rasul*. There was a scramble to get amicus curiae briefs ("friend of the court" statements) from people with some expertise or experience that might persuade the Court to take the case. Douglass Cassel, director of the Center for International Human Rights at Northwestern University Law School, spearheaded this amicus strategy. It yielded eight briefs, including from former American prisoners of war, lawyers from the United Kingdom and other Commonwealth nations, and former US officials and diplomats who warned that secret detention at Guantánamo would adversely affect US stature in the world. One brief came from Fred Korematsu, who had sued the US government in the Supreme Court in 1944 over the internment of himself and one hundred and twenty thousand other Japanese Americans and lost, to the shame of the Court and the nation.

Arguably the most important brief in support of certiorari—at least for the media attention it garnered—came from a group of retired high-ranking military officers. Gary Isaac was asked by Cassel to work on this brief and find people who would agree to sign it; he describes the process in *The Guantánamo Lawyers,* a collection of first-person essays by people involved in work on Guantánamo edited by Jonathan Hafetz and Mark Denbeaux. When Isaac and Jim Schroeder, his colleague at the Mayer Brown law firm, started, the only signature that was guaranteed was Admiral John Hutson. Isaac and Schroeder were having no luck persuading other retired officers to add their names. Some disagreed with the idea of challenging the president's wartime authority and others feared that signing would tarnish their reputations. Time was running out. In the eleventh hour, Hutson's Navy JAG successor, Admiral Donald Guter, agreed to sign. Isaac wanted at least one more signatory, ideally from a different branch of the military. He called Brigadier General David Brahms, who had served as the top lawyer for the Marine Corps and had overseen the repatriation of US prisoners of war from Vietnam. Brahms read the draft of the brief and emailed Isaac that he would be honored to be a signatory. Brahms's message continues:

> The measure of a country is how it acts in time of peril. We have not always measured up. Lincoln suspending habeas corpus, Roosevelt, the Supreme

Court countenancing displacement of the Japanese and the McCarthy debacle immediately come to mind. We cannot afford to fall short in today's world; we cannot forfeit our claim to moral leadership on the world stage.

The brief with the signatures of Hutson, Guter, and Brahms urged the Supreme Court to hear *Rasul* because, first, the rule of law must apply even in wartime, and second, the Bush administration's failure to provide detainees with any opportunity to challenge their detention, as the Geneva Conventions require, would put American soldiers at greater risk because foreign governments could follow the US government's example and do the same to them.

Brahms contributed an essay to *The Guantánamo Lawyers* titled "Thank You, *Zeyde.*" He recounts that when Isaac, whom he describes as a "civilian lawyer from a highfalutin Chicago law firm," called him, he surprised himself by saying yes for reasons he didn't thoroughly understand at the time. Upon reflection, he credits his *zeyde* (Yiddish for grandfather) for the strength to do the right thing. His grandfather was a Latvian Jew who immigrated to the United States at the turn of the twentieth century; he came for the American dream at the center of which is the rule of law and the promise of fair treatment by the government and courts. "I said yes," Brahms writes, "because the voice of my *zeyde* told me to. I did his bidding and became a part of defending the American way against those who would sully it for parochial ends."

Another influential amicus brief in support of certiorari was produced by a group of retired federal judges. John J. Gibbons, who became the spokesperson for this group, was a lifelong Republican. He had been appointed by President Richard Nixon to the Third Circuit Court of Appeals where he served for twenty years and as chief justice for a good part of his tenure. After he retired from the bench in 1997, he returned to private practice as a senior partner at a corporate law firm in Newark, New Jersey.

In November 2003, the Supreme Court granted certiorari to hear *Rasul*.

There was a new push for amicus briefs in support of the plaintiffs' case. In addition to some of those who had written briefs supporting certiorari and an assortment of human rights and civil rights organizations, briefs came from a range of interested parties, domestic and foreign. There was a brief from legal historians who expounded on the history of habeas corpus, one from law professors with specializations in international law jurisdiction, one from military lawyers who had been assigned to represent prisoners in the Guantánamo military commissions, and one from members of the

United Kingdom Parliament. One brief came from Hungarian Jews who had been victims of the Nazis and had used US courts to sue for return of their stolen property and wealth, and Bougainvilleans (an autonomous region of Papua New Guinea) who were suing the British-Australian corporation Rio Tinto in the United States for complicity in war crimes perpetrated by the PNG government; the Hungarian Jews and Bougainvilleans produced a joint brief to argue that if the DC Circuit Court dismissal of *Rasul* was not reversed, US courtroom doors could be closed to foreigners seeking justice.

The Supreme Court's decision to hear *Rasul* shook the Bush administration hard. The CIA, which was running two black sites at Guantánamo, panicked: if the government lost and lawyers were granted access to the base, its operations could be exposed. The CIA relocated the four detainees it was holding at Guantánamo to black sites elsewhere. The Pentagon must have feared that if lawyers representing Shafiq Rasul, Asif Iqbal, and Ruhal Ahmed won access to their clients, this would expose the baselessness of allegations that they were terrorists. On March 9, 2004, they were repatriated back to England, in chains and with no apologies. Hicks and Habib, however, remained at Guantánamo, because the government planned to prosecute them in the military commissions.

Because of the unexpected repatriation of the Tipton 3, CCR feared that the government would start transferring other prisoners out before the Supreme Court ruled, possibly sending them to countries where they might disappear entirely. There was a frantic push to find the names of more people detained at Guantánamo. Clive Stafford Smith went on expeditions to the Middle East in search of people with missing relatives in order to get authorizations to file habeas petitions on their behalf. On April 5, CCR filed two habeas petitions directly with the Supreme Court and one with the DC District Court for seven more detainees whose identities had become known. Their goal was to hold the line until the Supreme Court ruled on *Rasul*.

Because the key issue before the Supreme Court was whether federal courts have jurisdiction over Guantánamo, the *Rasul* attorneys developed two lines of attack. One, which had been successful in the Haitian refugee litigation, was to argue that habeas corpus extends to the Guantánamo naval base because the United States exercises exclusive control there. The potential weakness of the habeas argument in this context, Ratner explained to me, was that this was wartime. During World War II, the Supreme Court ruled in *Johnson v. Eisentrager* that enemy aliens imprisoned outside of the country didn't have the right to access federal courts. Indeed, Bush administration lawyers leaned on *Eisentrager* as the justification that there is no role for federal courts at Guantánamo now, and this case was cited by the lower courts in their orders to dismiss. The other line of attack was lifted from the *Filártiga* playbook. The Alien Tort Statute (ATS) permits lawsuits on behalf of foreigners whose fundamental rights have been violated. The *Rasul* team cultivated the argument that holding people incommunicado amounts to forced disappearance and arbitrary detention, which are violations of customary international law and the Geneva Conventions. Ratner reasoned that even if the Supreme Court decided that the habeas corpus statute doesn't apply at Guantánamo in wartime—although that would be a wrong decision—the ATS argument would make the case that customary international law does.

On the night of April 19, 2004, dozens of lawyers and other interested citizens who wanted to witness oral arguments in this historic case started lining up on the Supreme Court steps to ensure that they could get seats when the courtroom doors opened the following morning. One lawyer described this amassing as "Woodstock for nerds."

Lawyers who argue cases before the Supreme Court know that they have a short window of opportunity to emphasize their strongest points before justices start peppering them with questions. John Gibbons, who had been selected to argue the petitioners' case, went first. He began: "What is at stake in this case is the authority of the federal courts to uphold the rule of law. Respondents assert that their actions are absolutely immune from judicial examination whenever they elect to detain foreign nationals outside our borders. Under this theory, neither the length of the detention, the conditions of their confinement, nor the fact that they have been wrongfully detained makes the slightest difference. Respondents would create a lawless enclave insulating the executive branch from any judicial scrutiny now or in the future."

When the justices began asking questions, Gibbons deftly navigated the two jurisdictional tracks to argue that both habeas corpus and the Geneva Conventions are law of the land, and each requires hearings before an impartial tribunal or court. Justice Antonin Scalia, a conservative with a fulsome record of decisions and dissents supporting executive power against challengers, cited *Eisentrager* to push back against the argument that enemy aliens overseas should have access to federal courts. Gibbons explained the difference between that case and *Rasul:* these plaintiffs, unlike those in *Eisentrager,* claim they are not enemies of the United States, and unlike the plaintiffs in

Eisentrager who were tried and convicted in US military commissions in Nanking, these plaintiffs have not had any military hearings to determine their status.

Solicitor General Ted Olson, whose wife was killed in the Pentagon on 9/11, argued for the government. He began: "The United States is at war. Over 10,000 American troops are in Afghanistan today in response to a virtually unanimous declaration of an unusual and . . . extraordinary threat to our national security, and an authorization to the President to use all necessary and appropriate force to deter and prevent acts of terrorism against the United States. It's in that context that Petitioners ask this court to assert jurisdiction that is not authorized by Congress, does not arise from the Constitution, has never been exercised by this court—"

At that point, Olson was interrupted. As various justices questioned him or interjected their thoughts, through the hedges of jurisdictional contentions, the central question raised by this case could be seen clearly: Is the president's authority to make prisoner policies in wartime unreviewable by a federal court and does *Eisentrager* support this position, or do federal courts have a responsibility to exercise jurisdiction in a location under the total control of the United States and where human beings who claim they are innocent are being secretly detained?

Two months later, on June 28, in a six-to-three decision, the Supreme Court answered this question. Justice John Stevens, who authored the decision, wrote: "In the end, the answer to the question presented is clear . . . [The habeas statute] confers on the District Court jurisdiction to hear petitioners' habeas corpus challenges to the legality of their detention at the Guantánamo Bay Naval Base." He noted that neither *Eisentrager* nor any other federal case excludes people in military custody from "the privilege of litigation." He also noted that the Alien Tort Statute explicitly allows foreigners to sue over violations of customary law or treaties signed by the United States. "The fact that petitioners in these cases are being held in military custody is immaterial to the question of the District Court's jurisdiction . . ."

The two jurisdictional tracks developed by the *Rasul* lawyers, argued in court by Gibbons, and bolstered by amicus briefs for the plaintiffs had persuaded the majority. This was a landmark decision, and CCR and their allies had won.

In his dissenting opinion, Justice Scalia wrote, "Today, the Court springs a trap on the Executive, subjecting Guantánamo Bay to the oversight of the federal courts even though it has never before been thought to be within their jurisdiction—and thus making it a foolish place to have housed alien wartime detainees." He describes the majority's decision as "irresponsible" and "unprecedented," and the consequences as "breathtaking." "From this point forward, federal courts will entertain petitions from these prisoners, and others like them around the world, challenging actions and events far away, and forcing the courts to oversee one aspect of the Executive's conduct of a foreign war."

On the last point, at least, Scalia was correct.

TWO

_____

Enter the Warriors

ON A MORNING IN EARLY OCTOBER 2005, I went to a café in a strip mall near the Pentagon to meet Lieutenant Commander Charles Swift. The "war on terror" had just entered its fourth year and fighting had broken out on a second front in the war in court. Swift, who was representing a Guantánamo detainee named Salim Hamdan, had filed a lawsuit in 2004 against his boss, Defense Secretary Donald Rumsfeld. In the next few weeks, the Supreme Court would decide whether it would hear *Hamdan v. Rumsfeld.*

When I arrived at the café, none of the people in uniform sipping coffees and tapping away on their Blackberries appeared to be waiting for a lone female civilian. Surrounded by regulation haircuts, I was struck by how little time I had spent around American soldiers. I was in middle school when the Vietnam War ended. After that lost, costly, and unpopular war, the government ended the system of mandatory conscription and made military service voluntary. By the time I went to college, enlistment had become a matter of choice for those who wanted or were otherwise incentivized to volunteer. As an adult, my professional contacts and social circles didn't intersect with many people who volunteered for military service.

But that was changing. I had begun to meet and interview judge advocates general (JAGs) who were taking a principled stand in defense of the rule of law. The warrior wing of the war in court was emerging as a significant force, and a military–civilian alliance was being forged that would have been unimaginable before the "war on terror."

When Swift came through the café door, he was exactly what people who knew him told me to expect: a burly, grinning human cyclone. His first words of introduction were: "Call me Charlie! Everyone does."

Swift had become a national security celebrity because of his lawsuit. He had been interviewed by dozens of journalists, he had been the subject of a flattering profile in the *New York Times Magazine,* and he had testified in Congress about the problems with the military commissions. By the time I met him, he had his talking points down pat. "I'm a purveyor of truth." He made this statement in the context of expressing confidence that the Supreme Court would take his case, and if this happened, he and his co-counsels were going to purvey some hard truth to the government.

I wanted to get Swift's account of the origin story of *Hamdan,* and the one he offered was a blend of analysis, anecdotes, and unbuttoned personal details. I started by asking how he had been selected to be a military defense lawyer at Guantánamo—I had no idea how the military made these types of decisions. He told me his name had been put forward because he had experience defending soldiers who faced court martial. "Drugs, assaults, that kind of stuff. I was always winning my cases. It was fun!" He admitted that before he got the call about this assignment, he hadn't paid much attention to the Bush administration's legal policies. "I certainly wasn't thinking about the military commissions." He provided an embellishing detail: his only relevant training was one course in law school on US war powers and a two-week course in the military on the laws of war. "I had no prior knowledge of treaty law."

The call came from Colonel Will Gunn, who was tasked by the Pentagon to select a few JAGs to defend the first prisoners who would be charged in the military commissions. Gunn interviewed Swift, then offered him the job. When Swift accepted, his wife got upset that he had agreed to defend a terrorist. Swift recounted what she said: "You have one speed—full guns. Your loyalty is always to your clients." She was alarmed that this loyalty now would be attached to someone the government was branding "the worst of the worst." Unlike his wife's willingness to accept the allegation without question, which was in line with what the Bush administration expected of military service members, he was eager to defend any client assigned to him, and he planned to use every tool in the box to do the job well. "Zealous advocacy is the heart of defense lawyering. A defense lawyer can't do injustice by doing his job." He added wryly, "It's a totally different story for prosecutors."

To provide context for his decision to challenge the Pentagon over the legality of the military commissions, Swift described the effects of 9/11 and the "war on terror" as a sea change. He explained: "What they"—Bush administration officials—"are trying to do is fit a square peg in a round hole. Terror had never been fit into the laws of war before 9/11. Terrorism was always treated as an operational issue." In rapid fire, he shot off some examples. One was the fact that the United States never signed Additional Protocols I and II to the 1949 Geneva Conventions because "we refused to accept terrorism in the laws of war." (These two 1977 protocols extended the rules and protections of international humanitarian law to unconventional wars. Protocol I addresses armed conflicts in which non-state groups are fighting for their right of self-determination against colonial powers, foreign occupiers, or racist regimes, and Protocol II addresses civil wars. The US government refused to sign either because, in officialdom's view, they would grant terrorists a legal right to fight against states.) Another example Swift offered was the 1995 omnibus terrorism bill which made a nexus between terrorism and criminality, not war. (Actually, the 1995 bill was never put to a vote, but the following year Congress passed the Antiterrorism and Effective Death Penalty Act. One of its purposes, according to President Bill Clinton who signed it into law, was to provide federal criminal jurisdiction for international terrorism.) Swift was stressing the point that the Bush administration was making an unprecedented departure from legal traditions over the past half-century.

In March 2003, Swift was summoned to move from Florida, where he was stationed, to Washington, DC, to start his new job. For the first nine months, he didn't have a client because no one had been charged yet. He spent his time doing a crash course on the rules for the military commissions, and studying international law, military history, and Supreme Court decisions on wartime cases. "Trial lawyers teach themselves," he explained. One thing he read was the 1942 Supreme Court decision in *Ex Parte Quirin,* which influenced the Bush administration's decision to create new military commissions for the "war on terror." *Quirin* was a World War II case involving Nazi saboteurs who were captured in the United States. In June 1942, eight Germans—two of whom had US citizenship—traveled from occupied France by submarines; four came ashore at Amagansett on New York's Long Island, and the other four came ashore at Ponte Vedra Beach, Florida. They disembarked wearing German military uniforms in the event that, if they were captured, they could claim prisoner-of-war status. Once they landed, they ditched their uniforms, put on civilian clothing, and took off to fulfill their assignments to attack US war facilities. Soon after they started their mission, the two German Americans decided to surrender themselves, although the first one who contacted the FBI was initially regarded as a hoaxer. They provided information that led to the capture of the other six. President Franklin Roosevelt then issued an executive order to prosecute the saboteurs in a military commission. Their trial was conducted in secret inside the Justice Department building in Washington. All eight were found guilty and sentenced to death. Afterward, Roosevelt commuted the death sentences for the two who had turned themselves in and, when the war ended, President Harry Truman extradited those two to US-occupied Germany. The other six were hastily executed by electric chair. But while their trial was ongoing, their military defense lawyer, Colonel Kenneth Royall, filed *Ex Parte Quirin* in the Supreme Court to challenge the president's authority to prosecute them in a military commission when civilian courts were fully functioning. The Court reconvened from summer recess in an emergency session to hear the case. Attorney General Francis Biddle, arguing for the government, contended that these men had no right to a civilian trial because they were charged with war crimes. The Supreme Court ruled unanimously that a secret trial inside the United States without the usual due process protections was constitutionally acceptable. The Court also decided that the defendants didn't have status as prisoners of war because they had perfidiously disguised themselves as civilians, and therefore they could be executed. By the time the full decision was published, the six executed men were moldering in a potter's field.

Swift read the *Quirin* decision as a rush to an excessively deferential judgment to justify a presidential fait accompli, and he described the quality of the Court's reasoning "an abomination." He also thought *Quirin* should be read as an archaic relic of jurisprudence. The Geneva Conventions produced after the end of World War II created rules and rights that didn't exist at the time of *Quirin*. These conventions are now customary international law because every government in the world has signed or acceded to them, and they are law of the land in the United States because they are incorporated into the Uniform Code of Military Justice (UCMJ), which governs the four branches of the military. The Bush administration's use of *Quirin* to justify the Guantánamo military commissions, Swift analogized, is "like basing education policy today on *Plessy v. Ferguson*." (*Plessy*, the ignominious 1896 Supreme Court decision that separate-but-equal was constitutional, was overturned in 1954 by *Brown v. Board of Education* which ended de jure racial segregation.) On top of that, Swift said, *Quirin* only impacted eight people, not hundreds like the number of people being detained in Guantánamo.

Whatever Swift's views of the CIA prior to 9/11, by the time we met they were quite scathing. Shortly after he took this assignment, he said, his eyes were opened by a *Newsweek* article which referenced a quote by a CIA official: "The gloves are off." (That was counterterrorism analyst Cofer Black's line, delivered during his congressional testimony in September 2002.) Swift said, "To me, this meant something. Gloves off meant we don't have to follow the law. Intelligence agencies don't like the law anyway because spies are essentially criminals. Intelligence *is* ends justify means."

For the first few months on the job, Swift's only colleague was Lieutenant Commander Philip Sundel. Two other JAGs selected by Colonel Gunn had been deemed unacceptable by the Pentagon and were dismissed. Unlike Swift, Sundel came into this assignment with a solid understanding of international law because he had worked in the International Criminal Tribunal for Rwanda. He also had encyclopedic knowledge of the UCMJ.

Swift and Sundel quickly realized that the military commissions were designed not to produce justice but to guarantee convictions. Unlike a normal adversarial legal system where prosecutors and defense lawyers confront each other on a playing field that is supposed to be level, the new commission system was designed to skew power heavily in favor of the prosecution. They could bring charges and build cases on materials that would never pass muster in a regular military or civilian court, including secret evidence, hearsay, and statements elicited through coercion. The commissions made no accommodation for the presumption of innocence because, according to President Bush's November 2001 military order, anyone taken into US custody was an unlawful enemy combatant with no right to challenge his detention, which meant that everyone at Guantánamo was presumptively guilty. Even the right to mount a defense in the commissions was smoke and mirrors; defendants would not be able to see classified evidence against them, and there was no guarantee of confidentiality in their communications with their lawyers.

Swift told me that Sundel was confident that the government wouldn't go through with these commissions because cooler heads would realize that prosecuting people in a sham court would make them martyrs and boost recruitment for terrorist organizations. Swift said he concurred, but for a different reason: "I was convinced that we are not going to try them because coercive interrogations undermined their confessions." Swift's conviction derived from his experience and self-confidence as a trial lawyer; in the hands of a good attorney, tainted confessions can get tossed. He gave a defense lawyer explanation: "Interrogation is the only basis for the rights of defendants, since they have no other evidentiary or custodial rights."

But coercive interrogation was the raison d'etre of Guantánamo. The base had been selected because the Bush administration believed that it would be beyond the reach of federal courts, and because officials wanted to interrogate detainees using brutal and dehumanizing tactics. Swift and Sundel connected the dots: The government decided to use coercive interrogations and now wanted to use these new military commissions instead of regular military or civilian courts as a way of covering that up or making it irrelevant. Swift recounted: "It was becoming clear to us that the purpose of the commissions is to have your cake and eat it too: intelligence gathering and justice. But these two things are incompatible."

The administration's assumption at the start of the Guantánamo military commission experiment was that JAGs who were assigned to defend detainees would obediently fall into line and yes-sir their orders. The architects hadn't anticipated that military lawyers would prioritize their ethical duties as *lawyers* and that, as *soldiers,* they would be deeply offended by the manipulation of military justice for political purposes. According to Swift, "The irony is that this is not what the military is for. The military's role is to support and defend the Constitution. The reasons given for using the military commissions are b.s. [bullshit]. They are for the consumption of the American people." Swift and Sundel were vocal with their criticisms. Colonel William Lietzau, who had helped craft the rules for the commissions and was the first acting chief prosecutor, told Swift: "The biggest mistake we made was not sending you and Phil home."

On July 3, 2003, the Bush administration announced that six Guantánamo detainees had been selected for prosecution. They were transferred to Camp Echo and put in solitary confinement to await trial. Following the British government's criticism of the commissions, the two British citizens slated for prosecution were taken off the list and moved back into the general population. Meanwhile, three more JAGs joined Swift and Sundel as defense lawyers: Lieutenant Colonel Sharon Shaffer, Major Michael "Dan" Mori, and Major Mark Bridges.

I had met Shaffer in November 2003 when she attended a Middle East Studies Association conference in order to hear my presentation about the role of torture in Israeli military courts and what this might bode for the US "war on terror." During that encounter, she surprised me with her uncensored disdain for the military commissions and her intention to "fight everything" on behalf of her client.

When Shaffer and I continued our conversation by phone, she explained that her hackles were raised by the Bush administration's decision not to use the US court martial system, which had been perfected over decades, and instead to create a flawed system from scratch. Like Swift, she came into this assignment with limited knowledge of international law. To learn more, she made a trip to The Hague to consult with defense lawyers who worked in the International Criminal Tribunal for the former Yugoslavia, and to Oxford University to meet with Jordan Paust, one of the world's leading experts on international law. The more she learned, the more appalled she became about the Bush administration's "new paradigm" to wage the "war on terror." She said, "The United States can't just invent international law. There are statutes that are customary international law. The way [the civilian leadership is] picking and choosing parts of the Geneva Conventions they want to use and hacking off rules and procedures they don't like is mindboggling. They can't do that!"

The Military Commissions Defense Office became a hot spot in the fight over interrogation policy and law. But that fight began months before Swift and his colleagues made themselves part of the story. From the outset of the "war on terror," Secretary Rumsfeld saw an opportunity to transform what he regarded as overly cautious and excessively rule-bound military culture; in essence, he wanted to negate post–Vietnam War reforms in military doctrine and officer training that incorporated a heightened commitment to the laws of war. Rumsfeld, like his administration patron, Vice President Dick Cheney, bristled against the idea that the government should be bound by the Geneva Conventions in this new kind of war.

The administration's decision to disregard the Geneva Conventions began not as a well-articulated policy choice but out of chaotic urgency. Because the 9/11 terrorist attacks revealed the dearth of information about al-Qaeda, capture and interrogation were essential means of obtaining actionable intelligence. In Afghanistan, interrogators were under intense pressure to elicit information from the hundreds of people being taken into US custody. They were told with winks and nods rather than clear written orders that the old rules didn't apply. Some interrogators found themselves wrestling with their consciences as they tried to figure out how to balance the Army Field Manual rules that they had been trained to abide by with pressure to take the gloves off. Chris Mackey (pseudonym) was in the first cohort of military interrogators in Afghanistan. He and coauthor Greg Miller published *The Interrogators: Inside the Secret War against al-Qaeda,* which describes the challenges at the start of the war. None of the military interrogators spoke fluent Arabic or any of the Afghan languages, so they had to rely on local interpreters, and they were incapable of judging the accuracy of translated statements. They also knew little about the context in which they were working that might help them sort out who was who—who might be a member of al-Qaeda or the Taliban, and who might be some unlucky guy who ended up at Kandahar or Bagram because he had been rounded up in a military sweep or sold to the United States for bounty. This uncertainty and ignorance about who was being detained in Afghanistan led to decisions in Washington to send *every* captured non-Afghan to Guantánamo (although plenty of Afghans were sent along, too). The working presumption was that any non-Afghan who was in Afghanistan must be a terrorist.

If operations in Afghanistan in the fall of 2001 greased the skids for disregarding the Geneva Conventions, the selection of Guantánamo transformed that disregard into policy. David Addington, Cheney's legal counsel, directed a self-anointed "war council" of government lawyers to make the unitary executive case that neither federal nor international laws can fetter the president's wartime authority. The legal memo-writing front man for the war council was John Yoo, a deputy assistant attorney general in the Office of Legal Counsel (OLC). At the start of the "war on terror," Yoo wrote a memo arguing that the Geneva Conventions don't apply in Afghanistan because it is a "failed state" (a concept that does not exist in international law). In late December 2001, when Guantánamo was selected as the main site for long-term interrogation and detention, Yoo coauthored a memo with Patrick Philbin arguing that US courts have no jurisdiction over this offshore base. In early January 2002, he wrote a memo arguing that Geneva Convention rules are inapplicable to the treatment of people whom the president has declared to be "unlawful enemy combatants." He thought (incorrectly) that the president can disregard the Geneva Conventions because they only apply as a matter of reciprocity in conflicts with other states. Yoo and his handlers either misunderstood or chose to disregard the fact that the US military is bound by the Geneva Conventions, regardless of the nature of the enemy.

These legal memos, which formed the foundations for the Bush administration's new paradigm, were classified. The public had no way of knowing their details or the reasoning and ideological preferences of the war council lawyers who were providing legal cover for the administration's policy choices.

In early 2002, a fight erupted at the highest levels of government between the State Department, which insisted that the Geneva Conventions apply to the treatment of people in US custody, and the White House, Pentagon, and Justice Department, which—relying on the OLC memos—insisted that they don't. On January 25, White House counsel Alberto Gonzales sent a memo to President Bush inveigling him to accept as "definitive" the OLC position that the Geneva Conventions don't apply. (Three years later, the *Washington Post* reported that Gonzales's January 25 memo was ghostwritten by Addington.) The memo read, "As you have said, the war against terrorism is a new kind of war ... In my judgment, this new paradigm renders obsolete Geneva's strict limitations on questioning of enemy prisoners and renders quaint some of its provisions." Gonzales advised President Bush that one compelling reason to declare these conventions obsolete would be to shield people whose actions violated them from being prosecuted under the federal War Crimes Act, the 1996 law granting US courts the jurisdiction to prosecute anyone, including Americans, for grave breaches of the Geneva Conventions. He added, forebodingly: "It is difficult to predict the motives of prosecutors and independent counsels who may in the future decide to pursue unwarranted charges based on [the War Crimes Act]."

Secretary of State Colin Powell was the only member of the administration's top tier who had been a professional soldier of the highest rank; he had served in the military for thirty-five years and had been the head of the Joint Chiefs of Staff. To counter those voices advising the president to disregard the Geneva Conventions, Powell sent a memo to Gonzales criticizing the legal faultiness and political dangers of the OLC's reasoning. One of the dangers that he must have had in mind was the recent (1999) "Pinochet precedent" (i.e., no sovereign immunity for torture) because he warned that if the United States declined to adhere to the Geneva Conventions, the effect might be to "provoke some individual foreign prosecutors to investigate and prosecute our officials and troops." Moreover, Powell argued, a presidential decision to opt out of the Geneva Conventions would "reverse over a century of US policy and practice ... and undermine the protections of the law of war for our troops."

Attorney General John Ashcroft weighed in with his own memo. He presented the president with two clear choices: A "presidential determination" that the Geneva Conventions are inapplicable (the OLC position) would ensure that no court would be able to "entertain charges" against American military officers, intelligence agents, or other officials for any violations. A "presidential interpretation" that the Geneva Conventions do apply, even if POW status was not extended to the Taliban (the State Department position), would put US officials and state agents at risk because courts "occasionally refuse to defer to presidential interpretation."

On February 7, President Bush issued a memorandum to his national security team endorsing the OLC position that the Geneva Conventions don't apply. He sought to mollify the State Department with the line that US forces "shall continue to treat detainees humanely and, to the extent appropriate and consistent with military necessity, in a manner consistent with the principles of Geneva."

The Bush administration's decision to disregard the Geneva Conventions was further complicated by the role the CIA was assigned to play in the "war on terror." Six days after 9/11, the president authorized the Agency to engage in wartime functions typically reserved for the military, including capturing or killing enemies and running interrogation and detention operations. As a civilian agency, the CIA is not subject to the Geneva Conventions or the UCMJ. And unlike the military, which has mechanisms to deal with law violations by soldiers, the CIA operates under an impenetrable cover of top-secret classification that makes accountability for its law-violating activities nearly impossible. Even the CIA's footsteps are covered up when it is referred to by the acronym OGA, which means "other government agency."

President Bush decided to make the CIA the tip of the spear because its clandestine modus operandi comported well with the way the administration wanted to wage the "war on terror." The president, however, does not have the right to disregard the laws of the land—at least that that was the black letter understanding prior to 9/11. Cheney, Addington, Yoo, and the other members of the war council were pushing the unitary executive thesis that a US president has *constitutional authority* to disregard any law if he decides it is in the nation's security interests to do so. But for a nation that prides itself on legal traditions and commitments to the rule of law, this disregard could not just be asserted; it had to be justified through legal arguments. This was a job for the OLC. Within the vast bureaucracy of the executive branch, the OLC functions as "the government's lawyer" and its legal opinions are often compared to judicial opinions because they are supposed to provide the current and correct interpretations of laws that apply to the behavior and policies of all federal agencies.

The origin of the Bush administration's "legalization" of torture can be traced to the CIA's request to the OLC in July 2002 for an authoritative opinion about legal liability for torture. The request arose from concerns that interrogation techniques they wanted to use on the first "high value detainee" in CIA custody, Abu Zubaydah (the nom de guerre of Zayn al-Abedin Muhammad Hussein), might put agents or their bosses at risk of future prosecution. Abu Zubaydah had been arrested in Pakistan in late March and then was whisked off to a secret interrogation facility in Thailand. US officials believed—erroneously, as it turned out—that he was a top lieutenant in al-Qaeda and, therefore, that he must have lots of valuable information. In June, Langley had hired two contractor-psychologists, James Mitchell and Bruce Jessen, to run the black site program and asked them to come up with a list of techniques that would make Abu Zubaydah compliant so that he could be exploited for actionable intelligence. Mitchell and Jessen were not professional interrogators. What made them appealing to the CIA was their experience as trainers in the military's Survival, Evasion, Resistance, Escape (SERE) program. The SERE program was developed during the Cold War to prepare US soldiers to stay strong and silent if they were ever captured by a torturing regime. The psychologists proposed "re-engineering" SERE techniques and they submitted a list of violent and degrading tactics that they believed would be effective for interrogating detainees in CIA custody.

By early July, CIA headquarters was growing concerned that the techniques they planned to use on Abu Zubaydah might run afoul of Title 18 of the US Code Section 2340; this federal statute, passed after the United States ratified the UN Convention against Torture and Other Cruel, Inhuman, or Degrading Treatment or Punishment (CAT), makes torture a prosecutable offense in US courts. The CIA's own legal counsel, Scott Muller, had warned the Agency that it was at risk of violating that federal law if the reverse-engineered SERE tactics were utilized.

Decision-makers in the Bush administration wanted the techniques Mitchell and Jessen proposed to be interpreted as "legal." To do so, Yoo wrote two memos which were signed by OLC head Jay Bybee. One memo constructed a legal argument that violent and coercive interrogation techniques do not violate federal law if they do not rise to the level of torture, and therefore authorizing them is not "illegal." The other memo endorsed the specific techniques the CIA was proposing to use. Both memos were dated August 1, 2002.

The legal rationales in the first memo read like an object lesson in unitary executive thinking. Lesson one: US sovereignty is paramount and the only law that matters is American law. In his efforts to demarcate the line between torture and not torture, Yoo ignored international humanitarian and human rights laws and jurisprudence of international courts and tribunals. Instead, he combed federal law to "clarify" the meaning of torture. According to the federal torture statute (Section 2340), the prerequisite for physical torture is the intent to cause severe pain. Yoo found that the only federal law that contains the phrase "severe pain" pertains to medical professionals who are compelled to provide (or not withhold) emergency care to the uninsured who are experiencing severe pain. Yoo adapted the wording in that emergency care–related law to assert that "physical pain amounting to torture must be equivalent in intensity to the pain accompanying serious physical injury, such as organ failure, impairment of bodily function, or even death." Mental or psychological torture is defined in Section 2340 as "prolonged mental harm." Yoo found no reference to that phrase in US law, so he turned to dictionaries and medical reference books to clarify the meaning of "prolonged." He concluded that, to rise to the level of mental torture, the "harm must cause some lasting, though not necessarily permanent, damage." He elaborated, "The development of a mental disorder such as posttraumatic stress disorder, which can last months or even years, or even chronic depression, which also can last for a considerable period of time if untreated, might satisfy the prolonged harm requirement."

To evaluate the legality of specific interrogation tactics, Yoo surveyed the record of US judicial decisions in federal Torture Victims Protection Act (TVPA) cases. He found that courts had provided a civil remedy for victims who sued their foreign torturers for severe beatings, mock executions, burning with cigarettes, electric shocks, rape, sexual assault or injury to sex organs, and forcing a prisoner to watch the torture of others. But, Yoo argued, these TVPA lawsuits were not definitive because there are no US cases "that analyze the lowest boundary of what constitutes torture." To identify the lowest boundary as the line between torture and not torture, between crime and not crime, he turned for inspiration to a US ally, Israel. Specifically, he reproduced Israel's potted reasoning from the late 1980s (discussed in the Introduction) that "moderate physical pressure" does not constitute torture, and therefore is not illegal. But Yoo ignored the 1999 Israeli High Court of Justice ruling proscribing the government's prerogative to make routine use of violent and coercive practices.

Lesson 2: Adopt a formalistic approach and exalt the original intent of those who wrote the law. Yoo argued that when Congress passed the federal statute, it drew a distinction between torture and cruel, inhuman, or degrading treatment (CIDT). Indeed, both CAT and the federal law recognize different types and intensities of violence—that's the function of the word "and" between torture and CIDT. Yoo interpreted congressional intent to make torture a prosecutable offense while also intending to permit treatment that is *merely* cruel, inhuman or degrading.

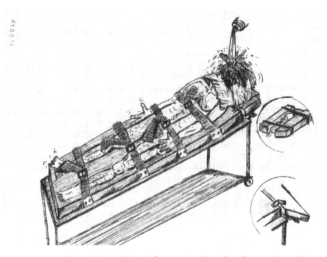

FIGURE 3. Abu Zubaydah self-portrait sketch of waterboarding. Copyright Abu Zubaydah 2019. Licensed by Professor Mark Denbeaux, Seton Hall Law School.

Lesson 3: The president's unitary executive power vests him with unfettered discretion to protect national security, including the right to authorize torture if he thinks it is necessary. Yoo crafted a golden shield for anyone who would follow the president's orders: "Even if an interrogation method arguably were to violate Section 2340A, the statute would be unconstitutional if it impermissibly encroached on the President's constitutional power to conduct a military campaign." But just in case the constitutional infringement argument might not survive challenges in the future, Yoo suggested a line of defense that Americans charged with torture could marshal. For this, he again borrowed from the Israeli model, circa 1987, that violent and degrading interrogation tactics may be necessary to combat terrorism and, therefore, are a legitimate national security option. The memo's final statement reads: "Even if an interrogation method might violate Section 2340A, necessity or self-defense could provide justifications that would eliminate any criminal liability."

These August 1 OLC memos provided the CIA with cover to use re-engineered SERE techniques. With approval from Washington, Abu Zubaydah was subjected to every one of the interrogation tactics Mitchell and Jessen had proposed, including waterboarding—he was waterboarded eighty-three times—as well as "persistent conditioning techniques" such as nudity and dietary manipulation to break his capacity to resist their questions. Abu Zubaydah was the guinea pig for the torture and human experimentation that would come to define the CIA's interrogation and detention program.

Although the August 1 OLC memos were written specifically for the CIA, the White House passed them along to the Pentagon where the civilian leadership seized upon them for military interrogators. In September 2002, Guantánamo interrogators were sent to Fort Bragg to learn about the SERE program so that they could apply the same re-engineered tactics that the CIA was using. On October 2, the CIA's chief counsel for counterterrorism, Jonathan Fredman, went to Guantánamo to brief senior military staff. According to minutes from that meeting, Fredman told them that the legal prohibition on torture "is basically subject to perception. If the detainee dies, you're doing it wrong."

A week later, the commander of Joint Task Force Guantánamo (JTF-GTMO), General Michael Dunleavy, sent a request for authorization to use coercive techniques, including stress positions, exploitation of phobias, forced nudity, isolation, sensory deprivation, exposure to extremes in temperature, and waterboarding, on a Saudi named Mohammed al-Qahtani who was assumed to be the most high-value detainee at Guantánamo. FBI investigators had fingered al-Qahtani as, possibly, the 9/11 plot's "missing 20th hijacker"; one of the four planes—the one that crashed in western Pennsylvania when passengers overpowered their hijackers—had one less muscle man onboard than the others. They speculated that the missing man might have been al-Qahtani because he had attempted to enter the United States in August 2001, but he was turned away at the border. He was captured in Afghanistan in December 2001 and shipped to Guantánamo in June 2002.

Secretary Rumsfeld responded to Dunleavy's request by verbally authorizing a "special interrogation plan" for al-Qahtani; he approved all the requested techniques as well as questioning for twenty hours in every twenty-four-hour cycle, and intimidation with military dogs. Two weeks later, Pentagon general counsel William "Jim" Haynes, who was also a member of the war council, turned the special plan into an action memo. When Rumsfeld signed it, he added a handwritten note at the bottom: "I stand for eight hours a day. Why is standing limited to four hours? D.R."

In November 2002, Major General Geoffrey Miller replaced Dunleavy as commander of JTF-GTMO. On December 10, Miller issued a new standard operating procedure for Guantánamo interrogators based on re-engineered SERE techniques that Rumsfeld had approved. According to Miller's order, "These tactics and techniques are used at SERE school to 'break' SERE detainees. The same tactics and techniques can be used to break real detainees during interrogation." Miller's signature innovation was to meld detention operations—that is, how detainees are treated by guards—with interrogation to ensure that they were suffering and humiliated on a constant basis.

The first sign of dissent over interrogation policy inside the Pentagon came from Alberto Mora, who was the top civilian lawyer for the Navy. In the late autumn of 2002, Mora saw excerpts of the logs from al-Qahtani's coercive interrogations. He started making inquiries about what was going on at Guantánamo, and he obtained copies of Dunleavy's request and Rumsfeld's approval for the use of coercion. Mora confronted Haynes, warning that the authorized techniques might constitute torture, and he complained that the legal reasoning to justify them was "incompetent." If Mora thought his warning would be sufficient, he was disabused of that idea in early January 2003, when he was informed that detainee abuse was ongoing.

On January 15, Mora sent a draft memo to Haynes criticizing the authorized techniques as "at a minimum, cruel and unusual treatment and, at worst, torture." He threatened to make his memo official if his concerns were not immediately addressed. Such exposure would create a real crisis for Bush administration officials who were insisting publicly that detainees were being treated humanely. The day Mora issued this warning, Rumsfeld rescinded his December 2, 2002, authorization and ordered the formation of a working group composed of senior officers to clarify the methods that military interrogators could use.

Haynes, who was in charge of this working group, made it clear that their mandate was to endorse the use of re-engineered SERE tactics that Rumsfeld previously had approved for Guantánamo. Some of the JAGs in the working group protested that any directive permitting soldiers to abuse prisoners not only would put them at risk of court martial for violating the UCMJ but would pose a threat to military discipline and, if it became public, could damage the reputation of the military. Their concerns were disregarded as examples of that excessively rule-bound military culture that Rumsfeld wanted to change. To silence their opposition, Haynes solicited Yoo to write a memo specifically for the military. The memo Yoo drafted reproduced the legal reasoning in the August 1 OLC memo he wrote for the CIA. With that draft in hand, Haynes demanded that the working group accept it as "definitive guidance."

The fight over interrogation policy and the law moved up the chain of command when the working group circulated a draft of its guidelines and recommendations. Between February 15 and March 13, the top JAG for each branch of the military wrote a memo decrying coercive interrogations as illegal, politically dangerous, and un-American. Major General Jack Rives, Deputy JAG of the Air Force, wrote: "[T]he use of the more extreme interrogation techniques simply is not how the US armed forces have operated in recent history ... We need to consider the overall impact of approving extreme interrogation techniques as giving official approval and legal sanction to the application of interrogation techniques that US forces have been consistently trained are unlawful." Brigadier General Kevin Sandkuhler, the Marine Corps's top lawyer, pointed out that "the OLC does not represent the [armed] services; thus, understandably, concern for servicemembers is not reflected in their memo. Notably, their opinion is silent on the UCMJ and foreign views of international law." Major General Thomas Romig, top JAG for the Army, assailed the "exceptionally broad concept of 'necessity'" to justify illegal practices. "I question whether this theory ultimately would prevail in either the US courts or in any international forum. If such a defense is not available, soldiers ordered to use otherwise illegal techniques run a substantial risk of criminal prosecution or personal liability arising from a civil lawsuit."

Rather than retreat in the face of these high-ranking JAGs' criticisms, Haynes and Yoo doubled down. On March 13, Yoo finalized his memo and Haynes pressed the working group to accept the reasoning and endorse the full gamut of techniques. On April 4, the working group's final report was submitted—without the knowledge of some of its members. That report contained sections of Yoo's memo verbatim while also, paradoxically, incorporating some wording that rebuts its reasoning as contrary to the UCMJ. On April 16, Rumsfeld secretly approved twenty-four of the thirty-five coercive techniques proposed in the working group report.

When other high-ranking military lawyers were "read in" (i.e., given access) to this legally schizophrenic Pentagon policy directive, they became alarmed. In the spring of 2003, several senior JAGs contacted Scott Horton, an expert on military and international law who, at the time, was head of the Human Rights Committee of the New York City Bar Association. They wanted to consult with Horton about the legal implications of policies that sanction the abuse of prisoners. Since interrogation policy was classified, they had to present their concerns in hypotheticals. Horton realized that the

JAGs needed expert analysis of the laws and rules governing wartime interrogations that would support their opposition to policies that violated the UCMJ. He assembled a team of lawyers and law professors with expertise in military affairs and human rights, and they went to work.

Resistance to Pentagon policy within the military, Swift explained, had consequences: "Because the JAGs were so opposed to coercive interrogations, the military commissions were taken away from them. Control was given to Haynes." Swift's assessment of Haynes was damning. "He totally misunderstood military justice. He repeatedly asked [acting chief prosecutor] Lietzau, 'How long will this take?' and 'the defense can file motions?' He doesn't understand justice and the rule of law." (After Haynes's decisions to override the opposition by top JAGs to coercive interrogations became public in 2004, retired military officers successfully lobbied Congress to block his nomination to the federal judiciary.)

Despite Swift's disdain for the military commissions, he may not have opened a second front in the war in court were it not for a fateful series of events. In May 2003, Neal Katyal, a Georgetown University law professor, sent an email to Colonel Gunn: "I would be willing to help you out with any legal strategy you might need." Katyal is an expert in constitutional and national security law. In November 2001, he had testified before the Senate Judiciary Committee about President Bush's military order. While Katyal's statements to the committee incorporated constitution-minded deference to presidential power in wartime, he contended that the establishment of a military commission system would require an act of Congress, not just an order by the president. Katyal and Harvard law professor Laurence Tribe, who made similar arguments in his testimony on the Hill, coauthored a *Yale Law Journal* article critical of the commissions. Gunn showed Katyal's email to Sundel and Swift. Sundel, who had already read the article, suggested that they meet Katyal.

Swift told me that, before their first meeting, he was expecting an ivory tower intellectual with "no experience in the real world" and, by his account, Katyal would be expecting "a C student too dumb to do anything else." Later, when I presented Swift's description to Katyal, he chuckled. He conceded that Swift's ivory tower stereotype wasn't entirely off the mark because his way of thinking is "very rule-bound and linear" and saturated with knowledge about international law and constitutional war powers. But, Katyal pointed out, he had prior experience working with JAGs from his time as a national security adviser in the Clinton administration's

Justice Department, so he knew how capable they were. Swift, Sundel, and Katyal spent the summer of 2003 developing arguments against the military commissions, not sure if they would ever get the chance to use them in court.

In September, Swift and several of his JAG colleagues decided to go to New York City. Part of their strategy in opposing the military commissions was to gain support and build relations with civil society organizations. One of the organizations they met with was the Center for Constitutional Rights, which had started the war in court in February 2002 by filing the first lawsuit against the government. Attorneys at CCR were working on Guantánamo from afar. The military defense lawyers, by contrast, were insiders with unique and valuable insights. Barbara Olshansky of CCR said that when she met these military lawyers for the first time, she was stunned by their ferocious attacks on the administration. "I started to have some hope. These lawyers helped forge connections for CCR with retired military commanders. This gave CCR's work some real juice."

In October, three of the military defense lawyers attended a conference of the National Association of Criminal Defense Lawyers (NACDL). At a reception, one of NACDL's board members introduced the JAGs to Joshua Dratel, who at the time was co-chair of the committee on military tribunals. They told Dratel about the ethical dilemmas they would face defending Guantánamo detainees. He assured them that NACDL, which was already concerned about these issues, would have their backs.

A critical turning point came in November 2003 when the Supreme Court granted certiorari to hear *Rasul v. Bush*. Katyal and the JAGs realized that this case, which turned on the question of whether federal courts have jurisdiction over Guantánamo, could have implications for the military commissions, too. They decided to submit an amicus brief that would stress the unconstitutionality of the military commissions and their deviation from the UCMJ. Because JAGs are in the chain of command, they had to obtain permission to file a brief, which—after some Pentagon foot dragging—they did. Swift credited their amicus brief for *Rasul* in bringing public attention to the fact that there was dissent in the ranks.

At the end of 2003, the five military defense lawyers were assigned clients. They were instructed that their only option would be to negotiate guilty pleas. The Pentagon was hoping that a couple of quick plea-bargained convictions could be sold to the public as victories in the "war on terror" and prove the effectiveness of the military commissions.

Swift's client, Salim Hamdan, had been selected as one of the first to be prosecuted, not because he was a terrorist mastermind or had played a role in plotting the 9/11 attacks, but because he had agreed to plead guilty. By the time Swift met Hamdan in January 2004, he had been in solitary confinement at Camp Echo for over ten months. Swift found a man so traumatized that he "was as close to a death penalty client as I've ever seen." In keeping with the standard operating paranoia of Guantánamo, in the room where their meeting took place, soldiers put two tables between Swift, who weighs in at around two hundred pounds, and Hamdan, a tiny man who was shackled to the floor. Swift's translator, Charles Schmitz, is an academic expert on Yemen. Swift was glowing in his praise of Schmitz's ability to speak a colloquial Yemeni dialect, and said these skills were critical to gradually winning Hamdan's trust.

At that first meeting, Swift had to explain the government's offer to his client: twenty years for charges that had not even been specified yet. He learned that Hamdan did not, in fact, want to plead guilty. What was he guilty of? Swift decided to refuse his orders to negotiate a plea bargain and started working to defend Hamdan. He explained, "All men have rights, including the right to a trial—a regular trial!"

Bush administration officials were billing Hamdan as a high-level al-Qaeda operative. In reality, Hamdan was an underemployed man with a fourth-grade education who had been driven by poverty to Afghanistan in the mid-1990s where he got a job as a driver for Osama bin Laden. After military operations started in October 2001, bin Laden was able to evade capture by fleeing the country while low-level functionaries were left behind. Hamdan was captured in November by bounty hunters and sold to the United States. Six months later, he was transferred to Guantánamo. Why, Swift wondered, did officials decide to prosecute Hamdan rather than make good use of him? "This is the kind of guy you turn into an informer, not a terrorist icon."

There was someone who might constitute a terrorist icon in Hamdan's family: his brother-in-law Nasser al-Bahri, whose nom de guerre is Abu Jandal, which means father of death. Abu Jandal began his calling as a mujahid (a Muslim who fights or struggles on behalf of the faith) in 1994 when he was nineteen and decided to go to Bosnia to help defend Muslims during the violent breakup of the former Yugoslavia. In 1996, Abu Jandal decided to take a group of mujahideen to Tajikistan. Hamdan joined them, not out of any political conviction but because he needed money to support his family.

On their journey, they were waylaid in Afghanistan. When bin Laden heard about Abu Jandal's group, he invited them to stay. Shortly after meeting bin Laden, Abu Jandal swore an oath of loyalty (a *bayat*). He soon became one of the al-Qaeda leader's inner-circle of bodyguards. He even had a special gun that he was supposed to use to kill bin Laden if he was ever at risk of being captured. Abu Jandal arranged for his brother-in-law to work as bin Laden's driver.

Abu Jandal endorsed bin Laden's January 2000 announcement of the plan to wage jihad on the United States. On October 12, 2000, he was back in Yemen when al-Qaeda suicide bombers smashed a bomb-laden dinghy into the USS Cole while the warship was refueling in the port of Aden. Seventeen sailors were killed. Abu Jandal was arrested by Yemeni security forces on the suspicion that he might have played a role in the attack. Six days after 9/11, while he was still detained in a Yemeni jail, two FBI agents, who had been tracking al-Qaeda for years, came to interrogate him. The agents, following FBI policy, read Abu Jandal his Miranda rights each day before they started. They used rapport-building methods to interrogate him and softened him up with sugar-free cakes (he is diabetic). When they told Abu Jandal that some of the men that he had identified from photographs were 9/11 hijackers, he broke down and began talking. Years later, he would tell filmmaker Laura Poitras, while she was shooting a documentary titled *The Oath* about Abu Jandal and Hamdan, that he decided to cooperate because the jihad he had signed onto didn't involve the mass murder of civilians.

According to FBI reports, Abu Jandal provided a vast amount of information about air defense and weapons systems in Afghanistan, munitions and training facilities, the location of tunnels, and details about bin Laden's security arrangements and strategic thinking. In fact, he provided so much actionable intelligence that the United States delayed the ground invasion until his interrogation was completed. Abu Jandal was never charged with any crime, and in 2003, he was released from jail after participating in the Yemeni government's reeducation program for militants. He became a taxi driver. Meanwhile, his brother-in-law was languishing in Guantánamo and facing trial by military commission.

Dan Mori was assigned to represent David Hicks, an Australian kangaroo skinner who converted to Islam in 1999 and went to Pakistan to study religion. A year later, he went to Afghanistan where he became a foot soldier in the Taliban's fight against the Northern Alliance. After the start of the war, Hicks was captured by the Northern Alliance and sold to the United States for five thousand dollars. The Bush administration's intent to prosecute Hicks begged the question: how was fighting in a civil war in Afghanistan prior to 9/11 a manifestation of international terrorism or a threat to the security of the United States? Only in these new military commissions could such a case be made. In a published interview, Mori said, "The same people writing the rules for this process are the same people who want to convict my client. They have a goal and they want to achieve it and unfortunately, an independent justice system would interfere with that goal."

Hicks was one of the plaintiffs in *Rasul,* which meant he was also represented by Joseph Margulies, lead counsel on the case. When Hicks was charged, Margulies realized that if any of his other Guantánamo clients was a source of evidence the government was planning to use against Hicks, he might have a conflict of interests. Since Margulies had not met any of his clients yet, this was an abstract concern. Margulies asked Josh Dratel to come aboard as "conflict counsel." Dratel agreed, assuming that "this would be a one-afternoon job." Two weeks later, after Mori's first meeting with Hicks, he called Dratel and said, "We have to talk." Mori flew to New York City and met Margulies and Dratel in the CCR offices. They decided that Margulies did, indeed, have a conflict. The Supreme Court case was too important for him to give up, so Dratel stepped into his place as Hicks's habeas counsel and Mori's co-counsel in the commission case.

In January 2004, Dratel became the first civilian lawyer in private practice to go to Guantánamo and meet with a detainee. The government wanted to control and limit his relationship with his client by imposing onerous restrictions on their communications. Dratel told me, "I refused to go along with the US government's original demands, so the government had to cave."

Sharon Shaffer was assigned to represent a Sudanese man named Ibrahim al-Qosi. In 1989, al-Qosi was hired as an accountant for a company in Khartoum owned by bin Laden. In 1996, when the Sudanese government, at the behest of the US government, ordered bin Laden to leave the country, he relocated to Afghanistan. Al-Qosi followed and got a job as bin Laden's cook. In November 2001, al-Qosi was captured in the Tora Bora region of Afghanistan, and he was one of the first to be transferred to Guantánamo in early 2002. The charges that the Pentagon leveled against al-Qosi included his activities dating back to 1989. As Shaffer said to me with some incredulity, "We were in an armed conflict with al-Qaeda in 1989?" And, "Being an accountant or a cook is a war crime?" These were not rhetorical questions. Shaffer was flagging two issues that would become major legal disputes in the war in court. First, according to the laws of war, there can be no war crimes without a war, which begs the question of when the war against al-Qaeda began. Second, the only people who can violate the laws of war are those subject to them: members of militaries. If people accused of being terrorists are not soldiers, how can they be charged with violating the laws of war? The charges against al-Qosi were indicative of the makeshift, outcome-driven approach to use military commissions to prosecute people captured in the "war on terror" for activities that did not constitute war crimes.

Phil Sundel and Mark Bridges were assigned to represent Ali Hamza al-Bahlul, a Yemeni propagandist for al-Qaeda. Unlike the other three men—Hamdan, al-Qosi, and Hicks—al-Bahlul proclaimed himself an important al-Qaeda facilitator and maintained unrepentant and unwavering support for violent jihad against the United States. And while Hamdan and al-Qosi overcame their initial reluctance to having US military lawyers represent them, al-Bahlul categorically rejected his.

As Swift got to work on Hamdan's defense, he learned about how his client had been violently interrogated, first in Afghanistan and then in Guantánamo. With outrage in his eyes, Swift told me, "The abuse of prisoners indicates that we don't think detainees are human." Although he couldn't share classified information about Hamdan's treatment with Katyal, he wanted to persuade his civilian ally that this might make a good test case for the theories they had been developing to challenge the military commissions. Katyal was skeptical at first because of Hamdan's personal connection to bin Laden. That skepticism subsided in April 2004 when photos of US soldiers torturing and abusing Iraqi detainees in the Abu Ghraib prison were published.

Swift said the publication of the Abu Ghraib photos "confirmed stuff I believed. I had talked to my client, I had seen the intelligence, so I knew what was happening." Shaffer said, "As a member of the military, it's scary to see Abu Ghraib and talk to my client about what he's been through. What will happen when our people are captured? We are supposed to be defenders of the rule of law. To lower ourselves with these tactics is not saying much about our commitments."

Scott Horton's team of experts submitted their report about the rules and laws governing wartime interrogations to the New York City Bar Association in mid-April. It didn't generate much buzz until after the Abu Ghraib scandal erupted and, two months later, the torture memos were released. The delayed impact of that report was like a law-of-war knowledge grenade tossed into the intellectually parochial swamplands of the unitary executive thesis camp.

FIGURE 4. Military commission hearing, August 24, 2004: Salim Hamdan standing between his interpreter, Charles Schmitz, and his lawyer, Lieutenant Commander Charles Swift. Drawing by Art Lien / Courtartist.

During that game-changing month of April 2004, Swift filed *Hamdan v. Rumsfeld* in the federal district court in his hometown, Seattle, Washington. He retained Katyal as his attorney out of concern that the government might retaliate against him. In its first iteration, *Hamdan* challenged the Pentagon's plan to prosecute Hamdan in a military commission because he had not been determined to be an enemy combatant by any competent tribunal. Because this issue overlapped with the matter before the Supreme Court in *Rasul,* the judge decided to stay *Hamdan* until after the Supreme Court ruled on that case.

The *Rasul* ruling was issued at the end of June. The Supreme Court decided that federal courts do have jurisdiction over Guantánamo and detainees do have habeas corpus rights. But that judicial rebuke didn't lead the Bush administration to overhaul its positions on law and policy. On the contrary, in July, the Pentagon charged Hamdan with conspiracy and material support for terrorism.

Meanwhile *Hamdan* was transferred from Seattle to the DC District Court. On November 9, 2004, Judge James Robertson ruled that Hamdan cannot be prosecuted by a military commission until his status has been determined by an impartial tribunal, adding "the president is not a 'tribunal.'" The ruling also found that the military commission rules violate the UCMJ. That day, Swift was at Guantánamo arguing some pretrial motions. Someone handed the presiding commission judge, Colonel Peter Brownback, a note with information about the federal court ruling. Judge Brownback put the case against Hamdan, which was supposed to start on December 7, into indefinite recess.

On the same day Judge Robertson issued his ruling in *Hamdan,* Shaffer filed a habeas petition for al-Qosi in the DC District Court which included allegations that he had been tortured by US forces. She told me, "This is an important piece of history to be part of. This is a battle. You do what you've got to do." She added, "I challenge everything I can because these are crucial issues for where our country is going."

The government appealed the District Court's ruling in *Hamdan* to the DC Circuit Court. The Bush administration had never wanted courts to intervene in policies pertaining to detainees captured in the "war on terror," but now that they had, the objective was to get a ruling that would validate the administration's new paradigm. While the *Hamdan* case was on the docket of the appeals court, Congress convened hearings about the military commissions. On June 15, 2005, Swift testified before the Senate Judiciary Committee. He used the opportunity to educate the committee about the bureaucratic problems and numerous legal flaws in the system, including the fact that his civilian superiors had exercised undue influence by trying to force him to negotiate a guilty plea for his client.

One month to the day after Swift testified on the Hill, the Bush administration got the ruling they were hoping for. The three-judge panel of the DC Circuit Court, one of whose members was John Roberts, unanimously reversed the lower court's ruling. Their decision endorsed the Bush administration's claims that the military commissions are a legitimate venue to prosecute foreign terror suspects. It went further down the new paradigm rabbit hole by ruling that the judicial branch has no jurisdiction to enforce the Geneva Conventions, and that US treaty obligations confer no right or remedies on accused terrorists.

Swift appealed the Circuit Court ruling to the Supreme Court. As he had predicted when I met him, on November 7, 2005, the Court agreed to hear the case. John Roberts, who became the new chief justice two month earlier, had to recuse himself.

In an *Esquire* article published in March 2007, Swift reflected on the significance of his case: "In most countries, when a military officer openly opposes the president, it is called a coup. In the United States, it is called *Hamdan v. Rumsfeld*."

THREE

Mapping the Lines of Battle

THERE WAS NO FIGHT AGAINST TORTURE, per se, while the existence of the torture program was a secret. That changed abruptly in the spring and early summer of 2004 when a trifecta of events exposed realities about interrogation and detention operations that had been hidden from the public. Before that, I was always on the lookout for news items that could confirm my sense that torture was being perpetrated in the shadows. Donald Rumsfeld gave that phenomenon a name: the known unknown. The phrase is one in a string of Rumsfeldisms delivered by the defense secretary at a Pentagon press briefing on February 12, 2002: "[A]s we know, there are known knowns; there are things we know we know. We also know there are known unknowns; that is to say we know there are some things we do not know. But there are also unknown unknowns—the ones we don't know we don't know."

Rumsfeld offered these comments to justify the Bush administration's plan to expand the "war on terror" to Iraq. The known unknown, in this context, was the allegation that Saddam Hussein still had weapons of mass destruction (WMD). Rumsfeld was casting doubt on UN weapons inspectors who, in the 1990s, had overseen the destruction of Iraqi WMD and the conclusion of a 1999 report by a UN panel of experts that "the bulk of Iraq's proscribed weapons programs has been eliminated." Rumsfeld was trying to persuade people that just because you can't see something doesn't mean it isn't there.

Rumsfeld did have a point about known unknowns, though. The "war on terror" was not launched with a well-stocked arsenal of hard, accurate information about the enemy. Rather, it began as a war for information, a transnational manhunt to find and capture terrorists in order to find and capture more terrorists and, in so doing, to avert the possibility of future attacks and destroy terrorist organizations and networks. As in most asymmetric wars in which states are fighting against unconventional enemies, human intelligence is essential to find people who don't wear uniforms or carry arms openly, don't control swaths of territory, and don't possess large weapons that could be spotted through aerial surveillance—which certainly was true of al-Qaeda. The most common way to obtain this kind of human intelligence is to capture people alive and interrogate them. But the decisions to authorize violent and degrading interrogation techniques were the fulfilment of ideological preferences, not rational imperatives.

The Bush administration was able to control the narrative about the "war on terror" for a solid year and a half by classifying so much of the information about war-related activities and policies. In October 2001, Attorney General John Ashcroft issued a memo to all federal agencies urging them to be hyper-vigilant when they processed Freedom of Information Act (FOIA) requests. State secrecy was critical to the administration's executive power grab because invisibility buttresses deniability about wrongdoing and fosters public compliance and gullibility. Whenever some troubling information about prisoner abuse or a homicide in an overseas detention facility was reported by investigative journalists or human rights organizations, officials typically responded with frothy assurances that the government was committed to humane treatment, topping them off with just-trust-us assertions that secrecy was essential for national security.

Secrecy and propaganda were quite effective means of controlling the public narrative until the claque of neoconservatives who dominated the upper echelons of the Bush administration began pushing and planning for war on Iraq. Neocons had been hankering to reinvade Iraq since the 1991 Gulf War ended without storming Baghdad and toppling the regime of Saddam Hussein. Immediately after the 9/11 attacks, Rumsfeld advocated starting the "war on terror" in Iraq because that country had better targets than Afghanistan. Although the Iraq-firsters didn't prevail at the time, they set about sidelining those in the intelligence community who didn't share their convictions and aspirations. In the Pentagon, an Office of Special Plans was set up and staffed with neocons whose mission was to interpret intelligence in ways that would validate Rumsfeld's and Deputy Secretary of Defense Paul Wolfowitz's contentions that Iraq posed an imminent threat to US national security.

In early 2002, when the neocons openly renewed their calls to attack Iraq, the post-9/11 patriotic esprit de corps began fraying at the margins. Anti-war activists sprang into action to try to stop this war before it started. But a sizable majority of Americans across the political spectrum supported a war on Iraq because they were persuaded by official propaganda that Saddam had secret stockpiles of chemical weapons that had eluded UN inspectors, and that he was somehow implicated in 9/11.

To make the case for war on Iraq, the WMD allegation was the workhorse. But what the administration really desired was evidence that Saddam was linked to 9/11. With the help of torture, they got it. Their source was a Libyan national named Ibn al-Sheikh al-Libi (nom de guerre for Ali Muhammad Abdul Aziz al-Fakheri). Al-Libi was a member of the Libyan Islamic Fighting Group, an organization whose enemy was the dictatorship of Muammar Qaddafi. Al-Libi left his homeland sometime in the 1980s and, like many Islamist militants, he went to Afghanistan to join the fight that the CIA was covertly supporting against the Soviet-backed communist regime. When the Soviets ended their occupation of Afghanistan in 1989, US interest in the country dissipated. When the communist regime fell in 1992, civil war intensified. The Taliban, led by veterans of the CIA-supported resistance to the communists, won control over most of the country in the mid-1990s. In 1995, al-Libi became the head of al-Khalden training camp, the largest and longest-running facility for Arab militants in Afghanistan (so-called "Afghan Arabs"). After 9/11, the Bush administration claimed that al-Khalden was an al-Qaeda camp, but in fact, it hosted individuals from various factions and al-Qaeda had its own camps.

In November 2001, al-Libi was fleeing the country when he was captured at the Pakistan border. He was sent back to Afghanistan where he was questioned by agents from the FBI and Britain's MI6. Then, over FBI protestations, the CIA took possession of al-Libi and spirited him off to the USS Bataan, which was being used as a floating detention facility in the Arabian Sea. That was January 2002, months before the CIA would get its black site program up and running.

Several weeks later, the CIA extraordinarily rendered al-Libi to Egypt. He was transported in a sealed coffin to the custody of Omar Suleiman, the long-time head of Egypt's General Intelligence Service. The United States had been rendering—that is, arresting or kidnapping and then extra-judicially transferring—suspects from one country to another for several decades. In 1989, William Barr, who headed the Office of Legal Counsel in the administration of George H. W. Bush, wrote a legal opinion to validate "the president's snatch authority." In the 1990s, the Clinton administration, often working in collaboration with Suleiman, used rendition at least seventy times to abduct Islamist militants and transfer them to the United States or their home country or a third country. But prior to 9/11, US rendition operations usually involved transporting suspects somewhere for trial. After 9/11, the purpose of renditions shifted from prosecution to interrogation. Egypt continued to figure large as a CIA rendition destination because Suleiman, in the words of former US ambassador to Egypt Edward Walker, was "not squeamish" about using violence. At least one person extraordinarily rendered to Egypt during the "war on terror"—Egyptian-born Australian citizen Mamdouh Habib—was tortured by Suleiman himself.

Egyptian interrogators were informed that al-Libi had said something while he was in CIA custody that suggested he knew about an al-Qaeda–Iraq connection. Their questioning focused on getting him to elaborate. Other prisoners in other places were being asked similar questions in 2002 because the Bush administration wanted evidence that Saddam was implicated in 9/11. Al-Libi couldn't even make up answers specific enough to satisfy his Egyptian interrogators, so they turned up the heat. He was placed in a small confinement box for about seventeen hours, but still he couldn't come up with anything. Then he was savagely beaten and warned that this was his "last opportunity to tell the truth." At that point, he told his interrogators that several al-Qaeda operatives had received training in Iraq for use of chemical and biological weapons. That statement made al-Libi the goose who laid the neocons' golden egg.

In August 2002, CIA analysts produced a report raising serious questions about the veracity of al-Libi's claim. The Defense Intelligence Agency had come to a similarly skeptical conclusion a month earlier. This reality-check, if it were made public, would have conflicted with the Bush administration's objective to link Iraq to 9/11 and might have strengthened the hands of those trying to prevent the war. Instead, in a stunning example of the deadliness of state secrets, the skeptical assessments stayed classified.

At a press briefing on September 27, Rumsfeld said that the link between al-Qaeda and Iraq is "accurate and not debatable." On October 7, as Congress was about to take up the White House–backed resolution to authorize war on Iraq, President Bush delivered a speech in Cleveland, Ohio, in which he claimed that the United States had evidence that Saddam had trained al-Qaeda members in bombmaking and the manufacture of chemical weapons. In the administration's failed gambit to obtain UN Security Council endorsement for the Iraq war, al-Libi's statement was one of the items that

Secretary of State Colin Powell presented on February 5, 2003. "I can trace the story of a senior terrorist operative telling how Iraq provided training in these weapons to al-Qaeda," Powell said. "Fortunately, this operative is now detained and he has told his story."

In January 2004, al-Libi was back in CIA custody. He told debriefers that the statement he had made in Egypt was false; he said what his interrogators wanted to hear to stop the abusive treatment. George Tenet, who was director of the CIA at the time, addresses al-Libi's recantation in his 2007 autobiography, *At the Center of the Storm:* "Now, suddenly, he was saying that there was no such cooperative training . . . and here is where the mystery begins . . . He clearly lied. We just don't know when. Did he lie when he first said that al-Qa'ida members received training in Iraq or did he lie when he said they did not? In my mind, either case might still be true . . . and since we don't know, we can assume nothing." But in 2006, a year before Tenet's book was published, the Senate Select Committee on Intelligence had affirmed that al-Libi's statement about the al-Qaeda–Iraq connection was false.

After al-Libi's statement was exploited to justify the Iraq war, he disappeared, like the other 118 or so "ghost detainees" in CIA custody who were shuttled around the archipelago of black sites and rendered to torture-by-proxy destinations. To follow al-Libi's story to its ignominious conclusion, in 2006, he was secretly transferred back to Libya. Qaddafi, who was trying to curry favor with the Bush administration, kept al-Libi's whereabouts a secret to shield the United States as well as Egypt from potential embarrassment. But in April 2009, Human Rights Watch investigators happened upon al-Libi in the courtyard of the notorious Abu Salim prison. He refused their request to be interviewed, but he did ask where they were when he was being tortured in American prisons. The publicization of his whereabouts sparked immediate international interest because of the role his false statement had played in the Iraq war. To manage the exposure, Omar Suleiman flew to Tripoli to consult with his Libyan counterpart. Before Suleiman's return flight had touched down in Cairo, the Qaddafi regime announced that al-Libi had committed suicide in his cell.

Although a majority of Americans bought the propaganda about the necessity of a war on Iraq, it didn't sell well on the international market. On the contrary, opposition was intense and furious. On February 15, 2003, with the declared start of the invasion a month away, millions of people in over eight hundred cities around the world participated in the largest coordinated protest in history. In the United States, demonstrations took place in at least

150 cities, including at least one hundred thousand protestors who converged near the United Nations in New York City. In Rome, three million demonstrators broke the Guinness Book of World Records for the largest anti-war rally ever.

Many of the governments that had joined the coalition that went to war in Afghanistan in 2001 refused to pony up troops for a war on Iraq. Britain and Australia agreed to join what President Bush took to calling the "coalition of the willing," but France said no. US politicians, who regarded the French refusal as an affront, expressed their displeasure by urging Americans to stop calling fried potatoes "French fries" and instead call them "freedom fries." The House of Representatives made the rename official in their cafeteria.

The neocons would not be deterred by opposition, foreign or domestic. Their propaganda manufacturing operation went into overdrive with claims that victory in Iraq would be a "cakewalk," that the invading military would be greeted as liberators, and that the war would pay for itself—with Iraqi oil.

The US-led invasion began on March 20 with an intense bombing campaign. When the Iraqi regime disintegrated in early April, Saddam and other top officials, rather than surrendering, just vanished. The neocons in the Pentagon, who believed their own rhetoric, had flatly rejected prewar advice from experts about the kinds of security measures and contingency plans that would be necessary to stabilize the country after the invasion. Their priority, to the exclusion of almost every other concern, was to secure the country's oil resources, and by their ideological standards, the quick fall of the regime amounted to a victory. On the ground, however, decisions to eschew planning meant that no measures were instituted to prevent mayhem or halt the pillaging of thousands of national treasures and priceless artifacts from unsecured museums. Rumsfeld downplayed the chaos by declaring that looting was Iraqis' means of expressing "pent-up feelings" after decades of oppression. "Freedom's untidy, and free people are free to make mistakes and commit crimes and do bad things," Rumsfeld said. "They're also free to live their lives and do wonderful things. And that's what's going to happen here."

On May 1, President Bush delivered a victory speech from the deck of the USS Abraham Lincoln, which was docked off the coast of San Diego. Standing under a banner that read "Mission Accomplished," he declared that "major combat operations in Iraq have ended." A week later, L. Paul Bremer assumed the position as head of the Coalition Provisional Authority to administer the occupied country. His first decree was to ban the Ba'ath Party

(Iraq had been a one-party state), and to purge its members from the public sector; at least one hundred thousand Iraqis, including forty thousand teachers, were cast out of their jobs. Bremer's second decree was to dismantle the Iraqi army, which made hundreds of thousands of armed, militarily trained, and battle-hardened soldiers unemployed as well. These decisions had catastrophic consequences. The country spiraled into a complex conflict that generated new enemies among the occupied population. Islamist militants from elsewhere gravitated to Iraq to capitalize on the opportunity to mete violence against US and coalition forces as well as Iraqi civilians, especially Shi'a and those who cooperated with the occupiers. In August 2003, a series of bombings, including one that devastated the building serving as the UN headquarters in Baghdad, buried the neocons' fantasies of easy victory in rubble. While there was no Iraq–al-Qaeda connection prior to the war, a year after the invasion, a Jordanian named Abu Musab al-Zarqawi established al-Qaeda in Iraq and declared loyalty to the original al-Qaeda in exchange for recognition.

Once again, the United States was fighting a war without information. Who and where were the people blowing up buildings, setting off improvised explosive devices (IEDs), and attacking coalition troops? In a desperate bid for actionable intelligence that might help turn the tide of what had quickly become a deadly and politically humiliating debacle, thousands of Iraqi men, as well as women and teenagers, were captured or randomly picked up in military sweeps and at checkpoints. Ten major facilities around the country were used to detain and interrogate them. US officials would later acknowledge that upwards of 90 percent of those detained in Iraq had no connection to anti-coalition violence.

At the end of August 2003, the Pentagon dispatched Major General Geoffrey Miller, commander of JTF-GTMO, to Iraq to provide some advice about how to run a successful intelligence-gathering operation. At the time, Guantánamo was still shrouded in secrecy. Miller brought a CD and a manual on the "advanced" techniques that Rumsfeld had approved and were now standard operating practice for Guantánamo interrogations. These included sensory disorientation and sleep deprivation, religious humiliation, sexual assault, and prolonged shackling in stress positions. In his briefing to military officials in Iraq, Miller extolled the efficacy of the Guantánamo detention-interrogation fusion model of using guards to "soften up" detainees for interrogators. General Ricardo Sanchez, top commander in the Iraq theater of war, adopted Miller's recommendation to "Gitmo-ize" detention operations in Iraq. He issued a memo authorizing interrogators to use an array of harsh techniques "to create fear, disorientate [the] detainee and prolong capture shock."

The largest detention facility was the Abu Ghraib prison on the outskirts of Baghdad, which had served as the main torture and execution center of the Saddam regime. By early autumn, it was packed well beyond capacity. The prison was also under near-constant attack by forces fighting against the US occupation. A unit of military interrogators headed by Captain Carolyn Wood was transferred from Afghanistan to Iraq and posted at Abu Ghraib. Back in December 2001, Wood's unit was trying to figure out what tactics were permissible for their use on detainees at Bagram. They were given no written guidelines from commanders up the chain or the Pentagon; all they were told was that the Geneva Conventions don't apply to "persons under custody," or PUCs. To try to figure things out for themselves, they searched the internet and contacted military interrogators working at Guantánamo, who told them about the harsh techniques that Rumsfeld had recently approved. Logically, Wood and her unit assumed that they had license to use those techniques, too. By the time Wood's unit got to Abu Ghraib, they were already experienced practitioners of coercion, degradation, and dehumanization.

Hundreds of journalists, including photojournalists, were in Iraq to cover the war. Despite Pentagon efforts to encourage members of the media to embed with military units, the war was going too badly to control the messaging, although little was known about what was happening inside detention facilities. On September 16, Brigadier General Janis Karpinski, who commanded the 800th Military Police Brigade and was in charge of detention facilities, told reporters that the United States was holding thousands of "security detainees." This concept, which has no basis in the Geneva Conventions or Army regulations, was created to categorize prisoners assumed to pose a threat to coalition forces or to have information about those who do. When asked by a journalist if these prisoners had any rights, Karpinski responded: "It's not that they don't have any rights . . . They have fewer rights than EPWs [enemy prisoners of war]."

But one organization knew exactly what was going on inside the detention facilities: the International Committee of the Red Cross (ICRC). Although ICRC representatives were barred from accessing or even knowing the identities of people held by the CIA, they were allowed to meet prisoners in military custody, on the condition that they would not publicize anything they saw or learned. To understand why the ICRC could see but not say what was going on, one must take account of the history of the ICRC and its unique international role as a neutral monitor in the context of armed conflicts.

When the ICRC was established in Geneva, Switzerland, in 1863, its original mandate was to imbue warfare with a humanitarian ethos by establishing rules and standards intended to prevent excessive violence and unnecessary suffering. The ICRC played a leading role in the development of international humanitarian law (IHL), also termed "Geneva law," whose core aims are to aid victims of war and protect nonbelligerents. The first Geneva Convention of 1864 proscribed the abandonment of wounded soldiers on battlefields. The Geneva Protocol of 1925 prohibited poison gas and other toxic weapons that cause excruciating injuries and slow death, and the 1929 Geneva Convention expanded the rules for the treatment of wounded soldiers and sailors and prisoners of war. As the official guardian of the Geneva Conventions, one of the ICRC's roles is to advocate that governments abide by IHL. Its other major role, dating back to 1918, is to monitor the treatment of prisoners on all sides of a war and to assess whether they are being treated in ways that comply with standards of the Geneva Conventions.

At the start of any war, the ICRC negotiates agreements with individual governments and in some cases with warring non-state groups for access to their prisoners. After Germany invaded Poland in September 1939, marking the start of World War II, the ICRC requested permission to send delegates to camps in occupied Poland where the Nazis were deporting Austrian Jews. The Nazis, who did not want to enter into a discussion about the treatment of Jews, categorically denied the request. In 1942, the German Red Cross informed the ICRC that it would not communicate any information about "non-Aryans," and instructed the organization to stop asking questions about their treatment. At that point, the ICRC debated whether to draw international attention to the Nazi refusal to allow their delegates into concentration camps. They decided against the idea because they feared that it might undermine their status as a neutral actor. The ICRC emerged from World War II with its humanitarian reputation tarnished for having failed to do more to protect the millions of Jews and other people whom the Nazis had exterminated.

The vast horrors of World War II, in addition to the Nazi Holocaust, included torture and inhumane treatment of prisoners in some theaters of war, obscene abuses of civilians in militarily occupied territories, such as the Japanese rape of Nanjing and the enslavement of women in Japanese-controlled countries to sexually service soldiers. Both sides used total-war tactics, including aerially bombing cities, with the US atomic bombing of Hiroshima and Nagasaki as the most cataclysmic examples. After the war ended in defeat for the Axis powers, the international community took steps to reform and expand IHL in order to prevent the recurrence of the humanitarian catastrophes of the immediate past. The four Geneva Conventions of 1949, which the United States played a major role in producing, established more comprehensive and clearer rules about what is lawful in the treatment of prisoners of war and civilians in militarily occupied territories. The ICRC's postwar lease on relevance hinged on vigorously defending the conventions, but its means of monitoring the treatment of wartime prisoners remained subject to the Faustian bargain of access in exchange for secrecy.

In 2001, Gabor Rona was the adviser in the legal division of the ICRC. His job was to represent the organization's positions on IHL, including in relation to counterterrorism policies and practices. When the "war on terror" started, this role put him in direct contact and, as it turned out, conflict with US officials. As ICRC delegates started obtaining firsthand knowledge about the abuse of prisoners in US custody in Afghanistan, Rona's duty was to report those findings to responsible authorities and make recommendations that he could deliver confidentially.

When I met Rona in 2005, he had recently quit the ICRC out of deep frustration that the Faustian bargain made him a complicit keeper of US government deceptions about its treatment of prisoners. In his new position as international law advisor for Human Rights First (HRF), he could ply his trade in the open. I asked about his prior ICRC experience. He explained that in the early months of the "war on terror," his off-the-record conversations with Bush administration officials generated "some good if superficial dialogue about legal status issues, but it got to the point quickly where no one would budge." At first, he was baffled by discordant messages coming out of Washington. His contacts in the State Department and the professional military were expressing their commitment to the Geneva Conventions, and Rona was heartened when, at the start of the war in Afghanistan, CENTCOM Commander General Tommy Franks issued an order that the Geneva Conventions were applicable to anyone taken into US custody in Afghanistan. In contrast, what he was hearing from officials in the White House, the Justice Department, and civilians in the Pentagon was that the administration would be "soft on terrorism" if it were to adhere to international law. These "hardliners," as Rona described them, were guided by "misapprehensions about what adherence to the law would permit, and false conclusions about the security liabilities of adhering to correct legal frameworks. Even if they were correct about the conventions being 'quaint'—and they weren't—you can't just ignore inconvenient legal frameworks."

But ignoring inconvenient legal frameworks was the essence of the Bush administration's new paradigm.

After Guantánamo opened for detention business in January 2002, and ICRC representatives began meeting detainees there, Rona's criticisms and recommendations were met with more uniform indifference. What he didn't know at the time—because it was classified—was that the president declared that the conventions don't apply to suspected terrorists, and therefore, complaints about violations were moot. What Rona did know was that public statements that all prisoners were being treated humanely as a matter of policy were lies. Rona described the civilian officials who opposed the Geneva Conventions as "the fringe," not because they were politically marginal—they weren't—but because their radical ideas were unmoored from US treaty obligations. "It's part of a certain mindset in this administration that reads its legal obligations differently than any past administration. The fringe took control of the wheel."

How, I asked, did Rona make sense of the abuse of prisoners in Afghanistan and Guantánamo when he first started receiving reports from ICRC delegates? He offered a blunt response: "Coercive interrogations are the product of a caveman mentality of some of our leaders. It's the politics of wanting to beat up on evil." Pentagon officials continued to pay lip service to humane treatment while insisting that they were under no *legal* obligation to treat detainees in accordance with the Geneva Conventions. Rona fumed, "The government has done an exquisite job utilizing creative ambiguity about when IHL applies and what it requires when it applies. This makes it very difficult for practitioners to press their critiques of violations."

Scott Horton, an expert on military and security law, had lots of personal connections to active-duty officers in the JAG corps, Special Forces, and other units serving in Afghanistan, as well as individuals working in the Pentagon and the intelligence community. In the early months of the "war on terror," some of his conversations with friends in the service made him aware that something was happening that was "not kosher." His initial instinct was to disbelieve the possibility that soldiers were being licensed to abuse prisoners because he had such faith and respect for the post-Vietnam reforms that were ingrained in officer training, and because the Geneva Conventions, which were integral to military ethics, were incorporated into the Uniform Code of Military Justice. But as he continued to hear disturbing reports from his contacts, he realized that the implausible might be true.

Horton began functioning like a clearinghouse, collecting information from his contacts about worrisome practices and policy decisions, and disseminating it to human rights organizations and journalists who could make good use of it. Horton learned that the Pentagon had discontinued the traditional presence of JAG officers at interrogation facilities so they could stop things if a line was crossed. He also learned that the military was using civilian contractors for interrogations and, because they aren't subject to the UCMJ, they couldn't be held accountable if they perpetrated abuses overseas. Horton passed this information to Rona and his ICRC colleague Bridget Oederline, and he urged them to look into these matters and raise them in conversations with officials.

Horton was an information clearinghouse in another, more public-service way. He wrote a column for *Harper's Magazine,* and he self-published a newsletter available to anyone who subscribed. In the newsletter, which he disseminated by email, he posted reports by human rights organizations and noteworthy articles from an array of media outlets—including, because he is a polyglot, pieces in French, German, and Russian. He preceded each entry with his own commentary on the political or legal significance or the historical context of the issues it raised. At a time when so much about the war was still unknown, Horton's newsletter put into circulation hard-to-get facts gleaned from his network of contacts, and his own expert insights.

The first major human rights organization to do field investigations of US detention operations was Human Rights Watch (HRW). When I visited their New York headquarters in 2005, I talked with John Sifton, a senior researcher for terrorism and counterterrorism. His work included investigating the US government's behavior in the "war on terror." He said, "*Every* detainee in 2002 was subjected to or witnessed *severe* and repeated abuse. But until 2004, HRW's criticism of prisoner abuse was a voice in the wilderness."

Sifton also noted that the bombing campaign in Afghanistan had generally conformed to Geneva Convention rules of proportionality. The fact that a human rights advocate was weighing in on something so overtly connected to military activity as proportionality—a legal standard to assess whether the amount of force used in an operation (e.g., the size or number of bombs) is proportional to a military objective—reflected a major change in the practice of international law in the last decades of the twentieth century. Following the end of the Cold War, the continuing rampancy of crimes against humanity, genocide, and torture, especially in the context of armed conflict, imbued human rights advocates with an interest in the legalities of warfare. Even more important was the establishment of new international tribunals and courts in the 1990s where individuals accused of perpetrating gross crimes could be prosecuted. This created new opportunities for human rights organizations to contribute and participate in the enforcement of international criminal law. One result of was a fusion of IHL and human rights laws, which preeminent international law expert Theodor Meron described as "the humanization of humanitarian law."

HRW first began reporting on bombing campaigns during the 1991 Gulf War, and in 1992, the organization created an Arms Watch division. By 2001, HRW and other human rights organizations already had acquired a competency in IHL. This expertise would become an enormously important resource in the fight against torture—once it started.

Unlike the ICRC, HRW representatives don't have access to people while they are in custody, but also unlike the ICRC, they aren't bound by any obligation to keep secrets about what they learn. HRW's research and data-collecting methods involved seeking out and interviewing people who were released from custody or had witnessed raids and arrests. They tried to cultivate contacts with soldiers and contractors who were working or had worked in detention facilities in the hope of obtaining insights about places and processes they were barred from seeing for themselves. They also scouted for military reports on criminal or disciplinary investigations of prisoner abuse.

One of Sifton's assignments was to investigate the CIA's rendition and detention operations. The Agency did not provide any information to HRW, which wasn't surprising, but what was surprising was their explanation: the reason that information was secret was a secret. Sifton and his colleagues had to function like detectives, ferreting out and piecing together various kinds of data. From official statements, they compiled a list of people who were in CIA custody, including Ibn al-Sheikh al-Libi, Abu Zubaydah, and Khalid Sheikh Mohammed, the alleged "mastermind" of 9/11 who was arrested in March 2003. They also relied on reporting by journalists and local human rights organizations for leads and clues. HRW's efforts to find the locations of people in CIA custody were boosted by the work of plane spotters, a worldwide network of data fetishists who track planes by their tail numbers, chat with each other online about what they see, and publish information on dedicated websites. In 2002, plane spotters started noticing planes owned by private companies flying strange routes with stops in Afghanistan, Libya,

Uzbekistan, Morocco, and Dulles Airport in Northern Virginia. One civilian plane with the tail number N313P was doing something especially strange: it was landing on US military bases in various parts of the world—including Guantánamo. The hobbyists were uncovering clues about one of the US government's most precious secrets.

Trevor Paglen, an artist with a PhD in geography and an abiding interest in state secrets, caught wind of the information being uncovered by plane spotters. Since the 1990s, much of Paglen's work has focused on what he calls "blank spots on the map," real places, often military, that are literally off the radar, like Area 51 in Nevada. Paglen and A. C. Thompson, an investigative journalist, teamed up and, in cooperation with human rights advocates, adopted the plane spotters' methods and mined their online forums for data about clandestine flights. Their research led them to a small airfield in Smithfield, North Carolina, which was the departure point for planes registered to what turned out to be a shell corporation. They figured out that the Smithfield airport was being used for extraordinary rendition operations. By tracking flights from departure to destination, Paglen and Thompson were able to reverse-engineer CIA travel itineraries to figure out in real time where these airborne "torture taxis" were going. In 2006, they published their findings in a book titled *Torture Taxis: On the Trail of the CIA's Rendition Flights.*

One of Paglen's dark geography sleuthing methods is photography. Sometimes this involves hauling heavy camera equipment to remote areas where he can situate himself to shoot places that contain secrets or are themselves secrets. He was the first person to photograph the Salt Pit, a decrepit brick factory north of Kabul that was repurposed for CIA use as a black site. When I met Paglen, he regaled me with his story of that trip to the dark side in May 2006. To find the exact location of the Salt Pit, he cross-checked publicly available satellite imagery with accounts by several former CIA prisoners who had been held there, including a German citizen named Khaled El Masri, who said that wherever it was, it was a ten-minute drive from the Kabul airport. Paglen figured out that it was located along a back road on a dusty plain north of the city. To find it, he needed a local guide—someone old enough to know the road that predated the Soviet invasion. Although he was well aware of the dangers of traveling that road and the possibility that his camera might be confiscated if he was caught near the site, his experience of reaching and photographing the Salt Pit proved less challenging than he expected. The moral of Paglen's Salt Pit story, one that informs much of his

FIGURE 5. The Salt Pit, CIA black site northeast of Kabul, Afghanistan. Photo by Trevor Paglen.

work, is that even the most secretive places and people can be found and, in his case, photographed.

Sifton told me about his experience of black site hunting in Morocco in early 2006. Thanks to plane spotting data, he knew the CIA was rendering people into that country. His mission was to find out exactly where they were being detained. He assumed that such a facility would be in a remote location, perhaps in the desert, or maybe on the outskirts of an interior city like Fez. He roamed the Moroccan countryside looking for clues. He didn't know what a black site would look like, but he reasoned that it would have to leave some kind of impression on its environment. He asked local farmers and shopkeepers and taxi drivers if they had seen any suspicious activities or people in their areas. As it turned out, the black site in Morocco was hiding in plain sight in a gated complex on Rue de Bucarest in the capital city of Rabat.

Following the 2003 invasion and occupation of Iraq, the ICRC, HRW, and other human rights organizations started investigating conditions in detention facilities and the treatment of prisoners there. According to Sifton, as bad as things were in Afghanistan—and they were *bad*—the situation in Iraq was much worse. In June, Amnesty International, whose representatives were interviewing people who were detained and then released, wrote to Paul Bremer to criticize the use of interrogation methods that constituted cruel, inhuman, and degrading treatment. The following month, Amnesty issued a report detailing cases of ill-treatment, including at Abu Ghraib, and a high-level mission registered those findings at a meeting with Coalition Provisional Authority officials.

ICRC's unique access gave it the capacity to develop a comparative perspective on patterns of abuse across US military detention facilities. Rona and his colleagues already had a pretty clear picture of how detention and interrogation operations in Afghanistan resembled those in Guantánamo; detainees interviewed by the ICRC could make those connections themselves since most of the people who ended up at Guantánamo had been imprisoned in Bagram first. Now the ICRC could apply that knowledge to what they were learning from prisoners in Iraq.

ICRC representatives made twenty-nine visits to detention facilities in Iraq in 2003. After each visit, they delivered oral and written reports to US officials and reminded them of their obligations under the Geneva Conventions. In May, they reported over two hundred allegations of ill-treatment. In early July, they delivered a working paper detailing abuses perpetrated by military interrogators at Camp Cropper, one of two facilities used to hold "high value" detainees; these abuses included mock executions and threats to capture and imprison detainees' family members, especially wives and daughters. (Years later, former Iraqi soldiers and members of al-Qaeda in Iraq who met each other at Camp Cropper and the other high-value detention facility, Camp Bucca, would form a new organization, ISIS, also known as Islamic State.) In response to ICRC complaints about terrible, ongoing abuses at Abu Ghraib, lawyers who reported directly to General Sanchez tried to curtail representatives' access to the facility.

The American Civil Liberties Union (ACLU) contributed in a different way to the quest for information. Created in 1920 with a mandate to defend the US Constitution, the ACLU is the largest organization of its kind with offices in all fifty states and half a million members. It is also a litigation powerhouse. After the start of the "war on terror," as plausible allegations that the government was violating the law began accumulating, the organization decided that, for the first time in its history, it had a role to play beyond US shores. When the organization decided to pursue official documentation about government policies, two staff attorneys, Jameel Jaffer and Amrit Singh, took charge of the organization's FOIA campaign.

In October 2003, Jaffer and Singh filed a FOIA request on behalf of the ACLU as well as the Center for Constitutional Rights, Physicians for

Human Rights, Veterans for Common Sense, and Veterans for Peace. The government agencies they targeted were the Pentagon, the State Department, the Justice Department, and the CIA. They wanted everything: records about detainees, policy documents, interrogation guidelines, medical reports, and findings of criminal investigations or disciplinary proceedings against soldiers, and they wanted this request expedited.

In January 2004, HRW wrote directly to Rumsfeld to protest incidents in which US forces arrested relatives of wanted suspects in order to pressure them to surrender; they pointed out that this constitutes hostage-taking which is a war crime. That month, the Pentagon learned that an Army specialist named Joseph Darby, who had asked fellow soldiers to send him interesting pictures of Iraq, had received an email with an attachment containing photos shot by military police (MP) at Abu Ghraib. Darby reported to his superiors that photos depicting shocking abuses were being circulated. The Pentagon assigned Major General Antonio Taguba to investigate the situation. Taguba discovered that prisoner abuse at Abu Ghraib was "systematic" and "wanton." But the public couldn't know that because his report was classified.

In February 2004, the ICRC delivered a comprehensive and devastating report based on investigations conducted between the previous March and November which noted in graphic detail that the patterns of abuse were "tantamount to torture." That month, the Pentagon responded to the ACLU's FOIA petition by refusing to expedite the release of documents because the subject matter was not "breaking news" or of "widespread and exceptional media interest."

Despite the fact that human rights organizations were reporting abuses, the ICRC was confidentially complaining to officials, several internal military reports including Taguba's were detailing extensive problems, and even Paul Bremer was warning the Pentagon that grotesque prison conditions were creating a blowback situation that was exacerbating anti-coalition violence, Rumsfeld never issued an order or any guidelines to prohibit interrogational violence. What he did do, in April 2004, was transfer General Miller from Guantánamo to Iraq to serve as the deputy commander of detention operations.

On April 28, 2004, photographs of prisoner abuse at Abu Ghraib that had been emailed to Darby were broadcast on the CBS program *60 Minutes II.* This was the first in a series of secrecy-busting events. Earlier that day, as coincidence would have it, the Supreme Court had heard oral arguments in *Rumsfeld v. Padilla,* a habeas case involving a US citizen whom President

Bush had classified as an unlawful enemy combatant. Jose Padilla was arrested in May 2002 when he flew into Chicago and was imprisoned as a material witness in a federal terrorism case. Two days before a court was to decide whether he could continue to be detained, Bush ordered him moved into military custody at a brig in South Carolina, where he was held incommunicado and in total isolation without any charges. After the government lost Padilla's habeas case, they appealed. During the April 28 Supreme Court hearing of that appeal, several justices posed some questions to Deputy Solicitor General Paul Clement about the kinds of legal power the executive claimed to have and how this affected the treatment of detainees. Justice Ruth Bader Ginsburg asked, "So what is it that would be a check against torture?" Clement assured the Court that the United States complies with its treaty obligations. Ginsburg asked, "Suppose the executive says, 'Mild torture, we think, will help get this information?'" Clement responded, "Well, our executive doesn't." Then he added: "You have to recognize that in situations where there is a war—where the government is on a war footing— that you have to trust the executive to make the kind of quintessential military judgments that are involved in things like that."

Several hours later, the Abu Ghraib photos were broadcast, showing US soldiers abusing, humiliating, and terrorizing Iraqi prisoners, most of whom were naked. Some were cowering from snarling dogs; others were bound in painful positions. One photo showed a dead prisoner on ice; he had died in CIA custody and his corpse was stashed at Abu Ghraib until it could be removed under the cover of night and disposed of in the desert.

The Abu Ghraib photos created a global scandal, but their catalytic significance for the fight against torture was provided by the legendary journalist Seymour Hersh, to whom someone leaked General Taguba's investigative report. Hersh published the scoop in the *New Yorker,* writing that Taguba's report "amounts to an unsparing study of collective wrongdoing and the failure of Army leadership at the highest levels."

Rumsfeld tried to deflect his own responsibility for the Abu Ghraib scandal by feigning shock and calling it "a body blow for all of us." Military officials tried to pin all the blame on "a few bad apples"—the MPs who had perpetrated the abuses captured in the photos, and who posed grinning and clowning in some. General Sanchez described Abu Ghraib as "an isolated incident." General Miller blamed the problem on "the conduct of a very small number of our leaders and soldiers." But those face-saving denials were contradicted by Taguba's report. The general had discovered that the immediate

FIGURE 6. Abu Ghraib prison in Iraq: detainee being terrorized by soldiers and military dogs. Source: Wiki Commons.

cause of the abuses at Abu Ghraib was the fact that military intelligence (MI) officers as well as CIA agents and private contractors had directed the MPs "to 'set the conditions' for MI interrogations" by beating, sleep depriving, and humiliating prisoners. Hersh's reporting of Taguba's findings pulled back the curtain to expose that coercive interrogations and degrading detention conditions were neither aberrations that could be pinned on "animals on the night shift" nor unique to Abu Ghraib. Rather, these practices, including photographing naked prisoners as a humiliation technique, had been occurring in Afghanistan and Guantánamo and had "migrated" to Iraq.

Until Abu Ghraib, the mainstream media walked delicately around the torture issue, putting the word in quotes or preceding it with "allegations of" and "what some might call." Now the word torture was used without any qualifications. At a press briefing on May 4, a reporter reminded Rumsfeld of his frequent comments that US troops don't engage in torture and then asked: "Is this one of those rare exceptions here that torture took place?" Rather than sticking to the bad-apple script or doing his I'm-flabbergasted routine, Rumsfeld answered: "I'm not a lawyer. My impression is that what has been charged thus far is abuse, which I believe technically is different from torture . . . I don't know if it is correct to say what you just said, that torture has taken place . . . And therefore, I'm not going to address the 'torture' word." With that answer, Rumsfeld was alluding to something that was still a secret: government lawyers had reinterpreted the law to empty the word "torture" of its basic meaning.

Congressional committees convened hearings throughout May to question civilian and military officials in an endeavor to discover what was really going on in detention facilities. Things got hotter for the administration on May 7 when the *Wall Street Journal* published the leaked executive summary of the ICRC's report that US abuses of prisoners were "tantamount to torture." Although the ICRC president denounced the leak, there was no denying that US officials had been receiving detailed information about torture and other violations, which undercut all their "we're shocked, shocked!" responses to the Abu Ghraib scandal.

On May 13, Scott Horton announced to the readers of his newsletter that he would be a guest on *The News Hour with Jim Lehrer* to discuss the Abu Ghraib scandal and the larger issue of prisoner abuse. The other guest was John Yoo, a law professor at the University of California—Berkeley. At that point, Yoo's role as a deputy assistant attorney general in the Justice Department's Office of Legal Counsel (OLC) from 2001 to 2003 and author of a number of key legal memos was not public knowledge. Horton had never heard of Yoo before they appeared together that evening.

Margaret Warner, who was hosting the show, began by asking Horton whether the administration had created a legal climate in which the Abu Ghraib abuses were able to occur. "Absolutely that's the case," he responded. He explained that the report about the legalities of wartime interrogation that he had submitted to the New York City Bar Association the previous month was undertaken *because* a group of very senior JAG officers had come to him in the spring of 2003 with "very profound concerns about the administration's departure from its norms of behavior in enforcing the Geneva Conventions. In fact, they told us that there was an atmosphere of ambiguity being created, that it served no legitimate purpose, and that there was a disaster waiting to happen."

Yoo asserted that it would be pure speculation to assume that the administration's interrogation policies for suspected terrorists at Guantánamo could possibly have "infected" the situation in Iraq. He elaborated: the government's position is that the Geneva Conventions do apply to the Iraq war but don't apply to the "war on terror" because the United States is not fighting a nation-state; the fight is against a collection of people who didn't sign the Geneva Conventions, who violate the laws of war and, therefore, who don't enjoy the protections of the conventions.

Horton was stunned by Yoo's "jaw droppingly outrageous" argument. At that point, he started wondering, who is this guy? In hindsight, Yoo was giving viewers a tour of the still-classified labyrinthine legal reasoning undergirding the Bush administration's prisoner policies.

Since Yoo was arguing that the status of Iraq and Guantánamo differ, Warner asked him whether the interrogation procedures approved by General Sanchez on the advice of General Miller really comport with the conventions. Yoo responded, "The Geneva Conventions do not contain a definition of torture or a definition of inhumane treatment," a dodge that called to mind Rumsfeld's response to a journalist nine days earlier. "It depends on the context." Using the example of sleep deprivation, Yoo said that "if someone were not allowed to sleep for days and days on end, that would amount to a violation of the Geneva Conventions. But what if someone is allowed to sleep five or six hours a day every day—is that a violation of the Geneva Conventions? The Geneva Conventions don't actually tell us. There is no definition of what torture is, what is inhumane treatment in the Convention."

Horton rolled his eyes and retorted that the legal rules that apply to interrogation include not only the Geneva Conventions but also the Convention against Torture (CAT). He pointed out that CAT contains a clear definition of torture, and on top of that, "there is a large jurisprudence applying both the torture definition and the cruel, inhuman and degrading treatment definition to this conduct."

Yoo's tour of the labyrinth then arrived at the inner chamber. "I'm glad you brought up the [Torture Convention]," he said. "[When] the United States ratified that convention, the Senate placed a very strict definition of torture. It's *the specific intent to cause severe physical or mental pain* ... But at the same time, it's important to realize that the Senate did *not* implement the other part of the Torture Convention, which was the prohibition on inhumane treatment. So to the extent that the Torture Convention is relevant, it only bars torture. It doesn't bar things that are less than torture. That's the gray area we're arguing about. What is it that's less than torture and still permissible in the war on terrorism?"

Horton got the last word: "That's an incorrect construction. I disagree with that. The Convention clearly precludes cruel, inhuman and degrading treatment. I think there's really no question about it. [F]or coercion to be effective, it really only becomes effective when pain is employed, and when pain is employed, you've crossed the threshold of the prohibitions. So it's just out."

As Horton was leaving the television station after the show, it dawned on him that Yoo's answers must be based on a legal memo that he knew about from his time in the OLC. Horton put out feelers and a few days later someone in the intelligence community passed him the August 1, 2002, memo. There it was in black and white, the Bush administration's "legalization" of torture. The author of the memo was Yoo.

Watching Horton and Yoo debate each other on *The News Hour* made me realize that I needed more knowledge about the laws of war and US jurisprudence. I used to joke that whatever I knew about the Geneva Conventions I had learned on the streets of Ramallah and Tel Aviv while I was researching the Israeli military court system, and most of what I knew about US law I had learned watching *Law & Order*. I signed up for a summer course on international humanitarian law at The American University that would begin in mid-June.

The Abu Ghraib scandal had no effect on the government's stonewalling of the ACLU's FOIA request for documentation; the only thing they received were some State Department talking points for the media. In June, Jaffer and Singh filed a FOIA lawsuit in the Southern District of New York, and they made use of information that had become public in the last month and a half. "Photographs and videos leaked to the press have established beyond any doubt that detainees held in Iraq have been subjected to humiliating and degrading treatment . . . There is growing evidence that the abuse of detainees was not aberrational but systemic . . . and that senior officials either approved of the abuse or were deliberately indifferent to it."

What did have an effect on the Bush administration, however, was pressure for information from Congress. In early June, several documents were declassified, including the March 2003 legal memo which Yoo had authored for the Pentagon to justify the use of coercive techniques by military interrogators. That memo, which the *Wall Street Journal* published on June 7, had been withdrawn the previous December by OLC head Jack Goldsmith, although he didn't withdraw Rumsfeld's policy directive that the legal memo was intended to support. The *Washington Post* published the leaked August 1 OLC memo on June 8. This one elicited such loud, scornful, and angry responses from lawyers across the country that Goldsmith decided to withdraw it, too. His decision to do so angered officials who were relying on it for legal cover. In July, Goldsmith resigned his OLC position and went back to his position at Harvard law school.

The publication of the "torture memos," as they were instantly branded, was the second secrecy-busting event that spring. The memos proved in no uncertain terms that prisoner abuse was policy and it had been authorized at the highest levels of government. Even more than the photos from Abu Ghraib, the memos catalyzed the fight against torture, because so many lawyers now realized that matters long-ago settled, like the absolute prohibition of torture and secret detention, and the fact that the president's powers are limited by law, had been unsettled by the Bush administration.

To be clear about the sequence of these events and their relation to each other: The Abu Ghraib scandal occurred because the Bush administration had given interrogators a license to torture, and that license traveled from Afghanistan and Guantánamo to Iraq. The torture memos became public because the Abu Ghraib scandal exposed the political malfeasance and disastrous consequences of decisions to invade and occupy Iraq, as well as the desperate reliance on torture everywhere the "war on terror" went. The contents of the memos undermined the government's denials that prisoner abuse was systemic, and this ignited the fight against torture.

The publication of the torture memos coincided with the start of my summer school course, which was taught by Robert Goldman, a towering figure in the fields where the laws of war and counterterrorism intersect. His fiery lecturing style was fueled by his unbridled disgust at the legal rationales that had been crafted by government lawyers to justify torture. Midway through the course, Goldman was appointed by the UN Human Rights Commission as an independent expert on the protection of human rights and fundamental freedoms while countering terrorism; his mandate included the US "war on terror."

Kim Scheppele, a sociologist of law, was scheduled to participate in a conference on national security law the second week of June. One of the other speakers on her panel was Yoo. When the August 1 memo was published a few days before this event, Scheppele decided to scrap her paper and instead present a critical reading of that memo. She was the first legal expert to call Yoo out in person in public for producing legal rationales to justify torture.

Law professors and other legal scholars started churning out blog posts about the torture memos in which they tried to analyze the administration's unprecedented and, in Horton's words, "bat-shit crazy" legal arguments. Legal bloggers were trying to navigate the uncharted terrain of the new paradigm and struggling to map it onto the familiar—US laws, jurisprudence, and treaty obligations. Two of the most prolific torture-memo bloggers were Georgetown University law professors Marty Lederman and David Luban. Lederman had served in the same OLC position during the Clinton administration that Yoo held during the first years of the Bush administration. Luban's areas of expertise include legal ethics and international law.

Scheppele's confrontation with Yoo inspired her to organize a gathering of scholars and practitioners to brainstorm about the now-exposed torture policy. The locale would be Princeton University's Law and Public Affairs Program, where, at the time, she was a visiting fellow. She reached out to Lederman and Luban, whom she knew by reputation because of their blogging about the memos. She also reached out to Sanford Levinson, a law professor at the University of Texas at Austin; he had just finished editing *Torture: A Collection,* composed of eighteen essays by philosophers, historians, and legal scholars who offered various perspectives on the post-9/11 torture debate. Scheppele recruited Lederman, Luban, and Levinson to help her come up with a list of invitees. Horton and Sifton were obvious choices. So was Deborah Pearlstein, a lawyer at Human Rights First who recently had coauthored a report on secret detentions. Some of the contributors to Levinson's volume were invited, including John Langbein, who is an authority on the history of torture, and the literature scholar Elaine Scarry, who had authored the highly influential book, *The Body in Pain.* I made the list because Scheppele and I knew each other through the Law and Society Association, and she had read some of my writings about torture.

On the day of the Princeton workshop, twenty of us convened in a conference room. This was my first opportunity to talk about torture for an entire day with so many experts. The conversation was a bonanza of diverse insights, experiences, and multifaceted debates over the finer points of law. At the end of the day, Scheppele suggested that we keep this conversation going. She volunteered to create a listserve. This was the origin of the "torturelist" which, over time, acquired about two hundred members—lawyers and law professors, JAGs, journalists, human rights activists, and scholars. The torturelist became a platform where people could share information and analysis, ask probing questions that generated riveting and deeply knowledgeable responses, engage in debates about evolving developments in the "war on terror," and get to know one another virtually.

In the exchanges and debates on the torturelist, one thing was clear: no one was a master of every domain. People needed each other's expertise and were generous with their own. At its core, the torturelist created a communicative alliance of learning and teaching as everyone strived to better understand what was going on in US detention facilities overseas and how that comported—or not—with applicable laws and legal norms. There were plenty of disagreements in the email exchanges, sometimes sharply expressed, but even those were edifying.

The third event in the secrecy-busting sequence occurred on June 28, 2004, when the Supreme Court handed down its decision in *Rasul v. Bush*. The Court ruled against the administration's new-paradigm claim that the president has the authority to secretly detain people at Guantánamo indefinitely. The significance of *Rasul* for the fight against torture was threefold: First, the Court affirmed that federal courts have jurisdiction to hear detainees' habeas petitions, which meant that they could be represented by lawyers. Second, because the timing of *Rasul* came so close on the heels of the Abu Ghraib scandal and the publication of the torture memos, many lawyers who were appalled and disgusted by revelations about the government's policies seized upon the opportunity to get involved by volunteering to represent detainees. Third, once lawyers started going to Guantánamo and hearing firsthand from their clients what had been done to them over their years in US custody, the official lies about humane treatment would become ammunition for the war in court.

FOUR

——————

The War in Court Takes Off

ON THE MORNING OF JUNE 29, 2004, the staff of the Center for Constitutional Rights got to the office a bit bleary eyed. The previous night, they had been out celebrating their stunning victory against the Bush administration in the Supreme Court case *Rasul v. Bush*. "Much champagne was had by all," recounted one paralegal. The leap of faith this progressive legal organization had taken back in February 2002 was vindicated by the Court's decision that people imprisoned on the Guantánamo naval base have the right to challenge their detention in federal court.

The phones were ringing off the hook. Amidst the congratulatory messages from friends and colleagues, lawyers around the country were calling with a surprising offer. They wanted to join the fight that CCR had started and were volunteering to represent Guantánamo detainees.

One of the lawyers who called that morning was Marc Falkoff. He remembers saying to the person who answered the phone, "You probably have lawyers lined up around the block, but if you need help, I'll try to get my firm on board." His offer was eagerly accepted, so he took the idea to the management committee of his firm, Covington & Burling. "To its credit," he told me, "the firm decided there was no conflict of interest in representing victims of terror"—they were representing 9/11 first-responder firefighters—"and fighting for the rule of law." He added, "It was in the best tradition of Covington & Burling." They had represented Fred Korematsu, one of the 120,000 Japanese Americans forcibly displaced and interned during World War II, who sued the government in the Supreme Court.

Unsure of what the Bush administration would do next, CCR wanted to lock in the victory. Around the clock from June 29 to July 3, staff lawyers worked to produce habeas petitions for the several dozen detainees whose names were known, which they filed in federal court. They assigned detainees to lawyers who had volunteered and started recruiting others.

The Bush administration wasn't chastened by the Supreme Court defeat. Rather, officials scrambled to figure out a way to put the habeas corpus genie back into the bottle that *Rasul* had uncorked. Nine days after the ruling, on July 5, the Pentagon announced the creation of Combatant Status Review Tribunals (CSRTs). This move was intended to minimally satisfy the Court's decision that detainees have a right to a hearing, but in a way that would subvert their access to federal courts.

The Bush administration's objective was to maintain the status quo, and this was evident in the establishment of CSRTs. According to the regulations, "[t]he Tribunal is not bound by the rules of evidence such as would apply in a court of law." Begging comparison to military tribunals in Brazil, Argentina, and other Latin American dictatorships during the dirty war years, these CSRTs could make their assessments on the basis of secret evidence and coerced statements. They would be composed of panels of three officers, none of whom had to be a lawyer, and whose identities would be classified. The panels would hold hearings to decide the fate of the hundreds of Guantánamo detainees, none of whom could be represented by a lawyer. Instead, each detainee would be assigned a "personal representative"—a soldier who, the rules specified, could not be a lawyer, and whose identity would be classified as well. The job of these anonymized representatives was not to make arguments on detainees' behalf, and not to help detainees understand the government's evidence because it was classified. The CSRT regulations stipulated that nothing a detainee said to his personal representative would be confidential, which meant that it could be used as new evidence against him. The personal representatives were window-dressing functionaries whose role was to help the tribunals achieve the preordained result that everyone imprisoned at Guantánamo belonged there.

The CSRTs started holding hearings on August 25, 2004. Six days a week, three sets of panels held concurrent hearings for four detainees a day. There were seventy-two hearings each week. Speed was of the essence because the administration wanted these CSRTs to create a fait accompli to moot detainees' habeas rights won through *Rasul*. Over the span of six months, the CSRTs held hearings for nearly six hundred detained men and boys.

The hearings were divided into two parts. In the first part, where the detainee was allowed to be present, a recorder—whose identity was also secret—would read out a declarative statement summarizing any unclassified evidence the government claimed to have against him. Then the panelists would ask him to respond. Detainees couldn't call witnesses to support their claims of innocence or question anyone who was a source of evidence. If, for example, a detainee said that his own self-incriminating statements were false, that he had said what his interrogators wanted to hear to stop the abuse, the panelists might tell him that this was not the forum to address those issues. If a detainee was accused of being associated with an al-Qaeda operative and he asked who this unnamed individual was, the presiding officer might say he did not know, or that the information was classified. The second part of the hearings took place in closed sessions to review evidence and reach decisions.

Unsurprisingly, these kangaroo courts decided that the vast majority of detainees had been legitimately classified as unlawful enemy combatants and could continue to be detained. In cases where the CSRT decided that the evidence did not justify continuing detention, the Pentagon ordered a do-over with a new panel. Thirty-eight individuals cleared that hurdle when panels decided that the evidence didn't support continuing detention. These men were not declared innocent, nor were their arrest and imprisonment acknowledged as a mistake. Instead, they were categorized as "no longer enemy combatants."

The Bush administration was pushing a narrow reading of *Rasul* by claiming that, while courts may have jurisdiction over Guantánamo, unlawful enemy combatants didn't have any court-enforceable *rights*. But that ploy did not succeed in keeping lawyers out. Even as the CSRTs were busy making a mockery of the rule of law, lawyers were applying for security clearances to get onto the base to meet their clients.

These lawyers called their collective endeavor the Guantánamo Bay Bar Association or Gitmo Bar. CCR functioned as the command center. They ran training sessions to advise volunteers how to understand the legal issues and navigate the bureaucratic hurdles, and they reviewed habeas petitions to ensure that each one was properly tailored to Guantánamo. Lawyers who had never handled habeas cases were mentored by those who did, especially death penalty lawyers, the sector of the legal profession most experienced with habeas litigation.

The Justice Department, facing the reality that the legal black hole was about to be invaded by lawyers, produced a protective order to gag them from revealing details about what was actually going on at Guantánamo. The rules and conditions lawyers would have to accept included the following: They would be required to treat anything a client said as classified and they could be prosecuted if they mishandled secret information. Their communications with their clients would not be privileged and confidential because their notes would be taken from them and held in a secure facility in Arlington, Virginia. All letters going either way would be censored by a "privilege review team," and there was no recourse to challenge whatever these teams decided to redact. If lawyers spoke on the phone or discussed their clients—and initially they could only speak to other security-cleared lawyers who were representing the same person—they would have to turn on white noise machines in their offices. If they wanted to review case materials, they would have to pull the blinds of their windows, even if their offices overlooked nothing. The fight over the protective order would soon end up in federal court, but in the meantime any lawyer who wanted to go to Guantánamo would have to sign it.

On August 31, 2004, Gitanjali Gutierrez became the first habeas counsel to journey to Guantánamo. At the time, she was working for the firm of Gibbons, Del Deo, Dolan, Griffinger & Vecchione. When I met her a year later, she told me about the fight she had to wage to get there. When the Justice Department denied her request to meet her clients, she responded with some "pit bull aggression." I tried to draw a mental picture of this elegant, soft-spoken woman shouting and threatening recalcitrant officials. The pit bull strategy didn't work, so she petitioned the DC District Court. The judge who handled her petition decided that *Rasul* established the right of detainees to have legal representation, which cleared Gutierrez's path. The last step was to sign the protective order, which she did even as she protested its terms.

The day before Gutierrez was scheduled to travel to the base, the Pentagon threw up a new obstacle: Each client would be required to sign a form authorizing that attorney to represent him. The hope was that detainees would refuse to sign these forms, and this would shut down the habeas track. Gutierrez feared that this requirement would raise "huge trust and mental health issues." By August 2004, dozens of detainees had attempted suicide and clinical depression was so rampant that about one-fifth of them were being given Prozac or other antidepressants. How, Gutierrez wondered, would people who were psychologically damaged by years of abuse and isolation respond when presented with a form obligating them to accept a lawyer they had never met before?

Gutierrez's first clients were British citizens Moazzam Begg and Feroz Abbasi. She was in a rush to get to Guantánamo because she was worried about them. Letters they had sent to their families via the ICRC indicated that they were suffering serious mental breakdowns caused by years of abuse and traumatizing uncertainty about their fates. Before Gutierrez met Begg, all she knew was that he had moved his family from London to Afghanistan in early 2001 to open an elementary school with funds raised from Britain's Muslim community. After 9/11, when it became clear that Afghanistan would be attacked, he moved his family to Pakistan. In January 2002, Begg was seized at night from his house in Islamabad and thrown into the trunk of a car. But his captors had missed the cell phone in his pocket which he used to call his father in England and relay what was happening to him. He was imprisoned for nine months in Afghanistan, first in Kandahar and then Bagram, before being transferred to Guantánamo. Gutierrez knew less about Abbasi, other than that he had gone to Afghanistan in 2000. He was captured in December 2001 by the Northern Alliance and sold for bounty to the United States. Abbasi was one of the first men to arrive at Guantánamo.

When Gutierrez got to the base, she was assigned a Department of Defense (DoD) handler who, she said, "was issuing new rules as we went." Her tense relations with the handler were made worse by the fact that he was encroaching on her client meetings. But Begg and Abbasi were intensely relieved to see her. She was the first person they met since being taken into US custody who wasn't on a mission to make them suffer. They readily signed the form authorizing her to represent them.

Like most of the lawyers who enlisted to represent Guantánamo detainees, Gutierrez had no firsthand experience dealing with people who had been tortured. And until that first meeting with her clients, she had limited knowledge of how they had been treated beyond the vague and government-censored complaints in letters to their families. Now she listened directly to Begg's and Abbasi's harrowing accounts of their experiences over the previous two-and-a-half years. She wrote down everything, knowing she would have to turn her notes over to government censors for security review. I asked Gutierrez what the experience was like for her. "Visits with clients aren't about intellectual and legal issues," she said. "It's hardcore human rights work. And even as I was trying to do my work, I was fighting with the DoD guy about basic rights—lawyer-client communication, confidentiality and other key issues." She was in no position to answer her clients' questions about what would happen to them, let alone when they might get out of Guantánamo. "What's hard is that at the end of each meeting you can't make promises. Part of the psychological torture is having promises broken and hope manipulated." The one psychological lift she could provide was to let her clients know that lawyers fighting for their rights had already won a battle in the Supreme Court, and Guantánamo had become an object of international ire and protest.

Officials controlling Guantánamo from Washington and soldiers in charge on the ground regarded Gutierrez as an interloper. As *New York Times* journalist Tim Golden later reported, a Pentagon official described her in a memo to the FBI as "pushy and deeply suspicious," and a military lawyer on the base said she was "difficult to please and very stubborn." These accusations were risible, considering that the men she was there to meet had been secretly detained for years.

The second habeas counsel to go to Guantánamo was George Brent Mickum IV, a partner with the Washington, DC, firm of Spriggs & Hollingsworth. In the spring of 2003, Joseph Margulies, lead counsel on the *Rasul* case, recruited Mickum to represent several British detainees. On paper, Mickum would not seem like an obvious candidate to join the fight against the government: he was a white-shoe lawyer who had served as a special assistant for the Justice Department and a senior counsel for the Senate Special Committee on Investigations. But he was appalled that the government would have the audacity to indefinitely detain people without any recourse to a fair hearing. When Margulies asked, Mickum said yes.

Mickum's first clients were British residents Bisher Al-Rawi and Jamil El-Banna, and Martin Mubanga, a dual citizen of Britain and Zambia. All three had been picked up in Africa by the CIA at the instigation, and with colluding assistance, of Britain's MI5. Mubanga was staying with relatives in Zambia when he was arrested. He was transported directly to Guantánamo. Al-Rawi and El-Banna were arrested in The Gambia where they had gone to start a new business venture developing mobile processors to make peanut oil. Before being sent to Guantánamo, they were extraordinarily rendered to Afghanistan where they were imprisoned for several months in a CIA black site which was described as the "dark prison" because people were held in total darkness.

As soon as Mickum learned of the CSRTs, he wrote letters to his clients advising them not to appear before these tribunals until he could meet them. When he made his first trip in September, he found out that his letters were not delivered until the day *after* their CSRT hearings. Someone on the base obviously was reading privileged lawyer-client mail. Although Mickum's clients were picked up in African countries, which belied the Bush administration's mantra that every detainee was "captured on the battlefield," and although they were not accused of having engaged in any acts of violence against the United States or being in possession of any weapons at the time of their arrests or anytime in the past, they were classified as unlawful enemy combatants. Adding insult to legal injury, Al-Rawi had worked as a go-between for MI5 in their investigation of a cleric in the United Kingdom named Abu Qatada who was suspected of having ties to al-Qaeda. The British government refused to confirm that Al-Rawi had assisted them, and his CSRT chose not to believe him. Instead, the tribunal decided that his "association" with Abu Qatada justified his continuing detention. El-Banna's crime of association was to have driven Abu Qatada's wife and son to visit him, once.

Like Gutierrez's clients, Mickum's were intensely relieved to see him. He, however, was disconcerted when he saw them. Al-Rawi, whom he met first, was chained by his feet to an O-ring on the floor with his hands cuffed to his waist and flanked by two guards. Mickum demanded that the guards unchain his client, but that went against their orders. After some tense back and forth, they agreed to remove the handcuffs but not the foot shackles. When Mickum met El-Banna the next day, he found a man who looked nothing like his pictures; his client had lost over one hundred pounds since his capture. El-Banna asked Mickum why he had not received any mail from his wife and children. Mickum asked the ICRC representatives who happened to be on base at the time, and they told him that they had delivered numerous letters for El-Banna, but none had reached him—nor would they reach him until the day before Mickum's next visit. Mickum deduced that El-Banna's love for his family was being exploited by his captors as a psychological weakness. The sixteen belatedly delivered letters were heavily redacted to obscure high-security information like "I love you, Daddy."

Baher Azmy, then a law professor at Seton Hall University, was the third habeas counsel to go to Guantánamo. His first client was Murat Kurnaz, a son of Turkish immigrants who grew up in Germany. Kurnaz had gone to Pakistan to study religion in order to be a better Muslim for his bride-to-be. He was in a bus on his way to the airport to return to Germany when he was pulled off at a security checkpoint. He was arrested and turned over to the United States for a three-thousand-dollar bounty. He was then detained at Kandahar for two months before being sent to Guantánamo. When Kurnaz's mother learned that her son was in Guantánamo, she hired a German lawyer, and he approached CCR and the Gibbons firm for help finding an American attorney. They recruited Azmy. When Azmy applied for his security clearance, he worried that his request might be delayed or even be denied because he is a dual citizen of the United States and Egypt. But he got his clearance, signed the protective order, and made his first trip on October 9, 2004.

Azmy began his first meeting by handing Kurnaz a note which read: "My dear son, it's me, your mother. I hope you're doing well. This man is Baher Azmy. You can trust him. He's your lawyer." Kurnaz stuffed his mother's letter into his shirt because he was afraid guards would take it away from him.

When attorneys began filing habeas petitions in federal court, the government's response was to file the detainee's CSRT records. Azmy learned that the main allegation linking Kurnaz to terrorism was his friendship with another Turkish national in Germany who later perpetrated a suicide bombing in Istanbul. Azmy easily discovered that the friend was alive and well in Germany and had nothing to do with the Istanbul bombing. "No one had any idea how shoddy and preposterous this case was until we actually got to Gitmo."

Kurnaz was classified by his CSRT as a member of al-Qaeda by "a preponderance of evidence" despite the fact that, back in 2002, US and German intelligence officials had decided that allegations linking him to terrorism were baseless. The information that it had long ago been decided that Kurnaz wasn't involved in terrorism became public in 2005, when accidentally unredacted records were released and reported by the *Washington Post*. Kurnaz became a political *cause célèbre* in Germany when the public learned that, because he is not a citizen, the German government refused to lift a diplomatic finger and planned to strip him of residency were he ever released. According to Azmy, "Habeas litigation *mattered* because it altered the narratives."

Clive Stafford Smith, one of the attorneys who took *Rasul* to the Supreme Court, made his first trip in November 2004. Several months earlier, he had moved from the United States to London to run Reprieve, an organization of human rights lawyers and investigators that he founded in 1999. When I met him in his Reprieve office, he recounted, "When I first started hearing about torture from my clients, it was horrifying, but I knew this is what would shut Gitmo down." One of his clients was Sami al-Haj, an *Al Jazeera* journalist who was taken into custody while en route to Afghanistan to report on the war. "Sami got me more facts than anyone else," he said.

Tom Wilner, who was representing twelve Kuwaitis, made his first trip in January 2005. "Before I got there and met my clients," he told me, "I couldn't imagine the US would engage in torture. There were rumors but I didn't want to believe it." He recounted being gut-wrenched when his clients told him that they had loved the United States and were enormously relieved when their Afghan or Pakistani captors turned them over to US soldiers. But that relief immediately dissipated. In US custody, they were stripped, shocked, hung upside down, threatened with dogs, and paraded naked in front of female soldiers. One client was sodomized. "All of my clients," Wilner said, "have been tortured by US agents, however you define the term." He explained how that first meeting with clients affected his thinking. "I got involved in this thing because I believed I was fighting for American principles. Secret detention was un-American no matter who was being detained. When I met these guys, I became convinced that they are really innocent—one of them is one of the best kids I've ever met. Now I see in a concrete way what due process means."

Traveling to the base took a day each way, and lawyers' time with clients was limited and subject to the discretion of JTF-GTMO soldiers. The meeting rooms in Camp Echo—which were also used for interrogations—were rigged with surveillance cameras which were monitored. Initially, the government's plan was to listen in on the meetings, which would have cast lawyers as unwilling accomplices in the ongoing quest for information, but that scheme didn't survive challenges. For lawyers whose clients did not speak English, they had to find and hire their own interpreters at a cost that ran about a thousand dollars per day. Some lawyers had a hard time finding qualified interpreters, either because their clients spoke obscure languages, like the Chinese Uighurs, or because so many Arabic-speaking linguists with security clearance were working for the US military or private contractors in Iraq. Every expense would have to be paid from lawyers' own pockets or law firm coffers.

All habeas petitions and other detainee-related matters were channeled to the DC District Court. Judge Joyce Hens Green was brought out of retirement to oversee Guantánamo cases because of her experience on the Foreign Intelligence Surveillance Act Court. One of the cases she handled was a lawsuit brought on behalf of sixty-two detainees, including Kurnaz, which challenged the legality of the CSRTs. In January 2005, Judge Green rejected the government's motion to dismiss all the habeas cases and ruled that the tribunals were no substitute for federal courts. She used Kurnaz's case to illustrate the fundamental unfairness of the CSRTs, including the fact that his panel disregarded evidence of his innocence.

The Pentagon had no intention of changing course just because a judge ruled against their procedures. They set up an Administrative Review Board

(ARB) as a follow-up to the CSRTs. Before Kurnaz's appearance before his ARB, Baher Azmy submitted a notarized affidavit from his client's friend, the non-suicide bomber. The ARB ignored it and voted unanimously to uphold Kurnaz's status as an unlawful enemy combatant.

Stafford Smith wanted the world to know about the inhumane ways his clients had been treated, but that information was imprisoned by a strict regime of censorship. "Then," he said, "I realized that all this secrecy is actually a wonderful thing because the coverup is always worse than the crime." He devised a public relations strategy to reverse-engineer the government's information blockade. In January 2005, he wrote a letter to Prime Minister Tony Blair that described some of the brutal and degrading ways several of his clients had been treated. The subject line of the letter was "Torture and Abuse of British Citizens in Guantanamo Bay." In the last paragraph he wrote, "Anything that has been censored or blacked out in this letter, your close allies in the United States don't think you should be allowed to hear." Then he sent the letter to the censor for review. When he got it back, 90 percent of the text was redacted, but the subject line and the last paragraph survived the black pen. He sent the redacted letter to the British Embassy in Washington for transmission to Downing Street and simultaneously published it in the British press. It made a sufficiently embarrassing splash for Blair to start pressing the Bush administration for the release of British citizens. By the end of the month, Begg, Abbasi, Mubanga, and Richard Belmar were flown home. Stafford Smith didn't pause his legal work, but in terms of what was working to get people out of Guantánamo, he said, "The real litigation is in the court of public opinion."

Joseph Margulies also turned to the court of public opinion, making strategic use of information about the treatment of one of his clients, Mamdouh Habib. In November 2004, Margulies filed a memorandum with the judge who was handling the habeas petition which contained Habib's own account of what had been done to him since he was arrested in Pakistan in October 2001. He was rendered by the CIA to Egypt, where he was subjected to horrifying abuses for six months. By the time he arrived at Guantánamo in May 2002, he had no fingernails, he bled from the nose, mouth, and ears when he slept, and he was unable to walk unassisted. The judge decided that nothing in Habib's first-person account was classified. This gave Margulies a license to use it. The day before the Bush administration was going to file military commission charges against Habib—based on his tortured statements— Margulies contacted Dana Priest of the *Washington Post* and shared the memo with Habib's story. She and Dan Eggen published a front-page exposé on January 6, 2005. The government immediately dropped the case against Habib and he was repatriated to Australia several days later.

Since late 2002, the Bush administration had been secretly repatriating detainees deemed to have no further intelligence value. The first ninety-seven transfers were to Afghanistan, Pakistan, and Saudi Arabia. But as some allied governments began turning up diplomatic pressure for release of their nationals, the destinations started diversifying. Between 2004 and 2005, among those who were repatriated by executive order were twenty-two citizens or residents of countries in Western Europe. Kurnaz was released in 2006 when Germany's new chancellor, Angela Merkel, pressed his cause in her first meeting with President Bush.

Some former detainees gave detail-laden interviews about their experiences to journalists, human rights researchers, and documentarians. Their revelations shattered whatever façade of "humane treatment" the US government had managed to maintain. In 2006, British filmmakers Michael Winterbottom and Mat Whitecross directed the first feature film about the "war on terror"; *The Road to Guantánamo,* a docudrama about the Tipton 3 (Shafiq Rasul, Asif Iqbal, and Ruhal Ahmed), included harrowing reenactments of their interrogations in Afghanistan and Guantánamo. The same year, Begg published the first detainee autobiography, coauthored with Victoria Brittain: *Enemy Combatant: My Imprisonment at Guantánamo, Bagram, and Kandahar.* While Begg had been imprisoned at Bagram, he witnessed the murder of two prisoners; one was an Afghan taxi driver named Dilawar who was beaten to death—"pulpified," according to a coroner's report—by soldiers guarding him. Alex Gibney's Oscar-winning 2007 documentary, *Taxi to the Dark Side,* centers on the killing of Dilawar, and Begg narrates the man's last hours. Begg participated in several other documentaries about the US torture program, and he became the outreach director for Cageprisoners (now CAGE), a British organization that was established to campaign for the release of Guantánamo prisoners and to support communities affected by the "war on terror." US officials responded to Begg's visibility and harsh criticisms with the threatening posture that his media activities met the criteria for him to be counted as a "recidivist" who had "returned to the fight."

One of the most pressing challenges for the Gitmo Bar was to figure out who was imprisoned there. The Bush administration, rather than acceding to the *Rasul* ruling that detainees have habeas rights, refused even to release the list of detainees' names. The literal meaning of habeas corpus is "we [the court] command you [the ruler] to produce the body [of the detained individual]." This proscription against secret detention originated in the 1166 Assize of Clarendon during the reign of King Henry II of England and was incorporated into the 1215 Magna Carta as "the great and efficacious writ in all manner of illegal confinement." The writ's medieval meaning, show us the body, was directly relevant to secret detention at Guantánamo. But this was not the commonplace understanding of habeas in the United States because secret and incommunicado detention had never been government policy prior to the "war on terror." In US jurisprudence, habeas corpus was used mainly by convicted prisoners, especially those sentenced to death, to challenge the constitutionality of their state trials in federal courts. In principle, *Rasul* won detainees the right to be seen and heard, but the government continued to treat their names as classified information. Lawyers had to learn who was at Guantánamo from other sources.

Some lawyers, including Stafford Smith, made trips through the Middle East to hunt for the names of people who had been disappeared. Amnesty International, local human rights organizations, and investigative journalists uncovered other names. CCR created a detainee database and added new names as they became known. Once detainees were identified, lawyers needed to get authorizations from their relatives (called "next-friend") in order to be allowed to represent them. Al-Rawi told Mickum the names of several men on his cell block who wanted lawyers. Mickum asked his client to sign the next-friend authorization for them. Officials would not stand for such prisoner-to-prisoner assistance and rejected those authorizations. This government-enforced secrecy meant that unidentified detainees had no way of requesting lawyers themselves, and if they weren't discovered by someone on the outside, there could be no next-friend authorization.

When I asked Marc Falkoff how he got his Guantánamo clients, he said that CCR provided a list of two dozen Yemenis. His firm, Covington, took on twelve prisoners and Allen & Overy, another multinational law firm, took the other half. When Falkoff first asked his firm about taking on habeas litigation, they decided that he could do it, but a senior partner would have to supervise. David Remes agreed to fill that role on the condition that he would not have to do any of the habeas work himself. Remes already had been drawn into work on Guantánamo when Neal Katyal, the Georgetown law professor who was involved in the *Hamdan v. Rumsfeld* case, asked him to write an amicus brief on behalf of retired military officers for that case.

In explaining why he called CCR to volunteer, Falkoff told me about his background, which was rather atypical for a corporate lawyer. He earned a PhD in literature in 1996, but he could only find part-time teaching work. He came to believe—and not just because of insecure employment—that "being a literary scholar wasn't much use." (His training as a literary scholar did serve a useful purpose, however, when he compiled and published *Poems from Guantánamo: The Detainees Speak* in 2007.) In 1995, the State of New York passed a death penalty law that created a public defenders' office. Falkoff got a job as a researcher and was surrounded by "brilliant people doing important things." He decided to go to law school with the intention of becoming a death penalty lawyer. As a law student at Columbia, Falkoff volunteered on Mumia Abu Jamal's habeas appeal of his death sentence, and during the summers he worked with the Southern Center for Human Rights to challenge inhumane conditions in US prisons in the South. Falkoff said, "I decided that death penalty wasn't what I wanted to do because all the work is devoted to getting a guilty or convicted person off death row. My eureka moment was when I worked on the SCHR's class action case about HIV-positive prisoners who were not being given their meds in prison. The settlement had an amazing impact on the lives of so many."

Falkoff's first job out of law school was clerking for a federal judge in the Eastern District of New York. Right around the time he was hired, his boss learned that there was a five-hundred-petition backlog of habeas appeals from prisoners just sitting on judges' desks. Falkoff was appointed special master and he worked with the court to resolve all of them in a year. After the clerkship ended, he took a corporate job at Covington & Burling. "I was pulling long hours and making plenty of money," he told me, "but I wasn't satisfied with the nature of the work I was doing." When the *Rasul* ruling was announced, he saw the opportunity to do to the kind of work he loved most: prisoner litigation.

Before Falkoff met his clients, he said, "I had no reason to *disbelieve* that these guys were the 'worst of the worst.'" When he made his first trip in November 2004, he was expecting to meet "Yemeni Hannibal Lecters." That wasn't the case. "You don't want to be too starry-eyed, but they were really nice and sweet. I will swear many of them were entirely innocent of all the allegations."

Falkoff found it challenging to navigate language and cultural barriers, and many of his clients were frightened and depressed. In order to establish a trusting relationship with them, he didn't want to ask lots of questions because he was concerned that they might think he was a "false flag interrogator." One strategy at Guantánamo was for interrogators to put on civilian clothes and pretend they were lawyers to induce detainees to talk. "We knew it was possible that they had been tortured, but if they didn't tell us, we didn't ask." Some clients wanted to tell him everything right away, and they hoped their innocence could be confirmed and their lawyers could get them released.

Another challenge to building trusting relations with clients was secrecy. Attorneys had access to their clients' CSRT records but, Falkoff explained, that was "classified information that we couldn't tell them about." I asked what he learned from his clients' records. "It was remarkable because there was no *there* there." The protective order prevented him from giving me any details, but he could tell me that they were full of double- or triple-hearsay and circular "evidence" (he used his hands to gesture scare quotes) of multiple accusations and factually confounding allegations. "It was so much like the Salem witchcraft trials."

When lawyers started going to Guantánamo and meeting their clients, they discovered how flagrantly false the government's claims of humane treatment were. One of the most critical factors for the fight against torture was the fact that it was lawyers, and only lawyers, who could penetrate the legal black hole and meet with detainees. Margulies told me that after the Supreme Court ruling in *Rasul,* he had been optimistic that things would change. "I thought, if you open Gitmo up, the government would close it down because secrecy was its raison d'etre. If a lawyer can bring a detainee a pan pizza and an orange, Gitmo loses its purpose."

But Guantánamo didn't lose its purpose for the Bush administration. To block lawyers' reality-based accounts about what was happening there, the protective order was like a sword of Damocles dangling over their heads; if they revealed information about the abuse of their clients, they could be prosecuted. They were made precarious because they were acquiring knowledge that could threaten the government's credibility if they were allowed to expose truths withheld from the public. The Bush administration must have hoped that imposing onerous rules and bureaucratic hurdles would induce lawyers to balk and quit the fight. That was a foolish assumption. Lawyers were being hit where it hurt: their professional ethics and commitments to the rule of law and due process. They fought back, hard.

David Remes, the Covington partner who had agreed to supervise Falkoff on the condition that he didn't have to do any of the work on habeas cases, decided he wanted to see Guantánamo for himself. He made his first trip in December 2004. Remes told me his story to contextualize why, after he got involved with Guantánamo, he decided to change his career from working for a big firm representing corporate clients to become a full-time human rights lawyer. He had grown up in New York City in a left-wing household and in the 1960s, he was in the teenaged vanguard of the counterculture. "When I was young," he said, "I had this great sense of outrage at what my own government was doing. I was very passionate about the injustice America was meting out on the Vietnamese, great outrage at the abuse of American power... When Nixon resigned and the counterculture had really conquered popular culture, there were still major political battles over accountability— for the CIA, for the Watergate masterminds and operatives... But then things cooled down. By 1976, efforts to cleanse the political system had spent themselves."

Remes responded to the political malaise by going to law school, a decision he attributed to the Chicago 8 trial. The Chicago 8 were prominent anti–Vietnam War protestors who were charged with conspiring to incite a riot at the 1968 Democratic Party convention. Remes read the arguments of their defense attorneys, William Kunstler and Leonard Weinglass, who had been founders of CCR. He was moved by their ability to demonstrate "the power of reason and words in the defense of basic civil liberties."

Remes hated his first year of law school at Harvard and considered dropping out. But he changed his mind when he took constitutional law with Laurence Tribe, then a young rising star. Awed by Tribe's brilliance, Remes became his research assistant and got to work on every prominent issue of the day, including school busing, abortion rights, and executive powers in relation to the Panama Canal treaty. "Tribe fought every battle with passion and originality," Remes said. "He became my inspiration and my influence. Working with him was like being on a speeding train, but always in the realm of speaking truth to power." The allure of speaking truth to power notwithstanding, "Harvard Law imbued me with a sense that the highest mountain to climb for power and prestige was to become a partner in a big, powerful law firm. If I had gone into public interest law after I graduated, I would always have wondered if I could have 'succeeded' in the terms promoted by Harvard." Remes romanticized his future as "an establishment figure crusading for justice."

When Remes was recruited by Covington, they sweetened the offer with the promise that he would work with Michael Boudin on appeals in regulatory law cases for corporate clients. Boudin, who later became a federal judge, was the son of left-wing civil rights attorney Leonard Boudin, who had made a career representing political dissidents; his clients included actor and activist Paul Robeson as well as Daniel Ellsberg, who leaked the Pentagon Papers about the Vietnam War. Michael's sister, Kathy Boudin, was a member of the radical Weather Underground who spent twenty-two years in prison.

Eventually, after working with Boudin, Remes began taking cases challenging restrictions on commercial free speech under the First Amendment and handling legislative matters for the firm's corporate clients, including Big Tobacco. This was a far cry from his youthful idealism, but it would turn out to be good preparation for the war in court.

When Remes made his first trip to Guantánamo, he found it "fascinating, appalling, surreal," but also invigorating. "I was so emotionally drained after the first meeting with men who had no hope until lawyers showed up. The things we heard, the encounters with those men who had been subjected to such terrible treatment during their capture and over hundreds of interrogations were astounding. I was hooked." He said that on his first trip, there were other corporate lawyers with no experience representing imprisoned clients. "We didn't know how extraordinarily burdensome the protective order was until we went to Gitmo. We accepted things that criminal lawyers never would have accepted, like limits on lawyer-client communications."

Remes believed his skill set of constitutional law litigation and government lobbying could be of service to the Gitmo Bar in the fight over the terms of the protective order. The government agreed to some modifications lawyers requested but refused to establish secure facilities in other major cities around the country in addition to the one in Arlington, or to grant lawyers permission to share information with those representing other clients, or to make public comments about Guantánamo. The protective order dispute was referred to Judge Green, who tried to resolve the contested issues through negotiations. When that failed, she set a briefing schedule. At the hearing on the Justice Department's motion to dismiss the challenge to the protective order, Remes joined lawyers who had started the war in court: Wilner, Margulies, and CCR's Barbara Olshansky.

Judge Green ruled in favor of the Gitmo Bar on two matters: They could comment on information about Guantánamo that was reported in the press, and lawyers working on different cases could share classified information with each other. CCR established a secure externet (a networking port) to facilitate the sharing of classified information. But Judge Green sided with the government in declining to order the establishment of any new secure facilities. This was a hardship and an added expense for lawyers living far from the Capitol who would have to travel long distances to see their own notes, prepare briefs and motions containing classified information, and write or read client mail. But having only one secure facility ended up fostering a sense of community among the lawyers who worked side by side there. According to Remes, the secure facility "looked and smelled like a college dorm room during finals."

The continuity of secret detention, despite *Rasul,* was a major hurdle for the Gitmo Bar. The Bush administration was not keeping detainees' identities classified for national security reasons, as officials claimed, but to prevent lawyers from signing on as their representatives. No knowledge, no lawyers, no habeas. Lieutenant Commander Matthew Diaz, a JAG officer who was working for JTF-GTMO in 2004, knew this was the reason because he was in the loop of Pentagon communications denying Barbara Olshansky's request for the full list of names which, she explained, was needed to provide detainees with lawyers. Diaz came to regard this policy decision as indefensible and patently unfair and he decided to do something about it. In early January 2005, he stayed in the office over several nights and printed out the full list of detainees' names, internment serial numbers (ISNs), and nationalities. On the last night of his six-month tour, he put the list into a Valentine's Day card that he had bought at a gift shop on the base and mailed it from the Guantánamo post office.

The recipient of this unsigned, list-bearing Valentine's Day card was Olshansky. She told me that when she opened the card, she thought it was a nasty prank. The idea that the list was sent by a JAG as an act of protest didn't cross her mind. She consulted with her CCR colleagues about what to do. Some suspected that the list was sent as a trap to put classified information into her possession which would provide an excuse for government agents to raid the office, make arrests, and seize files. Everyone started to worry that the offices were bugged and that they were under surveillance. But because the list was valuable information that they had been seeking through official channels, to no avail, CCR president Michael Ratner suggested that they turn it over to a journalist as a First Amendment–protected means of making it public. Olshansky rejected that option because she feared that the government might retaliate, and this could derail their work on Guantánamo.

After several weeks of mulling what to do, Olshansky sought the advice of court officers handling her habeas cases. They told her to notify the Justice

Department, which she did. This triggered an FBI investigation which led agents to Diaz. He was court martialed, convicted, sentenced to six months imprisonment, and dishonorably discharged. Diaz told me that when he sent Olshansky the list, he knew he was acting illegally, but at the time, it was a step he felt morally obligated to take. "My motivation for acting was two-fold: the process and the treatment. Habeas was the only real process that was outside of the executive branch . . . The treatment of detainees was unspeakable, and it had become clear that those detainees who had counsel were treated better than those who did not."

The government would keep the list of detainee identities classified until April 19, 2006, when they lost a Freedom of Information Act (FOIA) lawsuit brought by the Associated Press and were forced to release the names.

Meanwhile, the problem of secret detention was compounded by policy decisions aiming to scuttle habeas litigation by moving detainees beyond the reach of American lawyers. On March 11, 2005, the *New York Times* reported that the Pentagon was planning to transfer hundreds from Guantánamo to Saudi Arabia, Yemen, or Afghanistan for continued detention. Falkoff filed an emergency petition on behalf of his clients to prevent them from being transferred to other countries, at least until lawyers had the opportunity to challenge such transfers in court. This petition was submitted the same day the *Times* article came out, which was a Friday. In an emergency session on Saturday, Judge Rosemary Collyer issued a temporary injunction blocking any transfer of the clients Covington was representing. The Bush administration's unitary executive rejoinder was to tell the court that "there is no legal basis for judicial intervention in the processes by which enemy combatant detainees are repatriated or transferred, and any such interference would illegitimately encroach on the foreign relations and national security prerogatives of the Executive Branch."

CCR, which had not made use of the list of names that came into their possession the previous month, wanted to extend this injunction to unidentified detainees. They filed an emergency petition titled *John Does 1—570 v. Bush*. In American legal nomenclature, "John Doe" or the female variant "Jane Doe" is deployed to refer to a real person whose identity is unknown or for some reason is kept secret. *John Does 1—570* aimed to block the government from transferring *anyone* from Guantánamo under the metaphorical cover of night. On Sunday, Judge Collyer dismissed CCR's petition; she contended that "there are no facts that indicate that any of these particular petitioners are at risk of transfer . . . or imminent harm." The key difference in outcome between CCR's petition and Covington's was the fact that

Falkoff and Remes had access to classified information about their clients which was submitted to the court, including evidence of the Pentagon's plan to send one client to another country for torture.

Judge Collyer's dismissal of CCR's *John Does 1—570* petition was illustrative of a broader tendency of courts to defer to the executive branch on matters related to national security. Falkoff opined, "Judges were not used to dealing with these kinds of issues. At first, they were inclined to demur to government arguments because in their eyes, government lawyers are always the good guys because it was assumed that they wouldn't engage in frivolous litigation." He continued, "With Gitmo, the US attorneys used up their reservoir of trust. Every judge on these cases eventually realized that the government lawyers are bullshitting." To the extent that judges became increasingly skeptical, which Falkoff optimistically exaggerated with the phrase "every judge," it came slowly and unevenly, and only because members of the Gitmo Bar forced judges to face reality and think critically about government policies.

Because of the secrecy and official lying about humane treatment, lawyers only learned how bad things really were when they were able to travel to the base and meet their clients. Even hard-knock death penalty lawyers who had spent their careers working in some of the worst prisons in the United States found conditions at Guantánamo and the treatment of detainees shocking. Stafford Smith, who came to represent thirty-six men at Guantánamo, said that death rows in the most disgusting Louisiana or Mississippi prisons didn't compare negatively. One difference was that the men and boys detained in Guantánamo had not been charged, let alone convicted of any crime.

Even detainees who had lawyers continued to be interrogated and subjected to the standard operating abuses. If a detainee refused to submit to further questioning, he could be punished or deprived of "comfort items" such as a blanket or soap. If a detainee was beaten by guards, savaged by an Immediate Response Force (IRF) in the process of being "extracted" from his cell, had his Qur'an taken away, or was moved into isolation as reprisal for violating one of the ever-changing and poorly communicated rules, lawyers were the only ones who could complain or try to ameliorate their clients' immediate suffering. Falkoff found out that a client had his pants taken away for some disciplinary infraction, which meant that he was unable to pray. "I found that incredibly shocking to use religious humiliation as punishment." Another of Falkoff's clients, who refused to take back his Qur'an after it was mishandled by guards, was IRFed (one of the new words coined for Guantánamo) to force him to accept it.

Like other lawyers, Falkoff spent lots of his time on the base hammering out motions on issues of abuse. "It was very draining to be there, but at night it was important to file motions about things we were learning from our clients. Every time I went, I would become incensed anew. Working on Gitmo issues is intellectually innervating, but to get a letter or go down brings home the intensity of people's suffering."

Gita Gutierrez continued making monthly trips to Guantánamo and added many new clients to her roster. In 2005, she decided to become a full-time human rights lawyer, so she quit the Gibbons firm and joined the staff of CCR. One of her clients was Mohammed al-Qahtani who was like "Detainee Zero" at Guantánamo. In 2002, the Pentagon developed a special interrogation plan for him. The brutality and degradation meted on al-Qahtani was adapted as standard operating procedure for the interrogation of others. But, Guiterrez said, "his treatment was more extreme in terms of tactics and duration than anyone else." Al-Qahtani was interrogated almost around the clock for forty-nine straight days. At one point, his heartbeat dropped so precipitously that he had to be rushed to the prison clinic. When he stabilized, he was returned to interrogation.

Gutierrez met with al-Qahtani for the first time in December 2005. She knew from other clients that he was in bad shape. At their first meetings, he had a hard time focusing, but he was able to converse. She used her meetings with al-Qahtani to document his torture and abuse, including the roles behavioral psychologists and doctors played. Gutierrez said that if she could get a habeas hearing for al-Qahtani, she would challenge the evidence that his CSRT had relied on, including his own tortured statements. She would also challenge the core allegation that he was the so-called "missing twentieth hijacker" by presenting the 9/11 Commission Report, which found that if there was a missing hijacker, he had not been identified and could be any one of a number of people.

In 2005, Ramzi Kassem decided to get involved in Guantánamo "for rule of law reasons. When you go to law school, you are taught principles and rules. To see those things called into question is stirring to many lawyers. It was stirring to me." But there was also a more personal dimension: Kassem was born in Beirut, Lebanon, and grew up in Syria, Jordan, and Iraq. After 9/11, he worked with CCR and the ACLU on issues related to the roundup and detention of Muslims inside the United States. "I identified with the communities being targeted by the post-9/11 policies."

In order to get to Guantánamo, Kassem needed to find a way to subsidize himself. "I tried to pimp myself out. I could be an Arabic translator for other lawyers if they flew me down, and then I could do my own work as a lawyer. Surprisingly, no one jumped on my offer." He told me that his opportunity came when a Fordham University law student introduced him to Professor Martha Raynor. She, too, wanted to take on habeas work at Guantánamo. She offered Kassem an adjunct position in her clinic and he became habeas counsel for a dozen Guantánamo clients. Describing his clinical work with law students, he said, "They are dedicated. They have fresh ideas, and they are energetic. My students and I were learning at the same pace."

I asked Kassem whether being an Arab had any distinct advantages in relations with clients. He said, "My experience illustrated the double-edged aspects of a shared identity. Some clients could have heightened expectations and if I failed to deliver, this could lead to a backlash of strained relations or even being fired." But Kassem put this in context: "Many lawyers were fired by angry and frustrated clients, and *many* had their visits refused. At Gitmo, it's very difficult for anyone to establish rapport. This is tied to the fact that the well was poisoned by the time lawyers got there."

Long before the Abu Ghraib scandal broke in April 2004, Kassem had assumed prisoners were being abused. When he got to Guantánamo, this was confirmed in horrifying detail by his clients. Still, he said, "I never expected to become so versed in torture. Torture became a major issue in lawyers' thinking. In habeas petitions and judicial review, we have to argue that our clients were tortured in order to contest the government's evidence. Torture facilitates this work and focuses lawyers." Kassem was making a broader point: lawyers had to school themselves about torture in order to try to persuade skeptical and deferential judges to rule against the government.

Rick Wilson, who ran the human rights clinic at The American University law school, was already a torture expert when the "war on terror" started because of his long record of work on human rights violations in Latin America during the dictatorships. After *Rasul,* he thought that taking on Guantánamo cases could be a means of getting his students involved. This option, he quickly realized, would be very limited because the Justice Department was invoking national security to control access. Wilson did, however, get his students to do research for him and other Gitmo Bar lawyers and, later, to create a database to keep track of all filings in the military commissions and government responses.

CCR assigned Wilson to represent one of the child prisoners at Guantánamo because of his experience with torture and the juvenile death penalty. Wilson brought on his law school colleague, Muneer Ahmad. Their client, a Canadian citizen named Omar Khadr, was fifteen when he was arrested in Afghanistan and sixteen when he was transferred to Guantánamo.

Khadr's CSRT classified him as an al-Qaeda fighter because he had been captured near the Afghan city of Khost following a firefight. During that battle, one US soldier was killed and Khadr, badly wounded, was the only survivor in the compound. The Pentagon was planning to prosecute Khadr in the military commissions because he had confessed to interrogators that he threw the grenade that killed the soldier. Wilson and Ahmad learned from the Tipton 3 that they had witnessed Khadr at Bagram being denied medical treatment for his injuries until he confessed.

Wilson and Ahmad were concerned about Khadr's condition even before they met him. They petitioned the court for access to his medical records. But Judge John Bates sided with the government and refused to release Khadr's records. In hindsight, Wilson said, "Muneer and I were so naïve in our belief that Omar's story would make a judge do something." When they met Khadr for the first time in October 2004, he was obviously damaged psychologically. They sought permission to bring in a psychologist to evaluate him, but this request was denied. As a do-it-yourself alternative, they obtained a questionnaire designed to assess whether a person is suffering from post-traumatic stress disorder (PTSD). On their second visit, they worked with Khadr to fill out the questionnaire. When they showed the results to professional psychologists, the determination was that he exhibited acute PTSD symptoms.

Nancy Hollander, a senior partner in an Albuquerque law firm, joined the Gitmo Bar in early 2005 when a French lawyer, whom she had met in The Hague while she was running a training program for attorneys working at the International Criminal Tribunal for Yugoslavia, asked her to represent a Mauritanian named Mohamedou Ould Slahi. This was a fight she felt destined to join because, as she described herself, "I'm a down in the dirt criminal defense lawyer. When I was young, I was an activist—civil rights and anti-war—and then I went to law school to be a defense lawyer. My career morphed into human rights, national security cases, and international criminal law."

Hollander brought aboard her associates, Theresa "Teri" Duncan and Sylvia Royce. The information they had about Slahi at the outset was the official line that he was implicated in numerous terrorist plots, including recruiting two of the 9/11 hijackers. At their first meeting, Slahi surprised the attorneys by hugging them and saying, "My lawyers!" He had learned English at Guantánamo.

Slahi gave his lawyers a notebook in which he described some details of his torture, including that he had suffered several broken ribs. They discovered what a marvelously eloquent writer he was. Hollander credits Slahi for helping her learn about torture from the perspective of a victim. The lawyers, seeking more government information about their client, submitted a FOIA petition in October 2005. His medical records, which they eventually received, corroborated that his ribs had been broken at Guantánamo. But they wouldn't learn the full story of the horrors he had endured for several more years because, even in his letters to them, he resisted reliving all of his trauma.

In February 2006, Mark Denbeaux, a law professor at Seton Hall University, attorney Joshua Denbeaux, and seven law students published a report that profiled the 517 men and boys then imprisoned at Guantánamo. They used the Pentagon's own records from the CSRTs, which had been made public through a FOIA request by the Associated Press. The Seton Hall team reported that more than half (55 percent) of those classified as enemy combatants had not committed any hostile acts against the United States or its allies, 40 percent had no connection to al-Qaeda, and another 18 percent had no connection to either al-Qaeda or the Taliban. Of the minority who allegedly had a connection to some terrorist organization, 8 percent were classified as "fighters for," 30 percent were classified as "members of," and 60 percent were classified by the ill-defined concept of "associated with" a terrorist organization on a list of seventy-two that included fifty-two groups not even designated as terrorist by the Department of Homeland Security. The kinds of evidence that satisfied the CSRTs included having a Casio watch, wearing olive-drab clothing, staying in a guest house, owning a rifle and, of course, coerced self-incriminating or hearsay (third party) statements. The report's most significant rebuttal to the administration's credulous assertion that everyone at Guantánamo was an enemy taken off the battlefield was the finding that only 5 percent had been captured by US forces; the overwhelming majority (86 percent) were captured and sold for bounty by Pakistan or the Northern Alliance.

"The stunning fact of Guantanamo is that most detainees—more than 90 percent—have no connection with al-Qaeda or the Taliban," said Tom Wilner. "Most are there by mistake, sold for bounty and held under the 'worst

FIGURE 7. Attorney Gitanjali Gutierrez with an iguana at Guantánamo, May 22, 2008. Photo by Bryan Broyles.

of the worst' theory." He continued, "We need habeas hearings to get at the truth. Habeas is not abstract. It's about 'you have the wrong guy.'" Gutierrez expressed a similar view: "When will the Bush administration pull its head out of the sand? There are now so many reports that *confirm* that many detainees are not al-Qaeda and that the US *is* treating them all inhumanely."

In November 2006, the Seton Hall team published a second study analyzing the CSRT proceedings. In 96 percent of hearings, the government produced no witnesses and provided no evidence to detainees, not even unclassified material; the government's classified evidence was always treated as reliable and true; 100 percent of detainee requests for witnesses not detained at Guantánamo and 74 percent of requests for other detainees to serve as witnesses were denied.

In 2006, Gutierrez was making monthly trips, meeting not only her own clients but some of the 270 detainees who still had not met their lawyers because the Justice Department was holding up their security clearances. She tried to assure those clients that help was on the way. She complained that routines on the base were getting worse. Lawyers were subjected to lengthy briefings as they sat on the bus while their clients waited, chained, in meeting rooms. When they got inside, there was a second orientation that caused further delay.

But Gutierrez was optimistic that litigation, "which seems to be moving faster now, can overcome government stonewalling." Litigation was moving faster because the Gitmo Bar was growing as new lawyers and law firms joined up. She said, "These lawyers remind me of lawyers who participated in the civil rights movement and Freedom Summer. The Gitmo Bar is a huge spectrum, a cross-section of America. They are seeing a truth that has been hidden from the public by the executive." She added, "Human rights lawyers alone couldn't do what these lawyers can do. These are powerful lawyers from influential firms who have access and influence that is powerful."

At its peak, the Gitmo Bar counted among its ranks more than five hundred lawyers and over one hundred firms from all over the country. CCR hosted enormous meetings to discuss new developments and common problems with hundreds attending via secure phone lines. Olshansky painted a picture: "Our meeting room would be jammed with local lawyers and there would be like fifty [phone] lines, each with about five lawyers on it."

According to Seema Ahmad, who served as CCR's paralegal coordinator on Guantánamo, "Fighting to get detainees out of the legal black hole is the most important work many of these lawyers have ever done in their entire careers. They have a belief in the US legal system that trumps everything. It's a due process issue. But there is also the stark *human* issue because they are conduits for detainees and their families." Lawyers were the ones—the only ones—who could tell their clients about a birth or a death in the family or how their children were doing in school. Ahmad said, "The Gitmo Bar became a community. People would tell each other their stories. Little victories by one were celebrated by all. These little victories were important because the big goal—getting them released—is elusive, to say the least."

Neal Katyal, the Georgetown law professor who partnered with Lieutenant Commander Charles Swift to fight the government over the military commissions in *Hamdan v. Rumsfeld,* said that one day he was at Guantánamo to see Salim Hamdan when he ran into two former students who were meeting their clients. He was struck by the significance of this encounter. "This is the new civil rights movement," he told me. I asked him to elaborate. "Two things: First, it's a real change since *Rasul.* Before, there was a reluctance to challenge the government. Now people realize that the issues are more complicated than good versus evil. Second, the dense and diffuse networks of lawyers from private firms, academia, and the corporate world are deeply moving."

Buz Eisenberg, a private practice lawyer from Northampton, Massachusetts, described being part of the Gitmo Bar as an extraordinary experience. "We are working with corporate counsel from big firms that represent multinationals. I have been so impressed times thirty that these types of firms have been willing to declare that the wrongfulness of government actions merits *teams* at *great expense* and *time* to deal with these cases. They are amazing and their motivations are no different than mine. We all believe in the rule of law. We believe that torture is wrong, and that government power is limited." Indeed, big law firms played a role that went beyond the provision of their own attorneys working pro bono at the firms' expense. They contributed millions of dollars to subsidize the work of small-firm and solo-practice lawyers with funding to pay their interpreters and their travels to Guantánamo.

The fact that so many prestigious law firms were participating in the war in court was a sore spot for the Bush administration. In January 2007, Charles "Cully" Stimson, the Pentagon's deputy assistant for detainee affairs, gave a radio interview in which he criticized "major law firms in this country" for representing Guantánamo detainees. He mentioned a dozen firms by name in an attempt to shame them. "I think, quite honestly, when corporate CEOs see that those firms are representing the very terrorists who hit their bottom line back in 2001, those CEOs are going to make those law firms choose between representing terrorists or representing reputable firms . . . And we want to watch that play out." How it played out was that Stimson was assailed by lawyers, legal ethicists, and bar associations around the country. Karen Mathis, president of the American Bar Association, was quoted in the *New York Times:* "Lawyers represent people in criminal cases to fulfill a core American value: the treatment of all people equally before the law. To impugn those who are doing this critical work—and doing it on a volunteer basis—is deeply offensive to members of the legal profession, and we hope to all Americans." As a result of the controversy Stimson's comments provoked, he resigned from his job.

The Bush administration continued to insist that the fate of detainees remained the discretion of the executive branch. To effectively use courts to break through the executive line on Guantánamo, lawyers had to *shock the conscience* of judges. "Shock the conscience" is a legal standard in US jurisprudence that refers to treatment that is grossly unjust or manifestly unlawful. But what would shock the conscience of judges in the post-9/11 environment vis-à-vis the treatment of foreigners detained at an offshore facility and accused by the government of being terrorists? Gitmo Bar lawyers weaponized their habeas petitions to provide courts with information about the torturous treatment of their clients and the shoddiness of evidence the government was relying on to justify their continued detention.

Guantánamo was a manifestation of the way the Bush administration chose to wage the "war on terror," but it was not the only battleground for the war in court. A collaborative effort was taking shape to try to dismantle the entirety of the Bush administration's new paradigm. In the organizational division of labor, Human Rights First (HRF) played to its strengths in military and international humanitarian law by working with retired military officers, especially JAGs who were angry that the Pentagon had made policies that disregarded the Geneva Conventions and the UCMJ. Gabor Rona, HRF's international legal advisor, explained, "Circumstances dictate alliances. The administration's policies triggered the JAGs' willingness to work with us. They want to recapture the honor of the military, and they see a direct link between US policy failures to follow the law and future danger to US soldiers."

Deborah Pearlstein, who founded HRF's Law and Security Program in 2003, explained the organization's niche in the fight against torture. "HRF tries to bridge the gap between the human rights community and the national security community. For example, some in the human rights community aren't able to answer questions about what states legally *can* do to combat terrorism. On the national security side, few government lawyers knew anything about the Geneva Conventions and other international laws. They were making policies in a vacuum. That was evident in the torture memos." She added, "Part of what I do is build the bridge and try to bring people from these different communities together so that they can understand and learn from each other."

HRF's other strength is advocacy and lobbying political elites in Washington, DC. Jean Aylward, who joined the organization in 2005, described herself as "a bullhorn on Capitol Hill." She had extensive prior military and government experience that gave her advocacy credibility with those constituencies. She told me that during the first years of the "war on terror," she worked in the Justice Department, first in the Office of Intelligence and Policy Review, which gave her an early peek at the National Security Agency's massive spy operation that she described as "a fishing expedition, probably unconstitutional," and then in the international prisoner transfer unit. I asked how she responded to the torture memos when they became public in 2004. "Honestly, I wasn't paying much attention. My job and mothering kept me too busy." But when HRF hired her, torture was part of her billet. She described her mission "to help the cause of not screwing up intelligence collection and to repair our damaged international reputation."

I asked her opinion about one of the dominant subjects in debates at that time: Was there any validity to official claims that coercive interrogations were producing an abundance of valuable information? She responded, "I don't want to debate whether torture works. We just shouldn't go there." I asked her why the government had done so. "In order to look strong and out of a fear of missing something or even a ticking bomb situation. Coercion became standard operating procedure and part of the detention and interrogation culture where abuse is just routine." She added, "The interrogators we use are not properly trained. HUMINT [human intelligence] takes a lot more psychological work and training, not just brute force."

Aylward explained how HRF was working on the issue of torture. The Washington, DC, office where she was based took the information and analysis produced by HRF's legal experts in New York and used it to try to influence politicians and their staffs. "The DC office is the middleman between the experts and idealists in New York and government 'realism' which often takes the form of very politicized obstructionism. My job is to try to fix things which really involves baby stepping progress with the government."

The ACLU made a major contribution to the fight against torture by pursuing official documentation using FOIA and posting released materials on a public website (thetorturedatabase.org). This FOIA campaign was spearheaded by staff attorneys Jameel Jaffer and Amrit Singh. When I interviewed them together, I asked how this process worked. Jaffar explained, "The first step involves figuring out what documents to request and from which agencies. We are dealing with an information asymmetry: we know the class of documents we want, but it's hard to know specifics." Singh added, "We have to be on top of *everything* related to torture because so much information is secret. But we have to be practical, to prioritize, to pick our battles." Using information gleaned from journalists, human rights organizations, and other sources, they would submit requests with as much detail and justification as possible. If the government refused to release requested documents, they would bring a FOIA lawsuit. If the government responded by claiming that materials were exempted from FOIA, or even refused to confirm or deny the existence of such documents, they had to legally strategize to figure out which claimed exemptions could be challenged in court. "It's outrageous," Jaffar said, "that the government claims *legal opinion memos* should be exempted from disclosure. National security is invoked as a pretext for everything." Singh concurred, "Our overwhelming sense is that there is so much

FIGURE 8. ACLU attorneys Amrit Singh and Jameel Jaffer, August 29, 2009. Ruby Washington / New York Times Photos.

unnecessary secrecy. And everything is weighted in favor of the government. Even documents they release can be so heavily redacted that their contents are obscured." I asked whether there was any way to contest redactions. "Yes," Jaffar explained. "We have to litigate that too. One option—which the government consistently opposes—is to ask a judge to do a review in camera [behind closed doors] to compare the original with the redacted version to determine if some of the blacked-out material should be unredacted."

When the ACLU decided to expand their litigation work to target the US government's law violations overseas, they didn't have anyone in-house with international law expertise. In November 2004, they hired several people who did. One was Steven Watt, who had experience litigating international law cases in national courts and international tribunals. He moved over from CCR. Jamil Dakwar, a Palestinian with dual Israeli and US citizenship and strong ties to various UN human rights bodies, moved over from Human Rights Watch to help create the ACLU's new Human Rights Program. Early in his career as a lawyer in Israel, Dakwar represented many Palestinians administratively detained and tortured in Israeli custody. He was a co-founder of Adalah, the leading Palestinian Israeli civil and human rights organization. I became friends with Dakwar in the early 1990s when I was conducting research on the Israeli military court system. When I met up with him shortly after he started his ACLU job, he explained that in his first week, he went to Guantánamo to observe a military commission hearing in the Hamdan case. He joked, "The ACLU hired its first Palestinian human rights attorney and the first thing they do is send him to Guantanamo!"

I asked Dakwar how US and Israeli interrogation techniques compare. He replied, "Take the use of stress positions. US 'softening up' tactics are almost identical to Israeli tactics." In terms of interrogation strategy, he said, "There are strong similarities, including racist biases and intense dehumanizing 'othering.' But the Shabak [Israel's General Security Services] is legions ahead of the Americans in terms of an ability to effectively use persuasion, deception, and co-optation of prisoners. Americans have nothing to fall back on but violence in their desperation for information."

The war in court was being waged by a vast array of actors with different kinds of experience and expertise. But there was a broadly shared sense of common purpose to end torture and restore the rule of law. The Bush administration's recalcitrant refusal to bow to legal principles fortified the will of these lawyers and their allies to fight on and fight harder.

FIVE

Winning Some, Losing Some

ON JUNE 29, 2006, THE SUPREME COURT issued its decision in *Hamdan v. Rumsfeld*. In a landmark ruling, the Court decided that the Guantánamo military commissions created by President George W. Bush in his November 2001 military order were unconstitutional.

Hamdan was a hard loss for the Bush administration. The Court rejected the unitary executive proposition that the president has unilateral power, in this case to create a new legal system. The Court also rejected the administration's position that the Geneva Conventions don't apply to terror suspects captured and detained overseas. Everyone captured in the "war on terror," the Court decided, is protected under Common Article 3 (CA3) of the 1949 Geneva Conventions. Often referred to as the "humanitarian baseline," CA3 prohibits torture, cruel treatment, and outrages on human dignity. Violations of CA3 are war crimes.

A photo taken on the Supreme Court steps just after they won their case shows attorney Neal Katyal, in a dark suit and tie, pointing at Lieutenant Commander Charles Swift who is wearing Navy service dress blues. At the time, I saw this photo as an iconic depiction of the alliance of civilian and military lawyers that developed in the years after 9/11. Now, with that freeze-framed moment long past, I see this image depicting a pyrrhic victory because of all that has happened and not happened in the fight against torture since then.

The day the *Hamdan* decision came down, people on the torturelist responded with instantaneous jubilation and relief. The Supreme Court got it! Torture is illegal! The president's powers are limited! The Guantánamo military commissions are a failed experiment that can be relegated to the dustbin of history! Not so fast, one member on the list cautioned the rest of

FIGURE 9. Attorneys Neal Katyal and Lieutenant Commander Charles Swift in front of the US Supreme Court, June 29, 2006. Joshua Roberts / Getty Images.

us. The greater the victory seems, the worse the backlash will be. She was right, of course, and we should have known better, because there were enough recent negative developments to deter us from guzzling at the trough of hope.

After the trifecta of events in 2004—the Abu Ghraib scandal, the publication of the torture memos, and the Supreme Court's *Rasul v. Bush* decision that pried open the doors of Guantánamo to lawyers—the Bush administration could and indeed should have reversed course on its prisoner policies. Many of the people I was in conversation with at the time hoped that would happen.

One source of their hope after the torture policy was exposed was the knowledge that the prohibition of torture is a *jus cogens* norm (a universally accepted principle that cannot be set aside for any legal reason). But norms don't enforce themselves. The Bush administration decided to stay its course. The cruel, violent, dehumanizing interrogation tactics that had been assiduously denied before the secrets were revealed came to be branded "enhanced interrogation techniques" and publicly justified as "not torture" because they had been approved by government lawyers. In December 2004, the Office of Legal Counsel (OLC) produced a new memo at the CIA's request that resurrected the rationales of the withdrawn August 1, 2002, memo. Three more memos were produced in May 2005 approving even harsher techniques.

Another source of hope, especially among lawyers with ties or affinities to social movements, was the belief that "the people"—the US public—would be so repulsed by revelations of torture and the deviant legal reasoning crafted to justify it that they would clamor for a change in government policy. Deborah Pearlstein, who directed Human Rights First's program on Law and Security, said, "When the Abu Ghraib photos came out, it presented a public opportunity to mount an 'end torture now' campaign." But the general public failed to be repulsed; in fact, after Abu Ghraib, opinion polls showed that support for torture among Americans began rising. President Bush won a second term in the 2004 election and Alberto Gonzales, one of the government lawyers directly responsible for the torture policy, became attorney general, despite responding during his confirmation hearing to a question about whether US personnel can legally engage in torture: "I don't believe so, but I'd want to get back to you on that and make sure that I don't provide a misleading answer." John Yoo, who had authored several of the OLC torture memos, told *New Yorker* journalist Jane Mayer that Bush's electoral victory and the confirmation of Gonzales "are proof that the debate is over. The issue is dying out. The public has had its referendum."

One of the people who harbored hope that public opinion could be swayed was Gabor Rona, HRF's international legal advisor. He thought this could be achieved by linking the horrific treatment of detainees to narratives of humanity. "If people can be made aware of the facts, it's possible to mobilize them. Humanity isn't some specialized concern; it's part of the culture and something anyone can understand." To win the fight against torture, he was suggesting, depended in part on shaping the public narrative. "But," he conceded, "there are so many obstacles to bringing the facts to light. The government controls the methods, means and content of information about detainees and their conditions."

When I met David Cole in October 2004 in his office at Georgetown law school, he was also cautiously optimistic that Abu Ghraib might produce a political reckoning. Cole had begun his career working as a staff attorney at the Center for Constitutional Rights. After he became an academic, he continued to litigate cases for CCR. I was struck by how much he reminded me of CCR's president, Michael Ratner, because he exudes the same beatific affect that Ratner's friends describe as the "empathy gene." In the 1980s and 1990s, Cole specialized in cases of people and organizations whose First Amendment rights and civil liberties were violated by the government. Another track of his work involved challenging the criminalization of immigrants' political speech and association, the most famous of which was the "LA 8" case. In 1987, the Reagan administration sought to deport seven Palestinian men and a Kenyan woman, all lawful permanent residents living in Los Angeles, because they had distributed a magazine produced by the Popular Front for the Liberation of Palestine (PFLP) on college campuses. (The PFLP was the second-largest Palestinian nationalist faction at the time.) The government claimed that the PFLP advocated world communism and therefore, under the McCarthy-era McCarran-Walter Act (Immigration and Nationality Act of 1952, amended in 1965), noncitizens accused of being communists or sympathizers were deportable. Cole litigated the case for CCR, the National Lawyers Guild, and the ACLU—and won. The following year, Congress repealed the section of the immigration law allowing deportation for reasons of political belief. Not to be deterred, the government brought new charges against the LA 8, but lost again, because the court ruled that they were being selectively targeted for constitutionally protected political activities.

After 9/11, Cole emerged as a leading figure in defense of the rule of law. He fought the dragnets in which hundreds of Muslim immigrants were arrested without probable cause. His LA 8 work had another iteration when the Bush administration decided to recharge two of them, contending that their activities decades ago constituted "material support for terrorism." (The case finally ended in 2007 with a blistering judgment that described the government's conduct as "an embarrassment to the rule of law.")

Cole wanted to be optimistic that the public would be angered by the torture scandal, but he was frustrated that this political potential was undercut by the framing of issues in highly legalistic terms. He advocated bringing human rights principles into the conversation. "There is such a thing as *human* dignity, not just American dignity. Human dignity is at the center of human rights, and this is a language that people in other countries can speak, as opposed to talking in strictly constitutional terms." Why, I asked, did he think the public could be moved to protest torture? "Look at how people rallied against the PATRIOT Act," he answered. Indeed, a few weeks after Congress passed that omnibus legislation in October 2001, a women's peace group in Northampton, Massachusetts, formed a Bill of Rights Defense Committee, and in quick order succeeded in getting their city council to pass a resolution declaring Northampton a "civil liberties safe zone." This grassroots action model was emulated elsewhere and over the next two years over four hundred cities, towns, and even a few states passed similar resolutions.

Cole said, "We need a similar campaign against torture—a grassroots campaign, not just something of interest to elite intellectuals. If you can do grassroots around the PATRIOT Act, you should be able to do it around torture."

I was unpersuaded by Cole's suggestion that Americans taking action to protect their own civil liberties was a bellwether for popular mobilization to oppose the torture of foreigners. I was skeptical that even the most liberal sectors of the general public would rally in any significant way. But I wanted to understand why Cole thought differently, so I brought the issue up again in a second conversation several months later. His hopefulness, he explained, was rooted in the fact that "civil society organizations" like CCR, Human Rights Watch, and the American Bar Association were engaged in this fight, and their criticisms and challenges were having an impact. I agreed completely with him on that point, but I didn't agree with the implication that these organizations staffed with highly educated and high-skilled lawyers were in any way reflective of US society at large—and certainly not of majoritarian politics in the twenty-first century.

Cole and other lawyers I spoke with during that period who expressed hope that the American public would mobilize against torture seemed, to me, to be subscribing to the myth of social responsibility. Only a mythic American society would have the collective wherewithal and political motivation to oppose the government's authorization of custodial violence, kidnapping, and forced disappearance or demand legal accountability for their own leaders who authorized policies that criminally breached federal laws and ratified treaties. But neither did I embrace hopelessness and concur with Yoo that it was a game-over victory for the new paradigm because the public had spoken by reelecting Bush. Rather, my hope was vested fully and firmly with the lawyers who were waging the war in court. What I found paradoxical was that some of these lawyers bemoaned the dominant role that lawyers—themselves—were playing, as if they were crowding out the latent potential of laypeople. The Bush administration—that is, one political branch—had reinterpreted and disregarded laws in order to "legalize" torture. So far, Congress—the other political branch—had done nothing to stop it. The only kinds of people who *could* meaningfully contest the radical reinterpretations of law and their policy effects on prisoners were lawyers, with auxiliary support from human rights advocates, investigative journalists, and scholars with relevant specializations. And the place to wage that fight was in courts. Viva la litigation!

One litigation victory that would have broad ramifications for the war in court was the August 2004 decision in the ACLU's FOIA lawsuit for documentation about the treatment of prisoners. The court ordered the government to release all requested documents not exempted from FOIA. By October, the ACLU had obtained over six thousand pages, although many were heavily redacted. This cache included annexes to the Taguba report about Abu Ghraib and materials disclosing details about how Defense Secretary Donald Rumsfeld and some high-ranking military officials had chain-of-command culpability for the abuse of prisoners in military custody.

These revelations had an immediate effect. The ACLU was planning a civil lawsuit against Rumsfeld as well as three officers who bore responsibility for prisoner abuse in Iraq: General Ricardo Sanchez, who authorized the "Gitmo-ization" of interrogation operations; General Janis Karpinski, who was responsible for detention facilities; and Colonel Thomas Pappas, who oversaw military interrogations. The plaintiffs were five Iraqis and four Afghans who were tortured by US forces. While the ACLU was a litigation powerhouse, they wanted to partner with HRF which had strong ties to retired officers who were critical of Rumsfeld. According to Jamil Dakwar, director of the ACLU's Human Rights Program, "This partnership with HRF was crucial to mainstreaming the litigation. Since the issue is accountability at the highest levels of government, it's important to be able to say we have on our side people in the military, not just public interest lawyers." If that batch of materials had *not* become public as a result of FOIA, HRF would not have been able to persuade their military allies to support the lawsuit, and without their support, HRF probably would have declined to partner with the ACLU. Initially, the retired officers hoped that the scandal sparked by the Abu Ghraib photos, the Taguba report, and the torture memos would force the Pentagon to clean its own house. When it became clear that the administration would take no corrective action and was even promoting some of the culprits, the retired officers agreed to support the case—with the caveat that they supported suing Rumsfeld but not Sanchez, Karpinski, and Pappas; their position was that the command responsibility buck stopped with the secretary.

On March 1, 2005, the ACLU and HRF filed *Ali v. Rumsfeld*. Steven Watt, who was working on the case for the ACLU, said, "*Ali v. Rumsfeld* takes on those who promulgated the use of torture and CIDT [cruel, inhuman, and degrading treatment] against foreign detainees. The government keeps putting forward the 'bad apple' argument, but FOIA demonstrates the opposite. It was policy, and you can see it came from the highest levels." I asked Watt what impact he thought this case would have on the broader fight against torture. "This litigation is one means of trying to piece together the whole history and get it into the public domain. We want the public to understand that the government is lying."

Dakwar offered his view on the purpose of this lawsuit: "Since the administration is totally unresponsive to criticism and there has been no discernible change in policy and a total lack of accountability, going to court is a means of putting more pressure on the government." Dakwar had no confidence they would win. "But this case is important because it's the first time that major organizations filed a suit against the government for its handling of an aspect of the war in the middle of the war."

Hina Shamsi joined HRF as a senior counsel the day before *Ali* was filed. Her job was to develop strategy for the litigation and figure out arguments that would be persuasive to judges. "Demystifying issues for the court is crucial," she told me. "*Of course* national security is real and important, but the litigation must convey that some things—like clear, binding treaty obligations that prohibit torture and CID—*must be defended*." In the United States, she continued, "international law has an image as evil, but we have to convince judges that it's no different from any federal statute." How, as a litigator, did she prepare for a torture accountability case? "We have to use many and varied sources of law to make the point that the right not to be tortured is non-derogable." (Non-derogable rights are those of such importance that they cannot be limited or suspended under any circumstances.) "We also have to be persuasive in proving that torture doesn't work if the goal is to get accurate information. And we have to attack the terrible quality of the legal reasoning that was produced in the echo chamber in this administration. Some people think that the Justice Department's imprimatur legitimizes torture." Shamsi explained that the lawyers working on the case were getting important support from the networks of attorneys engaged in the war in court, including Cole and Katyal, and, she added, "an amazing and fantastic amount of amicus briefing."

In the course of preparing for the case, Shamsi spent a month overseas meeting with the nine *Ali* plaintiffs. "It changed my life. Twelve hours a day listening to survivors' tales. I still don't know how to talk about it." She knew that nothing could ever compensate them for the horrors they had endured, but "the case is *so* important to them. They want to do this. There's a lot of trust between these lawyers and clients. We take pains to explain this complicated legal system to them."

In the summer of 2005, three Republicans on the Senate Armed Services Committee (SASC)—John McCain, Lindsey Graham, and chair John Warner—geared up to challenge at least some aspects of the Bush administration's interrogation and detention policies. These three "Republican dissenters," as they were referred to in the media, were aggravated that policy decisions to deviate from the Uniform Code of Military Justice (UCMJ) were causing confusion in the ranks, undermining military discipline, and exposing low-ranking soldiers to the risk of court-martial while high-ranking officials were immune. Their SASC oversight role gave them a responsibility for the well-being of the nation's military. There were personal factors as well: Graham was a reservist Air Force JAG and McCain had survived five years of torture when he was a prisoner of war in North Vietnam.

Over the previous year, HRF and retired JAGs, as well as advocates from the Washington offices of Amnesty International and Human Rights Watch, had been lobbying McCain and Graham to get Congress to take action against the authorization of violent interrogations. The persuasion campaign got a lift in October 2004 when SASC got hold of memos written in early 2003 by top JAGs from all four branches of the military which criticized the deeply flawed legal reasoning in a memo produced by Yoo that was foisted upon the Pentagon working group assigned to develop guidelines for military interrogators. But the Pentagon refused Graham's request to declassify these memos, so the public could not know their contents.

On July 13, 2005, the executive summary of a military investigation into FBI allegations of prisoner abuse at Guantánamo was released. This was the last of twelve investigations into interrogation and detention operations, none of which had been authorized to probe the role of top officials in the government or military. This report, produced by Lieutenant General Randall Schmidt and Brigadier General John Furlow, confirmed that the abusive techniques used at Abu Ghraib had originated with Pentagon-approved techniques for Guantánamo, including threatening detainees with military dogs, chaining them up in painful positions, protracted sleep deprivation, and withholding food and water for long periods of time. However, the Schmidt-Furlow report concluded that these abusive, degrading techniques did not cross the line into torture and were not even inhumane. Rather, Schmidt and Furlow decided that they were perfectly in keeping with the Army Field Manual, which governs military interrogations and was designed to be consistent with the Geneva Conventions.

Schmidt and Furlow briefed the SASC about their report on July 13, the day it came out. During the hearing, Chairman Warner questioned them about how they reached the conclusion that the coercive techniques were neither torture nor inhumane. Schmidt's response was a textbook example of Orwellian doublespeak: "Sir, we made a distinction between what torture and inhumane treatment would be, given the general guidelines, and then what might be abusive and degrading. Something might be degrading but not necessarily torture, and it may not be inhumane. It may be humiliating, but it may not be torture. So we can say no torture, no physical pain, injury. There was a safe, secure environment the entire time. However, there was degrading and abusive treatment to [one] particular individual." He was referring to Mohammed al-Qahtani. When FBI agents found al-Qahtani lying semiconscious on the floor of an interrogation room with clumps of his hair in his hands, they reported that prisoner abuse was happening at Guantánamo. Schmidt and Furlow recommended that former JTF-GTMO commander Major General Geoffrey Miller be admonished for al-Qahtani's abuse.

General Bantz Craddock, commander of SOUTHCOM, had authorized the Schmidt-Furlow investigation. He testified that he had approved or accepted all the report's findings and recommendations except for one: "Major General Miller does not warrant admonishment under the circumstances." Craddock asserted that "the interrogation of ISN-063" (al-Qahtani) was "creative, aggressive and persistent" but "did not violate any US law or policy."

The following day, Graham convened a hearing of a SASC subcommittee to discuss military justice and detention policy. In his opening statement, Graham said: "Congress has been absent without leave (AWOL). We have criticized and we have applauded, but we have been absent when it comes to designing policies and dealing with the capture of people . . . who are involved in the war. That is a constitutional duty of Congress." This subcommittee hearing was intended to produce some clarity on three issues: who qualifies as an enemy combatant and what that designation means in terms of continued detention, how rules for the military commissions can be designed to comport with the UCMJ, and whether the Army Field Manual should be the standard for all interrogations.

During that day of hearings, widely divergent views about US prisoner policies got a full-throated airing. In the first session, the Pentagon's deputy general counsel, Daniel Dell'Orto, and three of the top JAGs who had authored the critical memos testified. Dell'Orto made a standard unitary executive argument against any congressional intervention into these policy matters and dismissed the need for new legislation to regulate interrogations. The JAGs, under questioning, delicately parsed their answers about the "concerns" they had expressed in their 2003 memos. An exasperated Senator Edward Kennedy said that their vague and wavering answers contradicted the fact they *had* objected strenuously, and those objections had *not* been seriously considered by Pentagon general counsel William Haynes. "I'd like to pursue that a bit, too," Graham chimed in. He suggested that the JAGs were alarmed "because you're not soft on terrorism, because . . . as military lawyers you don't want to get your troops in trouble by having a confusing legal situation. You don't want to do something that would violate the UCMJ." (When the Pentagon declassified the JAG memos on July 25, Graham read them into the Congressional Record and criticized the bad decision not to listen to those high-ranking officers because they "are not from the ACLU. These are not from people who are soft on terrorism, who want to coddle foreign terrorists.")

When the hearing turned to the issue of interrogation techniques, Admiral James McPherson testified that he believed Guantánamo detainees have been treated humanely. McCain responded, "You do? What about the use of dogs? Is that humane?" McPherson answered, "There are differences of opinion." McCain retorted: "Not according to the Geneva Conventions, there's not differences of opinion." As to other tactics, like forced nakedness and sexual humiliations, McPherson characterized them as "juvenile," but added, "I don't think that's inhumane treatment." McCain's ire was palpable.

The remainder of the day featured testimony from three legal experts: William Barr, who had served as attorney general in the administration of George H. W. Bush (and a decade-and-a-half later would hold the same position in the Trump administration); Stephen Saltzburg, a George Washington University law professor who had been serving on the American Bar Association's Task Force on Enemy Combatants and as general counsel to the National Institute for Military Justice, a nonpartisan organization with a mandate to educate the public about military matters; and Admiral John Hutson, who had served as the top JAG for the Navy and was now president and dean of the University of New Hampshire Law School. Hutson was among the most outspoken military critics of the administration's policies; he and seven other retired officers, in cooperation with HRF, had sent a letter on September 7, 2004, to President Bush urging him "to commit—immediately and publicly—to support the creation of a comprehensive, independent commission to investigate and report on the truth about all of these allegations, and to chart a course for how practices that violate the law should be addressed."

Barr was there to defend the Bush administration's policies as lawful and justified. He denounced the war in court and took aim at judges for interjecting themselves into the executive branch's policy decisions. "I think we would all recognize that over the past 30 years there has been expansion of judicial power. Judges are more and more willing to try to sort of second-guess and make decisions that heretofore they have relied on accountable political officials to make. That's now carrying over into the war area, unfortunately." Barr stated that fundamental decisions pertaining to war are the president's prerogative and his alone. "The framers [of the Constitution] did not give the commander in chief authority to the President because they played enie-meanie-miney-mo or flipped a coin; they felt that the President, that the executive, had to make the kinds of decisions that came up." McCain pushed back: "The executive is the commander in chief, but the Constitution says Congress shall make rules concerning captures on land and water." Barr followed up with a new paradigm argument that terror suspects don't have rights under the Geneva Conventions and that litigation pursuing the "due process theory" that they deserve habeas corpus is "frivolous."

Barr then turned to the issue of coercive interrogations to make the administration's case against any new legislation that would impose restrictions. "Now, I can understand if someone wants to say there is no right to coercive interrogation. I disagree with that as a moral matter . . . If you can use coercion in interrogation, the question is where you draw the line. This administration says they're not going to engage in torture, but they will engage in coercive interrogation, and I'm not sure if it would be helpful for Congress to try to figure out what exactly constitutes torture and what's coercion under the circumstances."

Saltzburg's testimony was a polite but determined rebuttal to Barr's claims that everything the administration was doing was obviously and inarguably legal and that therefore congressional involvement was neither necessary nor warranted. Saltzburg pointed out that the indefinite detention of people without charge or trial and the procedures for the military commissions were controversial within the US military and with crucial allies. This was a problem that begged for congressional intervention. He said, "While federal courts have not welcomed having to second guess the President as to the balance that should be struck between protecting the Nation and preserving individual rights, they have recognized their duty to decide the cases brought before them. The courts could not and did not shirk their responsibility to assure that basic constitutional values are not lost in the executive's war on terrorism. Yet, while the courts have met their responsibilities, Congress has provided the courts with no more guidance than it has provided the President. Congress has been silent for too long."

Hutson started his testimony by emphasizing that confusion in the ranks is both a problem in itself and the cause of other problems.

> I will bet that if you ask the Attorney General of the United States and Secretary Rumsfeld and Chairman of the Joint Chiefs and the judge advocates general and all the senior people who have worked on this issue to write down what their definition of [an enemy] combatant is, what they think the rules are that apply, to whom they apply, where they apply, when they apply, you would come up with as many different answers as the people you would ask the question. If those people can't write it down, if they don't understand it clearly, you surely can't expect the colonels and the captains and the staff sergeants to understand that. If you can't expect the staff sergeants to understand it, you're going to have the kind of problems that we have seen.

Hutson knew his audience: confusion in the ranks was exactly what was most concerning to McCain and Graham.

Then Hutson put the situation into a larger context: "I like to think of the United States as being above the law," not because the law can be ignored, but because "the law provides the floor." But, he said, "we are in the basement at this point." He continued, "We should be considering these things not so much from a legal point of view as from a moral point of view, a diplomatic point of view, what is right militarily, what is right practically, what makes common sense, what is going to work not only in this war but in the next war and the war after that . . ." He injected a nationalistic moral argument that "they may be terrorists, they may be evildoers, but they are human beings and we are Americans and we will treat them with the dignity and respect that Americans should always treat human beings, simply by virtue of their humanity." Hutson concluded by appealing to the senators' sense of civic responsibility. "When historians write the book on the war on terrorism, there will be a chapter entitled 'Treatment of Detainees.' The first part of that chapter has already been written and it's not pretty. We don't yet know how that chapter will end. Fortunately, we have the opportunity—*you have the opportunity*—to write that ending." Indeed, McCain already was working on legislation that would make the Army Field Manual applicable to all interrogations conducted by all US personnel and contractors everywhere.

When Hutson finished testifying, McCain asked Saltzburg and Barr whether they agreed with the recommendation to make the Army Field Manual's rules the standard. Saltzburg did. Barr said, "I agree that we are bound to treat all detainees humanely." McCain: "The question is, should the Army Field Manual apply to all detainees or not?" Barr: "Well, no, the Army Field Manual applies [only] to people that are . . . given the privileges of the Third Geneva Convention, [so] no . . ." McCain retorted, "Until we amend the Constitution because of its irrelevancy, I will use that as a reason for Congressional involvement."

McCain's substantive interventions during that hearing were interpreted by people engaged in the fight against torture as another source of hope. He had unique moral authority and stature as a torture survivor, and he had been willing to call out everyone who claimed that detainee treatment was humane and lawful and that the status quo should continue. McCain's position was so consistent, and so stirring, that it overshadowed a line of argument that Graham maintained throughout the day; he repeatedly pointed out that Supreme Court Justice Antonin Scalia was pleading for a "congressional buy-in" to provide legislative clarity about interrogation and detention policies, which Graham wanted heed. At the time, most people who were focused on these issues perceived McCain and Graham as two players going for the same goal: an end to torture through clarifying legislation. The reality, which would not become clear, at least to me, until later that year, was that Graham wanted to pass legislation that would eliminate any role for judges and lawyers regarding the treatment of prisoners. He wanted to end the war in court.

A week after these hearings, the White House issued a policy statement with a stern warning against the looming prospect that McCain and Graham might succeed in convincing Congress to pass new legislation. "*If legislation is presented that would restrict the President's authority to protect Americans effectively from terrorist attack and bring terrorists to justice, the President's senior advisers would recommend that he veto the bill*" (emphasis in original).

Marty Lederman, a Georgetown law professor, blogged his response: "Fancy that: Even *before* any amendments are offered—*by leading conservative*

Senators of the President's own party—and therefore before the White House has even seen what the statutory language might be, the President *categorically* concludes that the legislation *necessarily* 'would interfere with the protection of Americans from terrorism ... by restricting the President's ability to conduct the war effectively under existing law.' Heaven forbid Congress should have the nerve to actually exercise its authorities under Article I, section 8, clauses 10, 11 and 14 of the Constitution ..."

Vice President Dick Cheney took on the enforcer role for the administration. He lobbied Republicans in Congress to stay in their lane and not pass any legislation that would infringe on the president's discretion or impose any restrictions on interrogation policy; for this, the *Washington Post* editorial board labeled him "vice president for torture." Cheney evidently assumed that the siren song of political partisanship would succeed in separating McCain from the Republican herd.

In the midst of Cheney's aggressive campaign, McCain got relief supplies: on September 16, he received a letter from Captain Ian Fishback, which was published in the *Washington Post* on September 28. Fishback introduced himself to McCain as a West Point graduate who had done combat tours in Afghanistan and Iraq. Then the captain explained the purpose of his letter:

> For 17 months, I tried to determine what specific standards governed the treatment of detainees by consulting my chain of command through battalion commander, multiple JAG lawyers, multiple Democrat and Republican Congressmen and their aides, the Ft. Bragg Inspector General's office, multiple government reports, the Secretary of the Army and multiple general officers, a professional interrogator at Guantanamo Bay, the deputy head of the department at West Point responsible for teaching Just War Theory and Law of Land Warfare, and numerous peers who I regard as honorable and intelligent men ... Despite my efforts, I have been unable to get clear, consistent answers ... about what constitutes lawful and humane treatment of detainees. I am certain that this confusion contributed to a wide range of abuses including death threats, beatings, broken bones, murder, exposure to elements, extreme forced physical exertion, hostage-taking, stripping, sleep deprivation and degrading treatment. I and troops under my command witnessed some of these abuses in both Afghanistan and Iraq.

Fishback implored McCain: "That is in the past and there is nothing we can do about it now. But we can learn from our mistakes and ensure that this does not happen again. Take a major step in that direction; eliminate the confusion ... We owe our soldiers better than this." He concluded: "If we abandon our ideals in the face of adversity and aggression, then those ideals were never really in our possession. I would rather die fighting than give up even the smallest part of the idea that is 'America.'"

McCain used Fishback's powerful letter to shore up his position that new legislation was vital. John Sifton of Human Rights Watch offered his thoughts about the battle unfolding on Capitol Hill in the autumn of 2005: "You get no traction bringing criticisms to Rummy [Rumsfeld] and the DoD about detention issues. The only people who can jerk the administration's chain are McCain, Graham, and Warner. Their legislation would plug the CID gap and it would cover the CIA and all US personnel, including contractors." Sifton added, "The current confusion was created by Bush's statement that the Geneva Conventions don't apply. That was confusing to the military, and to the nation. Fishback's story proves this."

Sifton, at that time, was working with Meg Satterthwaite, the director of New York University's Center for Human Rights and Global Justice, and Hina Shamsi at HRF to build a database of all detainee abuse in the "war on terror." One source of information was records of disciplinary proceedings against soldiers. Sifton said, "Since Abu Ghraib we've seen well over four hundred allegations of serious abuse, including allegations from other soldiers." The majority of cases that triggered investigations—and, he said, most abuses never get reported—were resolved through nonjudicial proceedings (Article 15 hearings) that could only hand out administrative penalties like admonishments, reductions in pay or rank, or discharge from military service. "The Pentagon regularly trumpets its record of accountability, saying things like 'there have been over two hundred cases of people being punished.' But if you look at those numbers, over two-thirds are administrative. This includes people who were accused of killing detainees, perpetrating mock executions, et cetera. Even in actual courts martial, the majority result in punishments of less than a year." Sifton gave several examples: "Soldiers who electroshocked Iraqis got eight months. Soldiers who beat up juvenile detainees got two months. Soldiers who killed Afghan detainees got a suspended sentence."

McCain succeeded in outgunning Cheney's anti-legislation lobbying. By the end of September, it was clear that a veto-proof majority in the Senate was willing to pass McCain's legislation to prohibit all US personnel from engaging in cruel, inhuman, or degrading treatment. The McCain Amendment passed on October 5 by a vote of ninety to nine.

After Cheney lost that battle, he changed tack and started lobbying for a "CIA exception" to the prohibition. President Bush threatened to veto the whole defense appropriations bill unless the McCain Amendment was modified to exempt the CIA. Throughout the remainder of the year, McCain was engaged in tense negotiations with the White House. He was defending an absolute ban on cruel, inhuman, and degrading treatment, while the administration, aided by several key Republican senators, was fighting for loopholes.

The Bush administration's torture policy became the subject of intensified international criticism when *Washington Post* journalist Dana Priest published an article on November 2 exposing the fact that the CIA was running black sites in several Eastern European countries. However, the article did not name those countries "at the request of senior US officials." The CIA immediately scrambled to move detainees being held in European black sites off the continent.

Three days after the *Washington Post* story, Human Rights Watch released a statement filling in the blanks: those Eastern European countries were Poland and Romania. (Later, Lithuania was identified as a third country where the CIA had a black site.) HRW explained that its investigation into secret detention facilities had uncovered "flight records showing that a Boeing 737, registration number N313P—a plane that the CIA used to move several prisoners to and from Europe, Afghanistan, and the Middle East in 2003 and 2004—landed in Poland and Romania on direct flights from Afghanistan." HRW also revealed other countries that were implicated in the CIA's rendition operations: "The N313P airplane, and other planes allegedly used by the CIA to transport prisoners, have also repeatedly landed at airports in Jordan, Morocco, Egypt, and Libya, as well as in Germany, the United Kingdom, Switzerland, Spain, Portugal, Macedonia, Cyprus, the Czech Republic, and Greece." HRW concluded the statement by urging the United Nations and the European Union to launch investigations and urging Congress to demand that the Bush administration account for people the CIA had disappeared.

An exposé of a different kind was reported by the *Washington Post* on November 8. In an article about the Supreme Court's decision the previous day to grant certiorari to hear *Hamdan v. Rumsfeld,* an in-other-news paragraph at the end of the piece reported that Senator Graham "hopes to add language to the defense authorization bill that would eliminate habeas rights for detainees captured during the terrorism fight to halt the 'never-ending litigation that is coming from Guantanamo.'" Graham's immediate goal, which the White House shared, was to negate the Supreme Court's *Rasul* decision in order to drive lawyers out of Guantánamo. The larger goal was to strip courts of jurisdiction over all foreign detainees held anywhere overseas. Graham intended his legislation to be comprehensive and retroactive—to cancel detainees' right to file habeas petitions and dismiss all habeas cases already on the dockets of the DC District court. He also wanted *Hamdan* to be tossed before it was argued in the Supreme Court.

When David Remes read that paragraph about Graham's plans, he worried about what it would mean for the seventeen Guantánamo detainees he was representing. Remes sent an email to the Gitmo Bar listserve to alert the five hundred–plus habeas counsel that Graham's amendment, if it passed, could moot their petitions and possibly end their ability to represent their clients.

The Gitmo Bar, up to that point, had been focusing on the court battles over habeas which had come to an impasse in January 2005. Several months earlier, a decision had been made to consolidate all the Guantánamo habeas petitions and put them on the docket of Judge Joyce Hens Green, but it was conditioned on the agreement of the original judges to turn their cases over to her. Seven of the eight judges agreed to let Judge Green take their cases. The holdout was Judge Richard Leon, a Bush appointee with strong ties to Cheney. Leon and Green, presented with identical materials and arguments, issued contradictory decisions in January. Leon ruled in favor of the government motion to dismiss all habeas petitions on the grounds that "non-resident aliens captured and detained outside the territorial sovereignty of the United States" have no cognizable constitutional rights. Part of his ruling rehashed Justice Scalia's dissent in *Rasul.* In stark contrast, Judge Green ruled that the *Rasul* decision recognized that detainees do have rights to file habeas petitions in federal court and she rejected the motion to dismiss. Both decisions were quickly appealed to the DC Circuit Court.

The news about Graham's proposed legislation shifted the Gitmo Bar's attention from the courts to Congress. How would they fight legislation proposed by a Republican senator in a Republican-controlled Congress? "We are litigators, not lobbyists," was a common refrain. Gary Isaac writes about this in an essay he contributed to the edited volume titled *The Guantánamo Lawyers:* "Once the battle over habeas entered the halls of Congress, we lawyers needed to become political organizers and lobbyists, to press our case with members of Congress on both sides of the aisle, and to make them understand the importance of this fundamental—but potentially politically thorny—issue and the toll that would be exacted on the rule of law and our constitutional liberties if they made the wrong decisions."

The Gitmo Bar lawyers did what political campaigners do: they prepared talking points for the media, wrote op-eds, contacted their senators to make the case against jurisdiction-stripping legislation, and reached out to local bar associations and colleagues all over the country urging them to do the same. Isaac reached out to Admirals Hutson and Donald Guter. Hutson was already lobbying other retired military officers to speak out in opposition to Graham's scheme, but Guter was not convinced. He and Graham had a personal connection, and the senator was lobbying Guter to support his amendment. Hutson showed Guter a copy of Graham's amendment which stipulated that "no court, justice, or judge shall have jurisdiction to hear or consider an application for a writ of habeas corpus filed by or on behalf of an alien detained . . . at Guantanamo Bay, Cuba; or any other action against the United States or its agents relating to any aspect of the detention . . . of an alien at Guantanamo Bay." The legislation would grant one exception: the DC Circuit Court could retain jurisdiction to hear appeals of CSRT decisions, which determined whether a detainee was legitimately detained; and rulings in military commission cases. Guter agreed to oppose the legislation.

Graham presented his amendment on November 9, and the Republican Senate leadership limited discussion to two hours. According to Isaac, "Most of the country was unaware of what was being done to the Constitution that day in the Senate, but habeas counsel around the country anxiously watched the debate—if it could be called that—on C-SPAN . . . Graham took up most of the Republicans' time, delivering an utterly demagogic, but highly effective, speech ridiculing the supposed frivolousness of the habeas litigation and suggesting that some of the habeas lawyers were using the litigation to interfere with the mission of our armed forces."

The Gitmo Bar lawyers hoped that McCain would vote against the Graham Amendment because it essentially contradicted *his* amendment banning cruel, inhuman, and degrading treatment. Without a role for the courts, the protections provided in the McCain Amendment would be unenforceable. Hopes were dashed when McCain voted "aye" and the Graham Amendment passed by a vote of forty-nine to forty-two.

But that fight wasn't over. Senator Carl Levin, the ranking Democrat on the SASC, sought to negotiate a compromise by inserting a provision that the legislation would affect only future cases while preserving those already on the dockets of federal courts—in other words, to ensure that jurisdiction-stripping would not be retroactive. It worked: on November 15, the Senate passed "compromise" legislation, now referred to as the Graham-Levin Amendment.

The White House, meanwhile, was relentlessly pressuring McCain to agree to a CIA exception. Finally, he gave in and agreed to alter the amendment that bore his name to include language that would legally inoculate the CIA from accountability for torturing prisoners.

The CIA exception was, in an unsettling way, a testament to the efficacy of the war in court. As Gabor Rona put it, "People in the CIA were worried that they might be prosecuted or sued. That exception gave them cover."

On December 15, McCain and President Bush appeared together in the Oval Office to shake hands after Bush signed the McCain Amendment. The president used the occasion to stare into the cameras and declare that this legislation makes it "clear to the world that this government does not torture."

The McCain Amendment and the Graham-Levin Amendment were combined as the Detainee Treatment Act of 2005 (DTA). In December, a bipartisan majority passed it. The DTA could be interpreted as a congressional buy-in—or in the eyes of critics a congressional sell-out—for the Bush administration's new paradigm. Nevertheless, on December 30 when President Bush signed the legislation, he issued a signing statement (a written pronouncement about how the president intends to interpret the law) that he would enforce the DTA "in a manner consistent with the constitutional authority of the President to supervise the unitary executive branch and as Commander in Chief and consistent with the constitutional limitations on the judicial power."

The Bush administration made immediate use of the DTA's jurisdiction-stripping provisions. On January 3, 2006, the Justice Department, ignoring the nonretroactive clause Levin had negotiated into the legislation, notified federal judges that it would seek the immediate dismissal of the 160 habeas cases that had been filed on behalf of Guantánamo detainees. On January 10, the solicitor general asked the Supreme Court to dismiss *Hamdan* because federal courts no longer have jurisdiction over detainee-related matters. Although that initiative failed, the DTA meant that lawyers would have to relitigate the core question in *Rasul* over whether there was a role *for courts* to enforce the laws.

The first test of the DTA was *Hamdan*. Team Hamdan included Swift and Katyal as well as Harry Schneider, Joe McMillan, and David East from Perkins Coie, Seattle's largest law firm with a blue-chip corporate clientele that includes Boeing. Perkins Coie's involvement with the case traces back to March 2004 when Schneider gave a speech at a gathering of lawyers in which he emphasized the importance of doing pro bono work. Afterwards he realized he hadn't done much himself lately, so he told the firm's pro bono coordinator that he would take the next case. That day, Katyal reached out to East to ask for someone from the firm to represent Salim Hamdan. Schneider became Hamdan's habeas counsel. McMillan wanted in, too, because this work involved issues that he was very concerned, even alarmed about. When *Hamdan* was litigated in federal court, the Perkins Coie attorneys were part of the team.

I went to Seattle to interview McMillan in September 2008. Our conversation took place in one of his firm's swanky conference rooms with floor-to-ceiling windows looking out over downtown Seattle. I asked how he and the other attorneys developed their legal strategy for *Hamdan*. McMillan explained that Swift and Katyal's original plan was to build the case around the argument that Hamdan had been deprived of his right to a speedy trial, which violated Article 10 of the UCMJ. The Perkins Coie lawyers urged a broader and more ambitious approach. McMillan said, "It's got to challenge the executive's power to prosecute people before those military commissions. Our challenges had to be based on the full panoply of US and international laws."

Swift and Katyal had identified the issues that made the commissions so problematic and contrary to the UCMJ: protracted incommunicado detention, prosecutors' prerogative to use coerced statements and hearsay, infringements on lawyer-client relations, and rules that provided no guarantee of due process. But turning those problems into legal arguments persuasive to federal judges was a challenge. McMillan, who is a legal history buff, said he started reading to find problems of a similar sort and cases that raised relevant issues. When the team started hammering out arguments for their brief, their different skill sets sometimes clashed. McMillan and Schneider were seasoned litigators whereas Katyal was, foremost, a scholar. According to McMillan, "Neal would bury key stuff in footnotes. His writing would presume an academic audience. He loves obscure facts, but you don't get any credit for obscurity." McMillan also stressed that, unlike Katyal, he and Schneider were not inclined to be deferential to executive power. This case had to put the executive on trial by raising "well-documented and justified concerns" about the authorization of inhumane treatment and failure to adhere to the Geneva Conventions.

McMillan painted a picture: "We white boarded the case. We identified the major issues and then filled in details for each category." Category one was the Constitution and the separation of powers. "In Article 1, the Define and Punish Clause gives *Congress* power to define and punish violations of the laws of nations." Therefore, McMillan explained, they would have to argue that the president's November 2001 military order creating the commissions is unconstitutional. "The president doesn't have unilateral power." Category two was federal statutes. "The UCMJ . . . says the president has military commission authority only over those people—foreign enemy combatants—who are subject to the laws of war." That means soldiers. According to Common Article 3, which is incorporated in the UCMJ, prisoners of war can only be tried for war crimes in tribunals comparable to those used to court-martial soldiers. "If the government wants to prosecute Hamdan for violating the laws of war, let them treat him as a POW and court martial him."

Category three was international law, particularly the Geneva Conventions. There was some disagreement among the team about whether this would be persuasive because many judges simply don't understand international law. When the DC District Court heard the case, McMillan explained, "we had to argue to Judge Robertson that treaties *are* judicially enforceable to counter the government's argument that treaties are compacts between states and can't be enforced by individuals." He said that Robertson got it right and ruled in Hamdan's favor, but on appeal, the DC Circuit Court reversed Robertson by ruling that the Geneva Conventions are not judicially enforceable. For the Supreme Court, McMillan continued, "arguing customary international law would be a weak position. We have to argue that treaty law, according to the Supremacy Clause of the Constitution, *is law of the land.* The UCMJ incorporates the Geneva Conventions and domesticates it. We get the conventions in by putting the UCMJ out front in our arguments."

Before we concluded our conversation, I asked McMillan whether Hamdan's torture was a factor in their legal strategizing. He responded: "That requires a long and nuanced answer." There is no dispute that he was held in solitary confinement for a very long period. "Even if that doesn't qualify as torture, it's at least inhumane treatment. US *courts* have said this." At Bagram, he said, Hamdan's abuse included stress positions for protracted periods and numerous beatings. "At Gitmo, it wasn't the same raw brutality, but interrogation plans targeted the weaknesses and vulnerabilities of individual detainees. For Hamdan, this was sleep deprivation, nudity, and sexual humiliations. Plus, they withheld medical treatment." But for the Supreme Court, the details of his treatment were beside the point. They had to make the Court see the illegitimacy of a presidentially created legal system that disregarded and violated the UCMJ.

On March 28, 2006, the Supreme Court heard oral arguments. Katyal argued for the team. Sure enough, the question of whether the Court should even be hearing this case occupied the first half of his presentation because several justices wanted to know whether the DTA's jurisdiction-stripping provision applied. Katyal explained that the DTA was passed after the Supreme Court granted certiorari for *Hamdan* and, moreover, the DTA should have no bearing because it incorporated a nonretroactive clause. The second half of Katyal's presentation was consumed by the question of whether the main charge the government wanted to prosecute Hamdan for—conspiracy—was a violation of the laws of war and, therefore, a prosecutable offense in a military commission. Interjections by several of the conservative justices indicated that they were of the mind that the laws of war are whatever the president says they are.

On June 29, 2006, the Supreme Court issued a five-to-three decision. Justice John Stevens, who wrote for the majority, said that "the military commission convened to try Hamdan lacks power to proceed because its structure and procedures violate both the UCMJ and the Geneva Conventions." Thus, the presidentially created commissions were cancelled. Justices Anthony Kennedy and Stephen Breyer concurred with the majority but wrote their own opinions. Breyer's one-pager gave the administration a road map out of the loss: "Nothing prevents the President from returning to Congress to seek the authority he believes necessary." Justice Scalia wrote the main dissenting opinion and Samuel Alito and Clarence Thomas, while concurring with him, wrote separate opinions. Scalia argued that the DTA should have kicked the case off the docket, and he cited an amicus brief by Senators Graham and Jon Kyl that it was Congress's intent when the DTA was passed to have the *Hamdan* case dismissed before it was heard. Graham and Kyl's brief cited a colloquy (conversation) between the two of them in the Senate on the day the DTA was voted upon. The problem was that the colloquy—that is, what was actually said on the floor of the Senate—was a fake: Graham and Kyl had inserted a written text of a conversation that never took place into the Congressional record right before the vote for the specific purpose of giving Scalia ammunition if he needed it.

Despite the cacophony of multiple opinions coming out of the Supreme Court, people waging the war in court lauded *Hamdan* as a victory. But rather than bringing government policy back in line with the law, the political blowback opened new fronts, with wins and losses on both sides.

Those conflicting dynamics had a banner day on September 6, 2006. In the win-some column, the Pentagon released a revised Army Field Manual implementing the requirements of the McCain Amendment. A number of techniques that had been used by US interrogators in the "war on terror" were expressly prohibited, including forcing the detainee to be naked, perform sexual acts or pose in a sexual manner; placing hoods or sacks over the head of a detainee or using duct tape over the eyes; beatings, electric shock, burns, or other forms of physical pain; waterboarding; using military working dogs; inducing hypothermia or heat injury; conducting mock executions; and depriving the detainee of necessary food, water, or medical care.

In the lose-some column was President Bush's press conference, in which he criticized the *Hamdan* ruling and laid out the administration's combative responses. Because the Court had ruled that Common Article 3 applies to every prisoner in US custody, he felt it necessary to publicly acknowledge for the first time the existence of the CIA's top-secret rendition, detention, and interrogation program. He justified the program by spinning a yarn that Abu Zubaydah and other "high value detainees" in CIA custody fell like dominoes when subjected to "alternative" interrogation techniques, which he took credit for approving, and he claimed that they had divulged vital information that disrupted terrorist plots. (Many elements of his narrative about the CIA's program have, in the years since, been totally debunked.) By omitting facts and presenting a false account of the successes of interrogational violence, President Bush was laying the foundation for the grand deception that "this program has saved lives." He insisted that it "remains vital to the security of the United States and our friends and allies, and. . . deserves the support of the United States Congress and the American people."

The other cornerstone of this public deception was Bush's assertion that the techniques CIA agents and contractors were authorized to use were "designed to be safe, to comply with our laws, our Constitution and our treaty obligations." He added, "I want to be absolutely clear with our people and the world: The United States does not torture. It's against our laws and it's against our values. I have not authorized it and I will not authorize it." (That line might have been more plausible if he hadn't compelled McCain to concede to a CIA exception to the very techniques that the revised Army Field Manual had just prohibited.)

Bush complained that the Court's decision that Common Article 3 applies to "our war with Al Qaida could be interpreted in different ways by American or foreign judges." This possibility that a judge might regard waterboarding or months of naked solitary confinement in an ice-cold cell as outrageous or degrading could put "our military and intelligence personnel involved in capturing terrorists and questioning terrorists . . . at risk of prosecution under the War Crimes Act, simply for doing their jobs in a thorough and professional way. This is unacceptable." He pronounced his solution: soon the White House would send legislation to Congress that would "make it clear that captured terrorists cannot use the Geneva Conventions as a basis to sue our personnel in courts—in U.S. courts." He added, "The men and women who protect us should not have to fear lawsuits filed by terrorists because they are doing their jobs." This new legislation also would resurrect the military commissions that the *Hamdan* decision had wiped out. We need these commissions, Bush explained, because Khalid Sheikh Mohammed (referred to by his initials, KSM) who was the alleged "mastermind" of 9/11, Abu Zubaydah, and twelve others in CIA custody were about to be transferred from black sites to Guantánamo. "As soon as Congress acts to authorize the military commissions I have proposed, the men our intelligence officials believe orchestrated the deaths of nearly 3,000 Americans on September the 11th, 2001, can face justice."

The following month, Congress passed the Military Commissions Act (MCA) which Bush signed into law on October 17. The MCA sought to make US torture legally irrelevant by stripping away any recourse in federal court for foreign detainees to challenge their violent and degrading treatment or imprisonment without trial. The Bush administration and a congressional majority that voted for the law wanted an end to what they regarded as illegitimate judicial interference in the "war on terror." The MCA also incorporated a blanket grant of ex post facto immunity for violations of the War Crimes Act perpetrated by any US personnel. The MCA was more than just a congressional buy-in for the administration's policies. It was intended to terminate the war in court by salting the battlefield.

Scott Horton described the MCA as "a piece of legislation that will stand in history alongside the Alien and Sedition Acts and the Fugitive Slave Act as a reminder of the kind of constitutional vandalism that Congress is capable of when it really tries." Rick Wilson, who ran the human rights law clinic at The American University, was less pessimistic. "We keep losing but we can't back down now," he said, "because we are fighting for the rule of law itself. Besides, history always vindicates the lawyers who hang on and keep at it." He was alluding to the fact that since the late 1980s, Latin America had become a region of exceptional accountability because dozens of former officials, including heads of state, had been prosecuted for torture and other gross crimes perpetrated during the military dictatorships. Wilson added, "I hope someday I can look back and say that."

SIX

Fighting for Justice at Home and Abroad

TORTURE IS A GROSS CRIME under international law, in the same company as genocide and crimes against humanity. Torture is universally prohibited, and *legally*, there are no exceptions. This prohibition began mattering more tangibly in the last decades of the twentieth century when international criminal law started to be enforced in ways not seen since of close of the Nuremberg and Tokyo Tribunals after the end of World War II. In the 1990s, new international tribunals and courts were established to prosecute individual perpetrators and international lawyers began acquiring and honing the skills needed to bring those responsible for torture and other gross crimes to justice.

The US government affirmed its commitment to the universal consensus that torture is prohibited in its 1999 submission to the UN Committee on Torture: "Torture . . . is categorically denounced as a matter of policy and as a tool of state authority. . . . No official of the Government, federal or state, civilian or military, is authorized to commit or to instruct anyone else to commit torture. Nor may any official condone or tolerate torture in any form. No exceptional circumstances may be invoked as a justification of torture."

In 2000, I published an academic article that includes these lines: "No society on earth advances the claim that torture, as legally defined, is a valued or integral part of its cultural heritage or political culture. If such an argument could be made, it would be: the practice of torture would be acknowledged rather than denied."

That was true when I wrote it. It no longer is.

The Bush administration secretly authorized a torture policy in 2002. After it was exposed in 2004, President Bush and other top officials justified what they had done with an explanation that went like this: Yes, we coercively interrogated terrorists and evil doers, and we got lots of excellent information out of them because our "alternative" and "enhanced" techniques, which we used only as a last resort, were so effective. Those techniques may be "tough," but they do not rise to the level of torture, at least not when our guys use them, because our lawyers said so. Torture is bad, we are good, and there haven't been any mass casualty attacks on the United States since 9/11 thanks to the policies we instituted. Anyone who disagrees is soft on terrorism.

David Luban, a Georgetown law professor whose specialties include legal ethics and philosophy, accurately described this line of reasoning as "the liberal ideology of torture." Liberalism's opposite is not conservatism, but rather tyranny and authoritarianism. As a political system, liberalism rests on three pillars: the state represents society; the behavior of government officials and agencies is regulated by law; and all people have rights which are guaranteed by laws. Since torture is inherently illiberal, a liberal ideology of torture is, on its face, oxymoronic. When officials in a political democracy choose to authorize torture, they do it with euphemisms, calling torture "moderate physical pressure" as the Israeli government did, or "enhanced interrogation techniques" as the US government did. What Luban identifies as the liberal ideology of torture hinges on the significance of representative rule in a liberal democratic state: In fulfilling our responsibility to protect the nation, we used enhanced interrogation techniques *for you*.

The Bush administration tried to make the criminality of its own torture irrelevant, first, by reinterpreting the law to narrow the meaning of torture and to make the prohibition unenforceable against agents of the US government. Commenting on the torture memos when they became public in 2004, journalist Anthony Lewis compared them to "advice of a mob lawyer to a mafia don on how to skirt the law and stay out of prison. Avoiding prosecution is literally a theme of the memoranda." After the torture policy was exposed, the administration used the power of the state to oppose accountability for those responsible for this crime and to deny justice for victims. Since torture is a crime of state, unsurprisingly, zero US officials were prosecuted for their roles in the torture program. The Military Commissions Act of 2006 (MCA) cemented this impunity by granting ex post facto immunity for violations of the War Crimes Act perpetrated by American state agents.

With criminal prosecution off the table, the only option for torture-crime victims to seek justice in US courts was civil lawsuits (torts) for monetary damages against officials whose actions and decisions caused the wrongs they suffered. Michael Ratner, president of the Center for Constitutional Rights

(CCR), explained the purpose of civil litigation: "You have to open the door in some way to make high levels [officials] accountable. This fight takes everything—press accounts, lobbying Congress. Litigation for damages is one option. And besides, court cases are good for drawing attention to what these people are doing. It's the educative effect."

When the first civil lawsuits against government officials were filed in 2004 and 2005, I assumed that courts would have to vindicate the victims because there is no right to torture and no legal immunity for this gross crime—this was before the passage of the MCA. I wasn't naïve to the fact that courts often fail to provide justice for victims, but, I reasoned, torture is a special kind of crime. Even if some judges were politically hostile or indifferent to the suffering of foreign victims of US torture, they would nevertheless have to perform their primary institutional role to ensure that legal laws are lawfully enforced. Therefore, they would be duty-bound to rule against officials who bore responsibility for torture and its associated practices of kidnapping and forced disappearance.

The first civil lawsuit was *Arar v. Ashcroft*. David Cole, acting on behalf of CCR, filed the case in January 2004 in the Eastern District of New York. The plaintiff was a Canadian citizen of Syrian origin named Maher Arar. He was seized while transiting through the John F. Kennedy Airport (JFK) in New York. Two weeks later, the government secretly transported him to Syria where he was tortured for almost a year with the knowledge and collusion of US officials.

The lawsuit targeted the officials heading the agencies that bore responsibility for rendering Maher Arar to Syria: Attorney General John Ashcroft and his deputy Larry Thompson, FBI Director Robert Mueller, Secretary of Homeland Security Tom Ridge, Commissioner for the Immigration and Naturalization Service James Ziglar, plus three other named immigration officials and ten John Does (unnamed individuals) from the FBI and INS.

Arar's nightmare began on September 26, 2002, while he was changing planes on his way home to Canada from Tunisia where he had been visiting his wife's family. He traveled frequently to the United States because he worked as a consultant for a Boston-based engineering company. He had renewed his US work permit the previous April. After being detained at JFK, Arar was moved to a high-security section of the airport and held incommunicado. He was questioned about al-Qaeda, as well as his views on Palestine and the impending war on Iraq. At one point, he was shown a copy of a 1997 apartment rental agreement in which he had listed Abdullah Almalki, another Syrian Canadian, as an emergency contact.

In the mid-1990s, the Royal Canadian Mounted Police (RCMP) had put Almalki under surveillance as part of a broad investigation into possible terrorist activities among Muslims in Toronto and Ottawa. Almalki had aroused suspicion because, in the early 1990s, he worked in Pakistan for a Canadian charity providing relief to Afghan refugee women and children. The organization's regional director was Egyptian-born Canadian Ahmed Khadr. In 1994, Almalki quit the job after a dispute with Khadr and returned to Canada. But he remained an object of the Mounties' suspicion because of his previous ties to Khadr who, in 1997, moved his family to Afghanistan and developed a relationship with al-Qaeda leader Osama bin Laden. In 1999, Khadr was added to the UN list of people who support terrorism.

Arar attracted the Mounties' attention on October 12, 2001, when he met Almalki at a shawarma restaurant in Ottawa. The agents spying on Almalki found it suspicious that the two men spent some time that rainy day talking outside. Arar was added to the list of Canadian Muslims deemed to merit security scrutiny. In February 2002, an FBI agent met with his Canadian counterparts to exchange information about their respective post-9/11 investigations. At that meeting, a copy of Arar's rental lease was turned over to the FBI.

From the questions that interrogators were asking Arar while he was detained at JFK, he realized that they suspected that he was a member of some terrorist sleeper cell. They rejected his protestations that he was innocent. Although the Mounties had been the source of suspicion against him, there was no truth to the US agents' claims that Canada had refused to readmit him. They told him that he would be deported—"removed" in official parlance—to his native Syria. Arar pleaded with them not to send him to Syria where he feared he would be tortured.

Arar's family, frantic over his disappearance, hired a lawyer. Ten days after he was taken into custody, the lawyer was permitted to meet with him. In a *New York Review of Books* article, David Cole explains what happened after that meeting between Arar and his lawyer, which took place on a Saturday afternoon:

> [T]he government hastily scheduled an extraordinary hearing for the next night—Sunday evening—and only "notified" Arar's lawyer by leaving a voicemail on her office answering machine that Sunday afternoon. They then falsely told Arar that the lawyer had declined to participate, and questioned

him for six hours, until 3 am Monday. When Arar's lawyer retrieved the voicemail message later that Monday morning, she immediately called the Immigration and Naturalization Service. They told her falsely that Arar was being moved to New Jersey, and that she could contact him there the next day. In fact, he remained in New York until late that night, when he was put on a federally chartered jet and spirited out of the country. US officials never informed Arar's lawyer that he had been deported, much less that he had been delivered to Syrian security forces.

The officials making decisions about Arar were aware of the Syrian security services' propensity for torture, because it is well-documented in the State Department's annual country reports. By choosing to send Arar to Syria, they violated the customary international law principle of non-refoulement, which categorically prohibits any government from transferring any person to a country where there are "substantial grounds for believing" that he will be tortured. While Arar was detained in New York, an immigration review panel even concluded that he would be tortured if sent to Syria—a determination the officials dealing with him either chose to ignore or, cynically, were counting on. While Arar was held at JFK, the Bush administration, despite frequently accusing the Syrian regime of being a state sponsor of terrorism, asked Congress not to pass the Syrian Accountability Act because that would "tie its hands at a very important moment."

In Syria, Arar's torture began immediately with ferocious beatings. His interrogators asked the same questions he was asked in New York. On the third day, he later recounted, "I lost all my strength, and I told them what they wanted to hear." He falsely confessed to the allegation that he had trained at an al-Qaeda camp in Afghanistan. In fact, Arar has never been to Afghanistan. This allegation, forwarded from Washington, emanated from a broader web of tortured false confessions by other prisoners who were arrested months earlier.

One person caught in this web was Ahmad Abou El Maati, a Kuwaiti-born Canadian citizen. He traveled to Syria in November 2001 to marry his Syrian fiancée. He was arrested upon arrival and taken to military intelligence's Palestine Branch, one of Syria's premier torture centers. Between rounds of beating him with cables, dousing him with ice water, and threatening to rape his fiancée, his interrogators demanded that he confess that he and his brother were al-Qaeda operatives who were planning to bomb the US embassy in Ottawa. Fearing more torture, he falsely confessed verbally that he had planned to bomb the Canadian parliament building.

But when El Maati was forced to write his confession, he wrote the true account of the incident at the heart of the Canadian-sourced allegations: He was driving a company delivery truck when Canadian border agents found a map in the glove compartment that had been left by someone else. That map, which included government buildings, triggered the Mounties' suspicions that he was part of a sleeper cell. His Syrian interrogators were angered that his written statement did not reflect the confession they wanted, so they beat him and burned him with cigarettes. At that point he was incapable of writing anything, so they wrote a confession and forced him to sign it without allowing him to read it.

In January 2002, El Maati was transferred to Egypt where the torture continued. When he finally met a Canadian consular official in August 2002, he told them about his Syrian torture and the false confession he had signed but said nothing about his treatment in Egypt because Egyptian officials were present. It took two more years until he was released and, after several aborted attempts, was able to leave Egypt and return to Canada.

On May 26, 2004, during a joint press conference, Attorney General Ashcroft and FBI Director Mueller alluded to the confession El Maati had signed in Syria when they claimed that they had "hard" evidence of an impending attack on the United States. It is unknown whether Ashcroft and Mueller were aware that the confession was false and were lying to the public or actually believed their own claims of its veracity.

Arar's acquaintance Almalki was caught up in the web of torture and lies on May 3, 2002, when he traveled to Syria for the first time since emigrating as a teen in order to visit his sick grandmother. He, too, was arrested and, like El Maati, was transferred to Palestine Branch, and interrogated under torture. He was subjected to *falaqa* (beating on the bare soles of his feet), then forced to get up and jog in place while being doused with water to intensify the pain. He falsely confessed that he knew Osama bin Laden, concocting a story that they met when he was working in Pakistan. But the Syrians knew that bin Laden had been in Sudan during that period, so they beat him for lying. Interrogators later told Almalki that on his first day, he was lashed a thousand times with the cable, extraordinary even by Syrian standards. He was also subjected to electric shock, nail pulling, and the "German chair," a device resembling the medieval rack that hyper-extends the spine.

On Almalki's fortieth day of detention, he was interrogated by George Salloum, Syria's torturer-in-chief, who asked very specific questions about other Canadians, including Arar. Almalki realized that his Syrian interrogators were drawing on information provided by the Canadians from a search of his Ottawa apartment. In mid-July, the beatings intensified, and he confessed falsely that he had trained in Afghanistan.

On September 26, Salloum and five other interrogators questioned Almalki about Arar, who had been arrested at JFK four days earlier. They told Almalki to write down everything he knew and threatened that he would be beaten until he needed hospitalization if he lied. Almalki's questioning about Arar continued for days—the same days Arar was being interrogated in New York. When Almalki was asked if Arar had ever been to Afghanistan, he said no, not to his knowledge. Salloum told him that Arar would be there soon and if Almalki had lied, he would be put in the German chair until he was paralyzed.

Another Canadian who was questioned while Arar was at JFK was Omar Khadr, the fifteen-year-old son of Ahmed Khadr. In June 2002, Khadr senior had sent Omar from Pakistan into Afghanistan to serve as a translator for al-Qaeda militants because he spoke Arabic and Pashtu. Omar was captured in July following a firefight in a compound near Khost. He was transferred to Bagram and put into interrogation immediately despite being severely wounded. On October 7, an FBI agent named Robert Fuller interrogated Khadr and showed him a photo of Arar. Khadr didn't recognize the man but, when Fuller pressed him, he said that he might have seen Arar at an al-Qaeda training camp.

In the early hours of October 8, Arar was boarded onto the secret rendition flight to Jordan, and then transported by land to Syria. When Arar was not being interrogated under torture, he was confined in one of the prison's dank, filthy underground grave-like cells that was three feet wide and six feet long.

The Syrians finally concluded that Washington's allegations that Arar was a terrorist were baseless. On October 5, 2003, he was released to the custody of a Canadian embassy official in Damascus and was immediately repatriated. On November 4, Arar told his story publicly for the first time; he described his wrecked condition and stated that he had been imprisoned and tortured with Almalki. That day, Amnesty International issued an urgent action alert calling for Almalki's release. With media attention escalating and questions multiplying, the Canadian Crown moved to have evidence about domestic investigations of Arar, Almalki, and other Muslims sealed.

In Canada, Arar became a *cause célèbre* as a victim of a multilateral conspiracy to torture. Public outrage over his treatment intensified when an RCMP official insinuated to a journalist that he was indeed an al-Qaeda terrorist. In response to public anger, the government established an official commission of inquiry. The Arar Commission, which was tasked to investigate the actions of Canadians involved in his case, interviewed over seventy officials and reviewed approximately 21,500 documents. The Commission released its eleven-hundred-page report on September 18, 2006, concluding "categorically that there is no evidence to indicate that Mr. Arar has committed any offense or that his activities constitute a threat to the security of Canada." While the Commission found no evidence that Canadian officials played a direct role in the decisions to detain Arar at JFK or to send him to Syria, they decided that the Mounties had violated their own policies by providing information to US officials before and after his arrest that was "inaccurate, portrayed him in an unfairly negative fashion and overstated his importance in the RCMP investigation." The head of the RCMP resigned and, three months later, Canada's public safety minister announced the initiation of separate investigations into any role officials had played in the Syrian detention and torture of El Maati, Almalki and Iraqi-born Muayyed Nureddin.

On January 26, 2007, Prime Minister Stephen Harper issued an official apology to Arar on behalf of the Canadian government and announced that he would receive a $10.5 million (Canadian) settlement as compensation for his ordeal and an additional million to cover his legal fees. While no amount of money or apology can undo the effects of torture, the clearing of Arar's name and reform of the policies that had contributed to his rendition to Syria were vindicating.

The Bush administration made no moves to conduct an investigation, let alone hold US officials accountable for Arar's ordeal. A civil lawsuit was the only avenue for seeking justice. When David Cole filed the case, he was optimistic that Arar would win. "There are very few absolutes. Most rights can be limited in the face of compelling state interest and narrowly tailored means. But torture is absolutely prohibited and there is no legal basis for doing or abetting it." CCR attorney Maria LaHood, co-counsel on the case, explained their objective: "This case challenges the extraordinary rendition policy. We want to shed light and stop it." Cole said, "The Arar case has the best set of facts for this kind of challenge." He outlined how they would try to make the case: "We will argue that it is a violation of due process to send someone to be tortured. Due process ought to constrain the government. It also violates the TVPA [Torture Victim Protection Act] which creates a private cause of action"—a means by which an individual can sue officials—"for torture perpetrated by foreigners overseas. Arar's torturers were Syrians but the US conspired with them." To win damages, Cole explained, "we need a ruling that this is illegal under federal law."

The government moved immediately to shut down the lawsuit by invoking the state secrets privilege. This judicially created doctrine permits the government to withhold certain pieces of information if disclosure could harm national security. The doctrine originated with the 1953 Supreme Court ruling in *United States v. Reynolds;* after a military aircraft testing secret electronic equipment crashed in rural Georgia, the widows of civilian contractors on the flight sued for damages and requested the Air Force accident investigation report. The secretary of the Air Force invoked the privilege to withhold that information because the aircraft was engaged in a secret mission when it crashed. *Reynolds* created a precedent for courts to allow certain evidence to be withheld at the request of the government to protect state secrets.

The Bush administration made unprecedented use of state secrets. Instead of invoking the privilege to withhold some specific information, the government's motion to dismiss *Arar* claimed that the discovery of *any* information about the decisions that led to his rendition—why officials thought he was associated with al-Qaeda and why he was sent to Syria rather than Canada—would reveal sensitive intelligence-gathering methods and would be harmful to US national security and foreign relations.

Cole described this broad use of state secrets as "the nuclear option that would preclude any legal action against rendition." Steven Watt, a staff attorney at CCR when *Arar* was filed (he moved over to the ACLU in the following November), said, "The use of state secrets to end litigation started with *Arar.* The DoJ [Department of Justice] cooked up a theory that using state secrets will make the case go away. Litigating against state secrets is hard because there aren't many past cases that raise these issues." With a heavy sigh, Watt added: "We have to put our faith in the courts since there is no accountability from the government."

On February 16, 2006, Judge David Trager dismissed Arar's lawsuit, not for reasons of state secrets, but rather because what happened to Arar implicates policy considerations that are the purview of the political branches. Trager decided that even if officials' conduct violated US treaty obligations under the Convention against Torture or the customary international law prohibition of sending someone to a country where there is a high risk of torture, US law provides no remedy for a foreigner who suffered these violations. And he dismissed Arar's claim that his Fifth Amendment right to due process had been violated while he was detained at JFK on the grounds that he had not cleared customs and therefore he was not "in" the United States.

The day Trager dismissed *Arar*, I called Karen Greenberg, then director of New York University's Center for National Security and Law, to ask what she thought about the ruling. She replied, "Law has been brutalized by the war on terror."

Maria LaHood said Trager's dismissal of Arar's case devastated her. "This was a bad ruling and I'll admit it has affected my views. Trager's order implies that torture may be *constitutional* to prevent terrorist attacks. He's saying that it doesn't matter if what officials did is illegal. *The government didn't even raise this argument!*" She continued, "Trager never says what would give the executive the power to do this. As long as national security is invoked, the questions stop."

"Personally," Watt said, "the Arar case was the most difficult but also the most rewarding. Meeting someone who was tortured so harshly is tough. I met with him for nine hours. He spoke openly and with full details. He's amazing to be so strong after what he's been through. The fact that he kept his dignity and wants to keep fighting is inspiring."

On September 12, 2006, Arar's attorneys filed a notice that he would appeal the dismissal to the Second Circuit. Meanwhile, despite Arar's complete exoneration by the Canadian government, the US government barred him from traveling into the country in October 2007 to testify before Congress at a hearing that was examining *his experience* and the policy of extraordinary rendition. He testified by video link.

On June 30, 2008, in a two-to-one decision, the Second Circuit dismissed Arar's appeal for the same reason as the lower court: adjudicating his claims would interfere with national security and foreign policy. In August, the Second Circuit made an unusual move by deciding sua sponte (of its own volition) to rehear *Arar v. Ashcroft* en banc (with a full panel of judges).

On November 2, 2009, the Second Circuit issued its ruling. In a seven-to-four decision, the court affirmed the earlier rulings to dismiss the case. The majority held that "special factors" militated against awarding Arar any damages because to do otherwise "would enmesh the courts ineluctably in an assessment of the validity of the rationale of that policy and its implementation in this particular case, matters that directly affect significant diplomatic and national security concerns." The majority's ruling was a de facto judicial blessing for kidnapping, forced disappearance, and torture by proxy.

Judge Guido Calabresi dissented: "When the history of this distinguished court is written, today's majority decision will be viewed with dismay."

FIGURE 10. Maher Arar testifies via video conference before a House Joint Oversight Hearing on "Rendition to Torture: The Case of Maher Arar," October 18, 2007. Kevin Wolf / AP Photo.

Calabresi decried the majority's "utter subservience to the executive branch," along with its misunderstanding of the TVPA and the federal statute that prohibits refoulement. He also criticized their "extraordinary judicial activism." Such criticism typically is leveled by conservatives at judges who are deemed too attentive to the rights claims of victims, but Calabresi was criticizing judicial overreach to shield executive branch officials from legal accountability. The implications of this dismissal, he explained, are far-reaching: "The conduct that Arar alleges is repugnant, but the majority signals—whether it intends to or not—that it is not *constitutionally repugnant*."

Almost two years after CCR filed *Arar*, but before Judge Trager had issued his ruling to dismiss that case, the ACLU filed *El Masri v. Tenet*. The issues were similar: forced disappearance, extraordinary rendition, and torture, but in this case the kidnappers and torturers were CIA personnel. The plaintiff was Khaled El Masri, a German citizen of Lebanese origin, and the defendants were George Tenet, CIA director at the time that El Masri was abducted and rendered to a black site where he was tortured, as well as ten unnamed CIA agents and ten unnamed employees of three private corporations whose planes were used to transport El Masri.

El Masri's ordeal began on New Year's Eve in 2003, when he traveled by bus from his German hometown of Ulm to Macedonia for a holiday. When the bus reached the Macedonian border, local officials took him off and transferred him to a hotel in Skopje. Macedonian officials had arrested El Masri at the behest of the US intelligence agents who told them that El Masri was a suspected member of al-Qaeda named Khalid al-Masri. For twenty-three days, Macedonian interrogators, assuming El Masri was al-Masri, questioned him about an alleged meeting with an Egyptian in Jalalabad, and about possible contacts in Norway. El Masri had never been to Afghanistan, and he didn't know any Norwegians. The security agents guarding him denied his frequent requests to see a lawyer, a translator (he was interrogated in English despite his lack of proficiency), or a German consular official, or to call his wife to let her know where he was.

On January 23, while El Masri was still in Macedonian custody in the Skopje hotel, he was forced to make a video attesting that he had been well treated and acknowledging that he was about to be returned to Germany. What actually happened was that he was turned over to ski mask–wearing CIA agents who did what they do to people during an extraordinary rendition: he was beaten, stripped naked, anally raped with an enema tranquilizer, and then put in a diaper and dressed in a track suit. They put earmuffs, a blindfold, and a hood on his head, and frog-marched him to a plane where he was strapped facedown on the floor and given two injections that made him almost unconscious. His destination was the Salt Pit, a CIA black site north of Kabul.

A week into El Masri's detention in the Salt Pit, the CIA agents interrogating him realized that his German passport looked genuine and, therefore, he might not be the alleged al-Qaeda member. His passport was sent to CIA headquarters for authentication. In March, officials at Langley concluded that the passport was genuine. They had rendered the wrong guy. But rather than releasing and repatriating El Masri, the CIA continued to detain and interrogate him. In April, Director Tenet was informed that a German citizen who was not the alleged al-Qaeda member was in the Salt Pit. He did nothing. In May, four months into El Masri's black site detention, National Security Advisor Condoleezza Rice stepped in and ordered El Masri's release. A German-speaking agent who identified himself as "Sam" informed El Masri that, as a condition of his release, he must promise never to mention what happened to him because the Americans were determined to keep this a secret.

Rice's order to release El Masri presented the CIA with a dilemma of their own making: how could this be done without exposing their secret, illegal operations which would create an international incident? It took a second order from Rice for the Agency to act. El Masri was transferred out of Afghanistan, but rather than being flown to Germany where the Bush administration would have to acknowledge what had been done to an innocent citizen, El Masri was flown to Albania, driven for six hours into the mountains, dumped on a back road in the dead of night, given back his passport, and told to start walking and not look back.

The Albanian police who intercepted El Masri asked how he had entered the country without a visa. He told them he didn't even know where he was. They eventually believed that he was German and sent him home. When he got back to Ulm, he discovered that his house was deserted. Friends explained that when he disappeared, his wife didn't know what to do so she took the children to her family in Lebanon.

Like Arar upon his return to Canada, El Masri became a *cause célèbre* in Germany. The political scandal that he had been kidnapped and tortured by the CIA was compounded by revelations that he had been subjected to human experimentation, shot up with psychoactive drugs repeatedly over his months of captivity. This was proven through hair, nail, and skin samples. The German public's anger intensified in November 2005 when the *Washington Post* reported that the CIA was running black sites in Europe.

On December 5, 2005, the ACLU filed *El Masri v. Tenet* in the Eastern District of Virginia. The previous weekend, El Masri had traveled to the United States with his German lawyer, Manfred Gnjidic, to participate in a press conference with Steven Watt and his other American attorneys. Immigration officials in Atlanta denied both men entry into the country at the behest of an "other government agency" (OGA is a euphemizing codename for the CIA). El Masri participated in the press conference from Germany by video link. "I don't think I'm the human being I used to be," he said.

The filing of *El Masri* coincided with Condoleezza Rice's first official visit to Europe as Bush's secretary of state. In Romania, she signed a military agreement that would allow US and Romanian troops to train together at the Mihail Kogălniceanu air base (where the CIA black site had been located). In Germany, at press briefings, Rice was confronted with angry and probing questions about the US torture program. In her meeting with Germany's chancellor, Angela Merkel, one of their topics was El Masri. At a joint press conference after their meeting, Merkel openly discussed CIA flights through Europe and other matters that the United States regards as state secrets. Merkel told journalists, "The American administration has admitted that this man had been erroneously taken and that, as such, the American administration is not denying that it has taken place." Rice was in a tough spot because she could not publicly confirm anything about the top-secret CIA program, including the fact that El Masri had spent months being tortured in a black site. She said, "Any policy will sometimes result in error and when it happens, we do everything we can to correct it." Then she played the liberal-ideology-of-torture card: "We have an obligation to defend our people, and we will use every lawful means to do so." She added that any public debate or criticism of secret prisons ought to include "a healthy respect for the challenges we face" fighting terrorism.

One month after *El Masri* was filed, the Council of Europe released its investigative report about illegal US activities on the continent. It found that one hundred people—including El Masri—had been kidnapped in Europe by the CIA. The Council recommended that every European Union country review its bilateral military basing agreements and security operations with the United States to ensure that they conform to European law. The following year, the European Parliament issued a report, endorsed by a large majority, that exposed extensive collusion by European nations' security services with the CIA's illegal operations.

German prosecutors launched a criminal investigation into the US officials responsible for El Masri's kidnapping and torture, and they took note of a statement Rice had made to the *Washington Post* that it was she who ordered his release. Rice and John Bellinger, legal counsel for the National Security Agency, employed dark diplomacy to derail the German investigation, warning the German government that bilateral relations would be damaged if the inquiry into gross crimes perpetrated against their own citizen was to proceed. The German government took heed and the investigation was halted. However, in 2007, a German court issued arrest warrants for thirteen CIA agents who had been involved in El Masri's kidnapping and rendition.

When *El Masri* was filed, the government used the same strategy as they had in *Arar:* they invoked state secrets to shut down the litigation, arguing that to reveal any information about CIA operations—even confirmation that El Masri had been in CIA custody—would endanger national security. On May 12, 2006, Judge T. S. Ellis dismissed the case. "In the present circumstances," he wrote, "al-Masri's private interests must give way to the national interest in preserving state secrets."

El Masri's ACLU attorneys appealed the dismissal to the Fourth Circuit. Although *Arar* had started earlier, the *El Masri* appeal presented the first opportunity to try to litigate the Bush administration's unprecedented use of state secrets to block lawsuits alleging egregious government misconduct. That conduct, the attorneys wrote in their brief, "undoubtedly shocks the conscience." Apparently, the Fourth Circuit judges who heard the appeal were shockproof because they upheld the lower court's dismissal of the case. El Masri's last chance for justice in the United States was foreclosed on October 9, 2007, when the Supreme Court rejected the petition to hear his case.

Steven Watt put *Arar* and *El Masri* in context: "We use those cases as a vehicle for accountability. Losing a case isn't a loss if you are smart." How so? "When you file a suit, you also put together media and advocacy campaigns to bring these individuals' stories to the public. You use publicity to try to get Congress to hold hearings." I asked Watt how he experienced these losses. "The enormity of it all fell into place for me when I had to call Khaled. I found it hard to tell him that we lost. After I said my piece, he said he was glad for the call. The irony is that all he really wanted was an apology and an explanation." Despite these loses in court, Watt contended, "survivors like Khaled and Maher find telling their story cathartic. It's part of a healing process for them."

Arar managed to heal; he got a PhD and eventually started his own business. But El Masri's horrific experience left him with severe post-traumatic stress disorder and paranoia. In April 2007, he got into an altercation over a malfunctioning iPod when the store in Ulm where he purchased it refused to give him a refund. A month later, he burned down the store and was arrested. His attorney conceded that he had set the fire but blamed it on lasting psychological damage from his kidnapping and torture by the CIA and the insufficiency of treatment he received in Germany. The judge was sympathetic and sent El Masri to a mental institution for more intensive treatment rather than jail.

The first torture-victim lawsuit that targeted individuals in the military chain of command was *Ali v. Rumsfeld,* which was filed in March 2005 by the ACLU and Human Rights First on behalf of five Iraqi and four Afghan plaintiffs. All of the plaintiffs were suing Defense Secretary Donald Rumsfeld, and the Iraqis were also suing three high-ranking military officials responsible for interrogation and detention operations in Iraq: Lieutenant General Ricardo Sanchez, Brigadier General Janis Karpinski, and Colonel Thomas Pappas. By the time *Ali* was filed, there was abundant evidence, including several official investigations, that Rumsfeld's intentional disregard for federal laws and treaties and his policy decisions led directly to the suffering and abuse of thousands of detainees in military custody.

The treatment of each of the *Ali* plaintiffs was spelled out in the court filing. One man had endured "severe beatings to the point of unconsciousness, stabbing and mutilation, isolation while naked and hooded in a wooden phone booth-sized box, prolonged sleep deprivation enforced by beatings, deprivation of adequate food and water, mock execution and death threats." Another was subjected to "severe beatings, sexual assault and humiliation, deprivation of adequate food and water, intentional prolonged exposure to dangerously high temperatures, mock executions and death threats." Another was stepped and sat upon by soldiers

> while he was in extreme restraints and [soldiers humiliated] him by chanting racial epithets while videotaping and photographing him; keeping him in an outdoor cage at temperatures exceeding approximately 120 degrees Fahrenheit despite his suffering from chest pains; intentionally depriving him of sleep for long periods of time; and confiscating medications for his high blood pressure and heart disease and intentionally depriving him of medical care even after he suffered more than one heart attack and a possible stroke in detention.

Another plaintiff who was a juvenile when he was detained was subjected to "intentional infliction of pain after surgery by dragging him from one location to another and forcefully ripping away the surgical dressing, and by exposing him to infection by leaving his surgical wound half-bandaged; and intentional deprivation of adequate food and water."

The five Iraqis—like over 90 percent of people taken into US custody in Iraq—were innocent civilians picked up in sweeps or at checkpoints, and the four Afghans were arrested and detained on the basis of false statements by locals who sold them to the United States for bounty. All nine were eventually released without ever being charged with any crimes.

When the *Ali* case started, I was still of the mind that courts would have to provide justice to the victims of these crimes. I thought: how could Rumsfeld *not* lose?

But Rumsfeld did not lose. And key elements from Judge Thomas Hogan's ruling, issued on March 7, 2007, show why it is virtually, or at least jurisprudentially, impossible for US courts to provide justice when the defendants are officials, the plaintiffs are foreigners, and the crimes of state occurred overseas.

Judge Hogan began his decision: "This is a lamentable case . . ." He was lamenting that the plaintiffs' accounts of the gruesome treatment to which they were intentionally subjected were true, but as a matter of US law and Supreme Court precedent, he had to dismiss the case. Then he laid out his reasoning. The plaintiffs' claims that the defendants violated their Fifth Amendment right to due process and the Eighth Amendment prohibition of cruel and unusual punishment were deemed inapplicable because foreigners who are not present in the United States don't have constitutional rights. Regarding the Eighth Amendment claim, Judge Hogan found a further reason to reject it: That amendment only applies to "cruel and unusual punishments," and the plaintiffs were never charged or convicted of any crime so, therefore, what happened to them was not, technically, punishment.

Another leg of the plaintiffs' case was the quest for a "Bivens remedy," which is a judicially created doctrine to close a gap in the law by providing a means for a court to award monetary damages arising from constitutional violations by federal officials. The Bivens remedy originated with a 1971 Supreme Court case, *Bivens v. Six Unknown Agents of the Federal Narcotics Agency*. Six federal agents raided and searched the home of Webster Bivens and arrested him without a warrant. After he was released without charges, he sued the agents for violating his Fourth Amendment right to be free from unreasonable search and seizure. There is no remedy clause in the Fourth Amendment, so the Supreme Court decided to infer that the Constitution itself affords remedies for violations. Writing for the *Bivens* majority, Justice William Brennan held that every wrong must have a right, and that if Congress never legislated a remedy, the court could provide one. A Bivens remedy applies only to a narrow set of constitutional violations: unlawful searches and seizures (Fourth Amendment), cruel and unusual punishments (Eighth Amendment), and gender discrimination (Fourteenth Amendment).

Judge Hogan weighed the *Ali* plaintiffs' and defendants' arguments about whether a Bivens remedy should be available in this case. He had to contend with issues that had never been litigated because never before had the US government instituted a policy to torture prisoners captured in a war. By restricting his options to past precedents, Judge Hogan decided that the plaintiffs were asking the court to fashion an *unprecedented* remedy. While he acknowledged that the purpose of Bivens is to deter officials from violating the Constitution, he also acknowledged that this remedy "is clearly disfavored," as evidenced by the fact in the thirty-five years since *Bivens* was decided, "the Supreme Court has 'extended its holding only twice . . .'"

Hogan lamented that while it might be desirable to provide a Bivens remedy to vindicate the severe abuses perpetrated on the plaintiffs, he was compelled to conclude that they were not entitled to remedies because none are provided in US law. In a footnote, he added: "Regrettably, the facts stand as an indictment of the humanity with which the United States treats its detainees."

Judge Hogan also weighed the defendants' arguments that "special factors" should deter him from finding them liable for incidents that occurred while they were fulfilling their official functions against the plaintiffs' arguments that torture is not a legitimate part of any job. Hogan decided to scorn "the myopic approach advocated by the plaintiffs and *amici,* which essentially frames the issue as whether torture is universally prohibited . . ." He rejected that contention with a dollop of the liberal ideology of torture: "There is no getting around the fact that authorizing monetary damages remedies against military officials engaged in an active war would invite enemies to use our own federal courts to obstruct the Armed Forces' ability to act decisively and without hesitation in defense of our liberty and national interests." Moreover, "[m]ilitary discipline and morale surely would be eroded by the spectacle of high-ranking military officials being haled [*sic*] into our own courts to defend against our enemies' legal challenges, which might leave subordinate personnel questioning the authority by which they are being commanded and further encumber the military's ability to act decisively." And he punted on the illegality of torture: "Military, executive, and congressional officials might arrive at a different conclusion from the judiciary about where on the spectrum a particular interrogation technique falls and whether it was, or is, properly used to obtain information about our enemies while conducting a war."

But what about customary international law which is applicable everywhere? The plaintiffs argued that the prohibition of torture is a *jus cogens* (inviolable) norm and therefore there can be no immunity for it. The defendants claimed that they have absolute immunity for incidents that occurred when they were "acting within the scope of their employment." Judge Hogan sided with the defendants because "detaining and interrogating enemy aliens were the kinds of conduct the defendants were employed to perform." Moreover, he reasoned, the plaintiffs can't use the Geneva Conventions to sue for damages because treaties are not federal laws enacted by Congress; they are international agreements made by the executive. He noted that the 2006 MCA expressly prohibits foreigners detained by the United States overseas from suing for violations of the Geneva Conventions.

Collectively, the decisions in *Arar, El Masri,* and *Ali* are a testament that US law and jurisprudence never anticipated a government-authorized torture program. When the unfathomable became a reality, most federal judges were unwilling or regarded themselves as unable to hold perpetrators of crimes of *their* state accountable.

These cases and their outcomes were the subject of numerous exchanges and debates on the torturelist, which brought up distinct, sometimes clashing ideologies and understandings of law. While everyone on the list abhors torture, differences of opinion had not been as clear in the earlier stages of the war in court, when the Bush administration's stubborn refusal to admit wrongdoing and change course had a unifying effect. The accountability lawsuits allowed the differences to surface. For some, whom I would describe as "legal nationalists," their imaginative horizon of law was domestic, namely the constitutional powers of the executive, legislative history of the ratification of treaties, and US jurisprudence. The opinions of people in this category about these accountability cases seemed, to me, to be molded by what they believed was likely to prevail in US courts. In other words, what would work was what was right. For others, whom I would describe as "legal transnationalists," the imaginative horizon transcended the domestic arena; the lens through which they judged the quality of judgments were uncompromisable legal principles enshrined in international law. I fall into this camp, and though I am speaking only for myself—albeit with a view that is likely shared by some other transnationalists—I regarded the dismissals of these cases, which deprived victims of justice for one of the most egregious crimes in the world, as manifestations of judicial incompetence and evidence of a demonstrable lack of expertise about international law and US treaty obligations.

Beyond differences of opinion about accountability lawsuits among people on the torturelist, what I found confusing was the politesse that some lawyers and law professors displayed when commenting on even the most execrable views of other lawyers (not those on the list), as well as judicial opinions. My confusion was cleared up when I read an article by Alice Ristroph titled "Professors Strangelove." The premise of her article is a review of *Terror in the Balance: Security, Liberty, and the Courts* authored by two law professors, Eric Posner and Adrian Vermeule, whose book includes an aggressive defense of the president's prerogative to use whatever means he deems necessary to defend national security. Ristroph compares Posner and Vermeule as well as John Yoo and other like-minded lawyers and law professors "who advocate torture, executive absolutism, and other departures from the rule of law" to the characters in Stanley Kubrick's film, *Dr. Strangelove Or: How I Learned to Stop Worrying and Love the Bomb,* who clamored to deploy nuclear weapons: General Jack D. Ripper, General Buck Turgidson, and Major T. J. "King" Kong. Ristroph writes: "Insisting that the war on terror is too important to be left to anyone other than the President, scorning opponents of torture as sissies afraid to muss their hair, and rapidly collecting promotions and personal citations, these lawyers are teaching America to stop worrying and love the waterboard—and the wiretap, and the ethnic profiling, and the indefinite detention, and all the other strategies of our new war that might be funny if they weren't so deadly serious." She compares those law professors who politely oppose torture to the President Merkin Muffley character in *Dr. Strangelove* because he is the only one "who fully appreciates the moral implications of nuclear war, but his hesitancy and unfailing politeness render him a mostly ineffective counterweight to his war-mongering colleagues. He is the voice of reason, but that voice is timid and faltering."

The part of Ristroph's article that was clarifying for me was her contention that, in the legal academy, pro-torture professors "have been met with respectful, and inconsequential, disagreement." The academic Merkin Muffleys, she writes, "take exception to the bellicose program of the Professors Strangelove. But 'debates' over national security in the American legal academy are choreographed events among gentlemen, usually featuring excellent sportsmanship all around. Neither side wins or loses; everyone shakes hands at the end; and everyone keeps his job, his viewpoint, and his dignity."

Ristroph helped me make sense of why some law professors on the torturelist could be sanguine about the quality of judicial reasoning that resulted in the dismissals of the accountability lawsuits despite abundant evidence of criminality. They were trained and acculturated to *appreciate* the intellectual views and labors of their peers, even if they disagreed. When the outcomes of these accountability cases produce, in Ristroph's words, "a general jurisprudence of emergency that replaces the rule of law with the rule of the executive," I understood: what's a well-acculturated law professor to do but say "well played"?

But the incapacity or refusal of US courts to provide justice for torture victims and the judicially enforced unaccountability for officials who had violated the law had consequences unintended by those who cheered or meekly accepted these outcomes. The dismissal of these torture victim cases fueled and justified moves to take the fight for accountability to foreign courts and international tribunals where US jurisprudence has no sway.

Steven Watt articulated the legal transnationalist perspective perfectly when he told me, "We need to internationalize the issue and look outside Fortress America."

Michael Ratner and CCR's vice president, Peter Weiss, were among the first to start looking at overseas options in the summer of 2004, when it became clear that the only people who would face punitive consequences for torture at Abu Ghraib were low-ranking soldiers.

In the 1980s, Weiss and his CCR co-counsel Rhonda Copelon had litigated the *Filártiga v. Peña-Irala* case in which they sued one Paraguayan on behalf of another Paraguayan for torture perpetrated in Paraguay. The ruling in that case, which they won, included the admonition that torturers, like slave traders and pirates, are enemies of all mankind. *Filártiga* acquired international significance in the late 1990s, when the international criminal law doctrine of universal jurisdiction was brought out of retirement. The doctrine traces back to the nineteenth century; it was devised to create a means to prosecute people for piracy and slave trading (but not slavery itself). Those crimes took place on the high seas, which were legal *terra nulla*. In order to prosecute pirates and slave traders, the gap in existing jurisdictional doctrines (territorial, personal, and protective) had to be closed. The rationale for *universal* jurisdiction at the time of its conception was that pirates and slave traders were enemies of all mankind who deserved no sanctuary, and whose activities were so dangerous and deleterious to international peace and security that every state had an interest in either prosecuting perpetrators or extraditing them to another country for prosecution if petitioned to do so. By the turn of the twentieth century, universal jurisdiction fell into disuse, an archaic remnant of the maritime world. It was revived in 1998 when a Spanish judge, Baltazar Garzón, issued an arrest warrant and a request to extradite former Chilean dictator Augusto Pinochet from the United Kingdom, where he was visiting, to Spain to stand trial for torture and murder that occurred in Chile during Pinochet's dictatorship. Garzón, working in collaboration with Spanish and Chilean human rights lawyers and activists, believed that Pinochet's dirty-war crimes made him an enemy of all humankind and, because he had granted himself immunity from prosecution in his own country, the only way to punish him would be in a foreign court. The British police honored the Spanish warrant and arrested Pinochet. The British House of Lords weighed the charges in the warrant and decided that Pinochet could be extradited for torture (but not murder) because there is no sovereign immunity and no "scope of employment" justification for torture. Pinochet was never extradited to Spain because the British government, for political reasons, decided to allow him to return to Chile. But the case against him undermined his aura of untouchability. The Chilean government stripped him of the immunity he had granted himself and started the process of prosecuting him. He avoided a trial by dying.

The "Pinochet precedent," however, became a landmark in international criminal law enforcement because it held that anyone, even a former head of state, can be prosecuted for torture in a foreign court if he or she is not prosecuted at home or in the country where the crime occurred. The Pinochet precedent invigorated and altered debates about how and where justice for torture and other gross crimes could be pursued. A number of countries, mainly in Europe, created or strengthened national laws to incorporate the doctrine of universal jurisdiction.

Ratner and Weiss wanted to use universal jurisdiction to pursue accountability in the courts of other countries for US officials who were responsible for the torture program, since there was no accountability to be had in the United States. For Weiss, who had experience with wartime interrogations, this goal was personal. Born in Vienna, he fled from the Nazis in 1938. Several years later, when the US Army was looking for German speakers to help translate for the interrogation of high-level prisoners of war, he volunteered. The fact that the US military never tortured Nazis was a recurring theme in messages he posted to the torturelist. He regarded military torture in the "war on terror" as an egregious affront to that proud history and impunity for this gross crime as unconscionable.

In the summer of 2004, Ratner and Weiss read an article about Germany's universal jurisdiction law, passed in 2002, which gave prosecutors the authority to pursue cases of war crimes and crimes against humanity even where there is no connection to Germany. They reached out to the authors of the article to ask whether the German law could be used to go after the architects of the US torture program. The authors put them in touch with Wolfgang Kaleck, a criminal lawyer with decades of experience working with Argentinians to pursue justice for crimes perpetrated during the dictatorship in that country.

In August, Kaleck flew from Berlin to New York to meet Ratner and Weiss. A transnational alliance was immediately formed. In his autobiography, *Law versus Power: Our Global Fight for Human Rights,* Kaleck explains that he and his CCR allies weighed the pros and cons of submitting a criminal complaint against Rumsfeld and other officials responsible for torture at Abu Ghraib. They worried that if German prosecutors failed to act, it might damage the cause of enforcing international law. But they decided to go for it, and they set themselves a three-month deadline in order to submit their complaint shortly after the 2004 US presidential election. The best-case scenario they envisioned was that Bush, who was running for reelection against Democrat John Kerry, would be defeated and the new administration would be so embarrassed by a criminal complaint in Germany that they would pursue some form of accountability for the accused in the United States. The worst-case scenario would be political blowback that could undermine the doctrine of universal jurisdiction.

They were mindful of what had happened recently to Belgium's universal jurisdiction law. In 1993, Belgium had passed what was called the anti-atrocity law which established a special unit to investigate gross crimes perpetrated in foreign countries. The law also gave victims from any country the power to initiate such investigations. In 1999, the Belgian government, inspired by the Pinochet precedent, reformed that law to explicitly incorporate the doctrine of universal jurisdiction and availed its legal system to prosecute foreign violators of international human rights and humanitarian laws. Hunger for justice was so great, and options were so limited, that more than a dozen foreign officials quickly became targets of victim-initiated lawsuits. These included Ariel Sharon, prime minister of Israel; Saddam Hussein, president of Iraq; Yasir Arafat, head of the Palestinian Authority; Laurent Gbagbo, president of the Ivory Coast; Paul Kagame, president of Rwanda; and Hissène Habré, former dictator of Chad.

In June 2002, the Belgian Court of Appeals dismissed the case against Ariel Sharon for war crimes perpetrated in Lebanon in 1982—specifically his abetment of the massacre of one thousand civilians at the Sabra and Shatila Palestinian refugee camps in Beirut—because he was not present in Belgium. That ruling galvanized a broad-based coalition of Belgian parliamentarians, local and international human rights organizations, and victims from many countries. The following month, in response to that campaign, Belgian political parties came to an agreement to put forward an interpretative law that would strengthen the universal jurisdiction law. Despite vigorous foreign diplomatic pressure, the Belgian parliament passed the interpretative law, and in February 2003, the Supreme Court reversed the appeals court decision, deciding that Sharon's presence in Belgium was not a requirement to pursue a universal jurisdiction case against him.

Shortly after this ruling, the families of some of the hundreds of Iraqis who were killed when the United States bombed a civilian air raid shelter in

Baghdad during the 1991 Gulf War filed a criminal complaint in Belgium against former president George H. W. Bush; Dick Cheney, who was secretary of defense in 1991; Colin Powell, who was chairman of the Joint Chiefs of Staff; and General Norman Schwarzkopf, who was top commander in Iraq. The filing of this complaint coincided with President George W. Bush's announcement on March 18, 2003, that another US war on Iraq was about to commence. Powell, who was secretary of state, joked to reporters that "the next NATO ministerial meeting [in Brussels] might be short because of the prosecution threat." But he wasn't joking when he said, "We have cautioned our Belgian colleagues that they need to be very careful about this kind of effort, because it makes it hard for us to go places that put you at such easy risk. If you show up, next thing you know you're being. . . Who knows?" Rumsfeld put muscle into the threat by announcing that, unless Belgium gutted its universal jurisdiction law, he would relocate NATO headquarters from Brussels to Warsaw. The Belgian government responded to Rumsfeld's threat by amending the law to restrict criminal jurisdiction to Belgian citizens or residents, eliminating foreign victims' right to initiate cases, and guaranteeing legal immunity for visiting officials regardless of allegations against them.

Supporters of universal jurisdiction feared that this sharp narrowing of Belgium's national law might signal the death of the doctrine. But those fears were somewhat allayed when the Council of Europe declared that gross crimes "must not go unpunished and that their effective prosecution must be ensured by taking measures at the national level and by enhancing international cooperation." Germany's 2002 universal jurisdiction law was very much in keeping with the Council's demand for national measures.

Kaleck, Ratner, Weiss, and a team of CCR lawyers got to work preparing the criminal complaint on behalf of Iraqis who were tortured at Abu Ghraib. They gathered all publicly available information and created a dossier on every senior military, intelligence, and political official who bore responsibility. Law students from universities in New York City who had ties to CCR pitched in. When the lawyers divided up assignments, Kaleck was tasked with writing the legal analysis on whether the abuses perpetrated at Abu Ghraib meet the definition of torture under international and German law. "In doing this work," he wrote in his autobiography, "I see myself not as a European taking on the United States but rather as an anti-torture activist working with US colleagues to hold those responsible to account."

They submitted their two-hundred-page complaint in Berlin on November 30. Bush had won the election, so their best-case scenario was null and void.

But, as they reminded those who accused them of tilting at windmills, the Pinochet precedent still held, and there was abundant evidence that Rumsfeld was culpable for torture.

The US government put intense diplomatic pressure on the German government to dispose of what officials claimed was a "frivolous lawsuit." The German prosecutor dismissed the complaint on February 10, 2005, citing the reason offered up by the US State Department that if a case is being pursued at home, a foreign court cannot assert jurisdiction. This rationale is called the principle of subsidiarity, which holds that legal cases should be handled at the most relevant, usually local, level. But there was no criminal investigation of Rumsfeld or the others named in the complaint.

Kaleck and his CCR allies were undeterred by the dismissal. In 2005, they started working on a new complaint against Rumsfeld, and this time they broadened the scope because so much more evidence and information about the torture program had become public in the intervening period. The victims represented in the second complaint were eleven Iraqis and one Guantánamo detainee, Mohammed al-Qahtani. Rumsfeld's culpability for the torture of al-Qahtani was well-documented in interrogation logs, memos from FBI agents, several declassified torture memos, and an official investigative report. The new complaint also targeted five government lawyers who bore direct responsibility for the "legalization" of torture: Alberto Gonzales who, as White House counsel, had advised President Bush to "declare" the Geneva Conventions inapplicable; Jay Bybee, former head of the Office of Legal Counsel, who signed the infamous August 1, 2002 torture memo; John Yoo, who wrote that memo; Pentagon general counsel William J. Haynes, who oversaw the authorization of torture by military interrogators; and Vice President Cheney's counsel David Addington, who directed the criminal enterprise to legalize torture. There was a precedent for holding lawyers accountable for their role in facilitating gross crimes: At the post–World War II international tribunal in Nuremberg, German judges and lawyers were prosecuted for providing legal cover for Nazi programs of genocide, ethnic cleansing, and torture.

In order to thwart any contention that the new complaint should be dismissed on the basis of subsidiarity, the lawyers incorporated abundant evidence that there was no domestic US investigation, let alone criminal procedures against any of the accused. They also pointed out that three torture-victim lawsuits in the United States—*Arar*, *El Masri*, and *Ali*—had been dismissed by US courts.

In April 2006, while Kaleck was in New York working on the new complaint, he went to a public event at Columbia University. One of the speakers was Janis Karpinski, the retired general who had been in charge of detention facilities in Iraq. Afterwards, Kaleck introduced himself to her as the German lawyer who had filed the criminal complaint against Rumsfeld, herself, and others. "Very good" was Karpinski's reply.

Karpinski was positioning herself as an ally of those pursuing accountability for torture. She invited Kaleck to visit her in Boston for a longer conversation. When he went, she helped him understand the layout of Abu Ghraib, told him about the interrogation methods used there, and gave him details about the roles that high-ranking officials, including General Geoffrey Miller, had played. She also told Kaleck that she was prepared to give testimony in Germany.

Kaleck and CCR decided to file the new complaint after the November 2006 US midterm election. The day after the election, Bush announced that Rumsfeld was resigning as secretary of defense. The lawyers used his resignation to drum up publicity about the case against him, and they succeeded in getting international media attention refocused on the US torture program.

At six o'clock on the morning of November 14, they emailed their 383-page complaint to the federal prosecutor in Karlsruhe. At the press conference later that day, the attorneys were joined at the podium by Karpinski.

Kaleck, in his autobiography, put the new and expanded complaint in transnational context: "My friend Netta Amar, a lawyer from Jerusalem, told me how, on the day we lodged the complaint, she stood up during a court hearing with our press release in her hand and declared to legal advisors from the Israeli Army: 'Look at this. This is happening to Bush administration lawyers in Germany right now. Be careful what you do, or the same thing could happen to you.'"

Once again, the complaint was dismissed. This time, the prosecutor decided that, because none of the accused were present in Germany, there was no likelihood of convicting them. When I asked Ratner for his take on this dismissal, he reminded me that one of CCR's mottos is "success without victory." Just *trying* to try Rumsfeld and the torture lawyers was a show of fealty to the universal prohibition of torture and, despite not succeeding, it made powerful people responsible for gross crimes feel exposed and vulnerable.

Ratner was a master of the "outside track"—cultivating publicity about legal cases to try culprits in the court of public opinion. In 2008, he published *The Trial of Donald Rumsfeld: A Prosecution by Book,* which laid out all the

FIGURE 11. Left to right: Janis Karpinski, Michael Ratner, and Wolfgang Kaleck at a news conference in Berlin, November 14, 2006. Reuters / Alamy Stock Photo.

evidence against Rumsfeld and other officials who were targeted in the German complaint. He also presented readers with their defenses, gleaned from their own words in memos and other documents. A book is no substitute for actual justice, but it does help shape the narrative and contribute to the historical record of the "war on terror."

The same year Ratner published his Rumsfeld-on-trial book, Philippe Sands, a British-French law professor and international law practitioner, published *Torture Team: Rumsfeld's Memo and the Betrayal of American Values;* the titular memo was the one authorizing special measures for the interrogation of Mohammed al-Qahtani, which Rumsfeld signed on December 2, 2002. Sands had interviewed many Bush administration officials and his book was a forensic account of how torture was green-lighted for military interrogators. Sands's book fingered an additional lawyer involved in the "legalization" of torture: Douglas Feith, former undersecretary of defense for policy.

Sands testified before the Senate Judiciary Committee on June 10, 2008. He described the falseness of the administration's narrative that "the impetus for the new interrogation techniques came from the bottom-up. That is not true: the abuse was a result of pressures driven from the highest levels of government." Another false claim was that the administration followed the law. Sands said, "To the contrary, the Administration consciously sought legal advice to set aside international constraints on detainee interrogations . . . [T]his is an unhappy story. It points to the early and direct involvement of those at the highest levels of government, often through their lawyers." Sands also pointed out that Haynes, as Pentagon general counsel, gave intentionally false and misleading information when he testified before this committee in July 2006. He "did not tell you that in September 2002 he had visited Guantanamo, together with Mr. Gonzales and Mr. Addington, and discussed interrogations. This is a story not only of abuse and crime . . . but also of cover-up." Then, speaking directly to the question of whether torture "works," Sands stated: "That is not what I was told by those I interviewed. The coercive interrogations were illegal, did not work, have undermined moral authority, have migrated, have served as a recruiting tool for those who seek to do harm to the US, and have made it more difficult for allies to transfer detainees and cooperate in other ways. They have resulted in the very opposite of what was intended, contributing to an extension of the conflict and endangering the national security they were meant to protect."

Although the efforts to pursue accountability for US officials in a German court did not succeed, Kaleck was so inspired by his collaboration with CCR that he decided to set up a new organization to do the same kind of work in Germany. Ratner encouraged Kaleck to think bigger than a Germany-specific organization. Kaleck took that advice and founded the European Center for Constitutional and Human Rights (ECCHR). When I met Kaleck in Berlin shortly after the ECCHR was established in 2007, he explained that the Pinochet case would be its model, and its mission would be to pursue human rights violations anywhere in the world.

The pursuit of Rumsfeld didn't stop after he was out of office. CCR and ECCHR prepared another criminal complaint to be ready when an opportunity presented itself, and human rights organizations were tracking his movements. That opportunity came on October 26, 2007, when Rumsfeld was in Paris to give a talk at a *Foreign Policy*–sponsored conference. French criminal procedure requires a suspect to be in France for an indictment to be issued, but it allows the case to proceed even if the suspect subsequently leaves the country. When Rumsfeld was told that a criminal complaint was about to be filed, he slipped out a side door of the building where he was giving the speech and into the adjoining US embassy to avoid lawyers and reporters waiting for him outside. The following year, the Parisian prosecutor dismissed that complaint on the legally erroneous ground that that officials have immunity for activities connected to their work. There is no legal immunity for torture.

During the Bush years, the one accountability lawsuit that did get traction was an Italian case. In May 2005, an Italian court issued indictments for twenty-six CIA agents as well as four Italian security agents who, in February 2003, colluded in the kidnapping and extraordinary rendition of Hassan Mustafa Osama Nasr (aka Abu Omar). He was snatched off the street in Milan and sent to Egypt where he was brutally tortured. The Italian court was willing to issue these indictments because the snatch-and-grab operation was conducted without the knowledge of Italian police and it disrupted their own criminal investigation. Despite US diplomatic pressure and political opposition by Prime Minister Silvio Berlusconi, the court tried the CIA agents in absentia—which is legal in Italy. One of the agents, Sabrina de Sousa, sued the US government to invoke immunity on her behalf in order to shield her from the Italian charges. The Justice Department refused to support her request for a grant of immunity because it would constitute an admission of criminal culpability. At the government's request, de Sousa's lawsuit was dismissed.

On November 4, 2009, the Italian court handed down guilty verdicts for most of the indicted CIA agents. The heaviest sentence, eight years, went to Robert Seldon Lady, former head of the CIA's Milan station. Twenty-five others, including de Sousa, got five years each. Several higher-ranking CIA officials, including former Rome station chief Jeffrey Castelli, were neither convicted nor acquitted because the judge ruled that the unavailability (i.e., secrecy) of information about their roles in the crime stymied their in-absentia defense. The Berlusconi government refused to enforce the court's ruling by issuing Interpol warrants or requesting the extradition of the convicted agents, but Italian prosecutors can issue a European arrest warrant if any of the convicted were to set foot in any European Union country.

There was also some torture accountability action in the Western Hemisphere. After El Masri's US options were exhausted, the ACLU submitted a petition, *El Masri v. United States,* to the Inter-American Commission on Human Rights (IACHR) on April 28, 2008. The IACHR, whose motto is "more rights for more people," is authorized to examine human rights violations in North and South America and it accepts petitions submitted by or on behalf of individuals. Of all the regional human rights bodies, the IACHR has the richest record of dealing with forced disappearance and torture arising from terrorism and counterterrorism because of its involvement in cases and petitions for the dirty wars in South and Central America.

The United States never ratified the Inter-American Convention on Human Rights, but it is a member of the Organization of American States (OAS) and, as a signatory to the OAS Charter, is party to the American Declaration of Human Rights. Steven Watt explained, "We won't get a binding ruling—we can't, but the petition is part of the educational process." In preparing the petition, Watt and his colleagues laid out all the exhausted domestic remedies. "The basic thrust of the filing," he said, "is that states where egregious human rights violations are alleged have obligations to investigate and prosecute or provide civil redress. None of that happened for Khaled. We are using this filing to expose the US record of no accountability and no redress."

During the Bush years, none of the officials responsible for torture were made to pay for their crimes and none of the victims received any justice. But there is another way to interpret the significance of the battles for accountability, which continued after Bush left office. The fight for justice at home and abroad had what Ratner described as "an educative effect." These cases, regardless of their outcomes, helped publicize and disseminate the details of crimes of state. The legal legitimacy of the criminal complaints filed abroad forced the government to resort to *political* pressure to protect US officials. These accountability lawsuits may not have been enough to galvanize US public opinion in the ways that, just a couple years earlier, many lawyers hoped would happen. At minimum, though, the fact that there were cases against officials may have a deterrent effect if they dissuade future US administrations from repeating the kinds of legally disgraceful policy decisions that gave rise to the torture program.

But the Bush administration faced another torture problem. They wanted to prosecute some Guantánamo detainees in the military commissions, and everyone slated for trial had been tortured.

SEVEN

Trying Guantánamo

THE GUANTÁNAMO MILITARY COMMISSIONS were created to make it possible to prosecute people who had been tortured and to use evidence that would never make it through the door of a regular court. Before the Supreme Court's June 2006 *Hamdan v. Rumsfeld* decision canceled the commissions as unconstitutional, every case the Bush administration attempted to pursue was withdrawn or crashed. This record was early proof that torture cannot be made unimportant, even in a system created and designed to provide all advantages to prosecutors. The government's prospects didn't improve after the system was resurrected when Congress passed the Military Commissions Act.

One of the first detainees the Bush administration had put up for trial under the original commission system was a Mauritanian citizen named Mohamedou Ould Slahi. His was going to be the first death penalty case. When Slahi was charged in 2003, Lieutenant Colonel Stuart Couch was assigned to prosecute him. Couch was highly motivated to get a guilty verdict, not just because that was his job but because he was told that Slahi recruited several 9/11 hijackers, one of whom commandeered the plane piloted by a close friend of Couch's.

As a teenager in the 1980s, Slahi learned about the conflict in Afghanistan, which was attracting foreign mujahidin to fight against the Soviet occupiers. As a devout Muslim, he regarded fighting in defense of Muslims as a heroic cause. In 1988, he won a scholarship to study in Germany. The following year, the Soviets withdrew from Afghanistan, but the mujahidin kept on fighting against the communist Afghan regime. Slahi quit school in 1990 to join that fight. He went to Afghanistan and stayed for two months, then returned home to Mauritania. His younger cousin, Mahfouz Ould al-Walid, was inspired by Slahi's stories and set off for Afghanistan with the intention of meeting Osama bin Laden, which he did. Slahi went back to Afghanistan, but when the communist regime collapsed and the conflict became one of Muslims against Muslims, he quit and returned to Germany to resume his studies. His cousin, who came to be known as Abu Hafs al-Mauritani, became part of bin Laden's inner circle, eventually serving as his advisor on Shari'a law and a member of al-Qaeda's Shura Council. Because of Slahi's familial relationship with Abu Hafs and his continuing ties to other mujahidin, the German government flagged him as a person of interest.

In 1998, Slahi received a phone call from a satellite phone number he didn't recognize. It was Abu Hafs who asked for Slahi's help to transfer money to Mauritania for his family. The phone was bin Laden's. There was a second such call and request for help transferring money. Then Slahi learned that a relative in Mauritania who had taken a call from Abu Hafs was arrested and tortured. The third time Abu Hafs called Slahi, he hung up on his cousin. After the 1998 al-Qaeda bombings of US embassies in Kenya and Tanzania, the CIA began hunting for Abu Hafs. The earlier calls Slahi had taken and the money he had transferred on Abu Hafs's behalf would come to be interpreted as evidence that he, too, was active with al-Qaeda.

In 1999, Slahi agreed to a friend's request to let three Muslim men, whom he didn't know, crash for a night on the floor of his apartment as they passed through Germany on their way to Afghanistan. One of those men was Ramzi bin al-Shibh, who later would serve as al-Qaeda's coordinator for some of the 9/11 hijackers, and the other two became hijackers.

Although Slahi was under surveillance and was brought in for questioning several times, German intelligence did not regard him as a terrorist. When a friend living in Canada urged Slahi to come to Montreal because his ability to recite the entire Qur'an by memory would be a great asset in the Muslim community, he decided to make the move. Slahi began leading prayers in a large mosque. Someone who had worshipped at that mosque before Slahi arrived in Montreal was Ahmed Ressam, an Algerian who had trained in an al-Qaeda camp in Afghanistan and was living in Canada under a false identity.

On December 14, 1999, Ahmed Ressam was arrested while trying to cross the border into the United States with explosives and detonators in the trunk of his car. He was later charged and prosecuted for planning the so-called Millennium Plot to bomb the Los Angeles airport. Although Ressam implicated many people when he was interrogated, Slahi wasn't one of them because the men had never met. Nevertheless, Canadian intelligence agents made Slahi a person of interest and began surveilling him. Recordings of his phone conversations were passed along to US intelligence agents who heard him mention "tea and sugar" and other innocuous phrases which they began to spin into the whole cloth that he was a terrorist bigwig.

In January 2000, Slahi discovered hidden cameras in his apartment. He decided to leave Canada and return home to Mauritania. While transiting through Senegal, he was detained and interrogated for several days about the Millennium Plot, which he had never heard of. Senegalese agents did the interrogations but Americans who were present provided the questions. He was then flown to Mauritania where, again, he was detained and interrogated about the plot and about his cousin, Abu Hafs, but he was eventually released because the Mauritanians decided there was nothing to the US allegations that he was involved in terrorism.

In the summer of 2001, bin Laden told the al-Qaeda Shura Council the broad outlines of "the planes plot." Abu Hafs condemned the plot because mass murder of civilians went against the Qur'an. He broke ties with bin Laden. Nevertheless, after the planes plot came to fruition as 9/11, Abu Hafs was high on the list of known al-Qaeda operatives. This made Slahi a target as well.

In November 2001, the Mauritanian government, at the bidding of the United States, took Slahi into custody and then turned him over to US agents. Slahi was extraordinarily rendered to Jordan, where he was imprisoned and interrogated for seven months. He was one of at least thirteen people sent to Jordan by or at the behest of the CIA. The CIA made the Jordanians hide these prisoners when ICRC representatives visited. In July 2002, Slahi was rendered to Bagram, and on August 4, he was transported to Guantánamo.

When Slahi arrived, he bumped Mohammed al-Qahtani out of first place as the most high-value detainee in military custody. His first interrogators were FBI agents who were trying to figure out how Slahi figured in the various terrorist plots they were investigating. Soon he would ascend to the pinnacle of official suspicion as the person who recruited Ramzi bin al-Shibh. This allegation came from bin al-Shibh himself while he was being tortured—in official parlance, "custodially debriefed"—in CIA black sites. Only later would Slahi make the connection that bin al-Shibh was one of the three men who spent a night on the floor of his apartment in 1999.

On May 22, 2003, the FBI interrogations ended because Slahi did not confess to their allegations. Military interrogators took over. Slahi, like al-Qahtani, was subjected to the worst torture on offer at Guantánamo with the full knowledge of Defense Secretary Donald Rumsfeld. The man put in charge of instituting the Pentagon's "special plan" for Slahi was Richard Zuley, a Chicago police officer and Navy reservist who was recruited by JTF-GTMO commander General Geoffrey Miller. Zuley's main credential was his success in eliciting confessions that led to convictions of hundreds of poor and mostly Black and Brown Chicagoans. (In 2013, *Wall Street Journal* reporter Jess Bravin identified Zuley by name as Slahi's main interrogator in *The Terror Courts: Rough Justice at Guantanamo Bay.* In 2015, investigative journalist Spencer Ackerman broke the "Bad Lieutenant" story for the *Guardian* that Zuley's successes as a detective were largely the result of brutal interrogation tactics, including stress positions, threatening suspects' family members, and terrorizing people to confess to allegations against them, regardless of whether they were true.)

On July 1, 2003, Zuley, who went by the pseudonym "Captain Collins," got to work trying to get Slahi to confess to a myriad of accusations. For seventy days, Slahi was sleep deprived and terrorized with escalating abuses and threats. He was housed in a single-occupancy trailer called Echo Special, which was designed to block natural light. To heighten his fear, soldiers guarding him wore Darth Vader masks. Two of Slahi's personal "vulnerabilities" were his religious devotion, which includes modesty, and love for his family. He was repeatedly stripped and sexually molested by female interrogators. He was barred from praying and was punished if he was caught doing so, and he was denied all comfort items including toilet paper and soap, which made it impossible for him to do ablutions. Weeks into his ordeal, a military psychologist reported that Slahi appeared to be hallucinating. Despite being interrogated nearly around the clock for weeks, he didn't confess to the allegations his interrogators had cobbled together because they were untrue, and he continued to tell them so.

To try to break Slahi, Zuley showed him a fabricated letter stating that his mother had been taken into US custody and soon would be transported to Guantánamo where her presence in this all-male environment would pose some problems. The implication was that she inevitably would be raped by multiple men. What finally broke Slahi, though, was another deception that he was being taken to a place where he would be treated far worse. Slahi was hooded, shackled, and bundled out to a speedboat while dogs barked to intensify his fear. For four hours, he was sailed around while being beaten and kicked, causing several of his ribs to break. His hooded head was shoved into the water repeatedly to make him think he was about to be thrown into the sea. In the middle of this voyage to nowhere, the boat returned to shore and two men posing as foreign interrogators, one Egyptian and one Jordanian, got aboard to enhance the terrifying charade. In a letter Slahi later wrote to his habeas counsel, Nancy Hollander, he describes his traumatic seaborne episode as "a milestone in my interrogation history. . . . A thick line was drawn between my past and my future . . ."

After the boat ordeal, Slahi resigned himself that the only way to make the torment stop was to tell the interrogators what they wanted to hear. He concocted a string of wild stories inspired by questions interrogators had asked him over the years. One was a plot to blow up the CN Tower in Toronto, a structure he had never heard of before his imprisonment. The gold star confession was that he was a top al-Qaeda recruiter, which implicated him in the 9/11 attacks. He signed his self-incriminating statements, and as far as the US government was concerned, that made everything true and usable in the military commissions.

As Colonel Couch got to work prosecuting Slahi's case, he tried to corroborate the veracity of the self-incriminating statements. He had to overcome considerable bureaucratic resistance to obtain the logs from Slahi's interrogations that led to his confessions. When Couch discovered the forged letter about Slahi's mother and learned that Slahi had been reduced to a hallucinatory state, he decided to quit the case. To the ire of his military superiors, he warned that Slahi's statements were unusable because of the ordeals he had endured. Indeed, Slahi was never prosecuted. But neither was he released. The government's fallback was to detain him without trial indefinitely.

Another person the Bush administration attempted to prosecute early on was Binyam Mohamed, an Ethiopian national with British residency. In the summer of 2001, Mohamed, who had recently kicked a drug habit and converted to Islam, decided to go to Afghanistan to get away from temptations in London and learn more about his new religion. When the war started in October, Mohamed went to Pakistan. In April 2002, he was on his way home to England when he was arrested at the Karachi airport. During the three months he was detained in Pakistan, his interrogators included agents from Britain's MI5 and the FBI who threatened to send him to some Arab country, implying that his treatment there would be even worse. On July 21, Mohamed and two other detainees were turned over to CIA agents wearing ski masks. They were stripped, photographed, sodomized with tranquilizers, and flown to Morocco.

In Morocco, Mohamed's torturers were locals but the questions they were asking clearly came from British and US intelligence sources. Over the eighteen months he was held in that country, he suffered multiple broken bones, his penis was cut with a scalpel between twenty and thirty times, sometimes while stinging liquid was poured on the bleeding wounds, and he was threatened with rape, electrocution, and death. He was pressed to confess that he had associated with bin Laden and others in the top echelon of al-Qaeda. If the circumstances weren't so tragic, these allegations would be laughable, because he couldn't speak Arabic and was a recent convert. On January 21, 2004, he was extraordinarily rendered to Afghanistan where he was held in the CIA black site referred to as the "dark prison." There, he was beaten, sleep deprived, subjected to constant noise—"horror sounds"—at extreme levels, drugged, and nearly starved. In May, he was transferred to Bagram where he was forced to confess that he had plotted with Jose Padilla, a US citizen, to set off a "dirty bomb" in the United States. In September, he was transported to Guantánamo.

Clive Stafford Smith was Mohamed's habeas counsel. He met Mohamed for the first time on May 2, 2005. Stafford Smith described that encounter to me: "He talked for three days straight. I could barely keep up taking notes. I felt like I had PTSD, let alone him!" When the Bush administration charged Mohamed with conspiracy and material support for terrorism in November 2005, he was assigned a military defense lawyer, Lieutenant Colonel Yvonne Bradley. Stafford Smith shared his notes and other materials with Bradley. As she read through them, she realized that the charges against Mohamed were absurd. She wondered what these commissions were trying to achieve.

Before Mohamed's first hearing in April 2006, he asked Stafford Smith for several items: a long cotton tunic of the sort commonly worn by men in the Arab world which should be dyed the same orange as his prison uniform, a piece of paper and a black magic marker.

Back then, the hearings took place in a small, crowded courtroom in a building that had once served as the base's dental clinic. The journalists attending Mohamed's hearing included the *Miami Herald*'s Carol Rosenberg, dean of the Gitmo press corps, and reporters from the *New York Times,* the *Wall Street Journal,* and the *Los Angeles Times.* Observers from Human Rights Watch, Amnesty International, and the ACLU were there. Janet Hamlin, an artist who frequently did illustrations of commission proceedings (which had to be approved by censors), was seated at the front of the room. Joseph Margulies, Mohamed's other civilian lawyer, was there, too.

When Stafford Smith arrived in the courtroom, he started chatting with Rosenberg. A soldier immediately cut them off and admonished the reporter, "You can't be talking to the people taking part." Rosenberg retorted she had been attending hearings for months and knew a lot more about how things work than he did. When Mohamed arrived wearing his orange tunic, he was half-carried to his seat by guards because it was difficult to walk in shackles. Rosenberg leaned over to ask Stafford Smith for the correct spelling of his client's name, since it was spelled in different ways in court documents and the media. That ended up being a good setup for the political theater that Mohamed was about to direct.

The proceedings started when the judge, Colonel Ralph Kohlmann, arrived. (Military judges wear a black robe over their uniforms.) The judges' roles in these hearings were literally scripted by the Pentagon. As Judge Kohlmann started reading from his script, his first mistake was immediate: he referred to the defendant as Binyam Ahmed Muhammad. Mohamed, when it was his turn to speak, said: "Torture and they still don't get the right name. That means you've got the wrong person . . . The man you're looking for is not here. I am not Binyam Ahmed Muhammad . . . So now we have a problem." In the back-and-forth over the name of the person on trial, Mohamed said, "I can't call you Ralph Kallman rather than Kohlmann, can I, and arrest you and put you in jail? Because that's not you? Four years of—what do you call it?—enhanced torture techniques, and we have the wrong person in court. I mean, that bothers me. I don't know how it doesn't bother you."

Kohlmann stuck to the script and continued calling the defendant "Muhammad." When he got to the part about a defendant's rights, he said, "I hope your attorneys have told you . . . that as you come here and sit here today you are presumed to be innocent under commission law." Mohamed responded: "What is this rights you're talking about? Because I have been four years without rights and now all of a sudden I got rights. I am surprised." Kohlmann, thinking Mohamed was earnestly confused, explained that his rights come from Military Commission Order 1, and one was his right to be represented by a military lawyer. Mohamed pointed out the paradox of being represented by a soldier serving a government that regarded every detainee at Guantánamo as a guilty terrorist. He said he wanted to represent himself. Kohlmann didn't understand his point and tried luring Mohamed to say that he did not want Stafford Smith and Margulies. Mohamed punched back: "They're my advisers."

FIGURE 12. Military commission hearing, April 6, 2006: Binyam Mohamed and his lawyer, Lieutenant Colonel Yvonne Bradley. Court artist Janet Hamlin was asked by the security officer to blur Mohamed's features because drawing detainees' faces was forbidden at that time. Drawing by Janet Hamlin.

Bradley stood up to explain to Judge Kohlmann that she has an ethical conflict: She was working in an office with other military defense lawyers whose clients' cases were affected by statements Mohamed made against them under interrogation. Kohlmann pulled rank by lecturing her about correct decorum in the commission, implying that nothing should deviate from his script. Bradley pointed out the elephant in the room: "The problem is I don't understand commission law. I mean, I don't think anyone understands commission law."

Mohamed chimed in: "I'm happy that she stood up there and said she's confused, and I can understand why ... This is not a commission, this is a con-mission, a mission to con the world, and that's what it is." Then he pulled out the piece of paper on which he had written, in large black letters,

"CON-MISSION." He flashed it around so everyone could see. "You can execute me tomorrow, but don't try and cheat the world of what this really is ... You start playing around with con-missions here, then tomorrow we have another one in Canada, and then the next day have another in Australia, and the next day have it somewhere, another place, where certain non-citizens have to obey some rule that just got made up." After Mohamed finished, Kohlmann said, "I am not going to let you put up signs." Mohamed responded, "But it is not in the rules not to put up signs." "OK, so we have a new rule," Kohlmann said. "No more signs in court."

The judge turned back to the task of dressing down Bradley. "With all due respect, your honor," she responded, "I exercise my Fifth Amendment rights" to stay silent. Several minutes later, a soldier came into the courtroom and handed Kohlmann a note. He read it, then called a fifteen-minute recess. The Pentagon was monitoring the hearing by video and did not like the scene of a military lawyer being assailed by a military judge. The recess never ended. In June, the Supreme Court canceled the commissions with the *Hamdan* ruling.

After the MCA was passed in October 2006 and the commissions were resurrected, the Bush administration restarted the process of trying to extract some retributive justice from terrorists detained at Guantánamo. That, at least, was the public relations version of the situation. In reality, the MCA was designed to provide a workaround for torture.

The administration needed legislative help to reconcile its torture policy with the Supreme Court's *Hamdan* decision that Common Article 3 of the Geneva Conventions applies to everyone in US custody overseas. Although officials would not admit that *Hamdan* killed the torture program, for all intents and purposes it died but was denied a proper burial. The CIA black sites were emptied in September and fourteen "high value detainees" were transferred to Guantánamo. The administration wanted to prosecute at least some of these men and didn't want their torture to be a stumbling block on the path to guilty verdicts and executions.

The MCA, like every official statement and memo pertaining to the interrogation of detainees, cast torture as beyond the American pale while conforming to the denial-through-euphemism scheme. Military commission prosecutors would still be able to use statements obtained through *coercion* if they were deemed to be "reliable" and their use was "in the interest of justice." The responsibility to decide how to draw the line between prohibited torture and acceptable abuse and to discern the reliability of coerced statements would fall onto the narrow shoulders of military commission judges.

But the MCA had consequences unintended by the law's supporters. Military and civilian defense lawyers used the trials of their clients to bring long-hidden facts about torture into the light and, in doing so, exposed government lies. Seven military prosecutors, including two chief prosecutors, refused to collude in a system so ineluctably flawed. Two of them would take the stand as defense witnesses to testify about the government's dependence on dubious evidence and the political pressures that were exerted on prosecutors to dictate how cases should be handled.

The British government registered its opposition to the commissions because the rules bore no resemblance to international standards for fair trials. Nevertheless, the Bush administration recharged Binyam Mohamed. But the Pentagon was forced to drop all charges against him and four other detainees in October 2008, after the prosecutor handling those cases quit to protest the withholding of exculpatory evidence from the defense. Britain had been requesting Mohamed's repatriation since August 2007. After his charges were dropped, the Bush administration signaled its willingness to release him, but set conditions that were unacceptable. Mohamed would have to agree never to speak to the media about what his interrogators had done to him, and he would have to be put under electronic surveillance and other control measures that would violate British and European human rights laws. (Mohamed was finally repatriated without conditions in February 2009, a month after Bush was out of office.)

The MCA's jurisdiction-stripping component was intended to kill the habeas process, which meant indefinite detention without trial for those detainees whom the government had no intention of prosecuting and no motivation to release. The Gitmo Bar lawyers who had lobbied Congress against the MCA geared up for a new court battle to challenge the law as a breach of the Constitution's Suspension Clause. (This clause was inserted by the nation's founders to protect liberty by preventing the government from suspending habeas corpus except in the extraordinary circumstances of a foreign invasion or a rebellion.)

The Gitmo Bar also renewed their efforts to influence Congress, because Democrats had won control over the Senate and the House of Representatives in the 2006 election. On May 1, 2007, over seventy lawyers from all over the country went to Capitol Hill to lobby for legislation that would restore habeas rights for Guantánamo detainees. That effort went nowhere. Many Democratic politicians were fearful that, if they stood up for habeas, they would be portrayed as "soft on terrorism," and this might cost them in the next election. One of the exceptions was the junior senator from Illinois, Barack Obama, who had voted against the MCA. He provided invaluable support to Guantánamo lawyers during their lobbying efforts, and he endorsed the restoration of the Great Writ.

Two cases became the vehicle for the next battle over habeas: One was *Al Odah v. United States,* which Tom Wilner had started in 2002 on behalf of twelve Kuwaiti detainees. *Al Odah* had been merged with *Rasul* for the Supreme Court. After the decision in that case, and the subsequent repatriation of the *Rasul* plaintiffs, *Al Odah* remained; it now encompassed eleven separate cases and fifteen sets of lawyers and law firms, although Wilner and his Shearman & Sterling colleague Neil Koslowe continued as counsel of record. The other was *Boumediene v. Bush,* a case involving six Algerian-Bosnians who were represented by attorneys from the firm of WilmerHale. The named plaintiff in that case was Lakhdar Boumediene.

On February 20, 2007, the DC Circuit Court—where *Boumediene* had been in litigation for over two years—issued a two-to-one ruling dismissing the case on the grounds that the MCA had stripped the court of jurisdiction. One of the *Boumediene* attorneys was Seth Waxman, who had served as solicitor general during the Clinton administration. He advised his colleagues that if they wanted the Supreme Court to consider the case before summer recess, they would have to file a petition for a writ of certiorari immediately, and they would have to ask for an expedited consideration. They did, and so did the *Al Odah* attorneys.

On April 2, the Supreme Court declined to hear *Boumediene* and *Al Odah.* In an unusual move, the five nay-saying justices explained their reasoning: they wanted to wait and see how well the Combatant Status Review Tribunals (CSRT) worked because the Detainee Treatment Act, which Congress passed in 2005, stated that these tribunals were a valid alternative to habeas, and the only process detainees deserved.

The Supreme Court's refusal to hear these cases had immediate implications for the Gitmo Bar. Officials asserted that habeas was now over and, therefore, attorneys no longer had any right to visit or communicate with their clients. They were asked to turn over all of their documents, notes, and other client-related items for destruction.

The Bush administration assumed the Gitmo Bar would submit to this demand to surrender. Instead, the *Boumediene* and *Al Odah* attorneys filed petitions requesting the Supreme Court to reconsider. In their petition, Wilner and Koslowe argued that there was no reason for the Court to wait because the government had already demonstrated the inadequacy of the CSRT process: detainees were not allowed to present facts, confront evidence, or be aided by a lawyer, and as the Pentagon's own records proved, the on-paper right to call witnesses was an illusion. Moreover, they argued, the time was ripe for the Court to consider the constitutionality of the MCA because the DC Circuit's ruling in *Boumediene* contradicted the *Rasul* decision. Wilner and Koslowe got extra ammunition in the form of a declaration by Colonel Stephen Abraham, which they attached to their petition for reconsideration.

Abraham was a retired JAG officer who had been involved in the CSRT process; he had served as a liaison between the tribunals and intelligence agencies, he had evaluated the government's evidence, and he had presided at one panel. His experiences exposed him to problems that were endemic to the whole process. He wrote his declaration at the request of lawyers from the firm of Pillsbury Winthrop for their Guantánamo clients, and they shared it with other lawyers. The Abraham declaration explained the defects of the CSRTs to edify judges who were being misled by the government's false descriptions.

On June 29, 2007, the Supreme Court, for the first time in over sixty years, reversed itself and granted certiorari to hear the two cases which were consolidated as *Boumediene v. Bush*.

Everyone on the Gitmo Bar knew that *Boumediene* was a make-or-break case for the future of habeas, and lawyers representing other detainees pitched in to help. To win, they would have to relitigate the issue at the heart of *Rasul*—that federal courts have jurisdiction at Guantánamo because the United States exercises exclusive control there. They also would have to persuade the Court that the CSRT process was no substitute for habeas hearings in federal court. Oral arguments took place on December 5, 2007. Seth Waxman argued for the plaintiffs.

When the Supreme Court issued its *Boumediene* ruling on June 12, 2008, the Bush administration was handed its third big war-in-court defeat. Justice Anthony Kennedy, writing for the majority, didn't mince words. "We hold these petitioners do have the habeas corpus privilege . . . We hold that those [CSRT] procedures are not an adequate and effective substitute for habeas corpus. Therefore [section] 7 of the Military Commissions Act of 2006 . . . operates as an unconstitutional suspension of the writ." At the turn of the twenty-first century, US judges had no experience with the original, medieval "show us the body" purpose of habeas corpus because secret detention was not the function habeas served in US jurisprudence. But the Bush administration's policies gave medieval history contemporary relevance. In his ruling, Kennedy traced habeas corpus back to the Magna Carta, cited the famed English jurist William Blackstone who described the writ as "the stable bulwark of our liberties," and lauded its powerful influence on the nation's founding fathers, who incorporated the Suspension Clause into the Constitution even before they created a Bill of Rights. The most important outcome of *Boumediene* was the determination that the Constitution applies at Guantánamo. Without judicial oversight and a role for courts, Kennedy wrote, "it would be possible for the political branches to govern without legal constraint. Our basic charter cannot be contracted away like this."

Chief Justice John Roberts and Justice Antonin Scalia each wrote a dissenting opinion and signed onto each other's, and the two other conservative justices, Samuel Alito and Clarence Thomas, joined both. Roberts started his by complaining that the Court's majority has struck down "as inadequate the most generous set of procedural protections ever afforded aliens detained by this country as enemy combatants . . . One cannot help but think . . . that this decision is not really about the detainees at all, but about control of federal policy regarding enemy combatants." Roberts defended the CSRTs by regurgitating the administration's line that they worked well (enough) and served a vital purpose of keeping Americans safe. Scalia replicated the foot stomping that characterized his dissent in *Rasul:* "The writ of habeas corpus does not, and never has, run in favor of aliens abroad; the Suspension Clause thus has no application, and the Court's intervention in this military matter is entirely *ultra vires*" (acting beyond one's legal authority). In the view of these right-wing justices, corporations and fetuses are entitled to legal rights of personhood but people held in "executive detention" aren't.

Boumediene reopened the federal courtroom doors to habeas petitions. When the DC District Court started dealing with them in the summer of 2008, the evidence used to justify continuing imprisonment was put on trial, and it did not go well for the administration. Many of the incriminating statements on which the government was hanging its hat were rejected for what they were: at best unreliable, and at worst, complete concoctions elicited under extreme duress. Between October and November 2008, out of the first twenty-three petitions that were decided, twenty-two detainees—including seventeen Chinese Uighurs—prevailed. But the fight over habeas was far from over; it would continue throughout the next administration, and two more after that.

The Bush administration resumed charging people in the military commissions in 2007, confident that the MCA's government-favoring rules would grease the skids for quick guilty verdicts. Some detainees who had been charged before *Hamdan* were recharged, including Salim Hamdan. His attorneys tried to challenge the legality of the commissions again, but the Supreme Court was not willing to entertain their petition because the system now had Congress's blessing. The "new and improved" commission system was a lot like the old system, so all the work that defense lawyers and their legal academic and subject matter–expert allies had done before *Hamdan* would not go to waste. Arguably, the two most critical legal issues were whether people who are not soldiers can be prosecuted for violating the laws of war, and the fact that charges the government planned to level against defendants, including material support for terrorism and conspiracy, are not war crimes under international law.

David Hicks was the first detainee to be recharged in 2007. While the commissions were in abeyance, his military lawyer, Major Michael "Dan" Mori, had been hard at work trying to get his Australian client out of Guantánamo. Mori knew that some detainees were released because their governments put pressure on the Bush administration. Even senior Taliban officials had been released and repatriated to Afghanistan, while Hicks, accused of material support for terrorism for his role as a Taliban foot soldier, was facing charges and the prospect of a lengthy sentence. The Australian government resolutely refused to ask the Bush administration to release Hicks, and when he was recharged, endorsed his prosecution in the commissions.

Mori traveled to Australia seven times to wage a determined public relations campaign to build pressure for Hicks's release. Wearing his military uniform, Mori cut a swath across the country, giving lectures and interviews about prisoner abuse and the legal deficiencies of the commissions. He led a protest march to the office of the foreign minister, and he teamed up with Australian lawyers to sue the government for failure to act on Hicks's behalf. The court rejected the government's request to dismiss the case, which meant that the litigation could expose Australia's role in Hicks's continuing imprisonment.

Mori's PR campaign and the lawsuit made Hicks a political hot potato for Prime Minister John Howard who was running a tough race for reelection. Howard needed to demonstrate to his citizens that he was doing something, finally, to get Hicks out of Guantánamo. When Vice President Dick Cheney visited Australia in February 2007, Howard asked him for help. To the surprise and ire of the prosecutors handling Hicks's case, Cheney pressed Susan

Crawford, the convening authority for the military commissions, to offer Hicks a light deal to accommodate his conservative Australian ally.

Hicks's politically negotiated plea agreement gave the Bush administration its first conviction. On March 26, 2007, Hicks conceded to the charge of providing material support for terrorism in exchange for nine months of a suspended seven-year sentence, most of which he could serve in Australia. The agreement stipulated that Hicks would not speak to the media for a year and that he would never take legal action against the United States for the abuses he had suffered. On May 20, Hicks boarded an Australian-chartered plane and flew home. He was released from Australian prison on December 29. Howard still lost the election.

Salim Hamdan's case was the first to go to trial. Although Neal Katyal wasn't part of the defense team for the commission proceedings, the other lawyers who had taken *Hamdan* to the Supreme Court were on board: Lieutenant Commander Charles Swift, and Joe McMillan and Harry Schneider from the Seattle law firm Perkins Coie. The new lawyers on Team Hamdan were Captain Brian Mizer and Andrea Prasow. Charles Schmitz, the academic Yemen expert, continued on as the team's translator and he provided crucial emotional support for Hamdan, whose psychological condition was in freefall.

Hamdan had been in isolation for many months, which was exacerbating his suicidal thoughts, shattering flashbacks, and other symptoms of PTSD. On top of that, he was confused and despondent; although he had won what his lawyers told him was a major case in America's highest court, he was still imprisoned. Part of the team's work involved trying to give him some hope. Another part involved figuring out how to litigate the defects in the system—in essence, how to use Hamdan's commission trial to claw back elements of the Supreme Court decision that Congress had negated with the MCA.

Hamdan's lawyers' first move was to file a motion to dismiss the case for lack of personal jurisdiction (a challenge to the commission's authority to try him). Hamdan was classified as an enemy combatant by his CSRT, but according to the language of the MCA, the commissions have jurisdiction over *unlawful* enemy combatants. To their happy surprise, the judge, Captain Keith Allred, issued an oral ruling on the spot granting their motion and dismissing all the charges against Hamdan. At the same time, another judge dismissed all the charges against Omar Khadr for the same reason. The Pentagon responded by hastily assembling the Court of Military Commission

Review (CMCR), which previously only existed on paper. The CMCR decided that the commissions have the authority to determine who falls within their jurisdiction. When Judge Allred revisited the issue, he decided that Hamdan met criteria to be prosecuted. The case was back on.

Hamdan's pretrial hearings commenced on February 7, 2008—six years to the day from when President Bush had decreed the Geneva Conventions inapplicable to the "war on terror." Hamdan's lawyers put one legal flaw and illogical element of the system after another on trial. For example, if this was a war crimes trial, as the government contended, how could Hamdan be charged for activities that occurred before the "war on terror" started? They sought a ruling on the date the war against al-Qaeda began. In April, the defense moved to have the case dismissed on the grounds of unlawful command influence because the legal process was being directed and manipulated by political appointees. Colonel Morris Davis, who had resigned as chief prosecutor in October 2007 to protest interference by the convening authority's legal advisor, Brigadier General Thomas Hartmann, took the stand as a defense witness; he criticized the government's willingness to pursue weak cases on the basis of coerced statements and other unreliable forms of evidence, and he testified that Hartmann pressured prosecutors to handle cases in ways that would reflect well on the Bush administration. Judge Allred didn't dismiss Hamdan's case, but he did disqualify Hartmann from any further involvement.

At a pretrial hearing on April 29, Hamdan asked Judge Allred if he could talk to him. Permission granted. "Last night I told you that I did not want to come to this court, because there is no such thing as justice here. The law is clear. The law in America is clear. The international law is clear. If you ask me what the color of this paper is, I will tell you the color is white. You say black. I say, fine, it's black. Then you say, no, it's white. This is the American government. Do you understand what I have just said, your honor?" Judge Allred tried to reassure Hamdan: "I think you should have great faith in American law because you have already been to the Supreme Court . . . And you were the winner. Your name is printed in our law books. You beat the United States once . . . with these attorneys here with you today." Hamdan was not reassured. For all this talk of successes and victories, all he experienced was being locked up for five years, much of it in isolation. At the end of the hearing, he told the judge that he would not be returning to court and that his lawyers couldn't represent him in his absence. This threw into doubt what would happen next. Several months later, McMillan, Schneider and Schmitz visited Hamdan and persuaded him to let his lawyers continue to defend him.

Hamdan's trial began on July 21. After the voir dire process in which a panel of six military officers (the equivalent of a jury) was selected, the legal adversaries began battling it out. The first battle was over what evidence the prosecutors would be allowed to use to prove the charges of conspiracy and material support for terrorism. Judge Allred excluded all self-incriminating statements Hamdan had made at Bagram. "The interests of justice are not served by admitting these statements because of the highly coercive environments and conditions under which they were made." But he did allow statements from Guantánamo, despite that Hamdan had been subjected to many abuses there, including fifty straight days of sleep deprivation under "Operation Sandman."

The prosecutors were casting Hamdan as a linchpin in a vast terrorist conspiracy that included al-Qaeda's 1998 bombings of two US embassies in Africa, the bombing of the USS Cole in 2000, and the 9/11 attacks. There were two flaws in their position, as Swift explained to me. One flaw was legal: the MCA only prohibits "straight conspiracy," meaning personal involvement in a conspiracy, "not RICO-esque criminal enterprise conspiracy. The government was playing terrorism RICO." (RICO is the acronym for the Racketeer Influenced and Corrupt Organizations Act, which is often used in cases against members of the mafia to prosecute people for the crimes anyone else in the organization committed.) The other flaw was factual: there was no proof that Hamdan had conspired with the leadership of al-Qaeda. He was hired help, a driver for Osama bin Laden. The prosecutors' gambit was to implicate Hamdan in all of al-Qaeda's crimes. But when prosecutors played video of the collapse of the World Trade Center in court to persuade the panel that this was Hamdan's doing, it backfired. Hamdan had never seen this footage, and he broke down in tears. According to Swift, this reaction softened the panel in Hamdan's favor.

Swift was of the opinion that every military witness, by design or default, helped the defense. Colonel Louis Morgan Banks, an Army psychologist who was involved in Hamdan's interrogations in Afghanistan in November 2001, testified that he had advised senior officers either to recruit Hamdan as an informer or to release him. A soldier-witness for the prosecution testified about how he had saved Hamdan from being killed by anti-Taliban fighters, which appeared to elicit sympathy for Hamdan from members of the panel.

On August 6, after a three-week trial, the panel delivered its verdict. Hamdan was found guilty of one count of material support for terrorism but was acquitted of all conspiracy charges. At the sentencing hearing the following day, Hamdan said, "I personally represent my apologies if any think what I did has caused them any pain." The prosecutors scorned his apology and advised the panel to see Hamdan for what he was—an irredeemable terrorist. Despite having lost on the major charge, they still requested a sentence of "not one day less than thirty years" to send the world a message. Swift, arguing for the defense, laid out a set of reasons for leniency, including Hamdan's remorsefulness, and urged the panel that this would serve justice.

The panel deliberated for less than thirty minutes. When they returned, the president of the panel announced the sentence: "66 months," or five and a half years. They gave Hamdan credit for the sixty-one months he had already served at Guantánamo, which meant that his sentence would be over in five months. As Judge Allred was about to dismiss the panel, Hamdan asked to say something. "I would like to apologize one more time to all the members. And I would like to thank you for what you have done for me. And I would like also to thank the judge, and I would like to thank everybody. And I apologize once again."

After the panel left the courtroom, Judge Allred made some final remarks: "Well, this has been a long journey for Mr. Hamdan, who began in 2001; for Mr. Swift, who began in 2004 [actually it was 2003]; for Mr. McMillan and Schneider, who began, I guess, in 2004; and for others who have joined the case along the way . . . I commend you all for your professionalism and your courtesy to each other and the tremendous investment of hard work and your professional skills that have gone into the trial of this case." Then he directed a comment to Hamdan: "I hope the day comes that you return to your wife and your daughters and your country." Hamdan responded, "Inshallah" (God willing). Judge Allred reciprocated, "Inshallah." As Hamdan was leaving the courtroom, he waved his cuffed hands in the air and said, "Bye-bye everybody!"

Defense Secretary Robert Gates was incensed that Hamdan had been credited for time served and he ordered this option to be eliminated for future cases. The Pentagon refused to commit to releasing Hamdan after his sentence was up, insisting that he could continue to be detained as an enemy combatant. Then, in November 2008, Hamdan's lawyers were notified that he would be repatriated to Yemen in seventy-two hours to serve out the remainder of his sentence. In January 2009, Hamdan was freed and reunited with his family.

Because Hicks and Hamdan had been prosecuted, convicted, *and released,* some detainees started asking their lawyers if they could be charged. It was a sign of desperation to see a military commission conviction as the solution to the problem of indefinite detention. But this wasn't an entirely fantastical idea; the Pentagon was trying to speed up the process of charging people because there was concern that Guantánamo's days might be numbered. Both candidates in the 2008 race for the presidency, Republican John McCain and Democrat Barack Obama, had indicated that they would like to see Guantánamo closed.

Ali Hamza al-Bahlul, a Yemeni citizen, was the third person to be recharged when the commissions resumed. After going to Afghanistan in 1999 to join the Taliban's fight against the Northern Alliance, he became a propagandist for al-Qaeda and made recruitment videos glorifying violent jihad, including one featuring the attack on the USS Cole. Al-Bahlul fancied himself an important player because of his personal ties to bin Laden, and he regarded imprisonment as a continuation of his own jihad.

When al-Bahlul was first charged in 2004, he refused the services of his military lawyers, Lieutenant Commander Philip Sundel and Major Mark Bridges, and demanded a Yemeni lawyer, to no avail. His next military lawyer was Major Tom Fleener. At a hearing on January 11, 2006, the judge, Colonel Peter Brownback, asked al-Bahlul if he understood that Fleener's job was to defend him. He said that Fleener was being forced on him according to commission rules "that change from one minute to another." Al-Bahlul reiterated his position that he would not accept the services of any American lawyer. "This doesn't mean I hate all Americans," he said. "I regard them as enemies." Then he launched into a rehearsed statement criticizing the commissions as a farce. As he concluded, he held up a piece of paper with the word "boycott" on one side and his nine-point manifesto scribbled on the other. Brownback asked if the court could make a copy for the records. Al-Bahlul signed and dated it and handed it to a court officer for xeroxing. Then he pulled off the headset for translation, signaling that he was finished.

Judge Brownback denied al-Bahlul's request to represent himself because his intention to boycott demonstrated that he was incompetent. Fleener, who had been sitting behind al-Bahlul, was ordered to move to the defense table. He did, then immediately requested to be relieved. Request denied. Fleener told a *GQ* interviewer, "The concept of compelled representation has always bothered the crap out of me. You just don't force lawyers on people. You don't represent someone against his will. It's never, ever, ever done."

In 2007, al-Bahlul was recharged with conspiracy, providing material support for terrorism, and solicitation of murder (another invented war crime). When Fleener returned to civilian life, Major David Frakt took over as the lawyer not representing al-Bahlul. Frakt had served in the JAG corps in the 1990s and he reenlisted after 9/11. After the invasion of Iraq, which he characterized as an "illegal war" when I interviewed him, he resigned from active duty and became a law professor. In January 2008, the Pentagon sent a solicitation to all reservist JAGs asking for volunteers to serve as prosecutors or defense counsels. Whereas Frakt once had aspired to prosecute terrorists, now he volunteered to be a defense lawyer because, as he explained, "Maybe I could be part of an historic process." He was assigned to al-Bahlul whom he described as "a crafty committed al-Qaeda believer" with a propensity for bragging. "Everything they had about al-Bahlul they got from al-Bahlul."

The MCA had changed the rules slightly by incorporating a provision that a defendant can represent himself, and Judge Brownback granted al-Bahlul's request to go pro se. But this decision didn't stick because when Brownback was involuntarily retired from the Army days after announcing this decision, his replacement, Colonel Ronald Gregory, revoked it. At a pretrial hearing on August 15, al-Bahlul requested his boycott sign, which had been confiscated after his previous hearing. No one could find it. Al-Bahlul said, "If such a legal document is lost, what kind of court is this?" He told the judge that the only hearing he would attend would be the one where the verdict and the sentence are announced. As he departed the courtroom, he said, "You can continue your legal play." Frakt told Judge Gregory that he would represent the wishes of his client, which meant waiving all future pretrial motions so that the case could go immediately to trial.

When Al-Bahlul's trial began on October 27, Frakt declared, "I will be joining Mr. al-Bahlul's boycott of the proceedings, standing mute at the table." And so it went: There was no defense involvement in the selection of the panel, no defense witnesses, no cross-examination of prosecution witnesses. The case against al-Bahlul was unchallenged. On November 3, the panel deliberated for thirty minutes and then came in with the verdict: guilty of all charges. At the sentencing hearing, al-Bahlul taunted the panel by telling them he had volunteered to be one of the 9/11 hijackers. They sentenced him to life in prison. At a press conference afterward, Frakt told reporters, "I think the 20th hijacker comment sealed the deal." Al-Bahlul was moved to a section of the prison for people who were convicted. When Hamdan was repatriated to Yemen, he had it all to himself.

Frakt was assigned to another prisoner whom the administration was hustling to convict before the election: Mohammad Jawad, an Afghan who was estimated to be fifteen but may have been as young as twelve when he was captured in 2002. Jonathan Hafetz, on behalf of the ACLU, was Jawad's habeas counsel. The other lawyers on Jawad's defense team were Major Eric Montalvo and Commander Katherine Doxakis. Law students from Duke University were providing support.

When Frakt started this case, he recounted, "My working assumption was that Jawad was guilty. Why? First, generally defendants are guilty of what they are charged with. Second, Jawad was the fourth person to be charged [after passage of the MCA] so I assumed the evidence must be very good." Initially, Frakt's strategy was to avoid a trial. His first motion was to dismiss on the grounds that the commissions lacked jurisdiction to try a juvenile for war crimes. The Bush administration responded that if Congress had wanted to set an age limit, they would have included it in the MCA.

Even though Jawad had no ties to al-Qaeda or the Taliban, his case was given priority because he was accused of throwing a grenade that wounded two US soldiers and their translator. He was charged with attempted murder in violation of the laws of war (another made-up war crime). General Hartmann was pushing this case forward because it involved a bloodshed incident which, he said, would "capture the imagination of the American people."

The case against Jawad took an extraordinary turn over the spring and summer of 2008 as the prosecutor, Lieutenant Colonel Darrel Vandeveld, a devout Catholic, had a crisis of conscience. When he had started this assignment, he was gung-ho about the military commissions and, like other prosecutors, skeptical of defendants' allegations of abuse. But when he started examining the evidence, he realized that the case had all the makings of a gross miscarriage of justice. The chief prosecutor, Colonel Lawrence Davis, dismissed his concerns. Vandeveld could not confide in friends or family because the information that troubled him was classified. The one person with whom he could share his ethical struggles was his opposing counsel, Frakt. The two lawyers formed a collaboration that was cemented by mutual disgust over Jawad's treatment.

Frakt helped Vandeveld understand Jawad's prison logs, which had been turned over to the defense in discovery. In the summer of 2003, Jawad was removed from the Pashto-speaking wing of the prison and put into isolation without any comfort items. By September, interrogators reported that he appeared to be hallucinating because he was talking to himself. On Christmas

Day, he attempted suicide, first by smashing his head into metal bars in his cell and then by trying to hang himself. In May 2004, he was put into the "frequent flier program" (a sleep deprivation regimen) and moved from cell to cell every three hours for two straight weeks.

Jawad's attorneys filed motions to have his case dismissed on two grounds: unlawful command influence because of Hartmann's politicized interventions, and torture and outrageous government conduct. (The outrageous government conduct doctrine stipulates that a court may exclude evidence or even throw out a criminal case if the defendant was subjected to illegal or conscience-shocking treatment.) Frakt requested two days to argue these motions, but the judge, Colonel Stephen Henley, gave him only one.

On June 19, 2008, the torture motion was argued first. Frakt needed to persuade the judge that subjecting a person, in this case a juvenile, to weeks of sleep disruption constituted torture and therefore was outrageous. One of the witnesses testifying for the defense was a professor of neurology at Harvard medical school whose expertise was sleep research. When the prosecutors cross-examined her about the mental and physical effects of protracted sleep deprivation, Jawad became upset and asked to speak about his own experiences. Frakt hadn't anticipated this but he appreciated that the judge allowed it. When Jawad took the stand, he became the first defendant in the military commissions to describe his own torture on the record.

By the time they got to the motion on unlawful command influence, it was early evening. Former chief prosecutor Morris Davis testified about how Hartmann had pressured him on the charges and fast-tracking of Jawad's case. Testimony went on until ten p.m. Because Judge Henley had allocated only one day, despite the lateness of the hour, he gave Frakt the opportunity to make a closing argument on his torture motion. In a *Harvard Human Rights Journal* article, Frakt explains the strategy that went into preparing his closing argument.

> I did not want to deliver the typical motion argument, focusing on the specific facts of the case and the relevant legal precedents ... Rather, I wanted to put the torture of Mohammed Jawad into the larger context of the Global War on Terror and the extreme lawlessness that characterized the administration's response to the perceived threat of terrorism. What I had learned about the treatment of the detainees shamed me deeply. Conscious that the world would be watching and judging the commissions, I wanted to prove that someone in the US military was willing to stand up for real American values and the Constitution.

Frakt began his closing argument by describing President Bush's decision to disregard the Geneva Conventions as "fateful and ill-advised." That decision started the United States down a slippery slope, descending into "a dark Machiavellian world of 'the ends justify the means,' before plummeting further into the bleak underworld of barbarism and cruelty, of 'anything goes,' of torture. It was a path that led inexorably to the events that bring us here today, the pointless and sadistic treatment of Mohammed Jawad." Frakt leveled harsh criticism and named names of the civilian officials who cut the real experts, the JAGs, out of the loop. After tracing the evolution of the torture policy, Frakt pounded the point that members of the military and the president take oaths to defend the Constitution, and he criticized those who had failed that obligation by treating people in US custody as less than human. Then he brought his argument back to his client: "Why was Mohammed Jawad tortured? Why did military officials choose a teenage boy who had attempted suicide in his cell less than five months earlier to be the subject of this sadistic sleep deprivation experiment?" Jawad wasn't even interrogated after his weeks of sleep deprivation. Therefore, Frakt said, "we are left to conclude that it was simply gratuitous cruelty." He concluded by acknowledging that dismissal of Jawad's case would be a severe sanction on the government, "but it is the only sanction that might conceivably deter such conduct in the future."

In the government's response to the torture motion, Vandeveld conceded that Jawad had been abused. For this, he was reprimanded by his superiors and ordered to submit a revised response that made no concessions. When Judge Henley ruled on the motion, he refused to dismiss the charges because that would be an "unwarranted" penalty for the government, but, paradoxically, he did recommend that individuals directly involved in Jawad's protracted sleep deprivation be disciplined.

In July, Vandeveld happened upon the report of an investigation into the death of the Afghan taxi driver Dilawar at Bagram. A statement by Jawad, who was imprisoned at Bagram at the time, was recorded in the report. Jawad told the investigators that he (like Dilawar) had been hooded, shackled, forced to stand for prolonged periods of time, and frequently beaten. Vandeveld immediately told Frakt about the report, but when he realized that there was no means to put it into evidence as part of the discovery process, he became dismayed.

Vandeveld decided that the ethical thing to do, under the constricted options available to him, was to arrange a light sentence through a plea bargain that would include rehabilitative treatment for Jawad and repatriation back to Afghanistan. When the chief prosecutor nixed the idea of a deal, Vandeveld's personal and professional anguish intensified. He consulted an online priest for guidance. In an email, later published by the *Los Angeles Times,* he wrote: "I am beginning to have grave misgivings about what I am doing, and what we are doing as a country. I no longer want to participate in the system, but I lack the courage to quit. I am married, with four children, and not only will they suffer, I will lose a lot of friends." The priest counseled Vandeveld: "God does not want you to participate in any injustice, and GITMO is so bad, I hope and pray you will quietly, peacefully, prayerfully, just resign, and start your life over." Vandeveld didn't think quitting was the soldierly thing to do, so he kept trying to push the idea of a plea bargain on his superiors who remained stony in their refusal.

A motion hearing on undue command influence took place on August 13. One of the witnesses for the defense was an officer of rank equal to Hartmann, General Gregory Zanetti, who described Hartmann as "abusive, bullying and unprofessional . . . pretty much across the board." Judge Henley, again, didn't dismiss the case, but he banished Hartmann from any further involvement and ordered a top-level review of the charges against Jawad.

By September, Vandeveld concluded that the only principled thing to do was resign. He submitted a four-page sworn declaration explaining his decision: The government was withholding potentially exculpatory evidence from the defense, including an intelligence report that Jawad, who was an illiterate, homeless teenager when he was arrested, may have been duped or threatened to join Hizb-e Islami Gulbuddin (an Afghan organization headed by Gulbuddin Hekmatyar) and then drugged and sexually abused before being forced to engage in acts of violence. More concretely damning was the fact that two other men in US custody had reportedly confessed to throwing the grenade that Jawad was being charged for. Jawad's confession that he had thrown the grenade was elicited by Afghan police and, since he couldn't read, he didn't know what he signed. Vandeveld also stated that he was troubled that the Pentagon knew Jawad was a juvenile when he arrived at Guantánamo but never segregated him from the adult population.

At the motion hearing to suppress Jawad's confession, Vandeveld testified for the defense. In October, Judge Henley threw out Jawad's statement because he was persuaded it was coerced. That decision demolished the prosecution's chances of getting a conviction since the confession was the only "evidence" connecting Jawad to the grenade attack. The true believers on the prosecution side tried to minimize their loss by suggesting that they would pursue the case with different evidence. But they were unable to produce any. In the last week of Bush's time in office, prosecutors moved to have the suppressed statement readmitted because there was no evidence that Jawad was being tortured *while* he signed it.

Jawad's case extended into the next administration, and it illustrated a synchronicity between the two main battlegrounds in the war in court: the military commissions and federal courts. On July 30, 2009, Judge Ellen Huvelle, who was handling Jawad's habeas petition, cited Judge Henley's suppression of the confession, which was the sole basis for his continued detention. She ordered Jawad's release.

When Jawad was repatriated to Afghanistan in August 2009, one of his lawyers, Major Eric Montalvo, flew there early to stave off the likelihood that the Afghan government would transfer him to the Pul-e-Charkhi prison. (According to Human Rights First, more than 250 repatriated Afghan detainees were dispatched to Pul-e-Charkhi and 160 were put on trial, often on evidence deemed too flimsy even for the United States.) Montalvo went as a private citizen because the Pentagon refused to allow him to travel in his capacity as Jawad's military lawyer. When Montalvo arrived in Kabul, he went directly to the office of the attorney general and persuaded him to set Jawad free. When Jawad was reunited with his family, Montalvo was there to bear witness for the team.

Frakt reflected on the lessons he learned from Jawad's case: "For a defense lawyer, even a hopeless case can be one in which truth and justice can prevail, eventually. It might sound trite, but that's what working on this case taught me. Also, the skill of the lawyer *matters*. In this case, the system was so stacked that an ordinary level of advocacy would not have won. But I never accepted that I couldn't win. As a defense counsel, you have to believe that truth and justice will prevail."

Omar Khadr's situation was similar to Jawad's in several ways: He was a juvenile when he arrived at Guantánamo, he was accused of throwing a grenade that killed a US soldier, and he was one of the first to be charged by the Bush administration. One big difference was that Khadr had personal ties to Osama bin Laden.

When Khadr was captured on July 27, 2002, following a four-hour firefight near the Afghan village of Ayub Kheyl, everyone else inside the compound was dead. The soldiers who found him buried under rubble initially thought he was dead, too. He was alive but unconscious, shot twice in the chest and blinded in one eye by shrapnel. He was airlifted to Bagram, and his interrogation began as soon as he regained consciousness, while he was strapped to a hospital gurney. Eventually it would come to light that his interrogators withheld medical treatment until he made a confession.

The key to understanding the events that led to Khadr's capture is his father Ahmed, an Egyptian-born Canadian who was a devotee of a highly conservative interpretation of Islam. In the 1980s and '90s, he traveled frequently to Afghanistan and Pakistan to provide relief to widows and orphans with charitable donations from Canadian Muslim communities. Although Omar and his siblings were born in Canada, they spent significant periods of their childhood living in Peshawar. Locals knew them as "the Canadians."

In 1994, Ahmed sent his two eldest sons, Abdullah, thirteen, and Abdurahman, eleven, to al-Khalden training camp in Afghanistan to learn to fight. In 1995, he arranged a marriage for his eldest daughter, Zaynab, fifteen, to an Egyptian Islamist who, at the time, was suspected of involvement in a deadly embassy bombing in Cairo (and was later captured in Albania and rendered by the CIA to Egypt for trial). After the al-Qaeda leadership set up shop in Afghanistan in 1996, Ahmed became an intimate of Osama bin Laden. For a period, the Khadr family lived in bin Laden's compound south of Jalalabad. Following the US-led invasion and the fall of Kabul, the Khadrs fled to Pakistan, except Abdurahman, who got separated from the family and was captured by the Northern Alliance and handed over to the Americans.

In June 2002, Ahmed sent Omar back into Afghanistan with a Libyan al-Qaeda operative, Abu Laith al-Libi, to serve as a translator because he was fluent in Arabic and Pashtu. He was in the compound to translate on the day in July when there was the firefight that led to his capture. Ahmed was killed in October 2003 by Pakistani forces in Waziristan, and his youngest son, Kareem, was severely injured. The surviving members of the Khadr family who weren't in US custody returned to Canada. (The most comprehensive account of Khadr and his family is Canadian journalist Michelle Shephard's book, *Guantanamo's Child: The Untold Story of Omar Khadr*.)

When Omar Khadr arrived at Guantánamo on October 29 or 30, he had just turned sixteen. He was too young to grow a beard. Over the following two years, his interrogation regimen included being beaten and threatened with rape and dogs, having his hair pulled out, and being deprived of sleep for weeks. On one occasion when he was denied access to a toilet and urinated on himself, he was doused with pine-scented cleaner and used as a "human mop."

Canadian interrogators who were given access to him declined his desperate pleas for help. He was sequestered in isolation for protracted periods, and after he joined the sweeping hunger strike in 2005, he was force-fed, a process that involves being strapped to a restraint chair and having a feeding tube forced through the nose, down the throat, and into the stomach.

In 2005, the Bush administration selected Khadr as one of the first ten detainees to be prosecuted. He was charged with murder for allegedly throwing the grenade that killed Special Forces sergeant Christopher Speer. This charge rested heavily on Khadr's own statements to interrogators between 2002 and 2005. He was also charged with attempted murder because a video retrieved from the compound's rubble shows the teenager, among a group of adults, handling something with protruding wires, alleged to be an improvised explosive device that might have been planted along Afghan roads to attack US and allied forces. And he was charged with conspiracy and providing material support for terrorism. Khadr's first military lawyer was Lieutenant Colonel Colby Vokey. When he sought additional help, Lieutenant Commander William Kuebler and Lieutenant Rebecca Snyder were added to the defense team. Two Canadian lawyers, Nathan Whitling and Dennis Edney, provided legal counsel but, as non-Americans, they could not defend him before the military commissions.

Despite Khadr's youthfulness and, as his attorneys would argue, his lack of choice in engaging in activities that his father commanded, prosecutors insisted that he willfully conspired with al-Qaeda. Officials were confident that his would be one of the easiest cases to prove, an important consideration for an administration eager to demonstrate that this system was capable of producing convictions.

Khadr was arraigned for the first time in January 2006. The day before that hearing, the Defense Department convened a press conference for journalists present at Guantánamo. Muneer Ahmad, one of Khadr's civilian attorneys, spoke first. He denounced the government's decision to prosecute a juvenile for alleged war crimes and the prosecutors' plan to use evidence obtained through torture. He concluded his remarks by calling the commissions a sham. Chief prosecutor Colonel Lawrence Davis, who spoke next, described Khadr as a murderer, a terrorist, and an ally of Osama bin Laden; his comments got broad media coverage.

At the hearing the following day, Ahmad accused Davis of prosecutorial misconduct for making prejudicial statements intended to harm the accused. Prosecutors retaliated by saying Ahmad had opened the door with his statements that Khadr had been tortured and his description of the commissions as a sham.

In Canada, antipathy toward the Khadrs was so pervasive that they were referred to in the media as "Canada's first family of terrorism." The Canadian government refused to request Khadr's repatriation or oppose his trial by commission. In an effort to change this situation, Kuebler tried to "pull a Mori"—to emulate the public relations strategy that David Hicks's attorney had used so successfully to bring pressure on the Australian government. Kuebler made trips to Canada where he became the public voice shaming that government for its inaction on Khadr's behalf, and he provided journalists with a stream of press releases about Khadr's torture, the faultiness of the government's evidence, and information about prosecutorial malfeasance. On paper, Kuebler would seem an unlikely bare-knuckle brawler fighting on behalf of a person with a background so steeped in Islamist radicalism; Kuebler was a politically conservative born-again Christian who had never voted for a Democrat on principle. But as it turned out, Kuebler's Christian faith motivated his aggressive campaign on behalf of his client. As he told the *New York Times,* "It is a powerful way to be a witness for Christ, by demonstrating your capacity to not judge the way everybody else is judging and to serve unconditionally."

Khadr was recharged in April 2007. His lawyers' fierce criticisms of the military commissions had affected him; he absorbed the arguments that he was implicated in a sham. He fired Muneer Ahmad and Rick Wilson. His frustration and despondency were exacerbated by infighting among his lawyers. The two Canadians, Edney and Whitling, sometimes disagreed with his changing cast of military lawyers, but the latter sometimes disagreed with each other, too. Khadr grew increasingly close to Kuebler, who nourished his resentments, which took a further toll on relations among the lawyers. In September 2008, Commander Walter Ruiz and Michel Paradis, a civilian attorney working with the Military Commissions Defense Office, were added to the Khadr team. The judge assigned to the case, Colonel Patrick Parrish, rejected the defense motion that these commissions do not have jurisdiction over crimes of a child soldier. But in October 2008, Parrish suspended the case until after the November elections.

The Bush administration's hustle-and-bustle efforts to charge and convict lots of detainees before the election were something of a sideshow. The main act was the prosecution of some of the fourteen "high value" detainees who had been transferred from CIA black sites to Guantánamo in September

2006. The Pentagon began taking steps to prepare a case against Khalid Sheikh Mohammed, the alleged "mastermind" of the 9/11 attacks, and four other alleged 9/11 accomplices: Walid bin Attash, Ramzi bin al-Shibh, Ammar al-Baluchi (whom the government refers to as Ali Abdul Aziz Ali), and Mustafa al-Hawsawi. The sixth person they wanted to charge for 9/11 was Mohammed al-Qahtani who, unlike his codefendants, had spent his years in military custody at Guantánamo.

A new high-security military commission complex was designed specifically for the 9/11 trial. On the defense side of the courtroom, six rows of tables were installed for the six defendants and their lawyers. They would be seated in descending order of importance, with Mohammed in the front row and al-Qahtani in the last row. A gallery was built at the back of the courtroom to accommodate the public, which would consist of journalists, NGO observers, and family members of people killed on 9/11. The gallery had a window onto the courtroom so that people could watch proceedings, but it was soundproofed and the audio feed was rigged to run on a forty-second delay. These audio features were necessary to enable an ostensibly open trial while preventing the public from hearing something that a defendant or lawyer might blurt out in court which the government regarded as classified, namely anything pertaining to the CIA torture program.

The Bush administration was engaged in some high-grade magical thinking that they could put on a trial that would be widely perceived as fair while keeping details of the CIA's torture of the defendants a secret. Efforts to do so involved two distinct moves: One was the attempt to erase the relevance of their years in the black sites by pronouncing that nothing the defendants had said between the time they were captured and their arrival at Guantánamo would be used against them. In order to get self-incriminating statements that could be used at trial, the FBI dispatched "clean teams" to Guantánamo in January 2007 to interrogate them (and other former CIA prisoners) using conventional methods. The other move was to classify these detainees themselves because their own memories of their treatment in CIA custody were state secrets which the government claimed to own. They were housed in a maximum-security facility at an undisclosed location on the base. Even the name of this facility was a secret until it was revealed, by accident, on December 8, 2007, when a censor failed to redact a line in the client meeting notes of Gitanjali Gutierrez, a CCR attorney who represented one of the former CIA prisoners, Majid Khan. The revelation that the facility's name is Camp 7 created a crisis for military spokespeople, according to the

Miami Herald's Carol Rosenberg, because they were not permitted to talk about it and were rudderless in trying to respond to journalists' queries.

The administration was confident that this group trial would *really* capture the imagination of the American people, and the inevitable death penalty verdicts would vindicate the administration's "war on terror" policy choices.

On February 11, 2008, the six defendants were charged. When al-Qahtani learned that he was facing the death penalty, he attempted suicide. On May 12, for reasons unexplained at the time, the government announced that the charges against al-Qahtani had been dropped. Prosecutors said they intended to refile charges against him, but in November, Convening Authority Susan Crawford decided that he could not be prosecuted because "his treatment met the legal definition of torture." The difference between his torture and that of the other defendants was that his was perpetrated by the military and therefore wasn't secret in the same way. In a January 2009 interview with the *Washington Post,* Crawford explained: "We tortured Mohammed al-Qahtani.... The techniques [military interrogators] used were all authorized, but the manner in which they applied them was overly aggressive and too persistent ... It was abusive and uncalled for. And coercive. Clearly coercive." Crawford said that when she understood that al-Qahtani's torture required him to be hospitalized because his heart rate dropped, "that pushed me over the edge." Crawford's statement was the first and only time any Bush administration official acknowledged torture at Guantánamo. As a result of her decision, the high-security courtroom's sixth row would stand empty, a material relic of the Pentagon's decision to torture.

The 9/11 case moved forward with five defendants.

According to the MCA, any detainee facing charges in the military commissions had a right to a government-funded military lawyer. Because the 9/11 defendants were facing capital charges, they were allocated two. Khalid Sheikh Mohammed's military lawyers were Captain Prescott Prince and Lieutenant Colonel Michael Acuff; Walid bin Attash's were Lieutenant Commander James Hatcher and Captain Christina Jimenez; Ramzi bin al-Shibh's were Commander Suzanne Lachelier and Lieutenant Richard Federico; Ammar al-Baluchi's were Lieutenant Commander Brian Mizer (who was concurrently working on the Hamdan case) and Major Amy Fitzgibbons; and Mustafa al-Hawsawi's were Major Jon Jackson and Lieutenant Gretchen Sosbee. The administration was also pursuing a death penalty case against another former CIA detainee, Abd al-Rahim al-Nashiri, who was accused of being the "mastermind" of the 2000 bombing of the USS Cole which killed seventeen sailors.

None of the military lawyers assigned to these two cases had death penalty experience. To level the playing field and provide support for the under-resourced JAGs, the ACLU and the National Association of Criminal Defense Lawyers decided to bring in some big guns. They created the John Adams Project, named for the founding father who stood up for the right to a fair trial when he defended British soldiers who shot and killed several colonial American protestors in the 1770 event that became known as the Boston Massacre. Joshua Dratel, one of the organizers of the John Adams Project, explained: "We're recruiting lawyers with criminal defense experience on high profile cases involving national security and death penalty charges." I asked Dratel what characteristics he was looking for in the selection process. "Fearless, team players, not too ego-ish, willing to work for less money than they usually earn, and willing to stay in it for the long haul." The death penalty lawyers who were selected to be civilian co-counsels for the 9/11 defendants were David Nevin and Scott McKay for Mohammed, Edward MacMahon for bin-Attash, Thomas Durkin for bin al-Shibh, Jeff Robinson and Amanda Lee for al-Baluchi, and Nina Ginsberg and Jonathan Shapiro for al-Hawsawi. Dratel asked Nancy Hollander to represent al-Nashiri. She agreed to do it, and so did her colleague, Teri Duncan, if it didn't conflict with their habeas work on Slahi's case. Hollander, in turn, recruited Richard Kammen for the John Adams Project to head the team representing al-Nashiri.

Hollander told me that before she and Duncan met al-Nashiri in May 2008, they knew a lot more about the US torture program than they had when they met Slahi. But, Hollander said, "we didn't know how religious he was." Would he be offended to be represented by women? She recounted the first moments of their first meeting: "He grabbed my hand *hard*. He started talking very quickly about his torture." Hollander had prepared a document, which al-Nashiri signed, authorizing her and Duncan to represent him not just at Guantánamo but anywhere. (Several years later, she would use that authorization to take al-Nashiri's case against the two European countries that hosted black sites where he was tortured, Poland and Romania, to the European Court of Human Rights.)

The Pentagon's confidence that the 9/11 case would be wrapped up quickly was reflected in the proposed schedule, which was released on June 4, 2008. The arraignment would take place on June 5, the pretrial phase would begin on June 7, and the trial would start on September 15.

FIGURE 13. Left to right: John Adams Project attorneys Thomas Durkin, Edward MacMahon, and David Nevin at Guantánamo, September 23, 2008. Photo by Bryan Broyles.

They got one thing right. The arraignment hearing did occur on June 5.

Fifty-seven journalists traveled to Guantánamo for the 9/11 case arraignment. At a press conference, General Hartmann said, "It will be a battle *royale* in the courtroom. It will be what a trial is supposed to be, a very aggressive approach from the prosecution and the defense, bringing the matters of law to the judge, bringing the matters of fact to the jury, to allow them to decide. It will be an aggressive, intense experience, as a trial is supposed to be, to bring out the truth."

Media interest was most intensely focused on Mohammed who personified both the 9/11 attacks and the CIA torture program; at his 2007 CSRT hearing, he had claimed responsibility for the planning and execution of 9/11 "from A to Z," and it was widely reported that his treatment in the black sites was, relatively speaking, the most abusive—including being waterboarded 183 times. The arraignment hearing was also the occasion for the first delegation of 9/11 victim family members to attend and see for themselves the man who haunted their nightmares.

The judge was Colonel Kohlmann. He began the arraignment by stating that he intended to conduct this session just like the hundreds of other military cases he had presided over. But then he cautioned that the classified nature of materials might make this different from other proceedings. "The United States Government has determined that any statement by any of the accused is presumptively classified . . . A determination has been made that unauthorized release of this information would be harmful to national security." He explained, for the benefit of people in the gallery, that if anyone in the courtroom says something classified, a security specialist would hit the switch to cut off the audio feed.

After opening formalities, Kohlmann turned to the matter of whether the defendants wanted to be represented by the attorneys sitting at their tables. Some of the John Adams Project lawyers were missing because they hadn't received their security clearances yet. Those who were there had only met the defendants they were assigned to represent a day or two earlier. These seasoned death penalty lawyers knew how a capital case is supposed to be litigated, and what happened at Guantánamo that day bore no resemblance to the norms.

Kohlmann's fealty to the Pentagon script put him on a collision course with several of the attorneys who kept trying to ask for a postponement in order to have time to build relationships or advise the defendants about the importance of legal representation in a capital case. He rejected those requests and proceeded with his questions, one defendant at a time.

Mohammed, whom Judge Kohlmann questioned first, set the tone. "I will not accept any attorney. I will represent myself." He said the only law he accepts is Shari'a law and only God can judge him. Then he asked for permission to talk with his codefendants so that they could form a joint front. Kohlmann responded, "I do not believe it's going to be permitted under any of the rules governing these proceedings for you to engage in some sort of joint defense effort with the other accused in this case." Since Mohammed had stated his intention to represent himself, Kohlmann wanted assurance that he understood the implications. He told Mohammed that "if you are found guilty of the charges against you, the commission could ultimately sentence you to death. Do you understand that?" Mohammed responded, "Yes, this is what I wish. I am looking to be martyred for a long time."

Bin Attash, at table two, took the same position: "I don't want anyone to represent me. I will represent myself." Yes, he understood this could mean death. At one point he asked, "If we are executed, will our bodies be buried at Guantanamo or will our bodies be sent back to our countries?" Kohlmann declined to address that issue.

Thomas Durkin, the civilian lawyer assigned to bin al-Shibh, drew Kohlmann's attention to a motion he had submitted two weeks earlier which detailed systemic deficiencies and failure to provide even minimal due process standards for a capital case. "Although we are in Guantanamo," Durkin said, "this is still a US court." Kohlmann told Durkin that the motion had been denied in its entirety and unless he had something new to add, this discussion was over. Durkin responded: "What is new is what has transpired here . . . What is going on in this courtroom is creating an incredible ethical conflict for the lawyers." He added, "I believe what these gentlemen are saying to you is that they don't want to participate in these proceedings. I think they are incorrectly stating that they want to be representing themselves."

Bin al-Shibh disregarded Durkin's concern and emphatically stated that he, too, wanted to represent himself. When Kohlmann asked if he understood that this could mean a death sentence, he said, "I have been seeking martyrdom for five years." He explained that he had volunteered to be one of the 9/11 hijackers, but that hadn't worked out because he was denied a visa to the United States. "If this martyrdom happens today, we welcome it. God is great." But there was a glitch: bin al-Shibh was being treated with drugs for some unnamed mental or psychological condition. When Kohlmann asked about the medication, bin al-Shibh tried to explain that his condition was related to his treatment in the black sites. Kohlmann said this wasn't the time to hear about why he was medicated, just the kind of medication he was taking.

When their turns came, al-Baluchi and al-Hawsawi also stated their intentions to represent themselves. Their military lawyers, Brian Mizer and Jon Jackson, were concerned about how they had arrived at their decisions. Before the hearing, both of these defendants had indicated that they were willing to be represented by their lawyers. They apparently changed their minds after meeting the other defendants in the courtroom lockup. The implication was that they might have been pressured by Mohammed to follow his lead. This possibility of intimidation, which would have to be pursued at a future hearing, as well as bin al-Shibh's questionable mental competency, knocked the government's ambitious trial schedule off track.

Gita Gutierrez attended the arraignment of "the high five," which was how many attorneys described the 9/11 defendants to acknowledge their unique importance in the pantheon of military commission cases. "That was one of the most disturbing Gitmo experiences," she said. "It opened a door of a perspective I had not fully comprehended . . . There was this sophisticated court facility and lots of journalists bunking in Camp Justice tents. On the base there was lots of activity but no sight of the defendants until they were trotted out for the hearing. Meanwhile, 265 other guys in Gitmo were spending another day in solitary for their seventh year of detention." She added, "From now on, Gitmo will be all about the commissions and about twenty-six prisoners" who are slated for prosecution. "No one will even mention the habeas prisoners."

At a press briefing after the arraignment, a reporter asked General Hartmann if defense lawyers would be able to subpoena the CIA. "No," he responded.

After several more hearings over the summer, Judge Kohlmann decided that Mohammed, bin Attash, and al-Baluchi had knowingly made their decisions to represent themselves and could go pro se, but not bin al-Shibh or al-Hawsawi because their competency was an unresolved issue. In September, Kohlmann authorized the five defendants in this group trial to meet and consult with one another without any lawyers present, since three of them didn't have attorneys.

The result of these meetings became clear in December. The defendants sent a note to Colonel Stephen Henley, who had replaced Kohlmann the previous month. They wanted to forgo a trial and were ready to offer full confessions and plead guilty on the condition that they go directly to sentencing. A hearing was held on December 8 to address their offer. Henley didn't know—because the law was unclear—whether he had the authority to accept guilty pleas in lieu of a trial in a capital case. What he did know was that he could not accept pleas from bin al-Shibh and al-Hawsawi because they had not been granted permission to represent themselves. The other three decided to postpone entering their pleas until all five could act in unison. "We want everyone to plead together," Mohammed told the judge. With that, the fast-tracked trial of the century went off the rails.

By the time George W. Bush's term in office ended in January 2009, his "war on terror" record was a shambolic mess. His executive orders and policy decisions about interrogation and detention were attacked by dogged lawyers and their allies, and some didn't survive the war in court. The CIA torture program was an international disgrace and multiple foreign investigations were underway that promised to shed more light on those dark secrets. Over five hundred Guantánamo detainees who once were castigated as the worst of the worst and held incommunicado had been released by the administration without apology or explanation. Those who remained had won habeas corpus rights, thanks to the Supreme Court ruling in *Boumediene,* and when habeas hearings in federal courts commenced in August 2008, the government lost almost all cases. Only three people were convicted in the military commissions—a kangaroo skinner (Hicks), a driver (Hamdan), and a propagandist (al-Bahlul). Spoiler alert: most of those convictions would be nullified when they reached federal court on appeal, because the charges were not actually law of war offenses.

EIGHT

New Battles, Same War

ON JANUARY 20, 2009, as Barack Obama was being inaugurated the forty-fourth president of the United States, defense lawyers who were at Guantánamo formed a conga line and danced past the prosecutors' office trailers chanting "Rule of law!" Major Jon Jackson turned down the invitation to join the celebration. Although he was delighted that Obama had won, he was busy working on a motion for his client, Mustafa al-Hawsawi, one of the defendants in the 9/11 case. A little later, another 9/11 defense lawyer knocked on Jackson's door with news that Obama had announced a 120-day continuance for all military commission cases. Jackson still declined to conga and told his colleague, "There's nothing to celebrate until Guantanamo is closed."

Obama had campaigned on the slogan of "hope and change." He was the candidate of choice for people engaged in the fight against torture because he was a prominent critic of the Bush administration's interrogation and detention policies, and he promised that if he became president, he would put an end to "enhanced interrogation techniques" and restore the rule of law. The day after he took office, President Obama nourished hope for change by signing three executive orders. One terminated the CIA's prerogative to use harsh interrogation techniques and shuttered the black sites, which was hailed as a death knell for torture and forced disappearance. Another order pledged to close Guantánamo within a year. The third order suspended the military commissions. This was less than his rule-of-law-restoration supporters had hoped for—he could have just cancelled the commissions—but no one was in the mood to begrudge the new president the chance to reach that determination a little later. Besides, he had said that his administration would use federal courts to prosecute Guantánamo detainees.

The same day Obama signed those three executive orders, DC District Court judge John Bates invited the new administration's lawyers to notify the court if the government intended to alter its position on *Maqaleh v. Gates.* This was a habeas case for prisoners at the Bagram detention facility in Afghanistan, and one of many war-in-court inheritances the Bush administration bequeathed to the Obama administration.

Until the Supreme Court's *Boumediene v. Bush* decision in June 2008, the Bush administration's positions on Guantánamo and Bagram were essentially the same: Captured foreigners who were classified as unlawful enemy combatants and detained in either facility had no right to access federal courts for habeas or any other purpose. The preponderance of prisoner-related litigation focused on Guantánamo, but some court rulings had implications for Bagram, too. For example, a year after the Pentagon attempted to subvert the Supreme Court's *Rasul v. Bush* decision by establishing Combatant Status Review Tribunals for Guantánamo detainees, it established the Unlawful Enemy Combatant Review Board for Bagram detainees. These procedures, by the Pentagon's own account, were "less robust" than the CSRTs or the review process in Iraq, let alone Article 5 hearings the Geneva Conventions require. Detainees at Bagram had only one opportunity to appear before the review board; they were given no information about allegations against them, not even summaries; they had no option to call witnesses; and the transcripts of hearings were not verbatim.

Each Guantánamo case that the Bush administration lost cut deeper into that facility's utility. This was reflected in the fact that between March 2007 and March 2008, only six new prisoners were transferred in, and they were the last. The scheme to keep the identities of Guantánamo detainees classified didn't survive a Freedom of Information Act lawsuit that the government lost in 2006. By the time Bush left office, 532 detainees had been transferred out and five had died—one of natural causes and the other four of suicide, although the circumstances of three simultaneous deaths in June 2006 aroused suspicion. A guard on duty that night, Sergeant Joe Hickman, observed three prisoners being transported in a van to the CIA black site operating on the base at the time and, sometime later, three bodies were taken to the clinic where it was discovered that rags were stuffed deeply into their throats. The government claimed that they stuffed the rags into their own throats before hanging themselves in their cells simultaneously.

But the Bush administration never lost its taste for secret detention. Defeats in Guantánamo cases transformed Bagram's location in a faraway war zone into an advantage; what had once been a stop, or "collection point" on the way to Guantánamo became a place where the US military could hold people incommunicado indefinitely. Over the span of Bush's two terms, the total prisoner population at Bagram was triple the number ever held at Guantánamo. On September 28, 2006, the US government signed a lease for the Bagram facility with the Afghan government, which could continue "until the US or its successors determine that the premises are no longer required for its use."

The same day the Bagram lease was signed, attorney Tina Monshipour Foster filed the first habeas petition for a Bagram detainee. Fadi Al Maqaleh, a Yemeni who was twenty when he was arrested in Iraq in 2003, was imprisoned at Abu Ghraib before being shipped to Afghanistan and imprisoned in Bagram. Foster was a veteran of the war on court; she learned about Maqaleh from his father while she was in Yemen doing research for her Guantánamo cases. The next day, a petition was filed for Haji Wazir, an Afghan currency trader who was arrested in 2002 in Dubai where he had a shop. He, too, was transported to Afghanistan in order to be detained at Bagram. The two petitions were combined as *Maqaleh v. Rumsfeld*. When Donald Rumsfeld resigned two months later and was replaced by Robert Gates, the case was renamed *Maqaleh v. Gates*.

When Foster established the International Justice Network in 2006, she recruited Barbara Olshansky, with whom she had worked at CCR, to be the legal director. They led the charge to make Bagram a new front in the war in court.

In July 2007, Judge Bates rejected the government's motion to dismiss *Maqaleh* for lack of jurisdiction because, three weeks earlier, the Supreme Court had granted certiorari for *Boumediene*. Bates logically assumed that however the Court might rule in *Boumediene,* it would "likely directly" affect the Bagram petitions.

Boumediene was decided during the 2008 presidential campaign. The majority ruled that people detained at Guantánamo have habeas rights because the United States exercises exclusive control over the base and, therefore, the Constitution applies there. Republican candidate John McCain called it "one of the worst decisions in the history of this country," whereas Obama praised the Supreme Court for taking "an important step toward reestablishing our credibility as a nation committed to the rule of law and rejecting a false choice between fighting terrorism and respecting habeas corpus." The month after *Boumediene* was decided, Foster and Olshansky revised their petitions in an effort to extend that ruling to people detained at Bagram. They were joined by Ramzi Kassem, another veteran of the war in court. Kassem was teaching at Yale at the time, and he brought aboard his colleagues, Hope Metcalf and Michael Wishnie, and their students.

The attorneys submitted two new Bagram petitions. One was for Amin al-Bakri, a Yemeni gem and shrimp trader who disappeared in 2002 while on a business trip to Thailand. A year later, his family received a postcard via the International Committee of the Red Cross (ICRC) informing them that he was in Bagram. Before al-Bakri was transferred to that facility, he was held in a CIA black site for six months. The other petition was for Redha al-Najar, a Tunisian who was arrested at his home in Karachi in 2002. He spent two years in black sites before being transferred to Bagram.

On September 8, 2008, the Justice Department filed a response to al-Bakri's habeas petition with an argument pulled straight out of the Guantánamo playbook pre-*Boumediene.* They insisted that there was no role for federal courts to review, let alone second-guess military decisions in a war zone, and that doing so would infringe on executive power. The fact that al-Bakri was seized in Thailand and not captured on any battlefield was "immaterial." Kassem filed a response motion which highlighted the hypocrisy of the government's claim that the exercise of habeas jurisdiction at Bagram would "thrust" courts into the military's conduct of war when, in fact, it was the government that kidnapped al-Bakri off the peaceful streets of Bangkok and thrust *him* into the war zone.

Judge Bates held a hearing on the jurisdictional motions for *Maqaleh* on January 7, 2009, near the end of President Bush's lame duck period. This was the context for his question two days after Obama took office about whether the new administration intended to alter the government's position.

The answer came on February 20: no change. The government "adheres to its previously articulated position" that Bagram detainees have no habeas rights and federal courts have no jurisdiction. Thus, in his first month as president, Obama adopted one of the most ignominious policies of the Bush administration, which he had derided as a senator and campaigned for president on a promise to end: that people can be secretly detained for years.

Notwithstanding that Bush-like position on Bagram, Obama began his presidency exuding confidence that he could right the wrongs of his predecessor while unifying a deeply divided country. At his first address to a joint session of Congress on February 24, after outlining his administration's plans to deal with the worst economic crisis since the Great Depression, he offered some brief but optimistic comments on the "war on terror," which was then in its seventh year. "To overcome extremism," the president said, "we must . . . be vigilant in upholding the values our troops defend. [L]iving our values doesn't make us weaker, it makes us safer, it makes us stronger. And that is why I can stand here tonight and say without exception or equivocation that the United States of America does not torture."

In order to implement Obama's executive order to close Guantánamo, two inter-agency task forces were created. One was charged to review information about the remaining 242 detainees to decide what course of action to recommend: release, prosecution, or something else. To clear the decks for fresh determinations, in February, charges were withdrawn from all pending military commission cases. The other Guantánamo task force, which was headed by White House counsel Greg Craig, was charged to come up with a plan for how to close the detention facility within the year. The assumption in early 2009 was that shuttering this blighted symbol of injustice would not be controversial. Even Bush and McCain had expressed their support for closure.

But Obama made several decisions early on that would prove fatal to his lofty ambitions to be the Guantánamo-closing, anti-torture president. He appointed Rahm Emanuel as his chief of staff, and he installed John Brennan, deputy director of the CIA, as counterterrorism advisor to the White House. These two influential appointees responded to the partisan backlash that exploded immediately against the new president *not* by using the weight of the White House to support the principles Obama had touted during his campaign, but rather by urging caution and compromise with his critics. Emanuel regarded the expenditure of political capital to press the president's promises to restore the rule of law as a losing cause for Democrats. In his view, nothing should be done about Guantánamo that was unacceptable to Republican senator Lindsey Graham, who favored keeping it open, endorsed the military commissions, and was a fierce opponent of habeas rights for detainees. Brennan used his influence to steer the president away from accountability for those responsible for the torture program or damaging exposure of the CIA's recent inglorious record. Obama's other fatal decision was to retain Robert Gates as defense secretary, despite Gates's opposition to closing Guantánamo.

Former Vice President Dick Cheney took Obama's criticisms of the Bush administration's interrogation policies personally—as well he should. In the weeks and months after the political transition, this famously secretive man became uncharacteristically voluble, putting his Hobbesian sensibilities on full display. In television interviews, he propounded the message that brutal interrogation tactics, which he described as "tough" but not "torture," had produced excellent intelligence, and he admonished Obama for endangering national security by relinquishing methods that "work." In defiance of the public record, including a 2008 Senate Armed Services Committee report, he insisted that "our enhanced interrogation program . . . prevented the violent death of thousands, if not hundreds of thousands, of innocent people." (Cheney recycled the torture-kept-us-safe canard in his autobiography, *In My Time*.) Cheney's media offensive found a receptive audience among right-wing politicians and pundits who amplified his woolly speculations about the efficacy of torture. Senate Republican leader Mitch McConnell chimed in: "We were obviously doing something right."

Cheney was able to peddle fabricated narratives about all the plots uncovered and propagandistic talking points about all the lives saved because, at the time, so much of the truth about the torture program was still a secret. But there were reasons to hope that this might change. On his second day in office, in addition to the three executive orders, Obama had issued a memorandum pledging an unprecedented level of openness. "Transparency promotes accountability and provides information for citizens about what their Government is doing."

In February, the Senate Select Committee on Intelligence (SSCI) announced that it was launching an investigation into the CIA's now-defunct rendition, detention, and interrogation (RDI) program. The objective, as SSCI chair Dianne Feinstein explained, was to learn "how the CIA created, operated, and maintained its detention and interrogation program" and to make "an evaluation of intelligence information gained through the use of enhanced and standard interrogation techniques."

When CIA director Leon Panetta pledged to cooperate with the SSCI investigation, he was lambasted by Emanuel. As Panetta recounts in his autobiography, *Worthy Fights,* "I was summoned to a meeting in the Situation Room, where I was told I would have to 'explain' this deal to Rahm . . . 'The president wants to know who the f**k authorized this to the committees,' Rahm said, slamming his hand down on the table. 'I have a president with his hair on fire and I want to know what the f**k you did to f**k this up so bad.'" It was a telling sign of what was to become the Obama White House's position on the Senate investigation.

Abroad, the Obama administration got no honeymoon-period reprieve from the mounting costs and consequences of the US torture program. In

2008, Poland became the first country to begin a criminal investigation into the role its own security agents played in the CIA's clandestine operations in that country. Polish prosecutors began looking into allegations that three high value detainees—'Abd al-Rahim al-Nashiri, Abu Zubaydah, and Walid bin Attash—had been tortured in the CIA black site on Polish territory. In Spain, human rights attorney Gonzalo Boye filed a criminal complaint in March 2009 against six Bush administration lawyers—Alberto Gonzales, David Addington, William Haynes, John Yoo, Jay Bybee, and Douglas Feith—who bore responsibility for providing legalistic rationales for torture. Boye had worked with Spanish judge Baltasar Garzón and international lawyer Phillipe Sands on the 1998 universal jurisdiction case against Augusto Pinochet in the United Kingdom. Boye told the *New Yorker*'s Jane Mayer that Sands's 2008 book, *Torture Team: Rumsfeld's Memo and the Betrayal of American Values,* "showed me who the targets were." Sands, who supported the Spanish complaint, told Mayer, "If not for lawyers, none of these abuses would have ever occurred."

Two weeks after the Bush Six complaint was filed, a Spanish investigation into allegations of torture at Guantánamo was launched, and two months after that, prosecutors requested arrest warrants for thirteen CIA agents who had transited through Spain with forged documents on their way to Macedonia to kidnap Khaled El Masri.

In July 2009, El Masri submitted a complaint to the European Court of Human Rights (ECHR) against the government of Macedonia for its role in his abduction by the CIA and rendition to torture. In 2012, the ECHR ruled in El Masri's favor, ordering Macedonia to pay him compensation of sixty thousand euros. This was the first in a series of ECHR rulings against European countries whose security agencies colluded with the CIA and allowed black sites on their territory.

In the United Kingdom, soon after Binyam Mohamed was repatriated from Guantánamo in February 2009, public disclosures about his treatment and British security services' complicity sparked intense political controversy. Prosecutors began a criminal investigation into British involvement with CIA torture and extraordinary rendition. Mohamed and six other British torture victims—Moazzam Begg, Omar Deghayes, Bisher Al-Rawi, Jamil el-Banna, Richard Belmar, and Martin Mubanga—brought a civil lawsuit against five British agencies, including MI5 and MI6. Clive Stafford Smith, who represented some of the victims, gained access to forty-two documents that the United States had turned over to the United Kingdom. He said,

"Those documents are literally confessions to the crime of torture by interrogators." When Stafford Smith and the victims' other attorneys moved to enter these documents into evidence, the Obama administration responded, as the Bush administration would have, with a diplomatic stick, threatening to interrupt bilateral counterterrorism cooperation if classified information were exposed in the context of this lawsuit. This led the High Court to dismiss the case "in the interest of national security." But on appeal, the Court reversed that decision and ordered the documents to be made available, reasoning that allegations of wrongdoing must be heard in public. To avoid embarrassing disclosures in court, Prime Minister David Cameron authorized negotiations for a monetary settlement. He explained, "Our services are paralyzed by paperwork as they try to defend themselves in lengthy court cases with uncertain rules. Our reputation as a country that believes in human rights, justice, fairness and the rule of law—indeed, much of what the services exist to protect—risks being tarnished." In November 2010, the British government announced that it would pay an undisclosed amount (estimated to be between thirty and fifty million pounds) in compensation to fifteen former detainees plus Shaker Aamer, a British resident who was still imprisoned at Guantánamo. According to the terms of the settlement, the British government did not admit liability and the claimants did not retract their allegations of torture.

On the home front, the Obama administration's consuming priorities were economic recovery and the president's signature goal to reform the nation's health-care system. This left the field wide open for pro-torture voices to dominate media coverage of interrogation policy past and present. Cheney's relentless media offensive pushed Obama on his heels. The president strived to salve political tempers by saying that "we need to look forward as opposed to looking backward." Obama's conciliatory efforts included repeatedly stating that Bush administration officials who responded to terrorist threats by authorizing violent and degrading interrogation tactics, kidnapping, and forced disappearance, and those who had followed orders had acted in "good faith."

Obama's decision to excuse torture in this manner was a 180-degree turn from his preinaugural statements that "no one is above the law." That good-faith claim prompted lots of angry emails on the torturelist, so I knew I was not alone in wondering how Obama, or for that matter *anyone*, could think that a "reasonable person"—the legal subject of the good faith standard—believed at the time that the violent interrogation tactics authorized by the

Bush administration were not flagrantly illegal. By taking the position that the order-givers and the order-followers had acted in good faith, Obama was propagating the idea that their minds were such *tabulae rasae* that they had no prior knowledge or real-world sense of what constitutes torture. Anyone with the actual capacity to reason could have made the connection between interrogation techniques that were derived from the SERE program and the fact that the SERE program was created to train US forces to withstand *torture* if they were captured by a regime that disregarded the Geneva Conventions. Moreover, the kinds of treatment authorized by the Bush administration were banned by the Army Field Manual in effect in 2001. (The Manual was revised in 2006 to be more explicit about prohibited practices.)

Initially, Obama administration officials imagined that it was possible to reconcile unaccountability for state crimes with a new era of transparency in fulfillment of the president's pledge of greater openness. In March 2009, the Justice Department decided to declassify and release more Office of Legal Counsel (OLC) memos produced between 2002 and 2005 which described in detail tactics approved for use by the CIA. When Michael Hayden, the last CIA director under Bush, learned that these shameful memos were about to become public, he rallied other former CIA directors to lobby the White House to keep them classified. Brennan was their inside man. After entertaining a debate among his cabinet, Obama decided to release the memos but, to ameliorate CIA anxieties, he promised not to criminally investigate anyone except possibly those individuals who had engaged in practices that were not officially sanctioned.

When the OLC memos were released on April 16, Obama issued a public statement in which he hitched unaccountability for gross crimes to the creed of American exceptionalism: "[N]othing will be gained by spending our time and energy laying blame for the past. Our national greatness is embedded in America's ability to right its course in concert with our core values, and to move forward with confidence." Without apparent irony, he ended his statement: "The United States is a nation of laws."

These OLC memos, like those that had become public years earlier, described violent, cruel and degrading interrogation techniques in bland, obfuscating language: "removal of clothing," "stress positions," "dietary manipulation," "environmental manipulation," "sleep adjustment," "isolation," "use of noise to induce stress." On April 9, 2009, Mark Danner, a journalist-scholar who was one of the most outspoken critics of US torture, put these phrases into their flesh-and-blood context when he published a leaked ICRC report in the *New York Review of Books,* along with his analysis of its significance.

The leaked ICRC report was an account of visits representatives had made to Guantánamo in October and December 2006 to interview the fourteen detainees who had been transferred from CIA black sites in September. The report's publication provided the first opportunity for the public to read accounts from men who had been disappeared for years and who, for all intents and purposes, continued to be hermetically sealed up at Guantánamo to ensure that what was done to them remained a secret. One of the voices in the ICRC report is that of Abu Zubaydah, the first person detained by the CIA and the guinea pig for their torture program. He describes one of his eighty-three experiences of being waterboarded:

> I was then dragged from the small box, unable to walk properly and put on what looked like a hospital bed and strapped down very tightly with belts. A black cloth was then placed over my face and the interrogators used a mineral water bottle to pour water on the cloth so that I could not breathe. After a few minutes the cloth was removed and the bed was rotated into an upright position. The pressure of the straps on my wounds was very painful. I vomited. The bed was then again lowered to horizontal position and the same torture carried out again with the black cloth over my face and water poured on from a bottle. On this occasion my head was in a more backward, downwards position and the water was poured on for a longer time. I struggled against the straps, trying to breathe, but it was hopeless. I thought I was going to die. I lost control of my urine. Since then I still lose control of my urine when under stress.

The ICRC report contained first-person details from other detainees: "I collapsed," "I was not given any solid food," "I was naked," "The room was always cold."

Good faith?

That first spring of Obama's tenure as president was a season of increasingly hostile skirmishes across the political landscape, and debates about torture were in the thick of it. The ACLU was calling for criminal investigations with prosecution as a possibility. Human Rights Watch and Human Rights First were reporting new details about what former officials did to facilitate and abet torture. Democratic Representative John Conyers introduced legislation to create a commission, modeled on the 9/11 Commission, to investigate the Bush administration's prisoner policies. Democratic

Senator Patrick Leahy suggested the establishment of a bipartisan truth commission. "Rather than vengeance," Leahy explained, "we need a fair-minded pursuit of what actually happened. Sometimes the best way to move forward is getting to the truth, finding out what happened, so we can make sure it does not happen again." But without White House support for any of these accountability options, none gained traction among Democrats.

Republican politicians may have appreciated the president's charitable willingness to turn a blind eye to Bush administration crimes, but they regarded efforts to close Guantánamo as a weakness to be exploited for partisan gain. They found an ideal opportunity on April 24 when word leaked that Greg Craig's Guantánamo task force was planning to bring two Chinese Uighurs into the country for resettlement.

In the process of figuring out where to transfer detainees who were cleared for release, Craig's task force, working in collaboration with the State Department, realized that it would be easier to persuade other countries to accept some detainees if the United States did so too. Guantánamo was a problem the United States had created, after all, so why shouldn't it be part of the solution? Uighurs were regarded as ideal candidates for resettlement in the United States; they couldn't be repatriated to their homeland because China would imprison them as ethnic dissidents, and even the Bush administration had acknowledged that they were swept up by mistake in Afghanistan and posed no threat to US security. But in 2008, when Judge Ricardo Urbina granted seventeen Uighur detainees their writ of habeas corpus and ordered that all of them be resettled in the United States, the Bush administration appealed and the DC Circuit Court overturned Urbina's order on the grounds that courts don't have the authority to force the government to admit anyone into the country.

After the leak of the Craig team's plan to settle two detainees in a community of immigrant Uighurs in a suburb in Northern Virginia, critics went apoplectic. For three weeks, Mitch McConnell assailed the administration on a nearly daily basis for wanting to bring terrorists into the country, which resonated with those whose view of Guantánamo detainees was tinted a dull monochromatic shade of "worst of the worst." Emanuel, already at odds with Craig, made sure that the White House mounted no defense of the task force's plans.

On May 21, like duelers facing off to defend their honor and, in the process, lay low their rival, Obama and Cheney took to podiums to give speeches on national security. Obama chose the National Archives as his setting. He started his speech by rebutting the torture-works contentions that the former vice president and other historic revisionists were pushing: "I know some have argued that brutal methods like waterboarding were necessary to keep us safe. I could not disagree more. As Commander-in-Chief, I see the intelligence. I bear the responsibility for keeping this country safe. And I categorically reject the assertion that these are the most effective means of interrogation." He listed the adverse effects of the torture policy: they undermined the rule of law; they served as a recruitment tool for terrorists; and they decreased the will of allies to work with the United States. Most pointedly, he said, "They risk the lives of our troops by making it less likely that others will surrender to them in battle, and more likely that Americans will be mistreated if they are captured. In short, they did not advance our war and counterterrorism efforts—they undermined them, and that is why I ended them once and for all."

Obama was blunt about the complicated problems he inherited from the previous administration. "In dealing with this situation, we don't have the luxury of starting from scratch. We're cleaning up something that is, quite simply, a mess—a misguided experiment that has left in its wake a flood of legal challenges that my administration is forced to deal with on a constant, almost daily basis, and it consumes the time of government officials whose time should be spent on better protecting our country."

As Obama was delivering his speech, people on the torturelist were emailing running commentary with their reactions. I was heartened by the clarity of Obama's criticisms but, given the backpedaling on his promises over the previous three-and-a-half months, I was skeptical that he had the political wherewithal to dismantle the policies that he had criticized so harshly before he moved to the White House. The moment of truth came when Obama presented his plans for Guantánamo. Drawing on the recommendations of the detainee review task force, he explained that there were five categories and courses of action: First, those who violated federal terrorism laws would be prosecuted in federal courts. So far so good, I thought. Second, those who committed war crimes would be prosecuted in the military commissions. What? Obama tried to present this as something other than a surrender to expediency: "Instead of using the flawed commissions of the last seven years, my administration is bringing our commissions in line with the rule of law." He claimed that the planned reforms "will make our military commissions a more credible and effective means of administering justice."

The third and fourth categories Obama identified were, respectively, people who can be released because they have been cleared and deemed no longer threatening, and those who should be transferred to their own or another country for continuing confinement or surveillance to prevent them from posing a future risk to US security. The fifth category were those whom Obama termed "the toughest problem": "people who cannot be prosecuted yet who pose a clear danger to the American people." What he prescribed for this category was a full-body embrace of the Bush-era policy of indefinite detention without trial. (Several months later, the administration decided to emulate its predecessor's position by claiming that Congress had endorsed indefinite detention when it passed the Authorization for Use of Military Force in the aftermath of 9/11. This policy choice was further confirmed in the 2010 National Security Strategy.)

From a podium at the American Enterprise Institute (AEI), Cheney delivered his speech. He reiterated his pro-torture talking points. Then he lashed out at Obama's decision to release the OLC memos that cast the CIA program in a bad light while failing to release two other classified documents that, Cheney claimed, prove the efficacy of CIA interrogations. "For reasons the administration has yet to explain, they believe the public has a right to know the method of the questions, but not the content of the answers. Over on the left wing of the president's party, there appears to be little curiosity in finding out what was learned from the terrorists."

A week later, Democratic Senator Carl Levin delivered a speech to the Foreign Policy Association to rebut "Cheney's world view, which so dominated the Bush years and dishonored our nation . . . I do so because if the abusive interrogation techniques that he champions, the face of which were the pictures of abuse at Abu Ghraib, . . . are once more seen as representative of America, our security will be severely set back." Levin explained that the Senate Armed Services Committee, which he chaired, had examined the two documents Cheney had referred to in his AEI speech, which "gives the lie to Mr. Cheney's claims." They "say nothing about numbers of lives saved, nor do the documents connect acquisition of valuable intelligence to the use of abusive techniques. I hope that the documents are declassified, so that people can judge for themselves what is fact, and what is fiction."

But in the halls of Congress, politicians from both parties decided or conceded that maintaining the status quo was the best strategy and support for the closure of Guantánamo vanished like a mirage. By the end of May, Congress passed bipartisan legislation to prohibit any detainees from being resettled in the United States. In an interview with the *New Yorker*, Elisa Massimino, executive director of Human Rights First, offered an explanation: "It was Obama's lack of nerve to do what was politically difficult that created space for all the mischief that Congress made."

In order to accommodate Obama's decision to reform the military commissions for continued use, Congress passed a modestly revised Military Commission Act in October. The 2009 version did tighten up the evidentiary rules to prohibit the use of coerced statements, and it allocated government funding for learned counsel (lawyers with death penalty experience) to defend people facing capital charges. But it left intact the ex post facto immunity for war crimes from the 2006 version, as well as all the made-up law of war violations conceived during the Bush years. The Obama administration's contribution was to give these made-up violations the oxymoronic label "domestic humanitarian law."

November 13, 2009, was the eight-year anniversary of Bush's military order enshrining the new paradigm as government policy for people captured the "war on terror." It was also the day Greg Craig's imminent departure was announced, which was read by people eager to see progress on the closure of Guantánamo as a sign that the White House was dialing back those efforts. And it was the occasion for Attorney General Eric Holder to present details of the Obama administration's plans. At a press conference, Holder announced that ten detainees had been designated for immediate prosecution. The five men accused of playing roles in 9/11 would be prosecuted in federal court in the Southern District of New York. "After eight years of delay," Holder said, "those allegedly responsible for the attacks of September 11th will finally face justice. They will be brought to New York—*New York*," he emphasized, "to answer [for] their alleged crimes in a courthouse just blocks away from where the Twin Towers once stood." Five others would be prosecuted in the military commissions. The only name in this category that Holder mentioned during his speech was 'Abd al-Rahim al-Nashiri who was accused of being behind the 2000 bombing of the USS Cole off the coast of Aden.

During the question-and-answer session that followed, Holder identified another person who was slated for a military commission trial: Omar Khadr. He explained that Khadr was in this queue because he was accused of "an attack on one of our soldiers." Why, a journalist asked, is it necessary to use two different legal systems to prosecute Guantánamo detainees? Holder responded that decisions about how each case would be handled were based on Pentagon and Justice Department protocols, including the nature and location of the offense, the identity of the victims, and how the offense was investigated. "Just as a sustained campaign against terrorism requires a combination of intelligence, law enforcement, and military operations," he said, "so must our legal efforts to bring terrorists to justice involve both federal courts and reformed military commissions."

Another journalist asked Holder the obvious question: "Inevitably, defense lawyers are going to seek full disclosure about the circumstances of how these detainees were treated while they were in US custody . . . What is the [Justice Department's] position going to be on whether the defense will be entitled to know the full story of how these detainees were treated?" Holder was navigating a tightrope strung between the indisputable realities that everyone the Obama administration planned to prosecute had been violently abused for years and the aspirational goal that their trials would appear fair. He replied: "I don't know what the defense will try to do . . . But I'm quite confident, on the basis of the evidence, that we will be . . . successful in our attempts to convict those men."

Holder's announcement that the 9/11 "high five" would be moved from Guantánamo to New York for trial presented another opportunity for right-wing critics to assert that Obama was being "soft on terrorism." New York City and State officials' support for this trial collapsed and, once again, the White House didn't even bother trying to defend the administration's own plan. The following year, Congress closed the door on federal trials by passing legislation barring the use of funds to try Guantánamo detainees within the United States, which left military commissions as the only option.

The recurring national debate about torture resumed on Christmas Day 2009 when a Nigerian named Umar Farouk Abdulmutallab attempted to detonate an explosive device in his underwear while traveling on a transatlantic flight bound for Detroit. The pro-torture lobby excoriated Holder for allowing Abdulmutallab to be read his Miranda rights, and for not subjecting him to "enhanced" interrogation or shipping him off to Guantánamo, despite the fact that the Bush administration had followed an identical course of action with Richard Reid, who had attempted to detonate a bomb in his shoe. FBI interrogators, using conventional methods to question Abdulmutallab, learned that his actions could be traced to al-Qaeda in the Arabian Peninsula, particularly an influential US-born cleric named Anwar al-Awlaki. Because of this revelation, Obama decided to freeze the release and repatriation of cleared Yemeni detainees, thus adding eighty-six more to the category of "forever prisoners."

By the end of Obama's first year in office, any halcyon dreams that he would restore the rule of law had dissipated. He chose to own the legal mess he had inherited. He resurrected the military commissions, authorized indefinite detention without trial for dozens of prisoners, and endorsed the position that people at Bagram could remain in secret detention indefinitely, which earned that facility the nickname "Obama's Guantánamo." Of course, now the original Guantánamo was his, too.

At least Obama ended torture, right? In November 2009, the media began reporting ICRC concerns about continuing prisoner abuse in Afghanistan. In April 2010, the BBC published testimonies of nine prisoners who said they had been subjected to beatings, sexual humiliation, sleep deprivation, and other violent and degrading tactics at a facility on the Bagram airbase called "Tor jail," which translates in Pashtu as the "black jail." On May 11, the ICRC confirmed that its representatives were denied access to this secret prison. In October, the Open Society Foundation (OSF) published an investigative report into these allegations of torture in Tor jail; nine of the twenty released detainees who were interviewed by OSF had been imprisoned there in the period since Obama took office. This black site–like facility was run not by the CIA but by the Defense Intelligence Agency and the Joint Special Operations Command (JSOC) whose agents were authorized to use interrogation methods detailed in the classified Appendix M to the 2006 Army Field Manual. These tactics, which were otherwise expunged from US interrogators' playbook, are designed to induce debility, disorientation, and dread. Credible allegations also emerged that JSOC units were abusing captives held at undisclosed forward operating bases across Afghanistan.

Pentagon officials initially denied the existence of a secret detention facility at Bagram. As the evidence accreted and literal denial was no longer sustainable, the administration shifted to euphemistic denial, asserting that Tor jail is an "interrogation facility," not a "detention site," and therefore, the ICRC had no right to meet anyone held there.

If Obama had put up a good fight to achieve his policy-changing promises but failed because of insurmountable opposition in Congress, or because of institutional stasis molded to the Bush administration's new paradigm, his rule-of-law-restoration supporters might have given him credit for trying. But he chose the politically expedient path of conciliation, which his administration littered with excuses and the debris of abandoned principles. Even this might have been tolerated as the price of doing business in Washington were it not for his attempted sleight of hand in claiming that his administration's prisoner policies, many of which were rebooted and upgraded versions of Bush policies that he once had opposed, were somehow qualitatively different and better because they were his.

This was well illustrated in the Obama administration's position on the war in court. Whenever a Guantánamo detainee won his habeas case in the DC District Court, the Justice Department appealed, and every win was overturned by the DC Circuit Court, which would brook no court-ordered release of anyone. The appeals court provided "guidance" for the lower court to accept as presumptively accurate even the most shoddy or implausible government evidence. Thus, the habeas rights Guantánamo detainees had won in the last year of the Bush era were snuffed out by a de facto collusion between the Obama administration's appeals machinery and judges on the DC Circuit who fundamentally disagreed with *Boumediene*.

For example, when Mohamedou Ould Slahi's habeas petition was argued in 2009 before Judge James Robertson, he testified from Guantánamo by video link. Judge Robertson found ample evidence that Slahi had been badly abused, and that government evidence to support his continued detention was thin and riddled with implausible assertions. Robertson ordered Slahi's immediate release. The Obama administration, true to form, appealed the decision. Jonathan Hafetz, one of Slahi's habeas counsel, described this move as "a national disgrace." "Regrettably," Hafetz told a journalist, "rather than ending this shameful episode that flouts the rule of law, and repatriating Slahi, the government is seeking to prolong his illegal imprisonment." The DC Circuit Court vacated Robertson's decision to release Slahi.

Meanwhile, Nancy Hollander, another of Slahi's lawyers, decided to build a case for his release in the court of public opinion. With his permission, she moved to have his letters detailing his experiences in US custody declassified. It took seven years of litigating and negotiating with the government to get them cleared. When they were, Hollander recruited Larry Siems, an editor and director of PEN USA's Freedom to Write Program, to compile the letters into a book. *Guantánamo Diary* was published in 2015 with all the government redactions appearing as blacked-out passages, including the entirety of one of Slahi's poems and the female pronouns he used to describe interrogators who had sexually abused him. Siems was able to supply readers with some of the redacted information in footnotes. Slahi's was the fifth autobiography by a Guantánamo prisoner, but the only one to be published while the author was still incarcerated. *Guantánamo Diary* became an instant best seller and received wide media coverage in the United States and abroad. Hollander's bet that it could benefit him, eventually, was vindicated. On

October 17, 2016, almost seven years after Judge Robertson ordered his release, and almost fifteen years since he was taken into US custody, Slahi was repatriated to Mauritania. But the four other book manuscripts he had written while incarcerated didn't get to go with him. Slahi and Siems worked together to un-redact his book, which was published in 2017 as *Guantánamo Diary, Restored Edition.* (Slahi's story was brought to the silver screen in 2021 in a film directed by Kevin Macdonald titled *The Mauritanian.* When the film was released, Slahi told me he couldn't bring himself to watch the scenes in which Tahar Rahim, the actor who plays him, enacted his torture. Jodie Foster won a Golden Globe for her portrayal of Hollander.)

There was no sunlight between the Bush administration's and the Obama administration's overly broad (and previously unprecedented) use of state secrets to shut down civil lawsuits by torture victims. This was vividly demonstrated when Maher Arar's attorneys petitioned the Supreme Court over the dismissal of his lawsuit against former Attorney General John Ashcroft and other officials who had authorized his secret transfer to Syria in 2002. The government's motion urging the Court to deny certiorari for *Arar v. Ashcroft* was authored by Neal Katyal, who had fought the Bush administration and won the landmark case, *Hamdan v. Rumsfeld.* Now, in the role of acting solicitor general for the Obama Justice Department, Katyal made the case for unaccountability. He plumped his motion with obligatory pieties that the United States does not countenance torture—although, of course, this wasn't true when Arar was rendered to Syria to be tortured. Katyal followed the worn path of his Bush administration predecessors to argue that government wrongdoing is irrelevant—technically, "nonjusticiable"—by arguing that if the Supreme Court took the case, justices would have to "review sensitive intergovernmental communications, second-guess whether Syrian officials were credible enough for United States officials to rely on them, and assess the credibility of any information provided by foreign officials concerning petitioner's likely treatment in Syria, as well as the motives and sincerity of United States officials who concluded that the petitioner could be removed to Syria." The Obama administration prevailed when Arar's petition was rejected with a twenty-two-word statement, foreclosing forever any prospect that he could obtain justice in a US court.

The Obama administration's approach to the problem of torture could be summed up as follows: torture is bad, but holding US violators to account or providing justice for victims is worse. The intentionality and amount of energy that went into justifying the failure to deal with torture as a crime was a legacy-defining aspect of Obama's first term.

No amount of flowery rhetoric about the virtues of looking forward, not backward could negate the fact that laws on the books prohibiting and criminalizing torture set standards against which reality can be judged. As it sunk in that Obama was not going to turn the national page, the mood among people engaged in the war in court, who had once been hopeful and optimistic, turned to disappointment and angry determination to keep fighting. Clive Stafford Smith put the collective ethos succinctly: "Law is about figuring out how to bring about a change in the exercise of power."

Since the war in court had taken off in 2004, lawyers and their allies had gained increasing awareness about the dehumanizing, politically toxic, national security–compromising, lie-generating effects of torture. Their fight-must-go-on spirit during the Obama years reminded me of a quote by French social theorist Michel Foucault, which makes a virtue of pessimism: "My point is not that everything is bad, but that everything is dangerous, which is not exactly the same as bad. If everything is dangerous, then we always have something to do. So my position leads not to apathy but to a hyper- and pessimistic activism. I think that the ethico-political choice we have to make every day is to determine which is the main danger."

For those whose lodestar was justice and the rule of law, there was no shortage of main dangers.

The Obama administration made targeted killing the strategic centerpiece of the "war on terror." The strategic appeal of capture and detention had dissipated even before he took office, because the exposure of the torture policy had negative ramifications for the government. One political benefit of killing rather than arresting and detaining suspected enemies was that it deprived the clamorous pro-torture lobby of opportunities to land their demands to resurrect "enhanced interrogation techniques." In carrying out the policy to extrajudicially execute terror suspects, the Obama administration relied on the same unitary executive logic that the Bush administration had relied on to disappear and torture people, and both administrations marketed the same hubristic assertions that US intelligence about who is an enemy was flawless.

Although Bush inaugurated targeted killing in 2002 when he ordered an armed drone operation to eliminate a suspected al-Qaeda member in Yemen, the number of strikes per month escalated dramatically after Obama took office, and the geographic scope soon extended to countries in East and

North Africa. In May 2012, the *New York Times* and the *Daily Beast* published major investigations about how the Obama administration's kill policy was carried out. At a weekly event that insiders termed "Terror Tuesday," the *Times* reported, "more than 100 members of the government's sprawling national security apparatus gather, by secure video teleconference, to pore over terrorist suspects' biographies and recommend to the president who should be the next to die." The most grievous revelation was how the administration contrived its claim of low ("single-digit") civilian casualties, especially in "signature strikes" which target "groups of men who bear certain signatures, or defining characteristics associated with terrorist activity, but whose identities aren't known." According to unnamed officials, all "military-age males" (anyone sixteen and older) killed in drone strikes are counted as combatants "unless there is explicit intelligence posthumously proving them innocent." This assertion that any male who is killed is a terrorist or militant (unless posthumously cleared), and that the killing itself, even if done by an unmanned drone, is a military engagement was clearly reflected in the term used to describe casualties as "enemy killed in action." It was boilerplate new paradigm to assert that the president had unreviewable rights to authorize whatever violence he wanted to apply in the name of national security.

Contrary to Obama's pledge of greater transparency, everything about the kill policy was classified, including the criteria for being selected to die, and intelligence on the imminence of the threat targeted individuals ostensibly posed. To make this policy appear "legal," OLC lawyers reinterpreted the meaning of imminence to liberate the government from the requirement that lethality is a last option; according to a document leaked to NBC in 2013: "The condition that an operational leader present an 'imminent' threat of violent attack against the United States does not require the United States to have clear evidence that a specific attack on US persons and interests will take place in the immediate future."

Another Obama administration innovation was to place unindicted citizens on the kill list. The OLC attorney who coauthored a secret memo to support this policy was Marty Lederman, who had been such a prominent and effective critic of the Bush administration's OLC torture memos. On September 30, 2011, a joint CIA-JSOC drone operation targeted and killed Anwar al-Awlaki. This was the first government-authorized extrajudicial execution of a citizen since the Civil War. Another US citizen, Samir Khan, and two non-Americans were also killed in the strike. Obama made a public statement afterward that the attack had dealt a "major blow" to al-Qaeda. On October 14, another drone strike killed al-Awlaki's sixteen-year-old son, 'Abd al-Rahman, his seventeen-year-old cousin, and five others while they were dining outdoors. Officials tried to legitimize that killing by claiming that 'Abd al-Rahman was a twenty-one-year-old militant. His grandfather produced the boy's birth certificate, proving the lie, at which point the administration reverted to its default position that everything about drone operations is classified and cannot be commented upon.

The targeted killing policy became the focus of a handful of lawsuits. But these cases never got the traction that cases pertaining to torture and unlawful detention did. Torture is a clear violation of law and offenses can be traced to actions and policy decisions by specific individuals. Drone strikes, in contrast, can be framed as military operations that courts are loath to adjudicate, and responsibility for the process of killing is diffused. Consequently, in each of the few cases challenging this policy or seeking justice for victims, courts granted the government's request to dismiss them, thus leaving unaddressed the question of whether targeted killing is legal. The one area where there was some minor success was FOIA litigation, led by the ACLU, which eventually pried loose some documentation about drone warfare, including the OLC memo endorsing the execution of al-Awlaki.

Another main danger for people whose lodestar was the rule of law was the Obama administration's punitive response to whistleblowers who leaked information about crimes of state. The unauthorized disclosure of classified information is a criminal offense, but so are war crimes and torture. The only CIA agent who was prosecuted for something relating to torture was John Kiriakou. He had been present when Abu Zubaydah was captured and transferred to the first black site in March 2002, and he was privy to information about the torture program that ensued, although he was not involved in interrogations. Kiriakou retired from the CIA in 2004. In 2007, he did an interview with Brian Ross of ABC News in which he was the first to confirm that the CIA used waterboarding as one of its techniques. The Bush administration, whose dirty secret Kiriakou had spilled, didn't prosecute him. The Obama administration did.

Kiriakou was indicted in January 2012, and a year later, he was convicted and sentenced to two-and-a-half years in prison. "I've never believed my case was about a leak," Kiriakou told a reporter from *Vice* after his sentencing. "I've always believed my case was about torture." His attorney, Jesselyn Radack, who was also a whistleblower, told *Vice,* "The people who ordered the torture, the lawyers who justified it, the people who carried it out, and those who destroyed the videotapes of it—none of them are being held accountable. The only person going to jail . . . is the person who blew the whistle on it. In fact, if John had actually tortured someone, I don't think he would be going to jail."

Wikileaks, an anti-secrecy organization established in 2007, became a major repository for leaks exposing crimes and misdeeds of states around the world. In 2008, the US Army Counterintelligence office characterized Wikileaks as an enemy organization. In their report—which Wikileaks obtained and published—one example of the organization's dangerousness was its posting of a leaked manual for Guantánamo interrogations, which became the "subject of a lawsuit by international human rights groups and a domestic civil rights organization requesting the release of the document under the US Freedom of Information Act."

On April 10, 2010, Wikileaks released a classified military video under the title "Collateral Murder." This was the first leaked item in what would become the largest breach of classified material in US history to date. (It was exceeded by a far larger breach in 2013.) The video was shot on July 12, 2007, from an Apache helicopter during an aerial assault in Baghdad. The audio includes voices from a remote command center urging the gunners to shoot everyone in the vicinity. When the assault ended, eleven people were dead, including a Reuters photographer, his driver, and a man who had stopped his van during the attack to try to rescue one of the wounded. The audio captures someone laughing when an armored vehicle ran over one of the corpses. When soldiers arrived on the scene and discovered two badly wounded children in the Good Samaritan's van, one soldier can be heard saying: "Well, it's their fault bringing their kids to a battle."

The video debunked the Pentagon's explanation that the people on the ground had initiated the attack: only one of the men mulling in the street had a gun slung from his shoulder, and what was believed to be a grenade launcher was actually the photographer's telephoto lens.

After "Collateral Murder" went viral, a military intelligence analyst at a forward operating base in Iraq, Private Chelsea Manning, revealed herself to be the source of the leak to someone she met online named Adrian Lamo. (At the time, Manning was going by her given name, Bradley.) Manning told Lamo why she leaked the video: "I want people to see the truth . . . regardless of who they are . . . because without information, you cannot make informed decisions as a public." Manning tipped her hand to Lamo that she had leaked other materials as well, and for the same reason: "if you had free reign over classified networks for long periods of time . . . and you saw incredible things, awful things . . . things that belonged in the public domain, and not on some server stored in a dark room in Washington DC . . . what would you do?"

Lamo reported these chats to the FBI. On May 27, 2010, Manning was arrested and incarcerated at a US base in Kuwait before being transferred to the Marine brig at Quantico. She was held in solitary confinement for eight months, during which her treatment included forced nudity and sensory overload. Juan Mendez, the UN Special Rapporteur on Torture, investigated the conditions of Manning's detention and reported that it constituted cruel, inhuman, and degrading treatment, and possibly torture.

On November 28, Wikileaks released a trove of more than 250,000 State Department diplomatic cables that Manning had leaked. That day, I published an article about the significance of one of these cables, dated February 6, 2007, from the US embassy in Berlin to the State Department, which revealed previously unreported details about the Bush administration's pressure on the German government to prevent its prosecutors from pursuing a criminal case against the US officials responsible for German citizen Khaled El Masri's kidnapping and torture. I published my piece, which incorporated some direct quotes from the leaked cable, in the e-zine *Jadaliyya.* Then I pasted the article into the body of a message and emailed it to the torturelist. What I hadn't known (because I don't work for the federal government) was that government employees are not allowed to see classified material for which they don't have clearance, and these cables, despite that they were now in the public domain, retained their classified status. Several people on the list who were working for the government and opened my email had to submit their computers or cell phones for a scrubbing to remove all traces of the cable. This was nothing compared to the lengths the government had to go to prevent employees from reading the cables that were published in major newspapers. For example, on military bases, access to the *New York Times,* the *Washington Post,* the *Guardian,* and other major newspapers that were publishing the cables was blocked while they were headline news.

The cache of diplomatic cables included three from the US embassy in Madrid to the State Department, dated April 1, April 17, and May 5, 2009, which exposed the Obama administration's efforts to thwart the Spanish criminal investigation of the six Bush administration lawyers. The April 1 cable reports that the Spanish organization that filed the complaint "is attempting to have the case heard by Investigating Judge Baltasar Garzón, internationally known for his dogged pursuit of 'universal jurisdiction' cases." Chief Prosecutor Javier Zaragoza assured US embassy officials that he would try to get the case assigned to another judge, and was quoted saying, "Garzón's impartiality was very suspect, given his public criticism of Guantánamo and the US war on terror . . . and his August 2008 public statements that former President Bush should be tried for war crimes." Zargoza advised the US officials that the one sure way that Spain could dismiss the Bush Six case would be for the United States to open its own credible investigation of the accused.

According to the April 17 cable, the Obama administration dispatched two Republican senators, Mel Martinez and Judd Gregg, to lobby Spanish officials to dispose of this complaint. Their mission was to underscore "that the prosecutions would not be understood or accepted in the US and would have an enormous impact on the bilateral relationship." This pressure appeared tentatively successful when Spain's attorney general, Cándido Conde-Pumpido, denounced the criminal complaint as "fraudulent" and "a political statement to attack past USG [US government] policies." Conde-Pumpido, echoing Zaragoza, said that if there was evidence of criminal activity, it should be the US government that investigates.

The Bush Six case initially was assigned to Garzón, but he bowed to pressure from the attorney general and the chief prosecutor, and he let it be reassigned to Judge Eloy Velasco. On May 4, Velasco submitted an International Rogatory Letter (a request by a court in one country to legal officials in another country) to Attorney General Holder asking for information about "whether the facts to which the complaint makes reference are or not now being investigated or prosecuted." The May 5 cable concludes with a summary of where the case stood at the time: "Zaragoza is acting in good faith and playing a constructive role . . . Nevertheless, we do not share his optimism that this problem will go away anytime soon . . . In any event, we will probably be dealing with this issue for some time to come."

When these three cables were published in *El Pais* on November 29, 2010, they elicited an outcry among Spaniards who were angered by their officials' complicity with US officials to manipulate the Spanish legal system. On December 14, the Center for Constitutional Rights and the Berlin-based European Center for Constitutional and Human Rights, which had been assisting Gonzalo Boye and the other Spanish human rights lawyers who filed the complaint, submitted an expert opinion to the Spanish National Court with additional information about the US torture program that had come to light and, referencing the leaked cables, efforts by the US government to interfere politically with the Spanish legal process.

By the end of January 2011, Velasco had not received a reply to his letter requesting information about any US investigations of the Bush Six that might moot the Spanish complaints, so he issued an order that set March 1 as the deadline. On exactly that date, the Justice Department sent a letter authored by an attorney in the Criminal Division's Office of International Affairs. It contained gaslighting claims that the "government of the United States, in various fora, has undertaken numerous actions relating both to 1) the alleged mistreatment of detainees at issue in the complaint; and 2) legal advice provided in relation to the detainees."

The specific "numerous actions" taken in response to detainee mistreatment cited in the letter are two federal prosecutions: David Passaro, a CIA contractor, was convicted for brutally assaulting a detainee in Afghanistan; and Don Ayala, a private military contractor, was convicted of voluntary manslaughter for the death of a detainee in Afghanistan. The letter then proclaims that the "breadth of investigative actions . . . show that there are effective judicial processes under U.S. law for addressing violations." In reality, aside from court martial proceedings or administrative sanctions against approximately one hundred soldiers, the Justice Department never pursued criminal investigations targeting those up the chain of command. Nor was a single official ever held civilly liable for torture in a US court because of the Justice Department's successful efforts to either persuade judges that such cases are non-justiciable or to shut them down by invoking state secrets.

In regard to the torture-endorsing advice by government lawyers, the letter explains that the Justice Department's Office of Professional Responsibility (OPR) had investigated the activities of Yoo, who authored the August 1, 2002, memo, and Jay Bybee, who had signed it. The blithe description of that investigation and its outcome misrepresents the actual story, which is a sordid and politicized effort by the government to enforce unaccountability. A draft of the OPR investigation was completed in December 2008 while Bush was still in office, but not released. When a final draft of the OPR report was released in February 2010, as astute observers had expected, it contained substantial evidence that Yoo and Bybee had conspired with the White House to legalize torture tactics. That version of the OPR report concluded that this constituted "professional misconduct," which could have led to disbarment proceedings and, in the case of Bybee, his impeachment from the bench of the Ninth Circuit. But instead of allowing the conclusion of professional misconduct to be adopted, Holder authorized David Margolis, a career Justice Department official, to make the final determination. Margolis decided that the lawyers had merely exercised "poor judgment," although he did include this chiding comment: "I fear that John Yoo's loyalty to his own ideology and convictions clouded his view of his obligation to his client and led him to author opinions that reflected his own extreme, albeit sincerely held, view of executive power . . ." According to the letter sent to Judge Velasco, the OPR conclusion that Yoo and Bybee had not engaged in professional misconduct means there is no basis for criminal prosecution of them, or the other lawyers named in the Bush Six complaint.

The only forms of criminal conduct that the Obama administration authorized for investigation involved individual CIA agents who might have "exceeded" the legal advice provided by OLC lawyers, and those CIA officials who, in 2005, defied a court order to preserve evidence by destroying videos of several detainees being waterboarded and subjected to other forms of violent abuse in black sites. Assistant US Attorney John Durham was tasked with investigating these two matters. In November 2010, he concluded that "it was not appropriate to bring criminal charges with regard to the actual destruction of the tapes." He also decided that the CIA agents who exceeded the OLC guidelines by perpetrating mock executions should not be prosecuted.

Exposing the regime of secrecy, deception, and unaccountability for torture and other illegal actions by the US government was the reason Chelsea Manning decided to leak the massive cache of classified materials. Writing to Lamo, Manning had described the contents of the diplomatic cables in particular as "crazy, almost criminal political back dealings . . . the non-PR-versions of world events and crises . . . [it's] important that it gets out . . . i feel, for some bizarre reason . . . it might actually change something . . ."

In late April 2011, Wikileaks released 765 classified Detainee Assessment Briefs (DABs) containing information gleaned through interrogations of Guantánamo detainees. These briefs contained intelligence the government relied on to oppose detainees' habeas petitions, and which the DC Circuit Court had instructed the lower court to accept as presumptively true. What the leaked DABs revealed was that eight detainees were the source of information the government used against 255 others. Gitmo Bar attorneys were not allowed to use or even see—for risk of losing their security clearances—the briefs about their own clients, which would have been highly beneficial in their habeas cases.

The same month the Guantánamo briefs were released, Manning was transferred from Quantico to the maximum-security military prison at Fort Leavenworth. On February 24, 2012, she was arraigned for court martial and charged with twenty-two offenses under the Uniform Code of Military Justice. She was also charged under the draconian Espionage Act of 1917 for actions that allegedly aided the enemy. On July 30, 2013, Manning was found guilty of espionage, theft, and computer fraud, but was acquitted of the most serious charge of aiding the enemy. She was sentenced to thirty-five years in prison.

The Obama administration made an example of Manning to deter other would-be whistleblowers from leaking information about government malfeasance, deceptions, and crimes. By keeping truthful information secret, people were prevented from seeing evidence of past wrongdoing, and publicizing official accounts that were deceptive and untruthful was a means of sustaining public support, or at least public apathy, about aspects of the country's longest war. During the Obama administration, government classification and redaction reached levels unprecedented in US history, and more federal employee whistleblowers were prosecuted than under all previous presidents combined. But Manning's sentence made history as the harshest ever against a whistleblower.

In 2016, Nancy Hollander received a letter from Manning asking her to appeal the verdict, which she did. Hollander also strived to obtain clemency for Manning. The former effort failed but the latter effort succeeded. In 2017, Obama commuted Manning's sentence and she was released.

During Obama's presidency, the war in court remained a sustained, collective endeavor waged on multiple fronts, but rarely did the outcomes vindicate justice. The case that best epitomized Obama's unwillingness to restore the rule of law was his history-making decision to prosecute a child soldier for war crimes.

NINE

————

Obama's Guantánamo

NO GOVERNMENT SINCE THE END of World War II had prosecuted a child soldier for war crimes until President George W. Bush tried, twice. He failed. President Barack Obama, to his great shame, succeeded.

When Omar Khadr was put at the head of the queue for a military commission trial in late 2009, at twenty-three, he was the youngest person still imprisoned at Guantánamo. He had been there for eight years, over one-third of his life. He was the last citizen of a Western country remaining in detention, although one British resident, Shaker Aamer, still was locked up there, too.

The Obama administration chose to disregard the internationally preferred approach of rehabilitating child soldiers when it decided to bring charges against someone who was fifteen when he was captured on a battlefield. For people who still harbored some hope that Obama would part ways with his predecessor, that decision came as a shocking disappointment. In mid-April 2010, a week before Khadr's trial was scheduled to begin, New York University's Center for Law and Security hosted a conference about Guantánamo and international law. Much of the focus was on Khadr's case because it was so legally unprecedented. The Center's director, Karen Greenberg, summed up what many of us were thinking: "You can never get back on track when you're this far off."

Khadr was accused of war crimes invented by the US government in the post-9/11 era. The main charge was "murder in violation of the laws of war" for allegedly throwing a grenade that killed Sergeant Christopher Speer during a July 2002 battle in Afghanistan. The hot-war allegation that Khadr killed a soldier in battle distinguished his case from every other in the military commissions. He wasn't accused of killing civilians, like those charged for the 9/11 attacks. Nor was he accused of attacking a military target at a time and place where the United States was not at war, like the 2000 attack on the USS Cole. Khadr was involved in an actual war when he was a juvenile, but as a civilian, he was not subject to the laws of war. Moreover, soldiers are not protected persons under international humanitarian law. On what legal basis, then, could Khadr be charged with a war crime for killing Sergeant Speer? If these US-made war crimes were regarded and treated as universally applicable, by the same measure, CIA agents, who are civilians, also could be charged with murder in violation of the laws of war for operating Predator drones.

Many military and international law experts regard the post-9/11 legal edifice constructed for the "war on terror" as deeply flawed, even illegitimate. The Bush administration chose to disregard the Geneva Conventions in order to classify people in US custody as "unlawful enemy combatants." The only people with that status were foreign Muslim males. Any criminal activity that people with that status were accused of was characterized as a war crime to justify their prosecution in the military commissions. The charges leveled against Guantánamo detainees—including conspiracy, providing material support for terrorism, and solicitation of murder—are not actually war crimes; they are violations of other, nonmilitary kinds of laws. The Obama administration cosmetically rebranded unlawful enemy combatants as "unprivileged enemy belligerents" to shift the emphasis from status to action—that is, belligerency. But they retained their predecessor's made-up war crimes for the same reason: to prosecute Guantánamo detainees in the commissions.

Even on its own terms as a system that could bring terror suspects to justice, the military commissions were an abject failure. While hundreds of people accused of terrorism-related offenses were prosecuted in federal courts in the years and decades after 9/11, the number of prosecutions at Guantánamo could be counted on two hands with fingers to spare.

In the process of charging Khadr, the State Department and the Pentagon disagreed over the legality and wisdom of treating the battlefield killing of a soldier as a war crime. State argued in favor of restoring the pre-9/11 interpretation of the laws of war to bring the United States back into line with international consensus. Had State prevailed, which it didn't, the Pentagon would not have had any grounds for prosecuting Khadr. The Obama administration retained its predecessor's fabricated war crimes, in part, *for Khadr*.

The Khadr trial promised to be a barn burner because of the youthfulness of the defendant, the years of torture and abuse he had endured, and the dubious legality of the charges. Above all, it was the first military commission case of the Obama administration.

In March 2010, with the start of hearings a month away, I scheduled an interview with Khadr's military lawyer, Lieutenant Colonel Jon Jackson. (He had been promoted from major the previous October.) I went to the nondescript building in Roslyn, Virginia, which houses the Military Commissions Defense Office (MCDO). A soldier buzzed me in, searched my bag, and led me past a maze of cubicles to Jackson's office. When he stood up from his desk to shake my hand, I was struck by his towering height and his incongruously babyish face.

One of the first things Jackson said was: "I never imagined, when I was young, that someday I would be defending a child soldier who was tortured by my own government." I asked him to tell me a bit about his personal background. "I grew up in Tennessee," he said. "I was very very conservative." Then he asked if I understood what he meant by "very very conservative." I thought for a moment about how to respond. "Did you love Reagan?" He shouted, "I LOVED Reagan!" He continued, explaining that the younger him always voted Republican. He joined the military in 1996 as a JAG officer, and after 9/11, he chose to demonstrate his patriotism by reenlisting for active duty.

After President Bush announced the creation of a new military commission system in November 2001, Jackson volunteered to be a prosecutor, because he thought this would be a good way to use his skills to fight terrorists. But the Pentagon had other plans for him. His first post-9/11 posting was at Ramstein, the US base on German soil, where he defended soldiers who faced court martial. In early 2003, he gave briefings about the laws of war to US troops transiting through Germany on their way to deployment in Iraq. This was before the torture program was exposed. His boilerplate Uniform Code of Military Justice advice to them included the admonition to treat all prisoners of war humanely, "like you would expect if it was you or your buddy."

When the Abu Ghraib scandal broke in late April 2004, Jackson was teaching military justice, trial advocacy, and ethics at the Army JAG School in Charlottesville, Virginia. He recounted, "Abu Ghraib was a huge shattering event. My outlook changed." His initial confusion about how US soldiers could have done such things was cleared up a month and a half later when the first torture memos became public. Reflecting on what he learned since then, he said, "The military commissions are a logical progression of the torture policy."

In February 2008, Jackson was assigned to serve as a defense lawyer in the commissions. His first client was Mustafa al-Hawsawi, one of the detainees charged for 9/11, whom he described as "the smallest man I have ever seen. Just tiny. Bedraggled. But very kind and respectful. He was a very good client." About being assigned to the 9/11 case, he said, "I had no idea what I was getting into. I realized what a big deal it was when CNN reported that I had requested a delay in the arraignment."

The 9/11 case came to an abrupt stop in December 2008, after the defendants made the offer to plead guilty on the condition that they could go straight to sentencing and execution—a scenario that hadn't been anticipated by the people who crafted the rules. But the case was still on the books, and Jackson remained al-Hawsawi's lawyer. In November 2009, when Attorney General Eric Holder announced that the 9/11 case would be tried in federal court in New York City, Jackson assumed that civilian lawyers would take over al-Hawsawi's defense. The plan for a New York trial never materialized and, for lack of alternatives, the 9/11 case returned to the military commissions.

When the Obama administration began charging the first detainees it planned to prosecute, the Pentagon decided to shuffle some of the military defense lawyers around. Commander Walter Ruiz was shifted from Omar Khadr's team and assigned to represent al-Hawsawi because he had death penalty experience. Jackson was assigned to be Khadr's military lawyer.

Jackson would not have met al-Hawsawi or Khadr if he hadn't been their lawyer, and if he hadn't met them, he never would have fully appreciated the devastating effects of torture. But it was his work with Khadr in particular that transformed his worldview. Getting to know his physically brutalized and psychologically damaged client altered Jackson's way of seeing his own government, and invested him with the responsibility not just to represent Khadr's legal rights but his dignity as a human being.

Jackson abandoned his fealty to ideological conservatism because he was repelled that the defense of torture had become a Republican Party value. "Now," he told me, "I'm on the left wing of the Democratic Party—the human rights wing." Notwithstanding the sad fact that there is no human rights wing to the Democratic Party, Jackson was embracing a human rights critique of the party's mainstream acceptance of Obama's "look forward, not backward" impunity for torturers.

When Jackson and I finished talking, he introduced me to Katherine Newell, the MCDO's in-house torture expert. She was an Air Force veteran who previously worked for Human Rights Watch. Her role in the MCDO, she explained, was to advise and assist all the defense lawyers on their cases. "American military lawyers come into this job with no experience working on behalf of people who have been tortured," she said. "It's an added challenge defending people in this system because many of them are so damaged." Another lawyer who stopped by Newell's office while we were talking said, "Khadr is the poster child for this farce."

When Jackson began working with Khadr, he had to build rapport with a depressed and hopeless client whose relations with previous defense lawyers were sometimes acrimonious. Jackson also had to prepare to defend Khadr in a case that raised unprecedented legal issues. Part of his trial preparation involved finding witnesses who had firsthand knowledge of how Khadr had been treated in US custody. In a 2015 TED talk, Jackson recounts an experience he and his paralegal had when they went to the house of a man who had been an interrogator at Bagram. "We went inside and started to talk," Jackson said. "He was visibly shaking. He was very anxious, I could tell. We sat down at the table and I looked over to the right. I noticed a lot of pill bottles— prescription pill bottles. He saw me and, unprompted, said, 'I take medication for PTSD, for anxiety, for depression.' I said, 'Well, things happen at Bagram.' He said, 'No, it's not because of what happened to me after 9/11 or what happened at Bagram airbase. It's because of what I did. I tortured Omar Khadr, and I tortured other people.'" Jackson told his TED talk audience, "So when you hear people talk about when is torture justified, think about the people who have to do the torturing. They're victims, too."

Jackson had told me that Khadr's torture would be a central focus of his defense. In the weeks leading up to the start of the trial, I felt increasingly frustrated that there was no option for me to go to Guantánamo; I couldn't go as a scholar who works on torture and military courts, or as a concerned American citizen. The only kinds of people who were permitted to attend military commission proceedings (other than those involved in the cases) were journalists and representatives from a handful of authorized nongovernmental organizations (NGOs). When the pretrial hearings started on April 28, 2010, over three dozen journalists were there. Like the rest of the interested public, I would have to get information about what was happening from them.

Carol Rosenberg, whose *Miami Herald* beat was Guantánamo, had been reporting on the prison since it opened in 2002, and she attended almost every military commission proceeding since the first one in 2004. Her voluminous and detailed reporting exemplifies the best of the Fourth Estate. When Rosenberg began using Twitter on April 17, 2009, with the handle @carolrosenberg, she amplified her ability to relay all kinds of things about Guantánamo.

Twitter, which was created in 2006, became an enormously important medium for conveying information from Guantánamo in real time. To understand why, one must appreciate the eyes-of-the-world role that journalists play in reporting on this inaccessible locale. Electronic devices are prohibited in the courtroom, but journalists who stay in the Media Operations Center (MOC) can watch the proceedings, which are broadcast on closed circuit TV, and can tweet about courtroom interactions and quote things people say, 140 characters at a time. (Twitter increased the character maximum to 280 in 2017.) Those tweets coming out of the MOC contain some information and details that never make it into other, more conventional kinds of reporting that journalists also produce. They can be read by anyone who wants to know what is happening as it happens, including other journalists, lawyers, bloggers, human rights advocates, policy analysts, and government officials. It often took weeks for the official transcripts of hearings to be released, whereas tweets provided immediate, unredacted snapshots of events.

Being an effective tweeter of breaking news and colorful details is an acquired skill. When Rosenberg started, she used Twitter mainly to post links to her *Miami Herald* articles. The person she credits for modeling the potential of live tweeting from Guantánamo is investigative journalist Spencer Ackerman, who was reporting for *The Washington Independent* during the April–May 2010 hearings in the Khadr case. Ackerman, whose Twitter handle is @attackerman, zoomed in on all kinds of heretofore untweeted information, offering up witness-by-witness and question-by-question details about how events were playing out in court. Ackerman broke the news through a tweet that the new manual for the commissions, which implemented the 2009 Military Commission Act, didn't arrive on the island until the eve of the first hearing. Rosenberg was inspired by Ackerman's example, and live tweeting from Guantánamo has never been the same.

The judge in the Khadr case, Colonel Patrick Parrish, was nicknamed "Rocket Docket" by some journalists, because of the speed with which he liked to conduct business. He gave the parties half a day to study the 281-page manual containing rules of procedure and evidence, and the penal code. The manual's belated release was due to the fact that, until the last minute, government lawyers struggled to figure out how to write the section on murder in a way that wouldn't implicate the CIA's drone program. The solution the Pentagon came up with was to equate murder by an unprivileged combatant to espionage, which is a violation of domestic law.

The main issue being litigated over two weeks in April and May was what evidence Judge Parrish would allow prosecutors to use at trial. The 2009 MCA prohibits them from using statements elicited through cruel, inhuman, and degrading treatment, but it falls on military judges to determine what those standards are and how they apply in specific cases. Jackson and two civilian criminal defense lawyers, who recently had joined Khadr's team, Barry Coburn and Kobie Flowers, contended that all the self-incriminating statements Khadr had made between 2002 and 2005, which composed the bulk of the government's evidence, were coerced and should be suppressed.

The witnesses who testified in person or by video-link included several of Khadr's interrogators, soldiers who had guarded him, medical providers who had treated his injuries, and FBI agent Robert Fuller, who had interrogated him at Bagram in 2002. The first interrogator to question Khadr, while he was still strapped to a stretcher and awaiting medical treatment for his severe injuries, was identified in court as Interrogator #1. He testified that he believed Khadr was being untruthful in answers to his questions, so, to scare him, #1 capitalized on the universal fear of rape by making up a story about a young Afghan detainee who lied to his interrogators and was shipped to a prison in the United States where he was raped by "four big black guys" and died. (Interrogator #1 had been court martialed in 2005 for the abuse of other detainees.) Ackerman live-tweeted: "Interrog #1 says his use of Fear Up, story about rape/killing to #Khadr 'didnt help out, didnt release any actionable' intelligence #GTMO."

Another Bagram interrogator testified for the defense under his own name, Damien Corsetti, and acknowledged that his well-deserved nickname was "The Monster" because he is big, scary, and loud. Corsetti said that after Khadr was transferred from the hospital to the detention facility, he developed sympathy for him. "He was a child. That's it. He was a fifteen-year-old child who had been blown up, shot, grenaded, and he was in probably one of the worst places on earth. How could you not have compassion for him?" In a blog post that went online the following day, Jennifer Turner, who was there as an ACLU observer, reported:

> During Corsetti's testimony, the government military prosecutor, U.S. Marine Maj. Jeff Groharing, made frequent, strenuous objections whenever the defense asked Corsetti about abuse practices at Bagram while Khadr was detained there. In the few instances when the judge overruled the prosecutor's objections, Corsetti testified about the rampant abuse that was approved for use by interrogators ... which included screaming, breaking furniture,

shackling detainees in stress positions for hours, and threatening to send detainees to interrogation in Israel or Egypt. He also said that during the period of Khadr's detention at Bagram in 2002, interrogators were under tremendous pressure from the Secretary of Defense's office and other commanders to extract information from detainees.

Turner added that the judge's decisions to sustain most prosecution objections to testimony about the abusive environment at Bagram "is very relevant because Khadr doesn't recall that period."

I followed reporting and tweeting about the pretrial hearing closely, dependent on, and grateful for, these secondhand sources. It didn't dawn on me that there was an alternative until, in early June, I had lunch with Kate Porterfield.

Porterfield is a clinical psychologist with extensive experience treating torture survivors and children traumatized by war. We met in a diner in midtown Manhattan near Bellevue Hospital, where she worked. She said that, over the previous year, she had spent hundreds of hours with Khadr. Part of her work involved "piecing him together again and cleaning up Kuebler's mess." She was referring to Lieutenant Commander William Kuebler, one of Khadr's previous military lawyers who had wrangled with other attorneys over strategy and who had railed loudly and often against the injustice of it all, including to his superiors and to Khadr. Although Porterfield believed Kuebler's disruptive actions contributed to Khadr's depression and alienation, she was sympathetic. "His judgment was questionable because he lost perspective on Gitmo. His story exemplifies how someone's perspective can be distorted by injustice and frustration."

Our main topic of conversation was Porterfield's impressions of the April-May hearings, including Khadr's reactions to various witnesses' testimony. She was scheduled to take the stand when the pretrial hearings resumed in July. She admitted that she was nervous because she had seen how aggressively the prosecutors treated defense witnesses. She looked at me, paused for a beat, then said, "I wish you could be there" by which she meant that it would be nice to see a friendly face in the courtroom when she was under fire. "Me too!" I responded. "You could go as a journalist," she said. I felt as though a lightbulb had switched on in my brain. I wrote journalistically for several media outlets. Could I go to Guantánamo as a journalist? I didn't have the faintest idea how to even test the question, so Porterfield gave me Rosenberg's phone number and advised me to get in touch with her.

When I called Rosenberg, she gave me all the information I needed to apply to the Pentagon's office of public affairs to be part of the media delegation for the next hearing of the Khadr case. I applied to represent *Middle East Report,* my longest-running media affiliation. When I got the clearance to attend the July hearings, Rosenberg plied me with invaluable advice about what to pack for two weeks on the base.

I was going to Guantánamo!

But it wasn't clear if Rosenberg would be going. Right after the hearings recessed in May, the Pentagon banned her for life, along with three Canadian journalists—Michelle Shephard of the *Toronto Star,* Paul Koring of the Canadian *Globe and Mail,* and Steven Edwards of Canwest—for reporting the name of Interrogator #1, Joshua Claus. The banning flew in the face of the fact that Claus's name was already in the public domain; Shephard had interviewed him the previous year, and the other two Canadians had written articles that identified him by name. But the Pentagon regarded his identity as classified information and retaliated against the four reporters. Ackerman tweeted a link to the Pentagon's letter banning the reporters to his five thousand followers. According to Rosenberg, that significantly increased the number of her own Twitter followers.

The *Miami Herald* hired a First Amendment attorney to sue the government and won. Rosenberg was unbanned and could join the media delegation in July.

Meanwhile, during the recess, prosecutors attempted to negotiate a plea bargain with Khadr's lawyers. A deal would have spared the government not only the labor and expense of a trial, but also the embarrassment of more damning testimony about Khadr's torture and abuse. The negotiations collapsed in late June and, although it was not clear if there was a direct connection, on July 7, Khadr fired his three American lawyers—Jackson, Coburn, and Flowers.

Because this firing derailed the scheduled resumption of pretrial hearings, most of the journalists who had signed up for the July trip dropped out. The delegation that assembled at dawn at Andrews Air Force Base to board the plane for Guantánamo was small, and I wasn't the only first-timer. An Italian photojournalist and a reporter for a Russian-language paper in Israel, neither of whom cover national security matters, had signed up because they were curious. When we landed, Rosenberg took me under her wing. I learned so much from her, including how to live tweet @attackerman-style about proceedings in the military commissions.

Instead of the resumption of pretrial hearings that would have featured Porterfield and another psychiatrist, Stephen Xenakis, testifying for the defense, and two psychiatrists testifying for the prosecution, the only issue to be discussed at the one-day hearing on July 12 was Khadr's legal representation.

An hour before the start of the hearing, journalists were led by our military escorts up the hill from the MOC to the court building that had once been the base's dental clinic. In the courtroom, journalists were assigned specific seats behind a low wooden barrier that separated us from the defense table, and the NGO observers sat behind the barrier from the prosecution table. Everyone was sternly warned that any effort to communicate with the defendant would get us thrown off the island.

Shortly before 9:00 a.m., Khadr, dressed in a loose-fitting white tunic and pants, was brought into the courtroom by a contingent of guards and seated at the defense table beside his Canadian lawyer, Dennis Edney. On the other side of Edney sat his fired military lawyer, Jackson.

The hearing started as soon as Judge Parrish entered the room. He began by asking Khadr to confirm that he had in fact fired his civilian attorneys, Coburn and Flowers, and that no one had forced or pressured him to do so. Then Parrish asked, "How do you plan to proceed?" Khadr replied, "I plan to boycott the process. I have my reasons." Then he explained those reasons by reading a handwritten statement (copies of which were later distributed to journalists):

> Your Honor, I'm boycotting this military commission because: firstly, the unfairness and injustice of it. I say this because not one of the lawyers I've had, or human rights organizations or any person ever say that this commission is fair or looking for justice, but on the contrary they say it's unfair and unjust and that it has been constructed to convict detainees not to find the truth (so how can I ask for justice from a process that does not have it or offer it) and to accomplish political and public goal. And what I mean is when I was offered a plea bargain it was up to 30 years which I was going to spend only five years so I asked why the 30 years. I was told it make the US government look good in the public eyes and other political causes. Secondly: The unfairness of the rules that will make a person so depressed that he will admit to alligations made upon him or take a plea offer that will satisfy the US government and get him the least sentence possible and legitimize this sham process. Therefore I will not willingly let the US gov use me to fulfill its goal. I have been used many times when I was a child and that's why I'm here taking blame and paying for things I didn't have a chance in doing but was told

to do by elders. Lastly I will not take any plea offer because it will give excuse for the gov for torturing and abusing me when I was a child.

Judge Parrish apparently did not understand Khadr's intention to boycott, because he asked, "Will you represent yourself? I'm not going to release Lieutenant Jackson if you choose not to represent yourself." Khadr reiterated that he did not want any lawyer to represent him. Assuming Khadr meant that he wanted to go pro se, the judge asked, "Have you ever studied the law?" Khadr replied, "This is a military commission. You don't need to study the law." Judge Parrish: "What is your education?" Khadr: "Five years in the military commissions."

As if the judge knew nothing about Khadr's background, he asked, "Have you ever represented yourself or anyone else in this type of proceeding? Are you familiar with the rules of evidence?" Khadr responded, "The rules are always changing, so knowing the rules doesn't really matter." Parrish: "Are you familiar with the rules of the military commissions?" Khadr answered, "In general. My lawyers are as untrained as I am. No one has any experience in these military commissions." Indeed, the new rules had materialized on the first day of Khadr's trial.

Adopting a paternal tone, Parrish advised that effective legal representation must be objective and that "representing yourself is never a good idea." Khadr was resolute. Parrish: "So are you saying that in this process legal training makes no difference?" Khadr: "Yes."

The judge asked if there were any responses or questions from the prosecution. At their table sat the chief military prosecutor, Captain John Murphy; the lead prosecutor, Major Jeffrey Groharing, who had been on the case since the beginning; and Captains Chris Eason and Michael Grant. Groharing asked the judge to inquire about Khadr's "possible physical and psychological ailments" and "to clarify what about the system the accused thinks is unfair." Groharing also reminded the judge that if Khadr were to be granted the right to represent himself and is "incompetent," he would not be permitted to raise the issue on appeal. Judge Parrish duly asked Khadr, "Do you have any mental or physical issues that would prevent you from making these decisions?" Khadr replied, "This place is not a five-star hotel, so I'm sure it's going to have an effect on me. I don't know."

Jackson, who had sat silently, interjected a point for the judge's consideration. Citing *Edwards v. Indiana* and referencing the fact that Khadr said he did not know if he is suffering any psychological illness, Jackson urged serious consideration of the issue of competency. Parrish responded that Dr. Porterfield had assessed Khadr as competent to stand trial. Jackson retorted that competency to stand trial and competency to represent oneself are different standards. Groharing urged the judge to further inquire about PTSD, and he stated that the two psychiatrists hired by the government, Alan Hopewell and Michael Welner, had drawn different conclusions about Khadr's mental state than the defense experts, Porterfield and Xenakis.

In an effort to project an aura of impartiality about motions as yet undecided, Parrish tiptoed around the issue of torture that might have caused Khadr to be suffering PTSD. "After you were captured, you've been through a number of things, and this might affect your mental state." He asked whether Khadr would want him to consider the reports by the defense experts. Dennis Edney whispered in Khadr's ear, then Khadr said that if the judge was going to consider the reports by the prosecution's experts, then, yes, he should consider those of the defense, too.

Judge Parrish called a recess to deliberate on the issue of representation.

When the court reconvened, Parrish seemed uncertain how to navigate this confounding relationship between a defendant's legal rights and the inevitable public relations disaster that would result from allowing the prosecution of an unrepresented defendant for war crimes allegedly committed when he was a juvenile. The prospect that the Khadr trial might follow the Ali Hamza al-Bahlul model, in which another boycotting defendant and his military lawyer sat mute, could not have been a heartening thought for the judge or the prosecution. Hoping to persuade Khadr to rethink his position, Parrish pointed out some of the disadvantages, such as: "If I allow you to represent yourself, you won't have access to material that's classified." Khadr: "I'm boycotting." Then Parrish tried praising the zealous dedication of the lawyers who had worked on Khadr's case over the years. Khadr: "I'm boycotting and I don't want any attorneys." Parrish asked, "Is part of the boycott that you will represent yourself and not talk?" Khadr: "I don't know." Parrish: "If you show up, does that mean you are still boycotting?" Khadr: "I don't understand. I'm boycotting this whole thing. What's the point of representing myself?" Judge Parrish: "So you do not want to represent yourself?" Khadr: "I don't see the point. I don't want to represent myself, and I don't want anyone to represent me. If I was in a formal court, I wouldn't be doing this. But because I'm in this court, I am forced to do this." Judge Parrish: "Then I am not releasing Lieutenant Jackson. He will remain your detailed counsel." Khadr: "You are forcing him on me. I don't want him to represent me."

Parrish seemed satisfied that the representation issue had been resolved. Flipping through the court calendar, he mused that if the defense wanted to continue pretrial hearings on motions to suppress government evidence, they could resume on August 10. That would mean, he continued, that the trial could start in October. Groharing, who seemed vexed by that scenario, asked whether the defense would indeed want to hold additional pretrial hearings because, if the answer was no, they could go straight to trial in August. And with that, the representation conundrum returned. Who was empowered to make that decision? Khadr offered his preference: "I want this to finish as soon as possible. I'm not calling any witnesses." Parrish asked if that was the final word from the defense. Jackson, who had not spoken to Khadr since he was fired, said, "I don't know if the client would talk to me, but I'm willing to talk to him." The judge called another recess.

At the start of the third and last session of the day, Jackson said that before taking any position on how to proceed or making any scheduling commitments, he would have to consult with Khadr and with "my licensing authority in Arkansas and the professional licensing branch of the Army." By this point, the prosecutors were apoplectic about the prospect of more delays. Groharing, rifling through the commissions rule book, said that "the obligation is to proceed unless there is a decision that this would pose an ethical problem." He testily added that Jackson could have made these ethics inquiries weeks ago, since Khadr's decision to fire his lawyers was hardly a surprise. Jackson replied that he had no idea until that day that he would be detailed to represent a client whose intent was to boycott since he had not been privy to Khadr's statement before it was read in court.

The prosecutors huddled with the rule book for several minutes, trying to find something to persuade the judge to push forward to trial. Groharing finally stood up to say that "the rules applicable to the military commissions would be paramount over any other licensing authorities." He said that any further delay "would create a significant disadvantage for the government." Then he added, "This is the latest of many instances when the accused has attempted to manipulate this process. He's making a mockery of the military commissions." Parrish was unmoved. "I am not going to allow an unrepresented accused in here," he said. "That is not going to happen." The hearing ended with Parrish asking Jackson to report by August 2 about what he heard from his licensing authorities.

After the hearing ended, Captain David Iglesias, who recently had joined the Military Commission Prosecution Office as its official spokesperson, came to the MOC to speak to journalists. (Iglesias became a national figure in 2006 as the most visible of the seven US attorneys fired by Attorney General Alberto Gonzales for refusing to pursue voter fraud cases against Democrats after they concluded that the allegations emanating from the Bush White House were politically motivated and baseless.) One journalist asked Iglesias whether the prosecution was worried about political fallout from Khadr's trial. He replied, "Perfect cases don't go to trial." Asked what he thought of the quality of the government's case, he pled ignorance of the details but added, "We will go forward no matter what." What did he have to say about the novelty of prosecuting a child soldier on charges that were widely regarded as specious among international law experts? "A conviction is a conviction, whether it's for a historical war crime or a more recently added war crime," Iglesias responded.

The Obama administration was able to squeak out a conviction of another detainee in July when Ibrahim al-Qosi agreed to a plea bargain, thus relieving them of the embarrassment of having Khadr be the first. Al-Qosi was one of the first detainees to be charged in the military commissions back in 2004. The defense strategy of his first military lawyer, Lieutenant Colonel Sharon Shaffer, was to challenge everything, including government plans to reinterrogate her client after he had been charged. Shaffer also had sought to depose top officials, including former President Bill Clinton, because the conspiracy charge against al-Qosi alleged conduct dating to 1996 when he started working as Osama bin Laden's cook and driver in Afghanistan. She wanted an official answer to the question of whether the United States regarded itself as at war with al-Qaeda in 1996. Her motion was denied because the commissions in their first iteration had no rules on depositions. Shaffer also alleged prosecutorial misconduct because some exculpatory evidence was withheld and, she said, the whole process is a "travesty of justice."

When al-Qosi was recharged on February 9, 2008, he had a new military lawyer, Commander Suzanne Lachelier. When I interviewed her in Washington in 2009, she described al-Qosi's case as "Hamdan lite." She explained that, because al-Qosi refused to deal with her or any other American lawyer, she reached out to Abdullahi An-Na'im, a Sudanese-American who teaches law at Emory University and is an internationally renowned expert on human rights. She hoped that an-Na'im could persuade al-Qosi to cooperate with his defense lawyers, and she arranged for them to meet at Guantánamo in August 2008. The Sudanese Bar Association sent

Ahmad al-Mufti, head of the government-run Sudan Human Rights Commission, to attend al-Qosi's hearings.

At a December 2009 hearing, prosecutors announced their intention to add new charges alleging that al-Qosi's conspiracy with al-Qaeda dated back to 1992 when he worked as an accountant in a Khartoum company owned by bin Laden, but the judge refused to accept the change. On July 7, 2010, al-Qosi pled guilty to conspiracy and providing material support for terrorism. *Al Arabiya* journalist Muna Shikaki broke the story that the agreed-upon sentence was two more years at Guantánamo, after which al-Qosi would be repatriated to Sudan. The deal was confirmed at a sentencing hearing on August 9.

Al-Qosi's case was wrapped up while Khadr's was still in progress. On July 17, Rosenberg reported that Jackson had received the ethics opinion he was seeking and she published his statement: "I am ethically required to continue representing Mr. Khadr at this time. Therefore, I intend to provide him with a zealous defense." Jackson told Rosenberg, "I never envisioned a scenario in my career as an Army lawyer that would require me to defend a child soldier against war crimes charges levied by the United States. I always believed we were better than that."

Khadr, on the advice of his Canadian legal advisors, agreed to allow Jackson to defend him. Coburn and Flowers were not put back on the team, but Jackson got a new co-counsel, Major Matthew Schwartz. I signed up to attend the next round of pretrial hearings, which began on August 10. The media delegation was much larger this time, and NGOs sent their top experts on international law.

On the base, even though journalists and NGO observers are housed in tents in Camp Justice, military escorts try to keep the two groups apart. The original logic for separating them was the notion that the NGO observers were there to criticize the government, and if they intermingled with journalists, their harsh and skeptical views might adversely influence and taint the tone of reporting. Years later, while the goal of keeping the two groups separate remained intact, the logic was reversed: Gitmo-experienced journalists must be kept away from observers, who now were less likely to be experts on human rights but law school students on one-time trips to learn something.

Trying to keep journalists and NGO observers apart during the Khadr hearings was a fool's errand. Every evening, people from both groups would converge at the picnic tables near our tents, pour drinks into plastic cups purchased at the NEC (Navy Exchange), and engage in deep discussions and florid debates about the day's events. Some journalists hatched story ideas or fact-checked details about international law from the experts, and observers could hear from journalists about past hearings they hadn't attended.

Many trial observers expected Judge Parrish to follow the pattern of judges in previous military commission cases by allowing prosecutors to use statements derived from interrogations at Guantánamo, but to exclude those from Bagram. Instead, to the prosecutors' delight, on August 9, Parrish ruled that he found "no credible evidence" that Khadr had been abused in either facility or that his treatment constituted violations of US law, and therefore all his self-incriminating statements were admissible. Under the stars that night, journalists and observers dissected that decision and its implications for the case.

Jackson realized that, given Parrish's incapacity to recognize torture or cruel treatment, further pretrial hearings were pointless. His new strategy was to relitigate his client's torture at trial in order to discredit the self-incriminating statements. He planned to call many of the same witnesses to give the panel of officers (the military equivalent of a jury) the opportunity to decide whether Khadr's statements were reliable in light of what they would hear about the tactics used to elicit them and the conditions of his detention.

The August hearing began with the voir dire process in which seven officers were selected from a larger pool of candidates to serve on the panel. None of those selected had a legal background or admitted having any opinion about Guantánamo, good or bad. Two candidates who did claim some knowledge of the law and awareness of current events were dismissed by the prosecutors as unsuitable.

Khadr's trial began on August 12. During his opening statement, Groharing emphasized that Khadr was a terrorist and a murderer, and that his confessions to interrogators had been uncoerced. Jackson told the panel: "Omar Khadr is not a war criminal, and the US government is not going to be able to prove it."

The first prosecution witness, who testified by video, was identified as Lieutenant Colonel "W." He had written the military incident report about the 2002 firefight. The original version of the report stated that the person who hurled the explosive over the compound wall that killed Sergeant Speer was subsequently killed. Several years later, however, the report was altered to state that the grenade was thrown by someone who was injured—to implicate the only survivor, Khadr. The "revised" version was backdated to cover up the change in the original. In 2008, Khadr's defense lawyers obtained a copy of the original report, which the government never intended to provide, when it was inadvertently included in some discovery filings. W testified that he changed the report "for history's sake" because he believed at the time that Khadr—whom he insisted threw the grenade—had died. But the same reason W adduced that Khadr had died in the firefight was the defense's reason for casting doubt on whether he could have thrown the grenade: A photograph taken inside the ruins of compound moments after it was raided shows Khadr unconscious and buried face down in rubble.

Jackson clearly appreciated the historic significance of this case as he questioned W and the government's second witness, who also had been on hand for the 2002 firefight, about whether there had been any armed CIA agents present. Through this line of questioning, he was trying to create a record that would expose the broader contradictions and anomalies of the post-9/11 legal edifice in which his civilian client was being prosecuted for the murder of a soldier while CIA agents, who are also civilians, were immunized for their wartime killings. This line of questioning could also lay the ground for an appeal if his client were convicted—perhaps with an eye on the Supreme Court.

Around 4 p.m., Jackson was on his feet speaking when he fainted and crashed to the floor like a giant tree being felled. Groharing leapt over the prosecution table and rushed to the aid of his legal adversary. Everyone was hastily cleared out of the courtroom. Soon we could hear the siren of an ambulance. Journalists stood outside the MOC whispering questions to each other about what could have caused Jackson to collapse. Rosenberg, unsurprisingly, knew the answer: he had gallbladder surgery in June and, because of the pressures and tight schedule of the case, he hadn't given himself time to fully heal. She let her Twitter feed go dark because she didn't want Jackson's wife, who followed her, to learn what just happened from a tweet.

Jackson was medivacked off the island and the case was recessed. The following day, a chartered plane flew everyone else back to Andrews.

When Jackson recovered from his medical emergency, he took a hard look at where things stood and weighed the likelihood that the panel would acquit his client. He decided that the best option would be a plea bargain. He spent a month negotiating a complex deal that involved a diplomatic agreement between the State Department and the Canadian government. In exchange for Khadr agreeing to plead guilty, he would be sentenced to eight more years—with no credit for the eight he had already been imprisoned. After one year, he would be permitted to petition the Canadian government to repatriate him to serve out the rest in his homeland. Later, when the terms were made public, Jackson described it as "the deal of the century."

I was one of twenty-five journalists who went to Guantánamo in October for the conclusion of Khadr's case. The delegation included the three Canadian journalists who had been banned for life in May, then unbanned several months later. Michelle Shephard started tweeting several weeks before her return to Guantánamo, and by the October hearings, she had hundreds of followers. One of her tweets reflected the fraught political stakes of the Khadr proceedings in Canada: "Note to my dedicated emailers. Thanks for suggestions to stay here in #Gitmo, marry #Khadr, or just go and die. Don't shoot the messenger."

On the first day, October 25, Judge Parrish announced that the defense and prosecution had reached a plea agreement. Then as each specification (charge) was read aloud, the judge asked Khadr if he was guilty, and in a muted tone he replied "yes." When he said "yes" to the first charge, murder in violation of the laws of war for throwing the grenade that killed Sergeant Speer, his widow, Tabitha Speer, who was in the courtroom, broke down in tears. "Yes" to attempted murder for making and planting IEDs intended to kill US and allied forces; "yes" to material support for terrorism, conspiracy and spying. As Judge Parrish was wrapping up this part of the hearing, he explained that Khadr had waived any right to appeal his conviction and had agreed not to initiate any litigation against the US government in the future.

Some of the journalists who had been covering the Khadr case for years were surprised that the government had given up nothing in the way of charges, and that Khadr had conceded guilt to everything to reach a deal. Captain Murphy came to the old hangar where the MOC is located to address the press. He said, "Omar Khadr stands convicted of being a murderer and an al-Qaeda terrorist. The evidence is the strongest kind in law—his own words! He is not a child soldier, not a victim. He is a murderer and a terrorist." Then he said, "The government believes that this is an important landmark in the military commissions."

The same seven military jurors who had been seated in August for the trial were now brought in to hear the arguments in the sentencing phase, and then to decide Khadr's fate—or so they thought. They were not informed about the terms of the deal, nor did they know that, under the rules of the commissions, whichever sentence was lower—the negotiated agreement or the panel's decision—would prevail. Over four days of hearings, witnesses testified

FIGURE 14. Military commission hearing, August 9, 2010: Omar Khadr and his Canadian legal adviser, Dennis Edney, in foreground. Drawing by Janet Hamlin.

about aggravating (prosecution) or mitigating (defense) factors that the seven members should consider when they were sequestered. The possibility that the panel might pass a sentence lower than eight years, or significantly higher was narrated and debated by journalists who tweeted about the persuasiveness of witnesses and the effectiveness of lawyers' lines of questioning.

One of the prosecution witnesses was Dr. Michael Welner, a forensic psychiatrist, who had met Khadr once for seven hours. He said that Khadr poses a "high risk of future dangerousness" because he is an unrepentant jihadist who "is marinating in radical Islamism" in the "extremist" environment of Camp 4. Welner regarded Khadr's religious devotion, including the fact that he had inscribed the Qur'an to memory and was a popular leader of prayers, to be a significant "data point" in the risk assessment. "In my professional opinion, he has become more devout while in custody." Other risk factors included the fact that Khadr had met bin Laden and that his own father had been an al-Qaeda insider, which gave him the status of a "rock star" and "al-Qaeda royalty" in Guantánamo, which would add to his dangerousness if he were to be released. Welner also opined at length that Khadr's family are unrepentant Islamist radicals, and that Canada has no de-radicalization programs for jihadis. The doctor, who had no previous experience with risk assessment for Islamists, explained that he based his analytical framework in large part on the research of a Danish psychologist, Nicolai Sennels, who authored *Among Criminal Muslims* based on a study of prisoners in Copenhagen. Welner never read the book because it is in Danish. But, he explained, when he heard about it, he called Sennels to discuss the latter's findings and methods, which he adopted to assess Khadr.

Journalists in the MOC started googling Sennels and immediately found an interview he gave to the right-wing online publication, *Frontpagemag.com,* in which he propounds on various defects of the "Muslim personality." They also found an article Sennels wrote in which he says that Muslim "inbreeding" has adverse impacts on their "sanity" and "intelligence." Links to these articles were tweeted while Welner was still on the stand.

During Welner's cross-examination, Major Schwartz questioned him about Sennels's views, his own inexperience with Islamists, and the fact that he had never read the book on which he constructed his predictions about Khadr's future dangerousness. Schwartz pointedly asked, "Your sample size was Omar Khadr?" Before the hearing recessed for lunch, Schwartz asked Welner to read the interview and the article by Sennels. When the hearing resumed, I tweeted, "Welner on redirect says reading Sennels articles today makes him even 'more impressed' with his insights."

Tabitha Speer took the stand to give victim impact testimony about how the killing of her husband had affected her and her two children. She said that part of her toddler daughter died with her husband. Speer read aloud a letter addressed to Khadr, then she turned and spoke to him directly: "The victims, the children, they are my children. Not you." She was deriding the characterization of Khadr as a child soldier. When Shephard got back to the MOC, she tweeted about the atmosphere in the courtroom: "Extremely emotional testimony by Tabitha Speer. Many court spectators crying. #Khadr had head down."

Before court on the morning of the last day of sentencing hearings, I saw Dr. Xenakis and asked if he was up first. He looked at me oddly, then said, "We're not going to testify." It took a second for me to register what he meant. Then I asked, "Is that a strategy?" Xenakis replied, "Yes, it's strategy. Strategy. These guys think . . ." He didn't finish his sentence.

Jackson and Schwartz had decided not to make the sentencing hearing a battle of psychiatrists, but rather to put on two witnesses who could testify about Khadr's character in ways they hoped would appeal to the panel. The first was a JAG officer, Captain Patrick McCarthy, who testified by video from Afghanistan. He had served at Guantánamo from 2006 to 2008 and had many opportunities to interact with Khadr, whom he described as respectful and friendly. "Many other detainees were radical, fanatical. They would threaten the guard staff." Not Khadr. Rather, he played a leadership role as a positive influence in Camp 4 by trying to defuse other detainees' frustrations.

On cross-examination, Captain Murphy asked, "Did you know that he was a murderer in 2006?" Captain McCarthy answered, "I knew that he was accused of throwing a grenade." Murphy: "You say he is not a radical. But do you know that he is an admitted al-Qaeda terrorist?" Welner, who was seated behind the prosecution, scribbled on a piece of paper and handed it to Groharing; a journalist sitting behind him saw that it read: "Wasn't Ayman al-Zawahri only fifteen when he became a radical?"

The other character witness for the defense was Arlette Zinck, a Canadian professor of English literature at King's College, a small evangelical Christian liberal arts school in Edmonton. Her contact with Khadr had been through letters. When she entered the courtroom, it was the first time they had seen each other in person. Khadr beamed as he looked at her. She beamed back. I recognized that expression on Zinck's face: inner godliness. This was Jackson's strategy.

Zinck explained that in September 2008, Dennis Edney was invited to King's College to speak about Khadr at a symposium on "invisible dignity," which was part of the school's global justice initiative. Many students and faculty, including Zinck, learned about Khadr for the first time that day. She described that event as "a great teaching moment." After Edney finished his speech, a student asked what she could do to help. He suggested that people should write letters to their member of Parliament, but he concluded by saying that Khadr's situation was hopeless. That message of passivity and despair contradicted the school's mission to serve Jesus through action. Zinck said, "We don't do hopeless." She encouraged her students to start doing research about Khadr. Soon, she recounted, they wanted to use their research to teach people in Edmonton what they had learned.

On campus, a student-led movement animated by the injustice of Khadr's situation started building. Edney was invited back, this time with Michelle Shephard, to speak at an event attended by more than seven hundred people. Zinck and some of her students started writing to Khadr to express their sympathy and support, and he wrote back. Edney was the conduit for this correspondence. In her own letters, Zinck encouraged Khadr to find solace in books. Then she started sending him lesson plans, based on the books available in the prison library. Khadr did his homework for Zinck in the style of texts he was familiar with: legal briefs. She produced five of Khadr's homework-letters, which he had signed, "your future student." One of them was a book report about Nelson Mandela's autobiography, *Long Walk to Freedom*. Zinck testified, "The person I met in these letters is courteous, generous in spirit, remarkably outward-focused, intelligent, and thoughtful."

Captain Eason began his cross-examination of Zink by stating: "You are an advocate for Omar Khadr." She replied, "Absolutely." Eason: "He's a murderer." She responded by invoking the work of Jesus among the despised, and the importance of forgiveness. Her Christian charity was bulletproof. Then Eason asked whether King's College has a de-radicalization program. "No." Eason: "Do you have any convicted al-Qaeda terrorists at King's?" Zinck: "Not to my knowledge." When Eason asked what she had to say about the fact that Khadr once called a guard the N-word, she looked directly at Khadr and said, "That's not a nice thing to say." Khadr looked at her with a sheepish expression, then the two of them resumed smiling at each other. Someone tweeting about Zinck's testimony introduced the hashtag #jihadis4jesus.

The last person to take the stand was Khadr himself. He began, "I decided to plead guilty to take responsibility for my actions." Because the two main issues that would be of concern to the panel were his remorsefulness and his rehabilitative potential, he told the panel a few things about himself. Then he addressed Tabitha Speer: "I'm really sorry for the pain I caused you and your family. I wish I could do something that would take this pain away from you." Speer shook her head and mouthed the word "no," apology not accepted.

When Groharing delivered his closing argument, he stressed the personal loss to the Speer family. He said that while Khadr might have been young at the time of his capture, he was old enough to know right from wrong. He asked the panel to "send a message" to al-Qaeda and to the world by passing a sentence of twenty-five years. He concluded, "Ladies and gentlemen, the accused is no Nelson Mandela."

Jackson delivered his closing arguments, not from notes at the podium, as Groharing had done, but off the cuff, standing in front of the panel. He stressed Khadr's youthfulness, his lack of choice and the culpability of his father who sent him into Afghanistan in 2002, and the fact that al-Qaeda uses children. Jackson also asked the panel to consider that 5,736 US soldiers had been killed by enemy fire and bombings in the "war on terror," but Khadr alone was being prosecuted for a soldier's death. He asked for leniency in light of the abuses to which Khadr was subjected in US custody, and the fact that he already had spent eight years in Guantánamo. In a pointed reference to Welner and the consequences if the jury were to agree with the prosecution's request for a long sentence, Jackson said, "For the next 25 years at Guantanamo he's going to be marinating, marinating in this jihad sauce?" He urged them to disregard Welner's testimony as having "zero significance" because it is not based on "real science."

The panel's deliberations lasted eight hours, spanning two days. A few minutes before 5:00 p.m. on October 31, journalists were informed that the panel had arrived at a decision. Those of us who wanted to be in court raced up the hill. When the president of the panel stood to announce the verdict, he wasn't speaking into a microphone, and when he was finished the judge did not restate the sentence. Rosenberg, who was in the MOC, said she thought her head was going to explode. Pentagon spokeswoman Major Tanya Bradsher had to call up to the court to find out what the sentence was, and then she announced to those in the MOC that the panel had decided on forty years—almost double the symbolic sentence that Groharing had asked for.

When Shephard got back to her computer, she tweeted: "40 years. Wow. #Khadr looked straight ahead. Widow of soldier he was convicted of killing cheered out in court." I tweeted: "Jury sent message with 40-year sentence, alright: plea bargains rule."

The Khadr case concluded eight years and a day from his arrival at Guantánamo. Immediately after the decision was read, he was moved into the semi-isolation of Camp 5 where the two other convicted prisoners—al-Bahlul and al-Qosi—were housed.

After the case was finished, Jackson crafted a new role for himself: he became Khadr's teacher. On his monthly visits, he would bring lesson plans for courses in geometry, astronomy, and biology, which were not covered by Professor Zink's curriculum. Jackson was motivated by the goals of restoring Khadr's sense of his own humanity, and preparing him for life after Guantánamo.

It took not one but two years for Khadr to be repatriated because Canada's minister of public safety dragged his feet processing the request. When Khadr was returned to Canada on September 29, 2012, he was incarcerated in a maximum-security facility in Ontario. Eventually, he was transferred to a medium-security prison, and then on May 15, 2015, he was released on bail on the condition that he live under the supervision of his attorney Dennis Edney. On March 29, 2019, a Canadian judge ruled that his sentence was up and he was freed. He enrolled as a student at King's College.

In addition to Khadr and al-Qosi, who was repatriated to Sudan in July 2012, three other detainees were convicted during the Obama presidency. Ahmed al-Darbi, whose civilian lawyer was Ramzi Kassem, pled guilty to all the charges against him in February 2014 and, in exchange for his agreement to testify against another detainee, he received a reduced sentence. Darbi was repatriated to Saudi Arabia in 2018, the only detainee to leave Guantánamo during the administration of Obama's successor, Donald Trump. Noor Uthman Mohammed pled guilty to material support for terrorism and conspiracy in February 2011; he was repatriated to Sudan in 2013. Majid Khan, one of the former CIA prisoners, who was represented by CCR attorney Wells Dixon, pled guilty in 2012 and got a reduced sentence in exchange for agreeing to cooperate with prosecutors in the 9/11 case; he remains at Guantánamo, although according to his plea deal, he could be released as early as 2023.

The majority of Guantánamo detainees would never be prosecuted; some had been cleared but remained imprisoned because the Obama administration didn't release them, and others, the "forever prisoners," had no prospect of release. In January 2012, Tom Wilner and Andy Worthington, a British journalist and prodigious conveyor of information and personal stories about everyone ever held at Guantánamo, inaugurated Close Guantánamo Now! The mission of this campaign was to pressure the US government by keeping the prison in the news and raising public awareness about the men whose only hope was a political solution. The signatories to the campaign's mission statement included all of the organizations and many of the leading figures involved in the war in court.

In February 2013, the Guantánamo population stood at 166, with 86 cleared for release and another 46 designated for indefinite detention without trial. That month, more than two-thirds of them—104, reportedly—went on hunger strike. Hunger striking is a common method for prisoners all over the world to protest the conditions of their confinement by exercising the limited power that they have—the power to refuse to eat. Hunger strikes were a recurring phenomenon at Gitmo, but proportionally, the 2013 strike was the largest.

When it started, David Remes alerted people on the torturelist that over a dozen of his eighteen Yemeni clients had joined the hunger strike, and four were being force fed. In 2008, Remes had quit the firm of Covington &

Burling to create a human rights organization, Appeal for Justice, and now he was working full-time on Guantánamo at his own expense. He regularly posted messages to the list about events and developments in the prison, and about his clients' tragedies and travails. The client Remes wrote most frequently about was Adnan Latif, a poet who was so despairing of his continued detention, despite having been cleared for release four times since 2004, most recently in 2010, that he had attempted suicide on several occasions. In one of the letters that Remes shared, Latif wrote: "Anybody who is able to die will be able to achieve happiness for himself, he has no hope except that." On September 10, 2012, Latif, who had contracted pneumonia, was found dead in the punishment cell where he had been moved three days earlier from the prison clinic.

In April 2013, Remes posted a note from one of his hunger-striking clients: "A human being should defend himself, but if he were to become totally unable to do so, he should take the difficult and simple decision because he has no other options. Doing so, he achieves victory over injustice and humiliation and feels his dignity as a human being." Remes provided the torturelist with a summary of the events that precipitated this mass hunger strike. In September 2012, the new JTF-GTMO commander, Colonel John Bogdan, without provocation, ordered his men to storm Camp 6, where "compliant" detainees lived communally. During the autumn, the temperature in the cells was lowered to 62 degrees. In January, a guard posted in a tower fired into a group of detainees in the recreation area, wounding one. The strike started the following month. In an attempt to break it, Bogdan ordered guards to confiscate personal items, including family letters and photographs, legal papers, and extra blankets. He also ordered his officers to search the men's Qur'ans, thus resuming a malicious and offensive practice that was stopped in 2006. Remes explained that the detainees offered to surrender their Qur'ans to prevent them from being mishandled, but Bodgan refused to accept them or to stop the searches, and he would not even discuss their grievances until they ended their hunger strike.

According to the Standard Operating Procedure manual in effect at the time, "in the event of a mass hunger strike, isolating hunger striking patients from each other is vital to prevent them from achieving solidarity." During a predawn raid on April 13, more than one hundred detainees in Camp 6 were moved to solitary cells. The manual's "general algorithm" for assessing if people are hunger strikers is as follows: missing nine consecutive meals, and a drop in body weight below 85 percent of their ideal. Those assessed as hunger strikers could be force-fed. Captain Robert Durand, the JTF-GTMO spokesperson, told Rosenberg and other journalists on the base in March 2013: "Passing out constitutes consent to a tube feeding." Rosenberg collected and reported on the array of answers provided to journalists about why the prison military and medical staff were force-feeding strikers: it's not humane to let detainees starve themselves to death; letting captives starve is at odds with the ethics of US military medicine; it's un-American to let people in custody endanger their health or their lives; it would look bad if people died from self-starvation; and force-feeding is policy.

The number of prisoners being force-fed rose as the strike endured. The process involves strapping them into restraint chairs which resemble electric chairs, inserting a tube through the nose down into the stomach, and then pumping in Ensure (a nutrient-rich liquid). After the "nutrient infusion," detainees were placed in a "dry cell" and observed for up to sixty minutes to prevent them from vomiting. If someone vomited, he could be put through the whole process again.

If this coercive hunger management process were not appalling enough, another item in the manual authorized the use of a controversial drug, Metoclopramide, commonly known by its brand name Reglan, to "enhance digestion." Writing for *Al Jazeera*, Jason Leopold reported that in February 2009, the Food and Drug Administration had slapped Reglan "with a black box label—the agency's strongest warning—to inform patients about the dangers associated with chronic use of the drug. According to the FDA's own medication guide, additional side effects include depression, thoughts about depression and, in extreme cases, suicidal thoughts and suicide."

The American Medical Association, the ICRC, and the UN Office of the High Commissioner for Human Rights protested the practice of force-feeding at Guantánamo as illegal and unethical. They pointed out that doctors who administered or were involved in force-feeding were violating the World Medical Association's 1975 Tokyo Declaration and 1991 Malta Declaration.

In response to criticism by medical and human rights experts, the Pentagon adopted a strategy of euphemizing force-feeding as "enteral feeding" or "tube feeding." Apparently, President Obama did not get the memo because, on May 23, during a major national security speech (the second and last during his term in office), he described the hunger strike at Guantánamo as a crisis and a policy failure: "Look at the current situation, where we are force-feeding detainees who are holding a hunger strike. Is that who we are?

Is that something that our Founders foresaw? Is that the America we want to leave to our children?"

At a press conference on June 4, SOUTHCOM commander General John F. Kelly took issue with the president's statement. "We don't force-feed right now at Gitmo." Rather, troops "enterally feed" hunger strikers. A reporter asked White House spokesperson Caitlin Hayden whether Obama would retract his remarks about forced feedings. "The President's comments stand." According to Remes, who spoke by telephone with one of his clients on June 14, "the hunger strike is still going strong."

Fourteen detainees sent an open letter to the prison's medical staff. "Dear doctor," they wrote. "You may be able to keep me alive for a long time in a permanently debilitated state. But with so many of us on hunger strike, you are attempting a treatment experiment on an unprecedented scale ... Whether you remain in the military or return to civilian practice, you will have to live with what you have done and not done here at Guantánamo for the rest of your life." The detainees' message was endorsed by dozens of doctors and other health professionals in an open letter to President Obama; they urged the government to permit independent professionals to have full access to hunger striking prisoners and their medical records. That request came to naught.

When political prisoners are incarcerated for their involvement in a cause that has local or wide public support, hunger strikes and other protests against abusive treatment and inhumane conditions of detention can resonate beyond the prison walls. This was the case of Northern Irish members of the Irish Republican Army, whose cause was the reunification of Ireland and whose British custodians denied their demands to be treated as political prisoners. In 1981, IRA prisoners mounted a hunger strike to the death; eleven prisoners, including Bobby Sands, who was elected to Parliament while he was on strike, died. That strike and the resultant deaths had a transformative effect on politics in Northern Ireland, and Sands was hailed as a martyr for the cause. These circumstances do not apply to detainees at Guantánamo; being Muslim males was the only identity they shared. Imprisoned without trial on a remote island, and cut off from their families, there was no political constituency predisposed to care about their well-being except their attorneys, human rights activists, and aggrieved medical professionals. The mass hunger strike in 2013 was reported in the media, but no significant public mobilization ever emerged to challenge the conditions that precipitated it, or the practice of force-feeding. Obama decried the situation as "a crisis and a policy failure," while failing to use the power of his administration to end it.

On the military commission front, the roof started collapsing on the flimsy legal edifice of fabricated war crimes on October 16, 2012. That was the day the DC Circuit Court issued a unanimous opinion in the appeal of Salim Hamdan's conviction on the charge of material support for terrorism. The court ruled that material support was not a war crime, and vacated Hamdan's conviction. According to Judge Brett Kavanaugh, who authored the decision, Congress had stated its intent not to allow people to be prosecuted for activities that were not crimes at the time they were committed (the ex post facto clause). At the time Hamdan engaged in the activities for which he was convicted (between 1996 and 2001), material support for terrorism was not a crime under international laws of war. Therefore, even though the 2006 Military Commission Act made material support a war crime prosecutable in the commissions, it did not apply retroactively to past actions. The court's decision upheld the principle of "no crime without law" (*nullum crimen sine lege*). In a footnote, Kavanaugh wrote that Congress is not *constitutionally* constrained from making up new war crimes, but such legislation would apply only to actions that occur after it was signed into law.

Three months later, in an appeal of Ali al-Bahlul's conviction, the DC Circuit Court ruled that neither of the crimes for which he was serving a life sentence—material support and conspiracy—were international war crimes at the time of his actions. The government was forced to vacate not only al-Bahlul's conviction for material support, but also the convictions of David Hicks, the first person to plead guilty in the commissions, and Noor Uthman Mohammed. Ibrahim al-Qosi's conviction also would have been vacated, but he refused to agree to any appeal process. The impact of these decisions stripped the government of the ability to charge any other detainees for this invented war crime.

But the government decided to appeal its loss on al-Bahlul's conspiracy conviction, and requested a hearing en banc. On July 14, 2014, the court affirmed al-Bahlul's conviction for conspiracy, but stuck with the earlier decision that the other charges must be vacated. On further appeal, al-Bahlul's lawyers challenged the conspiracy conviction as a violation of the ex post facto rule. On June 12, 2015, the court vacated the conspiracy charge because the law it was based on violated the constitutional separation of powers. The government again petitioned for an en banc hearing, contending that if the ruling was not overturned, it would restrict "the authority of Congress and the President not simply over pre-2006 conduct in the current armed conflict, but over future combatants in future conflicts, in circumstances that we cannot foresee."

On February 13, 2016, President Obama made a statement about Guantánamo in which he said that other world leaders were asking him why the prison had not been closed yet. "As Americans, we pride ourselves on being a beacon to other nations, a model of the rule of law. But 15 years after 9/11 ... we're still having to defend the existence of a facility and a process where not a single verdict has been reached in those attacks—not a single one." Obama noted that he didn't have to worry about politics, because he would be out of office soon, but it would take an act of Congress to get the job of closing Guantánamo done. He concluded with the following:

> I don't want to pass this problem on to the next President, whoever it is. And if, as a nation, we don't deal with this now, when will we deal with it? Are we going to let this linger on for another 15 years, another 20 years, another 30 years? If we don't do what's required now, I think future generations are going to look back and ask why we failed to act when the right course, the right side of history, and of justice, and our best American traditions was clear.

More hollow words: If Obama wanted to do his part to close Guantánamo in the time he had left, the government should have withdrawn from the al-Bahlul appeal. That didn't happen. On October 20, 2016, a deeply divided ruling came out with a slim majority upholding al-Bahlul's conviction for conspiracy. Steve Vladek, a University of Texas law professor and a high-profile expert on national security law, described the panoply of DC Circuit Court opinions as "surprisingly sloppy" in a *Lawfare* blogpost. "Until and unless that question is conclusively resolved by the courts, the commissions will continue to operate under a long (and ever-lengthening) shadow of illegitimacy. In the end, I can't see how that's good for anybody, except perhaps as a continuing jobs program for military commission lawyers."

Only two cases stayed alive while Obama remained in office: the one against 'Abd al-Rahim al-Nashiri, who was charged with the 2000 bombing of the USS Cole, and the case against five defendants accused of responsibility for the 9/11 attacks. These two cases represent the last front in the fight against torture.

TEN

The Last Front

THE CASE AGAINST FIVE MEN accused of responsibility for the 9/11 terrorist attacks will be the largest criminal trial in US history because of the number of victims. The charge sheet lists the names of 2,976 people who were direct casualties of two hijacked commercial airliners that crashed into the World Trade Center, another that crashed into the Pentagon, and a fourth, probably aiming for the US Capitol Building, that was downed in a field in Shanksville, Pennsylvania, because several passengers overpowered their hijackers.

This case has spanned four presidencies. Throughout, the government's intertwining goals remained the same: to get guilty verdicts and death sentences for the accused, and in doing so, to provide justice for the thousands of victims of 9/11. But the defendants are also victims; they were tortured by the government that now seeks to convict and execute them. Nothing better illustrates the irreconcilability of torture and justice than the pretrial litigation in the 9/11 case.

On September 16, 2001, when President George Bush authorized the CIA's new mission to hunt and capture high-value terror suspects, and to detain and interrogate them in secret locales, the objective was not to gather evidence for future trials but rather to obtain actionable intelligence about terrorist plots and networks. The Agency was assured that people they would disappear could stay disappeared forever. That assurance was demolished by the Supreme Court's June 2006 decision in *Hamdan v. Rumsfeld*. To comply with the ruling, the Bush administration was compelled to empty the CIA black sites. Fourteen prisoners were transferred to Guantánamo in September. Because the things that were done to these men during their years in CIA custody are regarded as state secrets, their own memories are treated as classified information. To shield those secrets from exposure, they were housed in a secret facility on the naval base, later revealed through a redaction error to be Camp 7. The men could only speak to people with top-secret security clearance, and anything they said was presumptively classified. And yet, the government imagined that some of the fourteen could be tried in a legal process that would be perceived as fair.

After the Military Commission Act was passed by Congress and signed into law in October 2006, the Bush administration took immediate steps to put the men accused of playing roles in the 9/11 attacks on trial. Khalid Sheikh Mohammed, a Pakistani national whom the government refers to as KSM, is accused of being the mastermind of the plot. Walid bin Attash, a Saudi who went to Afghanistan when he was fourteen and lost part of a leg fighting against the Northern Alliance, is accused of training several of the hijackers to fight in close quarters using box cutters as weapons. Ramzi bin al-Shibh, a Yemeni, is accused of recruiting some of the hijackers who formed a cell in Hamburg, Germany, and serving as the intermediary between Mohammed and the head hijacker, Mohammed Atta. Ammar al-Baluchi, whom the government refers to as Ali Abdul-Aziz Ali or Triple A, is Mohammed's nephew. Al-Baluchi is accused of making money transfers to a bank account in the United States that some of the hijackers accessed. Mustafa al-Hawsawi, a Saudi, is also accused of transferring money and making travel arrangements for some of the hijackers. Mohammed al-Qahtani would have been the sixth defendant, but charges against him were dismissed in 2008 by the convening authority of the commissions because he had been tortured, not in CIA black sites like the others, but by military interrogators at Guantánamo.

When the five 9/11 defendants were arraigned in June 2008, the government hoped their trial would finish before Bush left office. Instead, the case fell apart in December when the defendants made the legally impossible offer to plead guilty on the condition that they go directly to execution. The Obama administration, after abandoning its plan to try the five in federal court in New York City, recharged them in the military commissions on April 4, 2011. In official filings, the case's abbreviated name is *KSM II* to denote that this the second time it is being tried in the commissions.

The Obama administration's efforts to reform the military commissions included appointing a new chief prosecutor with stellar bona fides: Brigadier General Mark Martins, a Rhodes scholar who had attended Harvard law school with Barack Obama and done many tours of duty, including in Iraq and Afghanistan, most recently had co-directed the administration's interagency detainee review task force. In 2011, he was put in direct charge of the two death penalty cases: 9/11 and the USS Cole, whose defendant is 'Abd al-Rahim al-Nashiri.

Another reform was the 2009 MCA's provision of government funding for lawyers with death penalty experience (learned counsel) for capital cases. Two of the lawyers recruited by the John Adams Project back in 2008, David Nevin and Gary Sowards, chose to continue representing Mohammed. Walter Ruiz, who had retired from the Navy reserves, remained the head of al-Hawsawi's team because he had death penalty experience as a public defender in Florida. New learned counsel were recruited for the other three defendants. Cheryl Bormann, a criminal defense attorney from Chicago, offered her services when Illinois ended its death penalty in 2011; she became the head of bin Attash's defense team. James Harrington, a senior partner in a Buffalo, New York, law firm, was chosen to head the team for bin al-Shibh. James Connell, a partner in a Northern Virginia law firm, was hired to head al-Baluchi's team. He had some prior experience on the case because he had helped write motions on capital law for *KSM I*.

As *KSM II* started taking shape, I wanted to get the perspectives of lawyers with years of experience in the system about how "reformed" they thought the commissions were likely to be. In December 2010, I met with Adam Thurschwell, general counsel for the Military Commissions Defense Office (MCDO). He has capital defense experience, and he was involved as a consultant in most of the commission cases since 2008. During our conversation, as he was explaining why he was skeptical that the reforms would significantly improve the system, he posed a rhetorical question: "Is the military commission a real court?" Then he said: "There are two rules. Rule 1: KSM must die. Rule 2: there are no other rules."

Katherine Newell, the MCDO's in-house torture expert, told me about one of the projects she had been working on for a year. She was gathering and analyzing all declassified official documents about the CIA's rendition, detention, and interrogation (RDI) program in order to assist the 9/11 and USS Cole defense teams to understand how their clients were *actually* treated in the black sites. She referred to the document with a tongue-in-cheek name as "the ass lesion memo." Ass lesions, she explained, can result from being kept immobilized for long periods of time. Medical protocols for doctors working in the black sites gave guidance for monitoring detainees' conditions and providing treatments, as needed, to enable interrogations to continue. "If someone got an ass lesion," she said, "I wanted to know at what point treatment would begin. When early signs that a lesion was forming? When the lesion became large and painful?" This singular example of lesions and their treatment was illustrative of the totality of control over the bodies and minds of people detained in black sites.

Newell finished the document several months later. I asked her for a copy, but she told me that, even though the materials she used were declassified, she couldn't circulate it until the CIA finished its review. It took over a year for the document to be cleared—with redactions. Someone passed Newell's document to Daniel Jones, the Senate staffer who was heading the Senate Select Committee on Intelligence (SSCI) investigation of the CIA's RDI program, which began in 2009. Jones later told Newell that her document came in very handy during his back-and-forth with CIA officials who were trying to redact declassified information.

In early October 2011, I met James Connell. He told me that he had been at Guantánamo for what he described as "the event": the December 2008 hearing when the defendants said they wanted to plead guilty and be executed. "Wanting to die is quite common in death penalty cases," he said. He made his first trip as al-Baluchi's lawyer two weeks before we met, but he couldn't see his client because the Pentagon was holding up his security clearance. I asked how he anticipated that politics would affect this highest of high-profile cases. He conceded that he hadn't formed an opinion yet. "I don't really follow the commissions because I'm not a news junky." Being a news junky myself, I remember thinking: strap in, buddy, because it's going to be a bumpy ride.

Connell explained that he planned to use an analytical tool called CaseMap to chronologically organize the vast and varied information relevant to this case, including "reports from military commission investigators, journalists, et cetera, and publicly available information from over two hundred habeas cases." He added, "So many people have done so many things, it's impossible to know who knows what. This program will help us." Connell mentioned that Stephen Grey used the same program to trace all the flights that moved CIA prisoners around the gulag of black sites for his book, *Ghost Plane*. Connell also outlined a plan he was hatching to reach out to the 9/11 victim community. "This is a standard part of capital defense in general. Sometimes victim outreach is transformative. Sometimes it is healing."

The first task for the 9/11 defense lawyers, Connell explained, was to prepare mitigation motions laying out all extenuating circumstances they want the court to consider in deciding whether to reduce charges or seek a lesser sentence for their clients. These mitigation motions were due in January 2012, hence the urgent need for well-organized information about the clients' black-site years. An argument Connell was developing for his motion was based on federal law: "One statutory mitigating factor is if people are equally or more culpable and didn't get the death penalty. The Moussaoui case is important here." Zacarias Moussaoui, a French citizen who was arrested in the United States in August 2001 and prosecuted in federal court, pled guilty in 2006 to all charges against him, including conspiring with al-Qaeda to kill US citizens. The jury decided to sentence him to life rather than death. "So in our mitigation submissions," Connell said, "we might argue that Mr. al-Baluchi is accused of transferring money, not the serious charges Moussaoui was convicted of." He added, "Courts generally don't execute people who are accessories before the fact. This would apply to Mr. al-Baluchi and maybe Mr. al-Hawsawi." He was alluding to the possibility that those two might have been unaware of the 9/11 plot before the attacks. Connell's then-untested reasoning was that the reformed military commissions would comport with federal laws and precedents.

Two days later, I met Cheryl Bormann and bin Attash's military lawyer, Major Michael Schwartz. Bormann had met bin Attash for the first time a week earlier. "Getting to see my client is very difficult," she said. "I have to give at least fourteen days' notice prior to a visit. Apparently, moving the clients is a big operation." Bormann exuded a no-nonsense attitude about how capital cases should proceed, which, she made clear, bore little resemblance to what she was encountering in this case. "It's prison policy to allow only four clients to meet lawyers on any given day. But there are five men on trial, so that's going to be a problem when all of us are down there at the same time." Another problem was that only four people could meet with a client at once, but her team had four lawyers, and they would always need to include an interpreter. She identified a third problem: "For example, a psychologist wants to conduct a series of IQ tests. For testing, no one else should be there, but the rules require a lawyer to be there."

Bormann explained that the 9/11 attorneys were waiting for "prereferral discovery," meaning information and evidence that prosecutors plan to use to refer charges against the accused. "This is similar to information in a civilian system of grand jury," she said. But the 9/11 defense teams had not received any discovery yet, and the deadline for the mitigation motion was looming. "In this system, the defense has no right to subpoena the government! On top of that, the convening authority has no power to order the prosecution or the government to produce discovery." Bormann said that representing her client would require "Herculean effort—there are parts of his life that are unknown." One source of information that she mentioned was former FBI agent Ali Soufan's 2011 book, *The Black Banners: The Inside Story of 9/11 and the War against al-Qaeda,* which has a chapter on bin Attash. (An unredacted version was published in 2020 with a new subtitle: *How Torture Derailed the War on Terror after 9/11.*)

I asked Bormann how she anticipated making her client's torture an element of the case. She had lots of experience challenging Chicago police interrogation tactics, including torture. But, she conceded, "that's different from CIA custody where torture occurred over years." The CIA's objective was to extract intelligence, whereas renegade Chicago police used violence and coercion to extract confessions for trials. "If my client was tortured in CIA custody, we need to consider what were the effects? What statements did he make? Are they reliable? All of this is relevant for mitigation."

The 9/11 arraignment hearing took place on May 5, 2012, with Colonel James Pohl presiding. Bin Attash was brought into court strapped to a restraint chair, apparently as punishment for disruptive behavior in the lockup. Bormann cut a surprising figure when she entered the courtroom covered head to toe in a black abaya. Other female defense attorneys who were not soldiers in uniform wore hijabs to show respect for their clients' religious beliefs.

Judge Pohl started the hearing by seeking confirmation that the defendants agreed to be represented by their lawyers. Several defense attorneys tried to get the judge first to address their motions about the lack of resources available to them, the onerousness of the obligation to treat anything their clients said as presumptively classified, and clients' mistreatment by guards, including being strip-searched before the hearing. Judge Pohl declined to address those motions and stayed on script, to the extent that he could. The five defendants refused to answer any of his questions, so he confirmed the attorneys without their endorsement. For the last session of what turned into a twelve-hour hearing, General Martins and other prosecutors read the eighty-seven-page charge sheet and, because the accused refused to wear their headphones, a translator spoke aloud for them to hear. They were arraigned.

At a hearing on January 28, 2013, David Nevin, Mohammed's learned counsel, was addressing Judge Pohl about the scheduling of a classified motion concerning the CIA's secret prisons. As soon as he said the word "secret," a red flashing light went off, white noise blasted the courtroom, and the audio feed to the gallery was cut. Nevin, the judge, and the court security officer looked at each other in puzzlement. Someone somewhere else was remote controlling the courtroom. Pohl's immediate response was anger: "If some external body is turning the commission off under their own view of what things ought to be, . . . then we are going to have a little meeting about who turns that light on or off." The remote controller, as it turned out, was someone in the service of the CIA or, as Pohl dutifully blurred the source the following day, the "original classifying authority." This red-light incident caused the defense lawyers to wonder whether the microphones on their tables were being monitored by government spies. Nevin asked if an expert witness could be called to explain how the court monitoring system worked, but Pohl averred that he didn't even know "what guy or gal to call."

The following month, someone on Nevin's team noticed that what appeared to be smoke detectors in Camp Echo II where lawyer-client meetings take place were actually listening devices. Research into the company that produces these devices revealed that they have state-of-the-art capability to pick up even the faintest whispers. What about the video cameras mounted on the walls? That technology was so sophisticated that it could record even the smallest writing on a notepad. The possibility that lawyer-client meetings were being monitored launched another set of motion battles. The challenge in resolving this issue was threefold: the government had deceived the defense with assurances that their meetings were not monitored; then when the spy equipment was discovered, their only recourse was to litigate the problem in the commission; and—most importantly—even if the judge ordered the monitoring devices to be removed in the interest of justice, he has no power to enforce the decision because the base's facilities are under the control of JTF-GTMO, whose rules and interests are unrelated and largely indifferent to the legal process. One manifestation of this latter point is that, while the defendants are ostensibly presumed innocent for the purpose of trial, the commanders and guards who control their lives and movements regard and treat them as guilty.

Every member of the defense teams has top-secret security clearance, and many have prior experience working with highly classified information in national security cases. They bristled at the stringent terms and accusatory tone of the memorandum of understanding, or MOU, which is the protective order they were required to sign before the government would allow them to receive any discovery. In addition to the standard features of protective orders for Guantánamo lawyers, such as lack of lawyer-client confidentiality in legal correspondence, the 9/11 defense lawyers were obligated to neither confirm nor deny any details relating to their clients' ghost years in CIA custody, even if those details are publicly known as a result of investigative journalism, human rights reporting, or international court cases. They were barred from showing or discussing classified materials with their clients. That included the men's own letters, which became classified. Most aggravating and onerous was the requirement to treat everything their clients say as presumptively classified, and not just ordinary classified but "TOP SECRET//SCI level, which requires extremely stringent security measures." The MOU also required detailed reporting on any substantive contacts with foreign nationals, which would expose the work product of their overseas investigations and could reveal the contours of their trial strategies to the prosecution.

At the start, the defense attorneys took a united stand by refusing to sign the MOU because its terms contradicted their professional needs and legal ethics and infringed on the rights of their clients to effective legal counsel. The government's position was that the terms of the order were necessary and legitimate to protect state secrets. Connell was the first to yield. For eighteen months, al-Baluchi refused to meet him in Camp Echo. To try to break this deadlock, he had to go to his client, which meant visiting him in Camp 7. To do so, Connell had to sign the protective order.

All five defense teams had submitted motions requesting permission to spend forty-eight hours in Camp 7 to get a full sense of their clients' conditions of confinement and the behavior of the guard force. Prosecutors countered with an offer of a two-hour escorted tour during which lawyers could see their clients' cells but not their clients in them, and no talking to guards. Judge Pohl split the difference: lawyers could visit Camp 7 for twelve hours, and they could spend time with their clients in their cells. On August 15, 2013, Connell, a psychiatrist, and a crime scene investigator boarded a van with blacked-out windows and black garbage bags hung inside to prevent them from seeing out the front window. They were taken on a circuitous forty-five-minute journey to further obscure the location of Camp 7. But the visit served its purpose: Connell and al-Baluchi talked, shared a meal, and bonded.

I made my first trip to Guantánamo for 9/11 hearings in December 2013. At the press conference the night after we arrived, Connell and al-Baluchi's military lawyer, Lieutenant Colonel Sterling Thomas, were the first to speak. They walked us journalists through the issues in the motions that would be argued that week; there was one on unlawful command influence, another challenging the death penalty referral as defective, and a third challenging the jurisdiction of the commissions. Connell explained, "Mr. al-Baluchi is a civilian who is accused of killing civilians. Why is he being prosecuted in a military court?" He also explained that there would be a closed hearing on a prosecution motion pertaining to the classification of information about CIA black sites. Connell wrapped up his comments by informing us that in the Hollywood film *Zero Dark 30*, which had premiered a year earlier, the character named "Ammar," who is tortured in the early scenes, is based on his client. While the CIA refused to give al-Baluchi's lawyers information about his torture, they had readily shared it with filmmakers Kathryn Bigelow and Mark Boals, who don't have top-secret clearance.

General Martins began his remarks at the press conference by describing his recent tour of the 9/11 memorial, a poignant reminder of the high stakes in this case. Then he stated that, while his job is to ensure "open and fair proceedings," this doesn't negate the legitimacy of hypervigilance in handing classified materials. He explained that the reason only Connell's team had started receiving classified discovery was because they alone had signed the protective order. He concluded by saying, "This is a methodical, law-governed process that will achieve justice, however long that takes."

The floor was opened for questions. Martins knew the other journalists by name and interjected friendly asides as he responded to them. When it was my turn, I asked if he could explain how the prosecution decides what kinds of information will be provided to the defense in discovery, and what laws guide those decisions. He said, "Let's analogize from the Ghailani trial." Ahmed Ghailani, a Tanzanian, was one of the fourteen CIA prisoners who arrived at Guantánamo in 2006. He was accused of conspiring in the 1998 al-Qaeda bombings of US embassies in Dar es Salaam and Nairobi. The Obama administration decided to make his case a test run for federal trials for Guantánamo detainees. In June 2009, Ghailani was transported to New York where he was tried. Martins's point was that Ghailani's attorneys were subject to a protective order requiring them to treat anything he said about his experiences in CIA custody as classified. "As that case demonstrated," Martins said, "there are still important sources and methods that need to be protected." Martins didn't mention the political controversies the Ghailani trial had aroused: Judge Lewis Kaplan decided to exclude a key prosecution witness because his statements incriminating Ghailani had been made while he was in a black site, and the jury convicted Ghailani of one count of conspiracy while acquitting him of 284 other charges, including murder.

Although Ghailani was sentenced to life in prison, opponents of federal trials lambasted the exclusion of a key witness and the single-charge verdict as proof that civilian judges and juries can't be trusted to be as tough as military judges and panels would be. The politically controversial outcome of Ghailani's case motivated Congress to pass legislation blocking future federal trials.

In answering my question, Martins explained that decisions about what to release in discovery are made by senior officials who have classification authority. He was implying—without directly stating—that the CIA was in control. For this trial, Martins said, prosecutors "are not going to use any evidence that will not be available in open hearings." That would exclude any statements made by anyone while they were in the CIA black sites. "But," Martins continued, "we must be careful about what evidence does become available. We don't want information to get out that will aid bad guys still on the run. Also, we don't want something to come out that will prevent accountability." The accountability he was referring to was for the 9/11 attacks, not for CIA torture. "The people," meaning the United States, "do not forfeit their chance to obtain accountability because the government may have crossed the line."

The next morning, journalists filed over to the high-security court complex. We were ushered into the gallery where we took our assigned seats. NGO observers sat behind us. On the other side of the gallery, approximately twenty 9/11 victim family members (VFMs) were seated. There was a curtain that could be drawn, if needed, to separate the gallery in half to provide some privacy for the family members.

Khalid Sheikh Mohammad was the first defendant to be escorted into the courtroom. He wore a camouflage jacket, a white turban, and a black-and-white kuffiya. I asked Carol Rosenberg, who was sitting beside me, how he dyed his massive beard a surrealistic shade of red. She wasn't sure, because that information was classified, but she suggested, "Henna?" The Pentagon's victim family liaison began guiding them one by one to the front of the gallery on the journalists' side so that they could get a better view of Mohammed. They gazed at him in somber silence.

Walid bin Attash and Ramzi bin al-Shibh also wore camouflage jackets. Rosenberg explained that they and Mohammed did so because they regarded themselves as prisoners of war. Ammar al-Baluchi and Mustafa al-Hawsawi wore white tunics. After the defendants were settled at their tables, seventeen soldiers took positions shoulder-to-shoulder along the wall to guard them.

At every defense table, there were three or four lawyers plus a paralegal and an interpreter. I hadn't met most of them yet. Rosenberg pointed out who was who. One of the people I recognized was Suzanne Lachelier, now a civilian, who had joined al-Hawsawi's team. Another was Denny LeBoeuf, one of the organizers of the John Adams Project, who was on Mohammed's team. On the prosecution side, in addition to General Martins, the trial counsel team was composed of two civilian lead prosecutors, Ed Ryan and Robert Swann, as well as Clayton Trivett and Jeffrey Groharing, who had been the lead prosecutor for the Omar Khadr case.

The hearing got off to a rocky start. Bin al-Shibh, whose assorted mental problems were an ongoing issue, said he did not understand Judge Pohl's opening instructions. He used the opportunity to protest his treatment by guards and said that he wanted to leave. His military lawyer, Lieutenant Colonel Kevin Bogucki, explained to the judge that his client can't sleep because of constant noises in his cell, then said: "We want you to order the government to force the prison commanders of Camp 7 to stop the noise and vibrations that disturb Mr. bin al-Shibh." Bogucki pointed out that the judge had already asked JTF-GTMO to resolve the issue, but they hadn't. "This meets the definition of contempt," Bogucki said. "Since we have no authority to end his abusive treatment, we must keep putting it on the record. This government contempt will affect the view of these proceedings as fair."

Judge Pohl said, "The government says it isn't happening, Mr. bin al-Shibh says it is. You have presented no evidence." Was bin al-Shibh being intentionally harassed, or were the noises and vibrations figments of his tortured imagination? Pohl advised Bogucki: "File a motion." Bogucki responded, "We continue making a record on this because we have no access." Pohl replied that statements by a lawyer in court don't make a record, "evidence does. The burden is on you. You are giving me problems with no remedy."

The problem was not a "lack" of evidence but rather the inability to obtain evidence about the conditions of confinement in Camp 7 because the CIA would not permit an inspection by independent investigators. Bogucki offered a workaround solution: the judge could order a recording device to be installed in his client's cell to learn whether the noises were real or imagined. As soon as he said that, the court security officer cut off the sound to the gallery. When it was restored, we could hear Judge Pohl ask, "What sounds?" Bogucki: "Banging and knocking." Pohl: "File a motion!" Then bin al-Shibh started yelling about waterboarding and CIA secret prisons. He was removed from the courtroom.

The rest of the day and, indeed, the rest of the week proceeded as a series of skirmishes between defense lawyers and prosecutors over motions. The common theme in defense lawyers' arguments was that overweening secrecy was adversely affecting the defendants' right to a fair trial. Cheryl Bormann told Judge Pohl about one specific way she was unable to provide effective counsel: The two lawyers who advised the convening authority to refer death penalty charges, Michael Breslin and Michael Chapman, had ignored "the torture of my client between 2003 and 2006. Due process requires—in a death penalty case especially—pre-indictment input" from the defense. She explained that if she had had information about the treatment of her client in CIA custody, unimpeded access to him at Guantánamo, and the opportunity to provide input to the convening authority, bin Attash's torture might have affected the death penalty referral, like it did in the dismissal of charges against Mohammed al-Qahtani. Judge Pohl's questions seemed to suggest that he did not understand how torture and secrecy affected due process. Bormann explained that if those two lawyers decided that bin Attash's torture didn't matter, to avoid an al-Qahtani-like situation, "that would be relevant to the defective referral motion."

In the spring of 2014, the defense teams learned that the FBI had been secretly investigating them since the previous November, when agents had begun attempting to persuade or intimidate some non-attorney members to inform on their colleagues. The operation was exposed when a member of Jim Harrington's team disregarded the FBI's instructions not to disclose that he had been approached. Harrington discovered that another team member had been spying for the FBI, and, to compound the problem, Harrington didn't have the authority to fire this Pentagon-provided contractor. When other lawyers questioned their team members, they learned that the FBI had attempted to turn others into informants as well. Although the prosecutors had no hand in the FBI's spy operation, as the government's representatives, they had to argue that the case was not too damaged to proceed.

To put the case back on track, a Justice Department special prosecutor was appointed to investigate. At a hearing on June 16, 2014, he testified that the FBI was "no longer" pursuing a criminal investigation of the defense teams. Because the investigation was "closed," the special prosecutor urged Judge Pohl to deny the defense requests for hearings to call representatives of the FBI to testify about who had ordered the investigation and why. Pohl took that advice and declined to order a hearing for FBI testimony. The defense lawyers were not assuaged by the special prosecutor's assurance that they were in the clear.

Every time I went to Guantánamo, I sought opportunities to interview people about the case. These conversations often took place at a picnic table outside the decrepit hangar where the Media Operations Center (MOC) is located. In June 2014, I talked with several of the defense attorneys. The first was Walter Ruiz, whom I had previously interviewed when he was on the Khadr case. Among the defense teams, Ruiz is regarded—and regards himself—as an outlier because his primary goal is to sever al-Hawsawi from the group trial. "We want a fair, honest assessment of his case, not guilt by association. The facts are dramatically different among the defendants." Ruiz also talked about a motion he was working on to try to challenge the inhumane conditions in Camp 7. "It's pseudo-isolation," he said. "They live in conditions where interactions are so limited that they are, for all intents and purposes, isolated. This borders on or could rise to the level of torture according to international law standards." He said he went to The Hague, the site of the UN ad hoc tribunal for the former Yugoslavia and the International Criminal Court, to learn about the conditions of confinement for defendants being tried in those venues for the most serious violations of international law. Unlike the people held in Camp 7, he said, they aren't isolated or prohibited from interacting with other people.

Ruiz connected the conditions in Camp 7 to his client's health. Of the five defendants, al-Hawsawi is certainly the most physically damaged. He is in constant pain from injuries he sustained in the black sites when he was sodomized so brutally that it caused a disfiguring medical condition called rectal prolapse. Every day, Ruiz explained, his client faces the hard choice of fasting or eating; when he eats, he has to defecate, and when he defecates, he has to reinsert his own anal tissue. Because of the pain, al-Hawsawi often forgoes hearings, and when he does attend, he sits in a specially padded chair. (He had rectal reconstructive surgery in 2016, but it didn't ameliorate his suffering.)

Bin al-Shibh seems the most psychologically fragile of the five, and his lawyers' incapacity to do anything to improve his situation intensifies his frustrations. When I spoke with Jim Harrington, he explained that relations with his client were getting worse because, two months earlier, Judge Pohl had ordered a competency hearing for bin al-Shibh. He refused to cooperate, and the mere questioning of his competency further angered him. "We are in a war of attrition with our client," Harrington said. As for the legal case, bin al-Shibh "does not want or care about mitigation. He wants the death penalty. He wants to be a martyr." Harrington has a wry sense of humor that comes out in court on occasion, but when discussing the particulars of the case, his frustration was palpable. He said the discovery that someone was spying for the FBI roiled his team and created a conflict of interest between the lawyers and their client. "The complications in this case are unique and everything is hard and slow," he said. "There is a constant ethical quandary."

The following month, the complications in bin al-Shibh's situation intensified: Judge Pohl made a unilateral decision to sever his case from the rest because of the unresolved questions about his mental condition and the conflicts of interest the FBI investigation had created. The prosecution appealed because they wanted the trial to go forward with all five defendants. In August, Pohl unilaterally decided to reverse himself and he unsevered bin al-Shibh.

David Nevin has a calm, studied demeanor and razor-sharp courtroom skills, which, long ago, earned him the nickname, "the velvet shiv." When we sat down together in June 2014, I began by asking how he would describe the state of the case, now that it was three years in. "The government's goal," he responded, "is to protect the torturers." Like Harrington, he was vexed by the conflicts of interest that had resulted from misbehavior by government actors. "Why was the FBI investigating us? Was there a reasonable cause for suspicion or was it just a pretext for snooping around? Of course, the government is interested in what we are doing," he said. "I'm interested in what they are doing. But there are rules governing these things." He elaborated: "Government tampering is what causes us to trim our sails. Every criminal defendant deserves a lawyer who is not afraid." But, Nevin said, he was afraid; five times, he had put a lawyer on retainer in the event that he was ensnared in some investigation. I asked what motivated him to keep going, under such challenging circumstances. "I've made commitments to Mr. Mohammed and it's important to do the work."

Nevin fully appreciated that his work put him on the front line in the fight against torture. "*This* system and the treatment of *these* defendants defeats any assumptions one might have about capital law. The torture my client endured for three-and-a-half years is unlike the worst treatment in the domestic [criminal justice] system." Nevin and I were joined by Major Jason Wright, Mohammed's military lawyer, who jumped into the conversation. "There have been eighty-odd cases involving US torture," Wright said, "and all of them failed." He was referring to the failure of US courts to provide justice for victims and accountability for perpetrators and abettors of torture. "This is the last judicial forum for accountability," Wright said, "and it's falling short." The two attorneys took turns explaining the ongoing push-and-pull over the protective order. "We challenged the idea that the government can classify the defendants' own memories," Nevin said. "The second version took out the requirement that we provide notice to the court if our client wants to say something. Are we mind readers? The third version takes out the classified memories *but* put back in the need to provide notification if they plan to testify." Wright added that they had filed a motion to use the UN Convention against Torture to challenge the protective order, but "Judge Pohl denied the motion."

Our conversation turned to a ruling on a defense motion for discovery that Judge Pohl had made two months earlier in the USS Cole case, over which he was also presiding. The judge ordered the prosecutors to provide substantially more information to 'Abd al-Rahim al-Nashiri's defense team, including a full chronological accounting of where he was held from his capture in 2002 until his transfer to Guantánamo in 2006; the names, employment records, and training manuals of all government agents, medical personnel, guards, contractors, and others who were involved in his renditions and interrogations; and all records, photos, videos, interrogation logs, assessments, and other materials about al-Nashiri and any other current or former prisoners who had been interrogated about the USS Cole bombing. Judge Pohl decided that, because this is a capital case, all this information should be made available to the defense.

Nevin was cautiously optimistic that this ruling might break the discovery logjam in the 9/11 case. "Information about torture should be available to the defense. But will Judge Pohl stick with it? Legally, it's obvious. Lawyers have security clearances, so we should get it." He continued: "The government has the right to make classification decisions, but if those decisions compromise our ability to put on a defense, the judge has the power to impose a sanction, including dismissing charges or taking the death penalty off the table."

As we were parting company, Wright said: "Practicing in the military commissions is like one of four books: *1984, Catch-22,* Kafka's *The Trial,* and *A Confederacy of Dunces.*" The following month, the Pentagon informed Wright that he was required to take a graduate course for his next promotion, which would force him to leave the case. He decided that leaving under those circumstances would be an unethical breach of confidence with his client so, with no other option, he resigned from the Army.

General Martins, who was also prosecuting the al-Nashiri case, filed a motion appealing Judge Pohl's ruling on expansive discovery. He challenged the judge's authority to order the government to provide classified information to the defense because that was not authorized by Congress in the MCA. Martins also requested that Pohl give the government more time to complete its declassification review of the Senate's sixty-three-hundred-page report on the CIA's RDI program, which was completed and voted for release back in December 2012.

The CIA, which "owns" all information about itself, was dragging its feet in the declassification process because the SSCI report, which relied on the CIA's own documentary record, drew the scathing conclusion that the program was an intelligence-gathering failure. In January 2014, Senator Dianne Feinstein, chair of the SSCI, and Senator Carl Levin had written a letter to President Obama urging him to resolve the declassification delays because enduring secrecy about the CIA's "now defunct" and "misguided" program was adversely affecting the work as well as the reputation of the Guantánamo military commissions.

When Judge Pohl ruled on Martins's appeal of his discovery decision, technically, he stood by his order that more information should be provided to the defense. But he granted prosecutors some "leeway in redacting, 'anonymizing,' and summarizing the details." The following month, Pohl passed the USS Cole case to a new judge, Colonel Vance Spath.

In August, the issues of classification and discovery were revisited during the USS Cole hearings, which I was attending. Al-Nashiri's learned counsel, Richard Kammen, expressed his frustration about the "trust-free zone" of Guantánamo. "We have all the clearances in the world, but we are still not trustworthy enough," in the government's estimation, to see the original CIA documents. One problem, Kammen said, is that the summaries of original documents, which are produced by the prosecution according to rules designed by the CIA, are "reasonably useless if not outright false." This was not the prosecution's fault, Kammen said, assuming that they were faithfully following the procedures; the problem is the inaccuracy of the underlying documents that were produced by CIA interrogators and analysts. Kammen pointed out that the CIA has a robust record of lying, deception, and misrepresentation to judges, Congress, and the 9/11 Commission, not to mention the spy operation it ran on the Senate staff while they were working on the SSCI report. Kammen asked Judge Spath, "What will you do if the CIA is lying in this case?" Spath responded, "I don't know." Kammen continued, "This is a government agency that has lied to everybody. They deserve a presumption of dishonesty."

Kammen then raised the problem that defense attorneys were relatively powerless when the government acted in ways that adversely affected the representation of their clients. "They have already removed one lawyer from the case on a pretext," he said. He was referring to Nancy Hollander, whose access to al-Nashiri had been cut by the Pentagon when she began representing him before the European Court of Human Rights in cases against the countries that hosted black sites where he was imprisoned. Kammen also said that "we are *constantly* reminded of Lynne Stewart." He was making the point that prosecutors often cited Stewart's experience to threaten defense lawyers. Stewart, a self-described left-wing radical lawyer, had represented "the blind sheikh," Omar Abdel Rahman, who was convicted for involvement in the 1993 bombing of the underground garage in the World Trade Center that killed six people. He was sentenced to life. In 2005, Stewart was prosecuted for passing messages in Arabic—a language she didn't read—to her client's Islamist followers in Egypt. She was sentenced to ten years in prison.

For many hearings in the 9/11 case, the media delegation had less than ten journalists, sometimes much less, because motion battles over discovery and complex, arcane points of law were not the stuff of headline news. But I attended as often as I could. Those motion battles helped me to understand that the case was spinning its wheels in the pretrial phase because it was caught in a triangulated set of conflicting interests. One side of the triangle, the defense was fighting for access to classified information about what happened to their clients in CIA custody, insisting on their right to have it because pretrial treatment is legally relevant in any criminal case and, in death penalty cases, heightened due process *should* apply. The prosecution, the second side of the triangle, insists that this trial is about the defendants' roles in the crime of 9/11, and that what happened to them afterward is unrelated to their involvement in these events. In lieu of giving the defense original CIA material, prosecutors produce summaries and substitutions, which obscure specific dates and locations and mask the identities of people with unique functional identifiers (UFIs), like "Interrogator 1," and pseudonyms, like "Dr. Shrek." The CIA is the third side of this triangle because it controls the information the defense seeks and the process that guides the prosecution's preparation of discoverable materials. The Agency has no institutional interest in due process or fair trials, only in maintaining its secrets. The core of the problem, as I came to understand, is not that the CIA's secrets must be protected in the interest of national security, but rather that the government has prioritized the protection of those secrets over basic tenets of the rule of law and due process in this capital case.

In one of my conversations with Connell, he described the classification of information about torture as one of the "original sins" of Guantánamo. "When we received the first ten thousand pages of discovery, every important piece of information and every useful fact was redacted. So we did a little calculation: If you were to cut out all the redactions using scissors and you were to tape them together, it would be exactly 2.01 miles long, which is exactly the distance that you have to take on the ferry at Guantanamo to get from the airport to the courthouse. And those were the unclassified documents!" He added, "We are a long way into this case already, but it's not only that there's no end in sight, there's no middle in sight. We are still fighting for access."

Whenever I asked Connell a general question relating to the torture of his client, he would look upward and pause while he thought about how to answer. Like the other defense attorneys, his brain was compartmented into unclassified things he could say and classified things he couldn't. Because he was not allowed to confirm or deny information about the CIA torture program that is public knowledge but is still regarded as a state secret, he had to remember *how* he knows what he knows and on which side of the red line the potential answer would lie.

In a conversation with Nevin about the red lines, he offered the example of how, in a regular criminal case, he might challenge how his client was interrogated by police: "They questioned him *continuously* for *three hours!* They didn't give him a glass of water! They didn't let him go to the bathroom! That's why he confessed. I'm going to get those police officers on the stand and grill them about that because it's not fair." Nevin continued, "Imagine a person who spent a lifetime, going on forty years, defending criminal cases fighting about things like that, and now having a client"—Mohammed— "who was held incommunicado for over three years and was tortured *by my government*. That's an astonishing, counterintuitive thing, but it's true."

The decision to torture Mohammed, Nevin explained, is the reason he was transferred to Guantánamo rather than to New York for trial. Only in Guantánamo could his words be classified and his memories be treated as state secrets. "In fact," Nevin said, "the government filed a document in our case in which they referred to him as a 'participant' in the torture program— although they don't refer to it as a torture program. They said, 'As a result of that, they acquired information about classified sources and methods.' A participant!" Nevin concluded his point by saying that if the government didn't want Mohammed to know classified information, they shouldn't have exposed him to it by torturing him.

In order to get information that the government was withholding, defense lawyers and investigators for their teams made overseas trips to see what they could dig up about their clients' time in the black sites. Lawyers also made trips to meet their clients' relatives and acquaintances to gather information about their backgrounds, or to speak with people who had expertise about the broader conditions in their clients' countries of origin and residence. Nevin put this dimension of his work in context by emphasizing that his job is not to justify or excuse the horrific violence that killed thousands of people on September 11, 2001, but rather to fight for a fair trial. At the most basic level, this means that Nevin had to understand his client in order to represent him as a complex human being rather than a two-dimensional monster. Mohammed spent part of his youth in Kuwait, where there is a sizeable Palestinian diaspora community. He was sympathetic to the plight of the Palestinian people. This embittered him to the US government's special relationship with Israel, which contributed to the ever-worsening conditions for Palestinians in the occupied territories. Other aspects of US policy also angered him and influenced his political choices, including the high death toll in Iraq that was caused by a decade of sanctions in the 1990s, and US support for some of the region's worst dictators, such as Egypt's Hosni Mubarak, and the corrupt and repressive ruling family in Saudi Arabia. Nevin made it his job to gain a deep and grounded understanding of these issues. "I don't believe that innocent people should be killed under any circumstances," he said. "But there are reasons why 9/11 occurred which are very much on Mr. Mohammed's mind. Those reasons are not well understood or even known by most Americans, but they must be aired in this legal process."

The long-awaited SSCI report about the CIA's RDI program was released on December 12, 2014. Although this document is referred to as "the report," the only part made public was the 525-page executive summary. Despite heavy redactions, the report confirmed that the black sites were laboratories of cruel science where detainees were experimented on to see and study how they reacted and responded to pain and degradation. At the helm of this human experimentation project were the two psychologists the CIA had hired as contractors in June 2002, James Mitchell and Bruce Jessen. (Their names were pseudonymized in the SSCI report but had been publicly known since 2007, when the *New Yorker*'s Jane Mayer reported them.) The CIA, which had paid Mitchell and Jessen $81 million to run interrogation operations, issued a statement justifying the decision to hire the duo: "We believe their expertise was so unique that we would have been derelict had we not sought them out when it became clear that the CIA would be heading into the uncharted territory of the program."

Mitchell and Jessen's qualifications were their experience as trainers in the military's Survival, Evasion, Resistance, Escape (SERE) program, and their willingness to implement theories of learned helplessness, derived from experiments on dogs, on humans held by the CIA. The SSCI report lays out in detail how "enhanced interrogation techniques" were applied as long as needed to destroy or debilitate detainees' psyches in order to make them compliant. The assumption was that their compliancy was necessary to facilitate the extraction of actionable intelligence. According to the report, at least thirty-eight people were subjected to psychological and physical torments in black sites, and the results were methodically documented and analyzed.

The SSCI report confirmed techniques that were already publicly known, including waterboarding, smashing people into walls ("walling"), and weeks or months of nakedness in total darkness and isolation. But it also revealed techniques that were previously unknown, including rectal rehydration and rectal feeding. One of the detainees subjected to these rectal procedures was Majid Khan; when he demonstrated "resistance" by refusing to eat, his "'lunch tray' consisting of hummus, pasta with sauce, nuts and raisins was 'pureed and rectally infused.'"

After the SSCI report was published, the ACLU filed a lawsuit against Mitchell and Jessen on behalf of three victims. In August 2017, weeks before the case was set to go to the jury, it was settled with the government paying an undisclosed amount of money to the plaintiffs.

On the national stage, right-wing politicians and pundits railed against the SSCI report for its harsh criticisms of interrogation policies authorized by the Bush administration. Former CIA director George Tenet rallied other former directors to wage a media counterattack to defend the Agency's reputation against the Senate's findings, especially the conclusion that the program failed to produce valuable intelligence. A month after the report was released, as a result of the 2014 election, Republicans regained control of the Senate. The new SSCI chair, Richard Burr, issued a demand that every copy of the report that had been distributed to government agencies be returned to the SSCI, with the plan of destroying them all. However, Judge Pohl, responding to 9/11 defense team motions for access to the full, unredacted version of the report, ordered one copy to be preserved in a safe in the Pentagon. But he did not order the copy to be handed over to them, and it remains locked away.

In September 2017, tensions in the 9/11 case escalated further when prosecutors imposed new, heightened restrictions on defense teams' prerogatives to conduct their own investigations. One restriction barred defense team members from traveling to countries that had hosted black sites, because this could be deemed to confirm classified information—despite the fact that those locations are publicly known, including through lawsuits in international courts. Another new restriction prohibited them from independently contacting any person who may have been associated with the CIA's RDI program. Following some courtroom skirmishing, prosecutors agreed to exempt the handful of CIA officials whose identities were public knowledge.

At the twenty-sixth round of pretrial hearings in December 2017, the defense caught a big break. Around 9:00 p.m. on December 4, two FBI memos, which defense teams had been requesting since 2013, were delivered to them, and copies were distributed to journalists. These documents were made available because Walter Ruiz had persuaded Judge Pohl to hear his personal jurisdiction motion that week. Ruiz intended to challenge the military commission as an appropriate venue to try his client. To fend off this challenge, the prosecution had to provide information about self-incriminating statements al-Hawsawi had made to FBI "clean team" interrogators in January 2007, which were an essential piece of the government's case.

The two FBI memos provide snapshots of the US torture program at different stages. The first, dated May 19, 2004, begins: "In light of the widely publicized abuses at the Abu Ghraib prison, Iraq, this [memo] reiterates and memorializes existing FBI policy with regard to the interrogation of prisoners, detainees, or persons under United States control . . . [and] as a reminder of existing FBI policy that has consistently provided that FBI personnel may not obtain statements during interrogations by the use of force, threats, physical abuse, threats of such abuse or severe physical conditions." The second page of the two-page document reads: "*FBI personnel shall not participate in any treatment or use any interrogation technique that is in violation of these [1997] guidelines . . .*" (emphasis in original). If such treatment occurs, the memo continues, agents must remove themselves, even "[i]f a co-interrogator is complying with the rules of his or her own agency . . ." This was a prescient bet that the Abu Ghraib scandal was going to expose the Bush administration's authorization of violent and coercive interrogation tactics. The FBI wanted to be on record—at least to itself, since the memo was not public—that its hands were "clean."

The second FBI memo, dated January 10, 2007, lays out the procedures for clean-team agents to interview detainees previously held in black sites. It instructs the agents not to use any statement the detainee made while in the custody of "an intelligence agency," meaning the CIA, "unless approved in advance by the assigned prosecutor and the appropriate intelligence agencies." In describing how such interviews shall be conducted, the memo instructs agents to determine that anything the detainee says is freely given and not coerced. If the detainee asks for an attorney, the agent should inform him that, because he has not (yet) been charged with a crime, he has no such right. Agents should also make clear that the detainee's circumstances have changed, for example by stating that they "do not work for and are independent of any organization that previously held" him and "that he will not be returning to the control of any of his previous custodians."

These instructions reflected official rhetoric about the role of the clean teams: nothing these men said during their time in CIA custody will be used by prosecutors, whereas any statements they made to FBI clean-team agents are court-worthy by virtue of the conduct of interrogations using conventional and lawful means. But this rhetoric presumes that the FBI was institutionally separate from the CIA and had not dirtied its hands by colluding in torture. It also presumes that time itself can be separated between torture time and post-torture time. The notion of institutional and temporal separation was belied by the contents of the second memo which exposed how the CIA controlled the clean-team process: Any information that may come up during the FBI interview about interrogation techniques or black-site locations, "even though coming from a detainee, is deemed by the CIA to be national security information." FBI agents were instructed to produce a "letterhead memorandum [LHM] prepared on a CIA-supplied laptop." A footnote states: "Allegations of misconduct will not be included in this LHM." It also instructs the agents to submit the LHM and their interrogation notes to the CIA for classification review. The for-public-consumption illusion of institutional separation is contradicted by the concept of "compartmented information," which engulfs anything pertaining to torture. "If the CIA determines that compartmented information is contained in the LHM, the interviewing agent should create a separate LHM."

The release of the two FBI documents proved to be a game changer for the case. What was immediately clear in the proceedings in court during the December 2017 hearings, as Harrington noted, was that this was the "first time there were warm bodies in the witness seat." The witnesses were FBI Special Agents Abigail Perkins (retired) and James Fitzgerald, who interrogated al-Hawsawi in 2007.

The hearings began with the prosecution examining Agent Perkins. They presented a compelling array of material evidence about financial dealings between al-Hawsawi and some of the 9/11 hijackers, which she had questioned him about in 2007. When Ruiz cross-examined Perkins, she testified that al-Hawsawi spoke freely and acknowledged his role in the 9/11 plot. She said he never mentioned any abuse by the CIA and she never asked. When Ruiz asked how she conducted the interrogation, she explained that she did so without an interpreter. Ruiz bore down on this point because his client is not fluent in English. When he asked whether the interrogation was taped, she said no, because the CIA ground rules prohibited it.

The bombshell in Perkins's testimony was that she reviewed CIA black-site cables to prepare questions and strategies for her interrogation. While this black-site leakage into the process to obtain court-worthy evidence was not surprising to Ruiz or the other defense attorneys, putting it on record in open court undermined the pretense of separation between CIA torture and the FBI clean teams.

At a press conference in the MOC at the end of the week, Alka Pradhan, who had worked for the London-based human rights organization Reprieve before joining al-Baluchi's team in 2015, described the implications of Perkins's testimony: "Torture-derived evidence affects every part of this process. In no court of law would the 2007 statements be permitted." Connell added, "Torture isn't a single event, it was a program."

During the January 2018 hearings, the fight resumed over the new restrictions imposed on the defense four months earlier. General Martins, who, the previous November, had announced that he would no longer speak to the press, defended the restrictions as a national security necessity: "The mere seeking of interviews with people—and wandering up and ambushing people at the Piggly Wiggly—is a serious thing." (Piggly Wiggly is a chain of grocery stores.) He castigated the defense teams for trying to become their own "private attorney general, or whatever disembodied investigative authority they think they have outside the commission." But the prosecution agreed to compensate the defense teams for the impact of the new restrictions by giving them a timeline of the CIA's RDI program, which was supposed to reflect and contextualize the seventeen thousand pages of discovery they had received.

The hearing on March 1, 2018, put the stakes of the long-running battle over discovery on full display. Alka Pradhan had spent more than a month poring over the RDI timeline and the substitutions and summaries of original CIA materials, and comparing that information to open-source materials, including the SSCI report. Setting the stage for what would follow, she said: "Torture is, Your Honor, the nasty center of this case, whether we like it or not, and we have to deal with it at some point." Then Pradhan proceeded to argue that the flaws and gaps in information provided to the defense were so great that it was imperative they be allowed to access the original CIA documents to do their own assessments. To illustrate the deficiencies, she contrasted the publicly available chronology of Gul Rahman's month-long detention at a black site in Afghanistan before he died of exposure in 2002, which is three pages long, with the classified chronological summary of al-Baluchi's three-and- a-half-years in multiple black sites, which is one-quarter of a page.

Judge Pohl asked if Pradhan was asking him to reconsider the summaries and substitutions, which he had approved before they were given to the defense. (Under the MCA, the defense has no right to ask for reconsideration.) She replied, "No, sir. I'm asking you to compel the government to provide us all the original documents." Judge Pohl asked, "How is that not a reconsideration?" This exchange exposed a core issue in the battle over discovery: If the CIA-directed, prosecution-provided material is incomplete or inaccurate, the defense must persuade the judge why they need the originals to obtain accurate "granular" details. Pradhan explained, "Mr. al-Baluchi's recollections of his own torture, while they may be helpful, are not reliable precisely because of his torture over a lengthy period of time." She reminded the judge that the recently exposed collaboration between the FBI and the CIA "is relevant and material" to the case. "So at a minimum, the government has spent nearly six years since the arraignment, frankly, wasting our time."

Prosecutor Jeffrey Groharing took the podium to defend the discovery process. "There was no intentional wrongdoing, no obfuscation, no information intentionally stripped, and the summaries are not, in any way grotesquely misleading." He described the request for original materials as an "extreme remedy," and urged the judge to reject it. Taking Pradhan's example of the blurring of dates in the timeline, he explained that it was necessary "to protect classified information." Then he offered what was intended to be an assuaging statement: "The original classification authority ... yesterday, issued guidance that would allow additional dates to be provided in certain materials, not all dates."

Cheryl Bormann took her turn at the podium, explaining to Judge Pohl what experienced death-penalty lawyers do with flawed discovery: "[I]f this were any other court and I had a detective on the stand . . . or a special agent from the FBI, and I needed to go into what happened to my client during a 36-hour interrogation, and I had [information that was] riddled with mistakes, my argument to the jury would be that they can't believe anything that FBI agent says because that FBI agent is so careless in his duties that everything that he says should be subject to being found unreliable by the trier of fact. And so here we have the same thing."

What if, asked David Nevin, "information we receive . . . about the locations of the torture" comes from our clients? Groharing responded that information from the defendants "can be determined to be classified when held by counsel." Connell retorted: "That is absolutely untrue . . . The government has never produced a single shred of authority . . . for the proposition that people who were simply abducted by the United States . . . can be the custodians of classified information."

Connell and Judge Pohl had an exchange about the purposes that detailed information about the defendants' torture would serve in this trial. Connell explained that it was pertinent not only to the sentencing phase to seek an alternative to execution if the men are found guilty (i.e., mitigation) but also to the guilt-or-innocence phase to try to suppress statements the defendants made to FBI agents as torture-tainted—in legal terms, "fruit of the poisonous tree." Pohl said that Connell seemed to be assuming that his motion to suppress the FBI statements would fail. Connell answered, "Yes, sir. I am." Pohl: "Okay. But if your suppression motion were to succeed . . .?" Connell: "Wow." Pohl: "[Y]ou know, the judges can rule both ways." Connell: "So I hear."

One element of defense attorneys' arguments throughout the day was that the discovery process problems could go a long way toward being resolved if the government made a choice: either prioritize the CIA's secrets and take the death penalty off the table, or continue to seek the death penalty and respect the adversarial process by enabling the defense to access more information—including, for example, the full, unredacted SSCI report. The prosecutors rejected the notion that they must make such a politically unpalatable choice. The secrets, Groharing explained, are "the most highly classified information that the government has. . . . [I]t's extremely important that we protect that information." But, he insisted, that doesn't force a choice because the defense teams already have enough information to "paint a very vivid picture . . . and they have the accused [who are] the best source of information about their experiences in the RDI program." Moreover, Groharing said, the prosecution will not contest whatever vivid picture the defense wishes to present at trial, as long as it's tethered to reality. "We're not going to quibble. We're not going to call witnesses and debate about whether Mr. Mohammed was waterboarded 183 times or 283 times. We, frankly, think that has little relevance to the commission and the issues before it."

Jim Harrington could barely contain his agitation. "[S]aying that we can get information from our clients and . . . that we should focus on the guilt or innocence part of the case and not the sentencing part . . . is total ignorance of what capital law is all about." He added that the prosecution has no right to "tell the court or us" how to defend our case. He said Groharing's assertion that the defendants—whose torture continues to affect them profoundly—can be reliable sources of classified information "is just preposterous."

Nevin highlighted another paradox of the government's position—namely that the defense should rely on open sources for black-site information. "It's only when I get lucky enough to have some NGO come forward and . . . develop the evidence . . . that I can kind of glom onto and use it as a stalking horse to get in the door to talk about conducting my investigation."

To illustrate the possible effects of the defendants' torture experiences on their subsequent statements to the FBI, Pradhan read from a declassified CIA document about one short period of al-Baluchi's time in the black sites. Prior to his interrogation on May 20, 2003, he "had been kept naked in the standing, sleep-deprivation position since his initial interrogation session on 17 May 2003." Al-Baluchi "was significantly fatigued during this session. . . . His resistance posture had begun to decline. He appears to be answering questions truthfully. He was presented naked for this session. He was allowed to sit in reward for his increased cooperation. . . . In any case, he was able to complete the interview successfully despite the sleepiness that he exhibited." Then Pradhan quoted an unnamed CIA psychologist: al-Baluchi "is still developing a sense of learned helplessness which is contributing to his compliance, and the team will continue to lessen the intensity of the interrogation sessions relative to [his] cooperation." Pradhan explained the long-term consequences of this treatment by citing the declarations of two neuroscientists that "memory is changed by torture . . . brain function is changed by torture."

The issue of brain function came up during the hearing on May 1, 2018. Gary Sowards, the other learned counsel for Mohammed, asked Judge Pohl to issue an emergency order to keep the MRI (magnetic resonance imaging) machine at Guantánamo. The machine had been shipped in the previous October and brain scans had been performed on the defendants. Now the defense teams were concerned that the machine was about to be shipped off before they made further use of it. Sowards explained that the Navy MRI technician had performed only 25 percent of the requested tests on his client. Yet even these limited results seem to indicate that Mohammed had suffered brain damage as a result of his treatment in the black sites. Sowards said that if Mohammed's brain damage is validated by further tests, it could be grounds for challenging the death penalty. Moreover, brain damage resulting from being waterboarded and having his head bashed into walls numerous times could bolster defense motions to dismiss the case on the grounds of outrageous government conduct. Some victim family members in the gallery gasped at this prospect.

In the weeks prior to the June 2018 hearings, bin al-Shibh was subjected to intensified discipline that echoed his treatment in CIA custody. He was put into an isolation cell with nothing but a half-inch rubber pad and a Qur'an. He could not have his legal materials even though he had hearings approaching, and he had to read all his mail and produce any responses within an hour. Bin al-Shibh told his attorneys that members of the Camp 7 guard force and medical staff taunted him and threatened to move him to a padded cell or even to send him back to the black sites. In protest, he went on hunger strike. He was then told he could be force-fed if his health declines. Speaking to journalists at the start of that week of hearings, Harrington explained that this experience severely retraumatized bin al-Shibh. "This week was one of the deepest valleys I've ever been in with my client." The damage, he added, may never be repaired.

In August 2018, Judge Pohl issued a ruling barring the prosecution from using the FBI statements. He did this as a legal remedy to compensate the defense for the heightened restrictions. Then he retired. Pohl's successor, Colonel Keith Parrella, set aside that decision and put the FBI statements back in. Then he transferred to a different job. In July 2019, a third judge, Colonel Shane Cohen, was appointed. He made headlines in August when he set a trial start date of January 11, 2021. By September, after he apprised himself of the case's complexities and unresolved issues, he acknowledged that this time frame might be unrealistic.

In September 2019, I made my thirteenth trip to Guantánamo. This was the thirty-eighth round of pretrial hearings in the 9/11 case. It was also the eighteenth anniversary of the 9/11 terrorist attacks.

At the start of the hearing on September 11, General Martins took a few moments to acknowledge the tragic significance of that date and all those who suffered and died as a result of the attacks. He also acknowledged that the number of fatalities is not static; over two hundred firefighters and police had died from cancer or other fatal diseases they contracted while working for months pulling bodies out of the toxic debris of the World Trade Center. Now they, too, were recognized as 9/11 victims. Relatives of some of these first responders were among the delegation of victim family members. During the hearing, that delegation quietly left the gallery and went outside four times to commemorate and grieve the moment when each of the planes crashed.

Judge Cohen decided neither to restore Pohl's ruling to exclude the FBI statements nor to accept Parrella's decision to put them back in. Rather, he opted to schedule hearings to allow the defense to make the case that the FBI statements should be suppressed. Although the suppression hearings have implications for all five defendants, Connell and his team took the lead because it was their twelve-hundred-page classified motion being litigated. The same two FBI agents who had testified in December 2017 about the clean-team process were among the witnesses there in September to testify.

At the start of the hearing on September 16, Connell asked Judge Cohen if he could make a brief statement before the first FBI witness was called to the stand. Permission granted. Connell took the opportunity to draw attention to another eighteenth anniversary. "Sir," he said,

> I would be remiss if I did not remark [that today is] the historic occasion of the ... decision of the United States, my government, to use torture as an instrument of policy and investigation. [W]e'll hear important testimony today about the events of 9/11, a mass murder in which many people were killed. The trajectory of our [nation's] history was changed and many people, some of whom are in this courthouse, suffered. The key to this hearing and, I would suggest as a policy matter above my pay grade, to the healing of our country is to understand that both of those narratives are true at the same time. Our nation suffered a grievous wound, and it failed to live up to its principles afterward. Both of those things are true at the same time.

The suppression hearings, which started on the eighteenth anniversary of the authorization of the CIA's RDI program, represented a major turn in the case from the defense teams' struggles to *get* information that the government is withholding to a new struggle to *exclude* statements the government wants to use at trial. For Connell, one of the objectives was to illuminate that the FBI was far more implicated in the CIA torture program than was publicly known. Under questioning, he elicited testimony from FBI witnesses that collusion and information-sharing with the CIA dated back to 2002. Because FBI agents were barred from direct access to prisoners in the black sites, they sent questions arising from their own investigations to be asked by CIA interrogators, even though they knew the Agency's methods included violence and brutality.

A larger objective was to use the suppression hearings to demonstrate persuasively that there is no "after torture." Hearing after hearing, and witness after witness, Connell and other defense attorneys pursued lines of questioning to support their contentions that years of intensive and deliberate psychic damage in black sites were highly relevant to how the defendants behaved and what they said to FBI interrogators in 2007. The defense was using these hearings to put the CIA on trial in order to discredit the FBI clean-team statements.

The hearings in January 2020 were the most momentous because James Mitchell and Bruce Jessen, the architects of the CIA's black site program, were there to testify.

The day before those hearings began, the prosecution issued new classification guidelines. At the first session on January 21, Walter Ruiz explained to Judge Cohen how this last-minute rule change affected their preparedness: "We have to adjust; we have to reorganize everything that we're doing right before we come in here and question critical witnesses. I would just say, Judge, that's not consistent with due process, and I think we've got to get to a point where the government has had 12 years to figure this out . . . Are we going to be trying to figure this out on the eve of trial as well?"

When Mitchell took the stand, the first order of business was to put on the record that he had been briefed by the prosecution about how to discuss UFIs and locations of black sites so as not to reveal classified information. He had a handout with the real identities and locales and their masked versions that he could refer to during his testimony. Groharing told him that the government had invoked national security privilege over that document, and he cautioned Mitchell to cover it up if any defense attorney approached the witness stand, "so that the information is not disclosed."

Connell began by thanking Mitchell for coming down to Guantánamo to testify. Mitchell replied, "I actually did it for the victims and families, not for you." Why, Connell asked, did Mitchell choose not to meet with him ahead of time to discuss the questions that would be asked and materials that would be used during this examination? "You folks have been saying untrue and malicious things about me and Dr. Jessen for years," he replied. "So you shouldn't be surprised that I don't want to spend a lot of time with you . . ."

Connell's first line of questioning focused on Mitchell's 2016 autobiography, *Enhanced Interrogation: Inside the Minds and Motives of Islamic Terrorists Trying to Destroy America,* and the process of getting it cleared by the CIA. Connell was using the book to illustrate the contradictions between what the CIA approved for publication and information they barred the defense from accessing. Connell asked, "Did you write about the physique and complexion of a Counterterrorism Center operational psychologist?" Mitchell: "Yes." Connell: "Did anyone ever suggest to you at any time that including the physique and complexion of a Counterterrorism Center operational psychologist would damage national security?" Mitchell: "In my book or in my testimony?" Connell: "In your book." Mitchell: "In my book, no. In my testimony, yes." (This contradiction carried over into the transcript which redacted some direct quotes from the book.)

Connell's diplomatic approach and affable air seemed to soften Mitchell's attitude. Questions about the interrogation of al-Baluchi provided Mitchell with the opportunity to reiterate complaints he had articulated in his book about the unprofessionalism of another interrogator, whose UFI is NX2. The first time Mitchell met this man, he referred to himself as "the new sheriff" of that black site, signaling that he was implementing a different, even harsher approach to handling detainees. Mitchell complained that the new sheriff used unauthorized techniques, like putting al-Baluchi in a kneeling stress position with a wooden rod behind his knees and keeping him in standing sleep deprivation for eighty-two hours straight. Connell questioned Mitchell about a declassified CIA Office of Inspector General report which said that interrogators took turns practicing the technique of walling on al-Baluchi in order to get certified in the use of "enhanced interrogation techniques." Mitchell said, "It looks like they used your client as a training prop."

Groharing objected to the relevance of questions about bad interrogators like the new sheriff. Connell countered: "Our outrageous government conduct theory is that the coercive physical pressures to which Mr. al Baluchi was subjected fall outside the approvals by the Department of Justice."

During Mitchell's third day on the stand, Connell probed him about the cause-and-effect relationship between terrorist activities and "enhanced interrogation techniques" (EITs). Mitchell said, "You could say they brought this on themselves because they voluntarily attacked us. They chose to do

FIGURE 15. Military commission hearing, January 22, 2020: Khalid Sheikh Mohammed speaks with his lead counsel, Gary Sowards, and other members of his legal team. Drawing by Janet Hamlin.

this. One of the natural consequences of trying to kill 3,000 people is that the people you're trying to kill aren't going to like it." Connell asked about the decision to use the "EIT" euphemism. Mitchell replied, "Well, I mean, it had to be called something, and I don't think they liked calling it . . . coercive physical pressure, which is what I was in favor of calling it because that's what I thought it was."

As Connell questioned Mitchell about some declassified CIA documents to get his interpretation of their meaning, Groharing objected: "Your Honor, anyone could answer these questions." Connell responded that the government had denied fifty of the fifty-two CIA witnesses his team asked for. "They produced two, Dr. Mitchell and Dr. Jessen, who don't actually work for the CIA and are green-badgers [contractors] . . . So the government, on behalf of the CIA, has agreed to exactly two witnesses who are supposed to carry the weight of thousands of pages of documents." Judge Cohen overruled Groharing's objection.

When Mitchell was questioned about his relationship with Mohammed, he explained that, after some time in the black sites, they began having what he called "fireside chats." "Khalid Shaikh Mohammed and I had lots of discussions during the fireside chat about his reactions to him being subjected to EITs . . . We were trying to understand how to get jihadi males to cooperate with us and answer our questions without using EITs. And so a big piece of our push was to try to understand their belief system so that we could couch our request so that it matched their belief system. And to do that, we had to discuss their reactions."

Connell wanted to put on record Mitchell's approach to Pavlovian conditioning to achieve learned helplessness. He used the example of the walling technique in which a towel is placed around the detainee's neck before he is thrown against a wall. Connell asked, "How did those two things"—the towel and the wall—"work together?" Mitchell explained:

> Let's imagine that you had a dog that you would spray meat powder into his mouth, right? The meat powder is considered an unconditioned stimulus . . . And salivation is considered an unconditional response . . . But if you turn a light on contiguously with spraying the meat powder, very soon that light will cause the dog to salivate. And so what we wanted to do is have some innocuous thing take the place of the light, like the towel, so that we didn't have to actually use EITs. [W]e would put that towel around their neck in the beginning . . . and cinch it up . . . , and we'd use it for walling, and we'd have it on them the entire time that we were using EITs. And then as they began to progress to where we used fewer EITs, we would take that towel off, set it somewhere where they could see it. And we'd usually say something like, "Are we going to need this today?" And they would say, "No." And we would set it down and say, "We'll put it right here in case we do." And then we would have a back-and-forth conversation, right? And if the person began to drift back into resisting in a way that we couldn't control . . . we would take up the towel again and that was almost always enough. And then eventually, I would say, "Do we even need to bring it in the room?" And they would say, "No." . . . So in our view, using that towel produced the same sense of . . .—I don't think there's another word for it—dread that the light would do in producing the salivation.

Connell asked Mitchell how detainees in black sites were debriefed (questioned for information without EITs) after they were deemed to have achieved learned helplessness. Connell's objective was to illuminate that the defendants might perceive CIA debriefings and FBI interrogations as part of a larger continuum. Mitchell began by explaining that the two agencies had different objectives: A CIA "intelligence debriefer is not focused on a confession. I never, ever, under any circumstances was at all interested in anything that the detainee said to me that sounded even remotely like a confession. We don't want [confessions because] they weren't useful for stopping attacks. . . . If they wanted to say, 'I blew up the Empire State Building.' Somebody cared about it,"—he was implying the FBI—"but I didn't care about it, and I wasn't interested collecting that kind of information." Connell asked how the questioning processes of both agencies compared. Mitchell responded: "The skills are the same, right? The questioning skills, the establishing rapport, understanding what the person is saying to you . . . But the goals are different."

After Connell was finished examining Mitchell, Judge Cohen took a turn to get a clear understanding about the relationship between coercive interrogations and learned helplessness. Mitchell explained that the purpose of administering EITs was to elicit "fear or despair or emotional distress . . . what would be called negative reinforcement." Mitchell said that when someone started answering any question, the use of EITs is paused, which would make them understand that the only way not to be coercively interrogated is to talk. "Because in order for learned helplessness to develop, the person has to come to believe that there is absolutely nothing they can do to get out of the current situation that they're in [by] not answering questions . . ."

When Nevin examined Mitchell, he pursued a line of questioning about what "worked" to make his client cooperative. Mitchell said that, for Mohammed, the waterboard was largely ineffective because he was able to expel or swallow large amounts of water as it was poured onto a cloth covering his face. To get around that resistance, Mitchell said, another interrogator cupped his hands around Mohammed's mouth so that the water would have nowhere to go but in. But it didn't have the desired effect of creating fear or distress because, at one point, Mohammed fell asleep on the waterboard. What did work on him was sleep deprivation and walling. Mitchell pantomimed how to wall someone "correctly." Then Nevin asked about Mitchell's threat to kill Mohammed's son, which was documented in the SSCI report. Mitchell explained that using this threat had been approved by a CIA lawyer as part of the conditioning process. "What I said to him was, 'If there is another catastrophic attack in the United States'—the first condition—'and I find out'—the second condition—'that you had information that would have . . . allowed us to stop it'—that's the third condition—'and another American child is killed'—that's the fourth condition—'then I will cut your son's throat.'" Mitchell added, "He killed eight children in the 9/11 attacks, eight children who did nothing . . . And it is, I think, in retrospect, distasteful, but it is what it is."

At the February 2020 hearings, Jim Harrington asked Judge Cohen for permission to step down for health reasons. "My trial days are over," he said. Prosecutors protested that there was no immediate medical emergency and urged the judge to deny Harrington's request, but they lost that one. In March, Judge Cohen made the surprise announcement that he was retiring from the military, meaning the case would need a new, fourth, judge. At the end of that month, the COVID-19 pandemic ground everything to a halt because no one was permitted to travel to Guantánamo. David Bruck, who was appointed to replace Harrington as bin al-Shibh's learned counsel, was unable to meet his new client until travel restrictions were lifted in July 2021.

In the summer of 2020, Colonel Stephen Keane was appointed to replace Judge Cohen. Two weeks later, he disqualified himself because he realized that he had ties to some victims of the 9/11 attacks. The next appointee, Colonel Matthew McCall, was withdrawn because he lacked the requisite experience of two years as a military judge.

Camp 7, which was not designed as a permanent facility, had fallen into a state of irremediable disrepair because Congress never approved the funding necessary to maintain it. By 2021, it had become uninhabitable—it was literally falling apart and there was black mold and flooding sewage. The first week of April 2021, all of the former CIA prisoners were transferred to the maximum-security Camp 5. Despite the defense teams' request for an order of preservation, after the prisoners were moved, Camp 7 was quickly "sanitized" to prevent them from seeing the actual conditions in which their clients had been confined.

On July 12, 2021, General Martins, who had received extensions in his military service to remain chief prosecutor and had pledged to stick with the case to the end, announced that he was retiring, effective September 30. In August, Colonel McCall, who had acquired additional judicial experience in the interim, was (re)appointed to preside over the case.

After an eighteen-month recess due to the pandemic, hearings resumed in September 2021, coinciding with the twentieth anniversary of 9/11. The main issues continued to be the defense's ongoing quest for discovery, and suppression of the FBI statements. During the November hearings, Connell achieved one of his goals by putting on the record previously unknown details about FBI-CIA collaborations: at least nine FBI agents *became* CIA agents, temporarily, when they were detailed to work in the black sites. At least five of these agents participated in CIA debriefings of defendants.

At the end of November, I called Connell to ask whether there was any truth to rumors that the Biden administration might consider authorizing plea bargains to bring this case to an end. "Nope," he responded. He estimated that the pretrial phase would last for another two years.

But in March 2022, the prosecution finally conceded to the possibility of resolving the 9/11 case through plea bargains and initiated negotiations with the defense teams. In addition to the delays caused by all of the recent personnel changes and the prospect of more years of pretrial hearings, one probable factor in that decision to consider eschewing a trial in favor of a deal was Cheryl Bormann's request to leave the case, which Judge McCall granted. There was no one in the wings to replace her and getting a new learned counsel for bin Attash up to speed would further delay the start of a trial.

Another likely reason was the outcome of Majid Khan's sentencing hearing in October 2021. In 2012, Khan had agreed to plead guilty to charges against him, including serving as a courier for al-Qaeda and transporting money that funded the bombing of a Marriott Hotel in Jakarta in August 2003 in which twelve people were killed. He also agreed to become an informer. As part of the plea bargain that his attorneys negotiated, he was granted permission to read in open court an unsworn statement, albeit one vetted to ensure that no CIA personnel or black site locations were named.

At the sentencing hearing on October 28, Khan became the first former CIA prisoner to speak about his experiences in public. He began by thanking the panel and everyone in court, including his father and sister, for letting him tell his story "with the hope that you better understand who I was and who I have become." He acknowledged that he had done all the things for which he was charged, explaining without excusing that he had exercised "poor judgment" at important crossroads in his life. After narrating the key events in his life that made him susceptible to being recruited by relatives in Pakistan who were members of al-Qaeda, including "GTMO propaganda videos," he said, "I don't have the same mindset now . . . I reject al-Qaeda. I reject terrorism. I reject violence and hatred." He asked forgiveness from all those he had wronged and said he forgave all those who had tortured him. His decision to plead guilty and cooperate with the US government was his way of making amends, and for that he has no regrets. "But I think it's important for you to understand what happened to me."

Khan described his arrest in Karachi on March 5, 2003. He said he willingly answered interrogators' questions and was forthcoming with information about his activities and al-Qaeda associates. But his interrogators had no way of knowing what was true and what might be a lie, so they chose not to believe him, or they pretended not to in order to justify escalating violence. The more he tried to answer honestly, the worse the abuse became. He was repeatedly drowned, beaten, hung by his wrists for days, kept naked, starved, and denied the opportunity to pray. After months of interrogations in several black sites, the questioning ended and he was held in isolation. To protest his treatment, he began hunger striking and he ardently resisted force feedings. For these reasons, his captors resumed torturing him, not under the pretense of collecting information but as punishment for being noncompliant. In September 2004, he said, "I was raped by the CIA medics." These anal rapes often involved a green garden hose connected to a faucet. Others involved the rectal infusion of pureed food. He also recounted that his utter desperation led to numerous suicide attempts. After he was transferred to Guantánamo in 2006, the abuse and humiliations continued. "That's when I knew GTMO was no different than the other places." He described Guantánamo as "death by a thousand cuts." Because he provided information about other Camp 7 detainees, he was totally isolated. "I have been essentially alone for almost a decade," he said.

For people familiar with the CIA's torturous procedures during renditions and interrogations and inhumane conditions in black sites, the details in Khan's harrowing account were all too familiar. But the members of the panel had been chosen during the voir dire because of their admitted lack of knowledge and opinion about the CIA program or "EITs." In accordance with the Potemkin-like military commission rules for plea bargains, the panel was not informed that Khan had agreed to plead guilty in exchange for a ten-year sentence whose clock had started running in 2012. Prosecutors instructed the panel to sentence Khan to between twenty-five and forty years.

The panel returned a sentence of twenty-six years. They also returned a hand-written letter urging clemency for Khan which seven of the eight officers had signed. Their letter characterized Khan's treatment as "a stain on the moral fiber of America" and said it "should be a source of shame for the U.S. government." They compared what was done to Khan in CIA custody to "torture performed by the most abusive regimes in modern history."

On March 11, 2022, the convening authority, Jeffrey Wood, issued an action memo stating that Khan's ten-year sentence has been served. Now the Biden administration must make arrangements to transfer and resettle him somewhere where he can be reunited with his wife and the daughter he has never met.

The March 2022 hearings in the 9/11 case turned into closed-door negotiations between the prosecution and the defense. A possible plea bargain agreement would involve guilty pleas in exchange for sentences of, at most, life in prison. Carol Rosenberg reported that neither side would speak publicly about the terms being discussed. Probing for an answer to why the prosecution was now willing to consider eschewing a trial and abandoning hope for executions, Rosenberg learned that Majid Khan's case was a factor. "Last year, a military jury's condemnation of CIA torture in another war crimes case raised questions of whether prosecutors could win a unanimous death-penalty decision even for Mr. Mohammed . . ." Charles "Cully" Stimson, who had worked on detainee matters at the Pentagon during the Bush administration, said recently that "the Khan case illustrated that, even if the prosecutors get the Sept. 11 defendants to trial and win conviction, 'the likelihood of their coming to a unanimous verdict with respect to the death penalty is close to zero.'"

The 9/11 case used to be described by officials as "the trial of the century." As the pretrial phase wore on, a more accurate description would be the "the forever-never trial." The dozens of hearings, cumulatively, provide persuasive evidence that decisions to authorize kidnapping, torture, and forced disappearance undermined the ability of the government to use this case to provide justice for the victims of 9/11. It has also damaged the proposition that government secrets and a fair trial with death on the table are compatible. If this case does, someday, end with a deal, the reason is torture.

Conclusion

THE AFTERLIVES OF TORTURE

THE TORTURE PROGRAM IS OVER. But its specter haunts US politics because there has been no meaningful acknowledgment that government policy constituted gross crimes, let alone redress for torture and cruel treatment intentionally perpetrated against thousands of people taken into US custody during the "war on terror." The political house remains a welcoming place for the unpunished, those who bear responsibility for violating the laws of this nation and the world. If a future administration seeks to resurrect violent interrogation techniques, it may succeed unless all the realities of this dark chapter are illuminated and lessons are learned.

This specter appeared in the 2016 election. Every Republican candidate running for president endorsed the reauthorization of "enhanced interrogation techniques," the official euphemism for US torture. Donald Trump's rhetoric was the most aggressive and least euphemistic; he promised to bring back the waterboard and "a hell of a lot more," and linked this to his campaign slogan, "Make America great again." Democratic Party candidate Hillary Clinton didn't share Republican candidates' nostalgia for the canceled program, but to burnish her liberal hawk credentials, she said that if a situation arose in which torture might be necessary, she would authorize it and accept the consequences. Thus, in 2016, there was no anti-torture candidate. Instead, torture served as a bipartisan litmus test for hard-eyed American nationalism. The principle of human dignity, to which the universal right not to be tortured is all-important, was either scorned as a politically correct fiction or treated as negotiable.

The day after Trump won that election, he listed the resurrection of waterboarding as one of his top five priorities. While he didn't succeed in making that happen, to shore up his pro-torture bona fides, he appointed Gina

Haspel as director of the CIA. He made this appointment not despite but because she had been directly involved in the black site program. In 2002, Haspel was the chief of base at the CIA's first black site in Thailand. In 2004, as chief of staff to Counterterrorism Center director Jose Rodriguez, Haspel had a direct hand in the destruction of ninety-one videotapes of torture sessions, which violated a court order to preserve evidence. Her promotion to the role of director was lauded by torture enthusiasts as a vindication of the Bush-era program. Despite Haspel's managerial role in the CIA torture program that was documented in the Senate Select Committee on Intelligence (SSCI) report, six Democratic senators voted to confirm her, thus giving her career elevation bipartisan support.

According to a 2017 Pew Research Center national opinion poll, more than 70 percent of Republicans regard the use of torture as an acceptable counterterrorism measure. While the totality was evenly split between those who would find torture acceptable under certain circumstances (48 percent) and those who oppose it under all circumstances (49 percent), majorities of men, whites, and people over sixty-five were in the former camp. These mixed results show that, while the appeal of torture has a partisan cast, it cannot be explained by partisanship alone. In many quarters, the idea of US torture, past and future, has been normalized or even glorified.

This was not always the case. There was no pro-torture constituency in the decades prior to the "war on terror." Emergent and increasing support was a direct result of the Bush administration's decisions to authorize torture as government policy. As Darius Rejali, a political science professor at Reed College, explained in a February 19, 2017, op-ed in the *LA Times,* the most dramatic uptick occurred in the immediate wake of President Barack Obama's January 2009 cancellation of the program. Citing research Rejali conducted with Paul Gronke and Peter Miller, "the most powerful predictor" of people's views on torture is "presidential signaling": "If a president condones torture, those who favor him will support torture. If a president does not, those who favor him will not." Rejali elaborates: "We discovered that, when it comes to torture, people appear to be driven more by social cues, superstition, resentment and indecision than by philosophy, morality or rational outcomes." Most hauntingly, "respondents who favor torture don't care whether it produces a positive or negative security outcome."

Even if torture supporters' sole standard is what is "good for America," or if they accept the use of any measures, no matter how illegal, to "keep Americans safe," it is, nevertheless, irrational to believe that torture "works."

Despite all the secrecy that still surrounds the torture program, there is abundant evidence that coercive interrogation techniques did not aid in the collection of accurate intelligence; rather, the use of torture wasted the time and resources of national intelligence agencies as they pursued false leads from coerced statements. There is also abundant evidence that the government's authorization of torture and its pervasive use damaged US national security and other national interests. But, as Rejali's research shows, people who support the use of torture don't care that it is ineffective and damaging. For them, it provides one more means to express nationalistic and racialized resentments. These predilections, which are characteristic of numerous dark chapters of US history, were emboldened and exacerbated by the "war on terror."

The most concrete and enduring legacy of the torture program is Guantánamo, which seems politically impossible to close because that would require politicians to acknowledge the flaws and failures of government policies across four administrations since the prison was opened in January 2002. It would also require a new official narrative about the people who remain imprisoned there that incorporates truth-telling about what was done to them. As of July 2022, Guantánamo's population stands at thirty-six; this includes nineteen never-charged men who have been recommended for transfer to another country under security arrangements that must satisfy the US government and five for whom release isn't even considered an option; ten who have been charged in the military commissions; and two who have been convicted, one of whom is serving a life sentence (Ali Hamza al-Bahlul) and the other (Majid Khan) whose sentence is up.

The insolubility of Guantánamo is perpetuated by the lack of a national consensus that it *is* a problem. President Trump rejected his predecessor's stated desire to close the prison, and he vowed to load it up with "bad dudes." His actual record, though, was similar to President Obama's in the sense that the status quo was maintained, with one notable exception: During the Obama administration, 197 detainees were transferred out whereas during the Trump administration, not a single detainee whose release had been recommended long ago was transferred. The only man to leave Guantánamo during Trump's presidency was Ahmed al-Darbi, who was repatriated to Saudi Arabia in 2018 to serve out the remainder of his sentence from a 2014 plea bargain agreement. President Joe Biden has adopted a position similar to Obama's by expressing a desire to close the prison and a willingness to release detainees who have been recommended for transfer if and when a suitable location can be found. But only four (as of this writing) have been released and repatriated by the Biden administration. One of them was Mohammed al-Qahtani whose severe mental illness—schizophrenia predating his capture and post-traumatic stress disorder that was the result of his torture in US custody—was finally acknowledged by the government; he was repatriated to Saudi Arabia on March 6, 2022, to receive mental health care.

What set Trump apart from the two previous presidents and their administrations was the aggressiveness of his anti-intellectualism and his open hostility to extant political norms. Officials in the Bush administration expended considerable energy to reinterpret the law in order to establish a "new paradigm." As egregious as the consequences were, that labor in and of itself was an homage to the importance of law. The Obama administration's record was replete with failures to fulfill many of the president's promises to restore the rule of law, but those failures, too, were belabored. In contrast, Trump's record on law, including the laws of war, manifested as bullying indifference. One example was his decisions to pardon and champion Americans who had been convicted of war crimes. Contrary to his "America first" rhetoric, Trump personalized government in myriad ways to put his own interests first. The Trump White House was brazenly corrupt, and the president and many of his political appointees mocked or attacked individuals and agencies deemed insufficiently loyal to the chief. Trump romanticized and emulated foreign authoritarian leaders, foremost Russia's Vladimir Putin, and engulfed as much of the federal government as he could bend to his will.

Although Trump lost his bid for reelection in 2020, publicly, he never accepted his defeat. He is reportedly eyeing the 2024 race as the chance to resume the position he claims is rightfully his but was "stolen." Out of office, Trump has become a singular force dominating his party. His national clout is bolstered by the support of politicians who continue to seek his approval, sometimes by mimicking his rhetoric and often by appropriating his political objectives. Legions of Trump-supporting citizens revel in the politics of xenophobia, racism, Islamophobia, and the penchant for political violence that are his brand. Regardless of whether Trump himself ever returns to office, Trumpism is the Republican Party's new normal. These political realities bode ill for the permanent banishment of torture.

But the possibility that a future administration could reauthorize torture is not explainable simply by the fact that many politicians and citizens desire and would applaud it. Rather, that possibility nests in changes in the exercise of executive power since 9/11 that have not been undone. Dick Cheney, the most influential vice president in US history, saw the 9/11 attacks as an opportunity to implement his long-held objective to "restore" the power of the president, and the "war on terror" was an opportunity to recreate a national security realpolitik unfettered by international law and US treaty obligations. The policies the Bush administration inaugurated under the guise of the unitary executive thesis were both *illiberal,* in the sense that they undermined the nation's system of checks and balances, and *anti-liberal* (in the classical sense) by castigating and treating certain categories of human beings as rightless, and instrumentalizing harms against "them" to benefit "us." This illiberal and anti-liberal vision called into being a new paradigm of unchecked executive power and institutionally enforced impunity for crimes of state.

The new paradigm's enduring vestiges can be seen in post-9/11 continuities in the realms of war and national security. Obama hewed to the unitary executive thesis to expand the targeted killing policy, which was initiated by Bush. Trump escalated drone warfare even further and canceled the few legal restraints that Obama had introduced in his second term. The end to US war in Afghanistan was negotiated by the Trump administration in 2020 and brought to fruition in cataclysmic ways by the Biden administration the following year. The three administrations since Bush's have preserved the new paradigm by, among other ways, resolutely sustaining official secrecy about torture and invoking the specious claim that the truth would damage national interests.

For these reasons, the specter of torture haunts the political house. As Avery Gordon explains in her book, *Ghostly Matters,* "Haunting is one way in which abusive systems of power make themselves known and their impacts felt in everyday life, especially when they are supposedly over and done with ... or when their oppressive nature is denied ... Haunting raises specters, and it alters the experience of being in time, the way we separate the past, the present, and the future."

Obama altered the experience of being in time when he rationalized his refusal to pursue accountability for those who had authorized torture by saying that it was time for the nation to "look forward, not backward." His cancelation of the CIA program did not negate its *existence,* and his administration made a national reckoning impossible by keeping its truths closeted through secrecy, excessive classification, and an unprecedented war on whistleblowers. Although Obama, for the most part, fulfilled his promise to end torture, it was not until August 2014 that he officially acknowledged it as the intentional actions of officials and their subordinates. Even then, his manner of acknowledgment was hardly a reckoning with the truth. He said: "We did a whole lot of things that were right [after 9/11]. But we tortured some folks."

The closest thing to a reckoning is the SSCI report. But only a heavily redacted fraction—the executive summary—was released in 2014, while the rest remains locked away. During Obama's last weeks in office, when it was clear that Republican senators intended to obliterate the SSCI report entirely, he ordered his copy to be preserved in the presidential archives, but he allied himself with the report's opponents by ordering that access to it must be restricted for the maximum time allowed by law.

The broader implications of these failures to reveal or acknowledge the truth create opportunities for lies and false narratives to continue to be bought and sold in the public square. In this environment, those who support torture wrap themselves in the American flag and tout their irrational views as "patriotic." Centrist liberals may not support torture, but because they are unwilling to challenge the status quo by demanding, at minimum, access to the hidden truths, they are left with nothing but hope that the system—the haunted system—will somehow miraculously keep the specter at bay.

Against this bleak backdrop, the contributions of hundreds of people who waged the long fight against torture are greater than their specific and limited victories in courts, although those must not be minimized. The lawyers and their allies who have waged this fight didn't know the gravity of the mission when it started, and they might not agree with my conclusion now, but they were—and some remain—engaged in a redemptive project. Fighting for information and truth is redemptive because there is no dignity in ignorance. Fighting for justice for victims and consequences for perpetrators is redemptive because there is no virtue in unaccountable crimes of state.

Michael Ratner, who started the war in court in February 2002 when he filed the first lawsuit, *Rasul v, Bush*, died in May 2016. As his friend and colleague David Cole wrote upon his passing, "Michael Ratner's army" endures; it is composed of the lawyers and advocates who joined the fight for rights that Ratner led. Joseph Margulies, who was the first to reach out to Ratner in November 2001 and became lead counsel in *Rasul*, is still fighting. One of Margulies's clients is Abu Zubaydah, the CIA's first "high-value" detainee who was taken into custody the month after *Rasul* was filed, and who was used as the guinea pig for the torture program. Abu Zubaydah, whom Margulies has represented since 2007, remains imprisoned at

Guantánamo, despite the fact that the government conceded long ago that he was not, as originally and erroneously assumed, a top figure in al-Qaeda—he wasn't even a member. Abu Zubaydah can't be tried because the government has no evidence that could be used to prosecute him, and he has never been granted a habeas hearing because the government can't—or, rather, won't—even entertain the idea of releasing him because of the state secrets he embodies. Alex Gibney appropriately titled his 2021 film about Abu Zubaydah's experiences and plight *The Forever Prisoner.*

Margulies and Abu Zubaydah's other attorneys are engaged in an ongoing battle for truth and consequences. In 2010, they filed a complaint in Poland asking the Polish government to hold its own officials accountable for their role in Abu Zubaydah's torture at the black site in that country. The Polish government decided to pursue a criminal investigation and requested information from the US government under the mutual legal assistance treaty. When the US government refused that request, the Polish investigation was closed.

In 2013, Margulies and his co-counsel filed a complaint against Poland in the European Court of Human Rights (ECHR) for failure to follow through with its domestic investigation, which is in itself a violation of international law. In its 2014 ruling, the ECHR affirmed, "beyond a reasonable doubt," that Abu Zubaydah was held at a black site in Poland from December 2002 until September 2003. The court found abundant circumstantial evidence that Polish officials "knew of the nature and purpose of the CIA's activities on its territory." Poland, therefore, violated Abu Zubaydah's rights through complicity with the CIA and its own failure to conduct an investigation. This ECHR ruling caused Poland to reactivate its criminal probe. Under Polish law, Abu Zubaydah is entitled to submit evidence and testimony to assist in the Polish investigation. The US government blocked him from doing so, claiming that state secrets would be revealed and national security would be harmed.

In order to support the Polish prosecutors' investigation, Margulies and his co-counsel filed a petition for discovery in the District Court in the Eastern District of Washington. The objective was to subpoena James Mitchell and Bruce Jessen, the architects of the CIA torture program, for testimony about what actually happened to Abu Zubaydah in Poland. The court granted the request, and Mitchell and Jessen were subpoenaed. Then Mike Pompeo, Haspel's successor as CIA director during the Trump administration, filed a formal claim of state secrets privilege to quash the subpoenas. The court accepted the claim and terminated the discovery.

Margulies and his co-counsel challenged that decision in the Ninth Circuit Court of Appeals. They argued that the District Court had erred by not determining if some of the requested information might *not* be subject to the state secrets privilege. The Ninth Circuit decided that while some information might be privileged, what was *not* a secret was the fact that the CIA had a black site in Poland, or the interrogation techniques used by the CIA at that site, or the fact that Abu Zubaydah was detained in Poland because that information was already widely known. "[I]n order to be a 'state secret,' a fact must first be a 'secret.'" The Ninth Circuit also decided that, because Mitchell and Jessen were contractors rather than government employees, nothing they testify to would constitute official confirmation or denial of matters the government regards as secret. The case was remanded back to the District Court to decide what if any information was not privileged.

In December 2020, the Trump administration petitioned the Supreme Court for a writ of certiorari to challenge the Ninth Circuit's decision. Employing boilerplate new paradigm logic, the petition asserted that no matter how widely known something might be, if the executive claims it is a state secret, courts should deferentially agree. The Biden administration inherited the case and chose to cling to the same reasoning.

Mitchell and Jessen are willing to be deposed about what they did, as contractors, to Abu Zubaydah. They have testified before about their activities in black sites, including the January 2020 hearings for the 9/11 military commission case. They have testified about what they did to Abu Zubaydah at another black site, and they have testified about what they did to others at the black site in Poland. But they never have testified about what they did to Abu Zubaydah in Poland. Although the US government now regards *how* Abu Zubaydah was treated as declassified information, *where* that treatment occurred remains a state secret.

On October 6, 2021, the Supreme Court heard arguments in *United States v. Husayn (Abu Zubaydah)*. During that hearing, the justices did not rely on euphemisms; starting with Justice Amy Coney Barrett, one after another called what was done to Abu Zubaydah "torture." According to Margulies, "that, in the fullness of time, may prove even more consequential to the war on terror than the [discovery] question before the Court." He adds, "That Justices would call torture by its name is a truth that cannot be unspoken."

Another occurrence during oral arguments, which exposed the frailty of the official line, was the question posed by Justice Neil Gorsuch to Acting Solicitor General Brian Fletcher: why can't Abu Zubaydah just testify himself? This,

Gorsuch suggested, would provide an "off ramp" by making the need for Mitchell and Jessen's testimony moot. Why not, indeed? Justices Stephen Breyer and Sonia Sotomayor continued this line of questioning, and Sotomayor pointedly asked whether the government would allow Abu Zubaydah to testify about his own experiences. Fletcher could offer no answer on the spot, because it has been taken for granted for so long that the only people Abu Zubaydah (or other former CIA prisoners) can talk to are those with top-secret security clearance, and anything said must be cleared by the CIA. The government filed its response to the question on October 15: making an exception to standing policy, Abu Zubaydah can provide his own testimony to Polish investigators, but it would have to be vetted by the CIA, and it must remain classified.

The Supreme Court issued its decision on March 3, 2022. By a vote of seven to two, the majority, albeit with several partial dissents and partial concurrences, submitted to the executive's demand for utmost deference while also acknowledging that Abu Zubaydah "was tortured; no one can credibly maintain otherwise." Justice Breyer wrote the majority decision: "In our view, the government has provided sufficient support for its claim of harm to warrant application of the privilege."

As a matter of US law and Supreme Court precedent, the dismissal of the case may be a "correct" decision. But this outcome exposes the desperate need for better laws that are capable of accommodating legitimate demands for justice for crimes of state. There was no acknowledgment in Breyer's decision that the state secret the Court was willing to protect is evidence of a criminal enterprise, and thus nothing prevents the same or similar crimes from being perpetrated in the future. "In a word," Breyer writes, "to confirm publicly the existence of a CIA site in Country A, can diminish the extent to which the intelligence services of Countries A, B, C, D, etc., will prove willing to cooperate with our own intelligence services in the future."

Justice Clarence Thomas's partially concurring opinion, signed by Justice Samuel Alito, demonstrated his renowned fealty to "'the utmost deference' owed to the Executive's national security judgments." Thomas insisted that blind deference is warranted "regardless of the Government's reasons for invoking the state-secrets privilege." Since the CIA has the ultimate authority to decide what is secret about its activities, the Agency is afforded the power to steer the ship of state, while the rest of the executive branch and the Court must follow in its wake like tugboats.

Justice Gorsuch, joined by Justice Sotomayor, wrote a blistering dissent which begins: "There comes a point where we should not be ignorant as judges of what we know to be true as citizens . . . This case takes us well past that point. Zubaydah seeks information about his torture at the hands of the CIA. The events in question took place two decades ago. They have long been declassified. Official reports have been published, books written, and movies made about them . . . Ending this suit may shield the government from some further modest measure of embarrassment. But respectfully, we should not pretend it will safeguard any secret."

Despite all that is known about the CIA program, Gorsuch writes, Abu "Zubaydah's story remains incomplete." What is not yet publicly documented are the specific details about his treatment from December 2002 until September 2003. Taking a swipe at executive excess, Gorsuch argues that the state secrets privilege is "no blunderbuss and courts may not flee from the field at its mere display." Rather, the judiciary, as an independent branch of government, has the constitutional power to evaluate the executive's claim of privilege. "The Constitution did not create a President in the King's image but envisioned an executive regularly checked and balanced by other authorities. Our Founders knew from hard experience the 'intolerable abuses' that flow from unchecked executive power." Several of the illegitimate uses of secrets that Gorsuch mentions are the false and flawed information that was deployed to justify the internment of 120,000 Japanese Americans during World War II, for which the government apologized decades later, and the very Supreme Court case that created the state secrets privilege, *United States v. Reynolds*, in which the government was permitted to withhold an accident report about a military airplane crash from family members of people who were killed. "Decades later, when the government released the report, it turned out to contain no state secrets—only convincing proof of governmental negligence." The report was withheld from people who had a legitimate right to that evidence because "this Court accepted the Executive's declaration at face value." Gorsuch concludes his dissent by spelling out the larger lesson that must be learned from the debacle that was the torture program:

> In the end, only one argument for dismissing this case at its outset begins to make sense. It has nothing to do with speculation that government agents might accidentally blurt out the word "Poland." It has nothing to do with the fiction that Zubaydah is free to testify about his experiences as he wishes. It has nothing to do with fears about courts being unable to apply familiar tools to disaggregate discovery regarding some issues (location, foreign nationals) from others (interrogation techniques, treatment, and conditions of confine-

ment). Really, it seems that the government wants this suit dismissed because it hopes to impede the Polish criminal investigation and avoid (or at least delay) further embarrassment for past misdeeds. Perhaps at one level this is easy enough to understand. The facts are hard to face. We know already that our government treated Zubaydah brutally—more than 80 waterboarding sessions, hundreds of hours of live burial, and what it calls "rectal rehydration." Further evidence along the same lines may lie in the government's vaults. But as embarrassing as these facts may be, there is no state secret here. This Court's duty is to the rule of law and the search for truth. We should not let shame obscure our vision.

Despite losing the case on a technicality—the unacceptability of mentioning Poland in the discovery request, Joe Margulies saw a potentially redemptive potential in the outcome: "The simple willingness of a Supreme Court justice to call torture by its name is bracingly refreshing. If the first step to a moral reckoning is official acknowledgment of a painful past, then the Court has taken that step. And when that reckoning finally comes, people will look to Justice Gorsuch's dissent for inspiration." Contrary to the opinions of many observers, Margulies was not surprised that one of the Court's most conservative members, joined by one of the Court's most liberal members, should convey this message. "There is a space where conservative and liberal voices join. It is the belief that government service is a privilege, but only when government is honorable. When elected leaders betray their allegiance to the law and abandon their faith in the cleansing power of the truth, they must find no quarter in the Court."

I share with Margulies the hope that, someday, the collaborative efforts that have constituted the long fight against torture will help produce a real, national reckoning. While the role of courts remains paramount in pursuit of this goal, its achievement will require wide *political* acknowledgment that the decisions to torture were a national disgrace and the officials who authorized and abetted it were wrong. That kind of reckoning might, finally, eradicate the specter.

ACKNOWLEDGMENTS

I am grateful to so many people who shared their knowledge and insights, and to those who supported and encouraged my research and writing about US torture in the "war on terror" and the long fight against it. The seeds of this book were sown almost twenty years ago. I offer a blanket thanks to anyone who, at any time during these many years, listened and talked to me about torture and the law for more than thirty minutes. Some of those conversations helped me learn things I didn't know; others encouraged me to believe that I had something worthwhile to say.

Some of the people and organizations to whom I am most grateful are identified by name in the book and can find themselves in these pages and in the index. But I am no less grateful to the nearly two hundred unnamed lawyers and human rights practitioners who let me interview them. I am also grateful to the dozens of journalists and NGO observers and several Pentagon public affairs officers with whom I attended Guantánamo military commission hearings and talked about those events and everything else under the stars at the picnic tables in Camp Justice. Two journalists deserve a special shout-out: The indefatigable Carol Rosenberg, who wrote for the *Miami Herald* when I met her and who now writes for the *New York Times,* has been a mentor to me and a national treasure to all; and John Ryan, editor of *Lawdragon,* who is a close watcher of the 9/11 case and has been an unparalleled interlocutor about the issues this case raises.

Because I am grateful to multitudes of people, I must identify some by category. Pride of place goes to people on the torturelist; this listserve, created by Kim Scheppele in 2005, became and endures as a platform where people share their own knowledge about torture and the law, learn from and teach each other, and collectively dissect and debate the legal implications and the twists and turns in the "war on terror." It is no exaggeration to say that I could not have written this book without people on the torturelist.

My colleagues in the Sociology Department at UCSB have been supportive and encouraging of my research, even when it wasn't clear to some of them what is so interesting about torture. Many UCSB friends and colleagues have been collaborators and allies in an array of public-facing activities that informed the work on this book. Elisabeth Weber and Julie Carlson partnered with me to put on a year of programming in 2007 about "Torture and the Future." Thanks also to Terrance Wooten, with whom I have embarked on a new project on Global Carceral States, and to my student and friend Basil Farraj, who is partnering with us on this project.

The friends and colleagues I worked and socialized with, and the students I taught during the three years I was a visiting professor at the American University of Beirut helped me see and understand the "war on terror" from perspectives that were not anchored in the United States. I learned so much about America during those years living in Lebanon. Among those many, I am particularly grateful to Alex Lubin, Patrick McGreevy, Omar Dewachi, Sonya Knox, Parine Jaddo, Jasbir Puar, Nadya Sbaiti, Adam Waterman, Jackson Allers, Nazanin Shahrokni, Fouad Marei, and Ghassan Hage.

When I decided to write this book for general readers rather than tailor it to academics and specialists, I leaned into my experience writing journalistically and benefited from the lessons I learned from great editors. I cut my journalistic teeth with the Middle East Research and Information Project (MERIP), and I got my press credentials to go to Guantánamo as the "legal correspondent" for MERIP's *Middle East Report.* Thank you, Chris Toensing, for helping me gain entry to Gitmo and for being a peerless editor, and thanks to Joe Stork for teaching me how to make words hit their mark. My other journalistic home is *Jadaliyya,* where I published many of my torture-themed articles. Thank you, *Jad* comrades and very dear friends, especially Sherene Seikaly, Noura Erakat, Mouin Rabbani, Bassam Haddad, and Ziad Abu Rish. I would be remiss if I did not mention *The Nation,* the largest platform where I published articles about torture and the law. Special thanks to Adam Shatz, who solicited and published my first *Nation* piece, which dissected the torture memos, and Roane Carey, who kept coming back to my well, including inviting me to review the Senate report on the CIA torture program, which, I think, was the first to note that this was all about human experimentation.

Some of my greatest intellectual inspirations are also dear friends. Thanks to Laleh Khalili, Neve Gordon, Nicola Perugini, and Avery Gordon with whom I share a propensity for writing about the worst political practices in the world. I am grateful to Asim Qureshi and Jamie Mayerfeld, who let me benefit from their expertise.

In the process of bringing this book into the world, many thanks to Niels Hooper, my editor at the University of California Press, who doggedly pursued me till I signed with him. Thanks to assistant editor, Naja Pulliam Collins, and to my development editor, Megan Pugh, whom I was so privileged to work with. I am grateful to the reviewers of the manuscript, whose positivity pushed the book into production so expeditiously.

I owe huge gratitude to Dru Burtz and Ana Maria "Ia" Carbonell, my best friends since our days as undergraduates at Tufts, and Shiva Balaghi, each of whom listened to me talk about torture for twenty years. My close circle of Santa Barbara friends and comrades, who were indispensable supporters over the years as I worked on this book, include my "sister in cynicism" Jennifer Holt; Paul Amar, whose work ethic and generous spirit inspire me; Sherene Seikaly (again) who embodies everything good in a scholar and friend; Chris Newfield, who makes me laugh and helps me learn; and France Winddance Twine, who constantly encouraged me to keep going when the end of the line seemed so far away. When I started the writing of this book, I spent my yearlong sabbatical at seas; my adventurous journey from sea to sea was made magical and productive thanks to Mandy Turner, as well as others who joined us along the way, including my lifelong friend from Harrisburg, Donna Orbach; and dear Lee O'Brien, who returned to the sea with me when the book was drafted and listened to me read the conclusion under the Belize stars. I am also grateful for the pure unintellectual inspiration that Ludo and the rest of the crew at Octopus Dives in Mauritius provided, where I got certified as a rescue diver. I am deeply grateful to my mentor and friend, Richard Falk, and my compadre, Hilal Elver, who let me write part of this book on their balcony in Yalikavak.

I dedicated this book to my father, who always encouraged me to write something for "regular folks," like him, by which he meant no academic jargon and no footnotes. My dad and my mother, Maija, came to Santa Barbara for my "torture and the future" talk in 2004, and that meant the world to me. I also thank the rest of my family, especially my beloved sister, Tammy del Sol.

And to the people whose pain and suffering are the heart and soul of this book, I acknowledge that nothing can take that away. The past cannot be erased. But I hope that some solace can be derived from the efforts of all the people who fought to expose and end it. To you and them, I owe the greatest thanks.

SOURCES AND FURTHER READINGS

The literature on torture, law, and the "war on terror" is vast. Some of the books, articles, reports, and films cited here are resources for this book, including sources of direct quotations. Other materials are included as further readings to provide more context or deeper dives or sources of abundant citations. The items are listed alphabetically, placed under the chapter where they are first mentioned or most directly relevant. Each item is listed only once, although some are relevant for multiple chapters. Only a few items include links to internet sites, and those are regarded as reliable and durable.

PREFACE

Finn, Peter, and Greg Miller. "Panetta Outlines Plan for bin Laden's Detention If al-Qaeda Leader Is Captured." *Washington Post,* February 17, 2011.

Goldsmith, Jack. "The Guantanamo Detainees: What Next?" [webcast]. The American University Washington College of Law, February 18, 2011; https://media.wcl.american.edu/Mediasite/Play/abade4e366cd4db699f25b639affa7891d.

Hajjar, Lisa. "Anatomy of the US Targeted Killing Policy." *Middle East Report* 264 (Fall 2012).

Mayer, Jane. *The Dark Side: The Inside Story of How the War on Terror Turned into a War on American Ideals.* Doubleday, 2008.

Suskind, Ron. *The One Percent Doctrine: Deep inside America's Pursuit of Its Enemies since 9/11.* Simon & Schuster, 2006.

INTRODUCTION. WHY TORTURE MATTERS

Black, Cofer. Unclassified Testimony before 9/11 Congressional Inquiry, September 26, 2002; https://irp.fas.org/congress/2002_hr/092602black.html.

Carlson, Julie, and Elisabeth Weber, eds. *Speaking about Torture*. Fordham University Press, 2012.

Cohen, Stanley. *States of Denial: Knowing about Atrocities and Suffering*. Polity Press, 2001.

Dayan, Colin. *The Story of Cruel and Unusual*. Boston Review Press, 2007.

Dershowitz, Alan. "Let America Take Its Cues from Israel Regarding Torture." *Jewish World Review,* January 30, 2002.

———. *Why Terrorism Works: Understanding the Threat, Responding to the Challenge*. Yale University Press, 2003.

Dorfman, Ariel. *Exorcising Terror: The Incredible Unending Trial of General Augusto Pinochet*. Seven Stories Press, 2002.

Dörmann, Knut. "The Legal Situation of 'Unlawful/Unprivileged Combatants.'" *International Review of the Red Cross* 85 (2003): 461–486.

DuBois, Paige. *Torture and Truth*. Routledge, 1991.

Greenberg, Karen J., ed. *The Torture Debate in America*. Cambridge University Press, 2005.

Hajjar, Lisa. *Courting Conflict: The Israeli Military Court System in the West Bank and Gaza*. University of California Press, 2005.

———. "Sovereign Bodies, Sovereign States and the Problem of Torture." *Studies in Law, Politics, and Society* 21 (2000): 101–134.

———. "Torture and the Future." *Middle East Report Online,* May 15, 2004.

———. *Torture: A Sociology of Violence and Human Rights*. Routledge, 2013.

Ignatieff, Michael. *The Lesser Evil: Political Ethics in an Age of Terror*. Princeton University Press, 2004.

Khalili, Laleh. *Time in the Shadows: Confinement in Counterinsurgencies*. Stanford University Press, 2012.

Landau, Moshe, Yaacov Maltz, and Itzhak Hoffi. *Report of the Landau Commission*. Jerusalem, 1987.

Langbein, John H. *Torture and the Law of Proof: Europe and England in the Ancien Regime*. University Chicago Press, 2006.

Levinson, Sanford, ed. *Torture: A Collection*. Oxford University Press, 2004.

Luban, David. "Carl Schmitt and the Critique of Lawfare." *Case Western Journal of International Law* 43 (2010): 457–471.

Mayerfeld, Jamie. "In Defense of the Absolute Prohibition of Torture." *Public Affairs Quarterly* 22 (2008): 109–128.

McCoy, Alfred. *A Question of Torture: CIA Interrogation, From the Cold War to the War on Terror*. Metropolitan Books, 2006.

Pacheco, Allegra, ed. *The Case against Torture in Israel: A Compilation of Petitions, Briefs and Other Documents Submitted to the Israeli High Court of Justice*. Public Committee against Torture in Israel, 1999.

Peters, Edward. *Torture*. University of Pennsylvania Press, 1996.

Priest, Dana, and Barton Gellman. "US Decries Abuse but Defends Interrogations: 'Stress and Duress' Tactics Used on Terrorism Suspects Held in Secret Overseas Facilities." *Washington Post,* December 26, 2002.

Rejali, Darius. *Torture and Democracy.* Princeton University Press, 2007.

Scarry, Elaine. *The Body in Pain: The Making and Unmaking of the World.* Oxford University Press, 1985.

Scheppele, Kim. "Hypothetical Torture in the 'War on Terrorism.'" *Journal of National Security Policy and Law* 1 (2005): 285–340.

US Senate Armed Services Committee. *Investigation into the Treatment of Detainees in US Custody: Executive Summary and Conclusions.* Senate, 2008; https://irp.fas.org/congress/2008_rpt/detainees.pdf.

Weschler, Lawrence. *A Miracle, A Universe: Settling Accounts with Torturers.* University of Chicago Press, 1998.

CHAPTER ONE. TAKING THE "WAR ON TERROR" TO COURT

Freedman, Eric M. *Habeas Corpus: Rethinking the Great Writ of Liberty.* New York University Press, 2002.

Greenberg, Karen. *The Least Worst Place: Guantanamo's First 100 Days.* Oxford University Press, 2009.

Hafetz, Jonathan, and Mark P. Denbeaux, eds. *The Guantánamo Lawyers: Inside a Prison Outside the Law.* New York University Press, 2009.

Margulies, Joseph. *Guantánamo and the Abuse of Presidential Power.* Simon & Schuster, 2006.

McKay, Adam. *Vice* (film). Annapurna Pictures, 2018.

Ortiz, Dianna, with Patricia Davis. *The Blindfold's Eyes: My Journey from Torture to Truth.* Orbis Books, 2002.

Ratner, Michael. "How We Closed the Guantanamo HIV Camp: The Intersection of Politics and Litigation." *Harvard Human Rights Journal* 11 (1998): 187–220.

Ratner, Michael, and Ellen Ray. *Guantánamo: What the World Should Know.* Chelsea Green Publishing, 2004.

Ratner, Michael, and Michael Smith. *Moving the Bar: My Life as a Radical Lawyer.* OR Books, 2021.

Rose, David. *Guantánamo: The War on Human Rights.* New Press, 2004.

CHAPTER TWO. ENTER THE WARRIORS

Association of the Bar of the City New York's Committees on International Human Rights and Military Affairs and Justice. *Human Rights Standards Applicable to the United States' Interrogation of Detainees,* ABCNY, April 2004; http://www.abcny.org/pdf/HUMANRIGHTS.pdf.

Greenberg, Karen J., and Joshua L. Dratel, eds. *The Enemy Combatant Papers: American Justice, the Courts, and the War on Terror.* Cambridge University Press, 2008.

Hajjar, Lisa. "International Humanitarian Law and 'Wars on Terror': A Comparative Analysis of Israeli and American Doctrines and Policies." *Journal of Palestine Studies* 36 (2006): 21–42.

———. "In the Penal Colony." *The Nation,* January 20, 2005.

Katyal, Neal K., and Laurence H. Tribe. "Waging War, Deciding Guilt: Trying the Military Tribunals." *Yale Law Journal* 111 (2002): 1259–1310.

Mackey, Chris, and Greg Miller. *The Interrogators: Inside the Secret War against al-Qaeda.* Little, Brown and Company, 2004.

Mahler, Jonathan. *The Challenge: Hamdan v. Rumsfeld and the Fight over Presidential Power.* Farrar, Straus, and Giroux, 2008.

———. "Commander Swift Objects." *New York Times Magazine,* June 13, 2004.

Poitras, Laura. *The Oath* (film). Zeitgeist Films, 2010.

Rumsfeld, Donald. "Opinion: A New Kind of War." *New York Times,* September 27, 2001.

Schmitz, Charles. "Beating a Slow, Stubborn Retreat at Guantanamo Bay." *Middle East Report Online,* May 15, 2005.

Soufan, Ali, with Daniel Freedman. *The Black Banners: The Inside Story of 9/11 and the War against al-Qaeda.* W. W. Norton, 2011.

Swift, Charles, Lieutenant Commander. "The American Way of Justice." *Esquire,* March 1, 2007.

———. Testimony before US Senate Committee on the Judiciary, June 15, 2005; https://www.c-span.org/video/?187193-1/guantanamo-detainees.

Yoo, John. *War by Other Means: An Insider's Account of the War on Terror.* Atlantic Monthly Press, 2006.

CHAPTER THREE. MAPPING THE LINES OF BATTLE

Alexander, Matthew. *How to Break a Terrorist: The US Interrogators Who Used Brains, Not Brutality, to Take Down the Deadliest Man in Iraq.* Free Press, 2008.

Chandrasekaran, Rajiv. *Imperial Life in the Emerald City: Inside Iraq's Green Zone.* Vintage, 2007.

Coll, Steve. *Ghost Wars: The Secret History of the CIA, Afghanistan, and Bin Laden, from the Soviet Invasion to September 10, 2001.* Penguin Books, 2004.

Danner, Mark. *Torture and Truth: America, Abu Ghraib, and the War on Terror.* New York Review of Books, 2004.

Forsythe, David P. *The Humanitarians: The International Committee of the Red Cross.* Cambridge University Press, 2005.

Greenberg, Karen J., and Joshua L. Dratel, eds. *The Torture Papers: The Road to Abu Ghraib.* Cambridge University Press, 2005.

Grey, Steven. *Ghost Plane: The True Story of the CIA Torture Program.* St. Martin's Press, 2006.

Hajjar, Lisa. "Omar Suleiman, the CIA's Man in Cairo and Egypt's Torturer-in-Chief." *Jadaliyya,* January 30, 2011.

Hersh, Seymour. "The General's Report." *New Yorker,* June 18, 2007.

———. "Torture at Abu Ghraib: American Soldiers Brutalized Iraqis." *New Yorker,* May 10, 2004.

Human Rights Watch. "List of 'Ghost Prisoners' Possibly in CIA Custody." HRW, November 30, 2005; https://www.hrw.org/news/2005/11/30/list-ghost-prisoners-possibly-cia-custody.

International Committee of the Red Cross. *Report of the International Committee of the Red Cross (ICRC) on the Treatment by the Coalition Forces of Prisoners of War and Other Protected Persons by the Geneva Conventions in Iraq during Arrest, Internment and Interrogation.* ICRC, February 2004.

Isikoff, Michael, and David Corn. *Hubris: The Inside Story of Spin, Scandal, and the Selling of the Iraq War.* Crown, 2006.

Johnsen, Gregory. *The Last Refuge: Yemen, al-Qaeda, and America's War in Arabia.* W. W. Norton and Company, 2012.

Kennedy, Rory. *Ghosts of Abu Ghraib* (film). HBO, 2007.

Lederman, Marty, ed. The Anti-Torture Memos: Balkinization Posts on Torture, Interrogation, Detention, War Powers, Executive Authority, DOJ and OLC. *Balkinization,* July 8., 2005; http://balkin.blogspot.com/2005/09/antitorture-memos-balkinization-posts.html.

Li, Darryl. *The Universal Enemy: Jihad, Empire, and the Challenge of Solidarity.* Stanford University Press, 2019.

McDermott, Terry, and Josh Meyer. *The Hunt for KSM: Inside the Pursuit and Takedown of the Real 9/11 Mastermind, Khalid Sheikh Mohammed.* Little, Brown and Company, 2012.

Meron, Theodor. *The Humanization of Humanitarian Law.* Martinus Nijhoff, 2006.

Paglen, Trevor. *Blank Spots on the Map: The Dark Geography of the Pentagon's Secret World.* Dutton Adult, 2009.

Paglen, Trevor, and A. C. Thompson. *Torture Taxi: On the Trail of the CIA's Rendition Flights.* Melville House, 2006.

PBS NewsHour. "Bending the Rules: International Law and the Treatment of Prisoners." PBS, May 13, 2004; https://www.pbs.org/newshour/show/bending-the-rulesinternational-law-and-the-treatment-of-prisoners#transcript.

Rosen, Nir. *Aftermath: Following the Bloodshed of America's Wars in the Muslim World.* Bold Type Books, 2010.

Rumsfeld, Donald. Department of Defense News Briefing, February 12, 2002; https://archive.ph/20180320091111/http://archive.defense.gov/Transcripts/Transcript.aspx?TranscriptID=2636.

Tenet, George, and Bill Harlow. *At the Center of the Storm: My Years at the CIA.* Harper Collins, 2007.

Begg, Moazzam, and Victoria Brittain. *Enemy Combatant: My Imprisonment at Guantánamo, Bagram, and Kandahar.* New Press, 2006.

Denbeaux, Mark, Joshua Denbeaux, and Joshua Gregorek. *Report on Guantánamo Detainees: A Profile of 517 Detainees Through Analysis of Department of Defense Data.* Seton Hall Public Law Research Paper No. 46, February 21, 2006.

Denbeaux, Mark and Joshua Denbeaux. *No-Hearing Hearings: CSRT—The Modern Habeas Corpus?* Seton Hall Public Law Research Paper No. 951245, November 17, 2006.

Falkoff, Marc, ed. *Poems from Guantánamo: The Detainees Speak.* University of Iowa Press, 2007.

Gibney, Alex. *Taxi to the Dark Side* (film). Velocity/ThinkFilm, 2007.

Golden, Tim. "Naming Names at Gitmo." *New York Times Magazine,* October 21, 2007.

Hafetz, Jonathan. *Habeas Corpus after 9/11: Confronting America's New Global Detention System.* New York University Press, 2011.

Jaffer, Jaffer, and Amrit Singh. *Administration of Torture: From Washington to Abu Ghraib and Beyond.* Columbia University Press, 2007.

Jehl, Douglas. "Pentagon Plans to Transfer More Detainees from Base in Cuba." *New York Times,* March 11, 2005.

Kurnaz, Murat. *Five Years of My Life: An Innocent Man in Guantanamo.* St. Martin's Press, 2008.

Lewis, Neil. "Official Attacks Top Law Firms over Detainees." *New York Times,* January 13, 2007.

Priest, Dana, and Dan Eggen. "Terror Suspect Alleges Torture." *Washington Post,* January 6, 2005.

Stafford Smith, Clive. 2007. *Eight O'Clock Ferry to the Windward Side: Seeking Justice in Guantánamo Bay.* Nation Books, 2007.

Wax, Steven. *Kafka Comes to America: Fighting for Justice in the War on Terror—A Public Defender's Inside Account.* Other Press, 2008.

Winterbottom, Michael, and Mat Whitecross. *The Road to Guantánamo* (film). Roadside Attractions, 2006.

CHAPTER FIVE. WINNING SOME, LOSING SOME

Bennis, Phyllis. "Ten Years of the Los Angeles Eight Deportation Case." *Middle East Report* 202 (Spring 1997).

Bush, George W. Press conference transcript. White House, September 6, 2006; https://www.nytimes.com/2006/09/06/washington/06bush_transcript.html.

Cole, David. "9/11 and the LA 8." *The Nation,* October 8, 2003.

———. "Terrorizing Immigrants in the Name of Fighting Terrorism." American Bar Association, *Human Rights Magazine* 29 (Winter 2002).

———. "Where Liberty Lies: Civil Society and Individual Rights after 9/11." *Georgetown Law Faculty Publications and Other Works* 1119 (2012).

Hafetz, Jonathan, and Mark P. Denbeaux, eds. *The Guantánamo Lawyers: Inside a Prison Outside the Law.* New York University Press, 2009.

Hajjar, Lisa. "In Defense of Lawfare: The Value of Litigation in Challenging Torture." In *Confronting Torture: Essays on the Ethics, Legality, History, and Psychology of Torture Today*, edited by Scott A. Anderson and Martha C. Nussbaum, 294–319. University of Chicago Press, 2018.

Human Rights Watch. "Statement on US Secret Detention Facilities in Europe." HRW, November 7, 2005.

Lederman, Marty. "President Tells Congress to Take a Hike on Interrogation and Detention." *Balkinization,* July 22, 2005.

Mayer, Jane. "Outsourcing Torture: The Secret History of America's 'Extraordinary Rendition' Program." *New Yorker,* February 6, 2005.

Priest, Dana. "CIA Holds Terror Suspects in Secret Prisons." *Washington Post,* November 2, 2005.

Schmidt, Randal M., and John T. Furlow. *Schmidt-Furlow Report: AR 15-6 Investigation into FBI Allegations of Detainee Abuse at Guantanamo Bay Detention Facility.* US Government, July 14, 2005.

Senate Armed Services Committee. "Review of Department of Defense Interrogation and Detention Policy and Operations in the Global War on Terrorism." Transcript of hearings, July 13, 14, 2005; https://www.govinfo.gov/content/pkg /CHRG-109shrg28578/html/CHRG-109shrg28578.htm.

CHAPTER SIX. FIGHTING FOR JUSTICE AT
HOME AND ABROAD

Brinkley, Joel. "Questions about Secret Prisons Follow Rice in Europe." *New York Times,* December 6, 2005.

Cole, David. "He Was Tortured, But He Can't Sue." *New York Review of Books,* June 15, 2010.

Council of Europe. *CIA Above the Law?: Secret Detentions and Unlawful Inter-State Transfer of Detainees in Europe.* Strasbourg, France, 2008.

Government of Canada. *Report of the Commission of Inquiry into the Actions of Canadian Officials in Relation to Maher Arar.* Ottawa, September 18, 2006.

Hajjar, Lisa. "Chaos as Utopia: International Criminal Prosecutions as a Challenge to State Power." *Studies in Law, Politics and Society* 31 (2004): 3–23.

———. "Grave Injustice: Maher Arar and Unaccountable America." *Middle East Report Online,* June 24, 2010.

———. "Universal Jurisdiction as Praxis: An Option to Pursue Legal Accountability for Superpower Torturers." In *When Governments Break the Law: The Rule of Law and the Prosecution of the Bush Administration*, edited by Austin Sarat and Nasser Hussain, 87–120. New York University Press, 2010.

Kaleck, Wolfgang. *Law versus Power: Our Global Fight for Human Rights.* OR Books, 2019.

Klein, Naomi. *The Shock Doctrine: The Rise of Disaster Capitalism.* Metropolitan Books, 2007.

Kornbluh, Peter. *The Pinochet File: A Declassified Dossier on Atrocity and Accountability.* New Press, 2003.

Lewis, Anthony. "Making Torture Legal." *New York Review of Books,* July 15, 2004.

Luban, David. "Liberalism, Torture, and the Ticking Bomb." *Virginia Law Review* 91 (2005): 1425–1461.

———. *Torture, Power, and Law.* Cambridge University Press, 2014.

Posner, Eric, and Adrian Vermeule. *Terror in the Balance: Security, Liberty, and the Courts.* Oxford University Press, 2007.

Ratner, Michael. *The Trial of Donald Rumsfeld: A Prosecution by Book.* New Press, 2008.

Ristroph, Alice. "Professors Strangelove." University of Utah S. J. Quinney College of Law Legal Studies Research Paper Series No. 08-06 (2008): 243–257.

Smith, Craig. "Rumsfeld Says Belgian Law Could Prompt NATO to Leave." *New York Times,* June 12, 2003.

Transcript: Ashcroft, Mueller press conference. CNN, May 26, 2004; https://www.cnn.com/2004/US/05/26/terror.threat.transcript/.

Whitlock, Craig. "Germans Charge 13 CIA Operatives." *Washington Post,* February 1, 2007.

CHAPTER SEVEN. TRYING GUANTÁNAMO

Ackerman, Spencer. "Bad Lieutenant: American Police Brutality, Exported from Chicago to Guantánamo." *Guardian,* February 18, 2015.

———. "The Disappeared: Chicago Police Detain Americans at Abuse-Laden 'Black Site.'" *Guardian,* February 24, 2015.

Ahmad, Muneer I. "Resisting Guantanamo: Rights at the Brink of Dehumanization." *Northwestern University Law Review* 103 (2009): 1683–1763.

Bravin, Jess. "The Conscience of a Colonel." *Wall Street Journal,* March 31, 2007.

———. *The Terror Courts: Rough Justice at Guantanamo Bay.* Yale University Press, 2013.

Flynn, Sean. "The Defense Will Not Rest." *GQ,* July 14, 2007.

Frakt, David. "Closing Argument at Guantanamo: The Torture of Mohammed Jawad." *Harvard Human Rights Journal* 22 (2009): 401–423.

Glaberson, William. "An Unlikely Antagonist in the Detainees' Corner." *New York Times,* June 19, 2008.

Resnick, Judith. "Detention, the War on Terror, and the Federal Courts." *Columbia Law Review* 110 (2010): 579–686.

Shephard, Michelle. *Guantanamo's Child: The Untold Story of Omar Khadr.* Wiley, 2008.

Woodward, Bob. "Guantanamo Detainee Was Tortured, Says Official Overseeing Military Trials." *Washington Post,* January 14, 2009.

Worthington, Andy. *The Guantánamo Files: The Stories of the 759 Detainees in America's Illegal Prison.* Pluto Press, 2007.

CHAPTER EIGHT. NEW BATTLES, SAME WAR

ABC News. "Transcript: Barack Obama." *This Week with George Stephanopoulos,* January 10, 2009; https://abcnews.go.com/ThisWeek/Economy/Story?id=6618199&page=1.

Andersson, Hilary. "Red Cross Confirms 'Second Jail' at Bagram, Afghanistan." *BBC News,* May 11, 2010.

Becker, Jo, and Scott Shane. "Secret 'Kill List' Proves a Test of Obama's Principles and Will." *New York Times,* May 29, 2012.

Bruck, Connie. "Why Obama Has Failed to Close Guantánamo." *New Yorker,* July 25, 2016.

Burns, Scott Z. *The Report* (film). VICE Media, 2019.

Cheney, Dick, with Liz Cheney. *In My Time: A Personal and Political Memoir.* Threshold Editions, 2012.

Cheney, Richard B. "Remarks" [transcript]. American Enterprise Institute, May 21, 2009; https://www.aei.org/research-products/speech/remarks-by-richard-b-cheney/.

Corn, David. "Obama and GOPers Worked Together to Kill Bush Torture Probe." *Mother Jones,* December 1, 2010.

Danner, Mark. "The Red Cross Torture Report: What It Means." *New York Review of Books,* April 30, 2009.

———. "US Torture: Voices from the Black Sites." *New York Review of Books,* April 9, 2009.

Deeks, Ashley. "Domestic Humanitarian Law: Developing the Law of War in Domestic Courts." Virginia Public Law and Legal Theory Research Paper No. 2013-39, October 9, 2013.

"Eric Holder on Terrorist Trials in New York" [press conference video]. C-SPAN, November 13, 2009; https://www.c-span.org/video/?290007-1/eric-holder-terrorist-trials-york.

Fisher, William. "US: Guantanamo Detainee Ordered Freed." *Inter Press Service,* April 12, 2010.

Foucault, Michel. "On the Genealogy of Ethics: An Overview of Work in Progress." In *The Foucault Reader,* edited by Paul Rabinow, 340–372. Pantheon Books, 1984.

Greenwald, Robert. *The War on Whistleblowers: Free Press and the National Security State* (film). Brave New Foundation, 2013.

Hajjar, Lisa. "Bagram, Obama's Gitmo." *Middle East Report* 260 (Fall 2011).

———. "It Is Raining Documents, Hallelujah!" *Jadaliyya,* November 28, 2010.

———. "Wikileaking the Truth about American Unaccountability for Torture." *Societies Without Borders* 7 (2012): 192–225.

Horton, Scott. "The Guantanamo 'Suicides': A Camp Delta Sergeant Blows the Whistle." *Harper's Magazine*, March 2010.

———. "The Guantánamo 'Suicides,' Revisited: A Missing Document Suggests a CIA Cover-Up." *Harper's Magazine*, June 2014.

———. *Lords of Secrecy: The National Security Elite and America's Stealth Warfare.* Nation Books, 2015.

———. "The Margolis Memo." *Harper's Magazine*, February 24, 2010.

———. "Obama's Black Sites." *Harper's Magazine*, May 12, 2010.

Human Rights Watch. *Getting Away with Torture: The Bush Administration and Mistreatment of Detainees.* HRW, July 12, 2011.

"Independent UN Expert on Torture Calls for Unrestricted Access to US Detainees." *UN News*, July 12, 2011.

Jaffer, Jameel. "The Drone Memo Cometh." *Just Security*, June 21, 2014.

Junod, Tom. "The Lethal Presidency of Barack Obama." *Esquire*, July 9, 2012.

Kaye, Jeff. "Soros' Foundation Links Army's Field Manual Appendix M to US Torture in Afghanistan." *Shadowproof*, October 19, 2010.

Klaidman, Daniel. "Drones: How Obama Learned to Kill." *Daily Beast*, May 28, 2012.

———. *Kill or Capture: The War on Terror and the Soul of the Obama Presidency.* Houghton Mifflin Harcourt, 2012.

Macdonald, Kevin. *The Mauritanian* (film). STX Films 2021.

Mayer, Jane. "The Bush Six." *New Yorker*, April 6, 2009.

———. "The Trial: Eric Holder and the Battle over Khalid Sheikh Mohammed." *New Yorker*, February 3, 2010.

Obama, Barack. "Remarks by the President on National Security." White House Press Office, May 21, 2009; https://obamawhitehouse.archives.gov/the-press-office/remarks-President-national-security-5-21-09.

Panetta, Leon, and Jim Newton. *Worthy Fights: A Memoir of Leadership in War and Peace.* Penguin Press, 2014.

Parks, Lisa, and Caren Kaplan, eds. *Life in the Age of Drone Warfare.* Duke University Press, 2017.

Pasternack, Alex. "How the Government Turned a Former CIA Officer into a 'Dissident.'" *Vice*, April 8, 2015.

Ratner, Michael. "Bringing the 'Bush Six' to Justice." *Guardian*, January 7, 2011.

Roht-Arriaza, Naomi. "The Pinochet Precedent and Universal Jurisdiction." *New England Law Review* 35 (2001): 311–319.

Sands, Philippe. *Torture Team: Rumsfeld's Memo and the Betrayal of American Values.* St. Martin's Press, 2008.

Sikkink, Katheryn. *The Justice Cascade: How Human Rights Prosecutions Are Changing World Politics.* W. W. Norton and Company, 2011.

Singh, Amrit. "Europe's Human Rights Court Shines More Light on the CIA's Black Site Torture Program." Open Society Justice Initiative, June 8, 2018.

Slahi, Mohamedou Ould, and Larry Siems, ed. *Guantánamo Diary.* Little, Brown and Company, 2015.

———. *Guantánamo Diary: Restored Edition.* Little, Brown and Company, 2017.

Weaver, Christopher. "After Memos' Release, Push for Torture Commission Grows." *ProPublica,* March 4, 2009.

CHAPTER NINE. OBAMA'S GUANTÁNAMO

Crabapple, Molly. "It Don't Gitmo Better than This." *Vice,* July 31, 2013.

Feldman, Allen. *Formations of Violence: The Narrative of the Body and Political Terror in Northern Ireland.* University of Chicago Press, 1991.

Hafetz, Jonathan. *Obama's Guantánamo: Stories from an Enduring Prison.* New York University Press, 2016.

Hajjar, Lisa. "The Agony and the Irony of Guantanamo's Mass Hunger Strike." *Jadaliyya,* June 20, 2013.

———. "The Counterterrorism War Paradigm versus International Humanitarian Law: The Legal Contradictions and Global Consequences of the US 'War on Terror.'" *Law & Social Inquiry* 44 (2019): 922–956.

———. "Travesty in Progress: Omar Khadr and the US Military Commissions." *Middle East Report Online,* July 26, 2010.

———. "Tweeting from Guantanamo: Recording History 140 Characters at a Time." *Jadaliyya,* November 3, 2010.

Jackson, Jon S. "When Is Torture Justified?" *TEDx Memphis,* September 14, 2015; https://www.youtube.com/watch?v=3548Ac9wGN8.

Kaye, Jeff. "David Remes on the Tragic Death of Adnan Latif: What Is the Military Trying to Hide?" *Shadowproof,* December 17, 2012.

Khalili, Mustafa, Guy Grandjean, and Sherbert and Fonic. "Guantánamo Bay: The Hunger Strikes—Video Animation." *Guardian,* October 11, 2013; https://www.theguardian.com/world/video/2013/oct/11/guantanamo-bay-hunger-strikes-video-animation?CMP=twt_gu.

Knefel, John. "Guantanamo Prisoner's Tragic Letter." *AlterNet,* September 16, 2012.

Leopold, Jason. "Gitmo Officials Alter Hunger Strike Protocols." *Al Jazeera,* December 6, 2013.

———. "Guantanamo Manual Supports Controversial Drug." *Al Jazeera,* June 17, 2013.

Mitchell, Luke. "God Mode: Force-Feeding at Guantánamo." *Harper's Magazine,* August 4, 2006.

———. "Six Questions for Cynthia Smith on Legality of Force-feeding at Guantánamo." *Harper's Magazine,* June 4, 2009.

Reilly, Ryan J. "Guantanamo Hunger Strike Lays Bare Detainees' Growing Desperation." *HuffPost,* May 2, 2013.

Rosenberg, Carol. "Tracking the Hunger Strike." *Miami Herald,* June 25, 2013.

———. "Why US Doesn't Let Detainees Starve at Guantánamo Bay." *Miami Herald,* September 27, 2014.

Turner, Jennifer. "The Monster of Bagram." *Daily Kos,* May 7, 2010.

Vladeck, Steve. *"Al Bahlul* and the Long Shadow of Illegitimacy." *Lawfare,* October 22, 2016.

CHAPTER TEN. THE LAST FRONT

Bigelow, Kathryn. *Zero Dark Thirty* (film). Annapurna Pictures, 2012.

"CIA Torture Psychologists Settle Lawsuit." ACLU, August 17, 2017; https://www .aclu.org/press-releases/cia-torture-psychologists-settle-lawsuit.

Fallon, Mark. *Unjustifiable Means: The Inside Story of How the CIA, Pentagon, and US Government Conspired to Torture.* Regan Arts, 2017.

Hajjar, Lisa. "The CIA Didn't Just Torture, It Experimented on Human Beings." *The Nation,* December 14, 2014.

———. "The Long Shadow of the CIA at Guantanamo." *Middle East Report* 273 (Winter 2014).

———. "Torture Is the Nasty Center of the 9/11 Case at Guantánamo." *Jadaliyya,* March 24, 2021.

Hawkins, Katherine. "At Least One Copy of the Senate Torture Report Will Be Preserved. What about the Others?" *Just Security,* December 13, 2016.

Hirsch, Susan. "Ghailani Trial and Sentence Affirms US Federal Court System." *HuffPost,* January 25, 2011.

Isikoff, Michael. "Senate Report on Torture Is One Step Closer to Disappearing." *Yahoo News,* May 16, 2016.

Jacobson, Sid, and Ernie Colon. *The Torture Report: A Graphic Adaptation.* Bold Type Books, 2017.

Mayer, Jane. "Zero Conscience in 'Zero Dark Thirty.'" *New Yorker,* December 14, 2012.

Mitchell, James E., and Bill Harlow. *Enhanced Interrogation: Inside the Minds and Motives of the Islamic Terrorists Trying to Destroy America.* Crown Forum, 2016.

Pradhan, Alka. "Kafka's Court: Seeking Law and Justice at Guantanamo Bay." *Northwestern University Law Review* 114 (2020): 251–257.

Raphael, Sam, Crofton Black, and Ruth Blakely. *CIA Torture Unredacted.* The Rendition Project, 2019; https://www.therenditionproject.org.uk/#.

Rosenberg, Carol. "Inside the Most Secret Place at Guantánamo Bay." *New York Times,* March 14, 2020.

———. "Judge Tells Alleged 9/11 Plotter's Lawyer to Seek Funding for More Brain Scans." *Miami Herald,* May 2, 2018.

———. "Military Closes Failing Facility at Guantánamo to Consolidate Prisoners." *New York Times,* April 4, 2021.

———. "9/11 Attorneys Say They Can't Defend Clients without Questioning CIA about Torture." *Miami Herald,* June 29, 2018.

———. "Trial Guide: The Sept. 11 Case at Guantánamo Bay." *New York Times,* December 3, 2021 (periodically updated).

Ryan, John. "Pretrial of the Century: The Sept. 11 Case at Guantanamo Bay." *Lawdragon,* September 21, 2016.

Soufan, Ali, and Daniel Freedman. *The Black Banners (Declassified): How Torture Derailed the War on Terror after 9/11.* W. W. Norton and Company, 2020.

US Senate Select Committee on Intelligence. *Report of the Committee Study of the Central Intelligence Agency's Detention and Interrogation Program.* US Senate, December 14, 2014.

Yachot, Noa. "Out of the Darkness: How Two Psychologists Teamed Up with the CIA to Devise a Torture Program and Experiment on Human Beings." ACLU, October 13, 2015; https://www.aclu.org/issues/national-security/torture/out-darkness?redirect=feature/out-darkness.

CONCLUSION. THE AFTERLIVES OF TORTURE

Bonner, Raymond. "Will the United States Officially Acknowledge That It Had a Secret Torture Site in Poland?" *ProPublica,* October 1, 2021.

Church, Charles R. "What Politics and the Media Still Get Wrong about Abu Zubaydah." *Lawfare,* August 1, 2018.

Cohen, Stanley. "State Crimes of Previous Regimes: Knowledge, Accountability, and the Policing of the Past." *Law & Social Inquiry* 20 (1995): 7–50.

Fallon, Mark. "State Secrets and the Blinding of Justice." *SpyTalk*, March 24, 2022.

Gibney, Alex. *The Forever Prisoner* (film). HBO, 2021.

Gordon, Avery. *Ghostly Matters: Haunting and the Sociological Imagination.* University of Minnesota Press, 2008.

"The Guantánamo Docket." *New York Times,* June 26, 2022 (updated periodically).

Hajjar, Lisa. "Making American Torture Great Again." *Jadaliyya,* December 14, 2016.

Hajjar, Lisa, and Hedi Viterbo. "Seeing State Secrets: The Significance of Abu Zubaydah's Self-Portraits of Torture." *Jadaliyya,* June 4, 2020.

Margulies, Joseph. "The Innocence of Abu Zubaydah." *New York Review of Books,* September 28, 2018.

———. "Military Officers' Handwritten Clemency Letter at Guantanamo—What It Says about Who We Are." *Just Security,* November 8, 2021.

———. "9/11 Forever." *Boston Review,* September 9, 2021.

———. "Ruminations on the Abu Zubaydah Supreme Court Oral Arguments: Three Surprising Turns." *Just Security,* October 18, 2021.

———. "In US v. Husayn (Abu Zubaydah), the Supreme Court Calls Torture What It Is." *Just Security*, March 11, 2022.

———. *What Changed When Everything Changed? 9/11 and the Making of National History.* Yale University Press, 2013.

Miller, Peter, Paul Gronke, and Darius Rejali. "Torture and Public Opinion: The Partisan Dimension." In *Examining Torture: Empirical Studies of State Repression,* edited by Tracy Lightcap and James P. Pfiffner, 11–41. Palgrave Macmillan, 2014.

Moss, Ian. "There Is a Way to Close Guantanamo." *Just Security,* September 10, 2021.

Rejali, Darius. "Op-Ed: Donald Trump's Pro-Torture Rhetoric Could Help Bring Abuse to a Neighborhood Near You." *Los Angeles Times,* February 19, 2017.

Roehm, Scott. "A Torture Survivor Speaks at the Guantanamo Military Commission." *Just Security,* November 4, 2021.

Rosenberg, Carol. "For the First Time in Public, a Detainee Describes Torture at CIA Black Sites." *New York Times,* October 28, 2021.

———. "The 9/11 Trial: Why Are Plea Bargain Talks Underway?" *New York Times,* March 20, 2022.

Scheer, Robert. "J. Wells Dixon: Why 7 Military Officers Just Blasted the CIA" (podcast). *Scheerpost,* November 5, 2021; https://scheerpost.com/2021/11/05/j-dixon-wells-why-7-u-s-military-officers-just-blasted-the-cia/.

Tyson, Alec. "Americans Divided in Views of Use of Torture in US Anti-Terror Efforts." Pew Research Center, January 26, 2017; https://www.pewresearch.org/fact-tank/2017/01/26/americans-divided-in-views-of-use-of-torture-in-u-s-anti-terror-efforts/.

Worthington, Andy. "In Abu Zubaydah Case, Justice Gorsuch Lays Bare the US Government's Shameful and Enduring Torture Problem." Close Guantanamo, March 24, 2022.

INDEX

Note: Page numbers in italics indicate an illustration.

Bush Six, 220, 236–39
Bybee, Jay, 53, 172, 220, 238–39

Cageprisoners (CAGE), 103
Calabresi, Guido, 157–58
Cameron, David, 221
Camp Cropper (Iraq), 83
Camp Echo (Guantánamo), 48, 61, 100–101
Camp 7 (Guantánamo), 206, 277, 280, 282, 303
Canadian government, 154–55, 179–80, 257, 263–64
Canadian journalists, 249
Canadian Muslims, 151–54, 203
Canwest, 249
Cardozo, Michael, 28
Carlson, Tucker, 6
CaseMap, 273
Cassel, Douglass, 37
Castelli, Jeffrey, 176
Catholic Workers Movement, 26
Center for Constitutional Rights (CCR): accountability case of, 171–73; civil lawsuits of, 150–55; Cole at, 125; Falkoff and, 104; *Filártiga* and, 21–22, 168; Gitmo Bar in relation to, 95–96; *Habib,* 34; history and mission of, 21–23; in international courts, 16; *John Doe I-570 v. Bush,* 110–11; Kunstler and Weinglass at, 107; motto of, 35; Olshansky and, 24–25; principles of, 26; *Rasul* in relation to, 93–94; relations with JAGs, 60. *See also* Ratner, Michael
Center for International Human Rights (Northwestern University), 37
Center for Justice and International Law, 32
Central Intelligence Agency (CIA): aka OGA, 160; declassification process of, 285; Haspel at, 308; interests of, 286; kill-or-capture mission of, 10; al-Libi and, 70; *El Masri v. Tenet* and, 158; McCain Amendment and, 137–38; in Poland, 313–14; relations in Europe, 219–20; relations with FBI, 297–98, 303–4; role in "war on terror," 52. *See also* rendition, detention, and interrogation (RDI) program

certiorari, writ of, 37–39
chemical and biological weapons, 68
Cheney, Dick: counsel for, 7, 36; on executive power, 310–11; media offensive of, 218–19; national security speech (2009) of, 226; presidential power and, 23; relations with Howard, John, 191–92; response to 9/11, 2, 6; response to SASC hearings, 136; role in interrogation decisions, xviii; war council, 7
Chicago 8, 107
child soldiers, 241
Chinese Uighurs, 224
CIDT (cruel, inhuman, or degrading treatment), 54, 89, 128–29, 140
civilian contractors, 79
civil lawsuits, 149–50
classified information, 286–88, 293–94
Claus, Joshua, 249
Clement, Paul, 85
Clinton, Hillary, 307
Clinton administration, 27–28, 45
Close Guantánamo Now!, 264
CMCR (Court of Military Commission Review), 192–93
CNN *Crossfire,* 6
Coalition Provisional Authority (Iraq), 73, 74, 84
Coburn, Barry, 247, 249, 250, 255
coercive interrogation tactics: at Abu Ghraib, 84–87, 89; Aylward on, 120; Barr on, 133; Cheney and, xviii, 7; effectiveness of, 17, 175, 308; FBI memos and, 290–91; Israel and, 3–4; JAGs on, 58–59; learned helplessness in relation to, 302; military commissions in relation to, 47–48; Mora and, 57; Rona on, 78; Yoo on, 53. *See also* euphemisms for torture; torture
Cohen, Shane, 297, 303
Cole, David, 125–27, 150, 151–52, 155, 156, 312
"Collateral Murder" video, 235
Collyer, Rosemary, 110–11
Combatant Status Review Tribunals (CSRTs), 94–95, 101, 115, 188–90
Common Article 3 (CA3), 123, 143, 145, 146
Conde-Pumpido, Cándido, 237

enemy prisoners of war (EPWs), 75
enhanced interrogation techniques (EITs):
approval of, 124; in the authorization of
torture, 149; Mitchell on, 299–302;
Obama and, 17–18, 214; reauthorization
of, 307; SSCI report on, 288–89; Trump
and, xviii. *See also* torture
EPWs (enemy prisoners of war), 75
Espionage Act of 1917, 240
Esquire, 67
euphemisms for torture, 3, 5, 10, 54, 149,
300. *See also* coercive interrogation
tactics; enhanced interrogation techniques (EITs); torture
Europe, accountability lawsuits in, 175–77
Europe, relations with the CIA, 220
European Center for Constitutional and
Human Rights (ECCHR), 175, 237
European Court of Human Rights
(ECHR), 3, 220, 313
executive orders, 17, 46, 103, 214, 218,
240–41
executive power: Cheney and, 23–24,
310–11; expansion of, 8–9; Geneva
Conventions in relation to, 50, 52;
Gorsuch on, 316; in legalization of
torture, 53–55; under Obama, 232–34
Ex Parte Quirin, 45–46

falaqa, 153
Falkoff, Marc, 104, 105, 110–11, 112
false flag interrogations, 106
FBI (Federal Bureau of Investigation):
informants, 281; memos, 290–91; rela-
tions with the CIA, 297–98, 303–4;
statements, 296–97
Federalist Society, 22
federal trials, 278–79
Federico, Richard, 207
Feinstein, Dianne, 219, 285
Feith, Douglas, 174, 220
Filártiga v. Peña-Irala, 21–22, 40, 168
films and filmmakers, 62, 103, 167, 231,
278, 313
Fishback, Ian, 136–37
Fitzgerald, James, 291
Fitzgibbons, Amy, 207
five techniques (British), 3

Fleener, Tom, 196
Fletcher, Brian, 314, 315
Flowers, Kobie, 247, 249, 250, 255
Food and Drug Administration, 266
force-feeding policy, 266–68
Fordham University, 113
The Forever Prisoner (Gibney), 313
Foster, Tina Monshipour, 216
Foucault, Michel, 232
Four Key Principles of Being a Radical
Lawyer (Ratner), 26
Fourth Amendment, 164
Frakt, David, 197–200, 202
Franks, Tommy, 77
Fredman, Jonathan, 56
Freedman, Eric, 30
Freedom of Information Act (FOIA):
lawsuits, 110, 128, 234; requests, 69, 83,
120
Freedom to Write, 230
Fuller, Robert, 154, 247
Furlow, John, 130–31

Garzón, Baltasar, 168, 220, 236–37
Gates, Robert, xvi, 195, 215–16, 217, 218
Gbagbo, Laurent, 170
Gellman, Barton, 10
Geneva Conventions: Barr on, 133; Bush
administration and, 8; CA3, 123; disre-
gard for, 49–52, 78; *Hamdan* and, 16,
143; historical aspects of, 76; McCain
on, 132; PUCs and, 75; Torture Conven-
tion, 53, 88; on unconventional wars, 45
Georgetown University, 91, 125, 135, 149
George Washington University, 132
German accountability case, 171–73
German universal jurisdiction law, 169, 171
Germany, *El Masri* and, 159–61
Ghailani, Ahmed, 278–79
Ghostly Matters (Gordon), 311
Ghost Plane (Grey), 273
Gibbons, Del Deo, Dolan, Griffinger &
Vecchione (law firm), 96
Gibbons, John J., 38, 40
Gibney, Alex, 103, 313
Ginsberg, Nina, 208
Ginsburg, Ruth Bader, 85
Globe and Mail, 249

gations under, 239; detainee convictions, 264; executive orders of, 17, 214, 240–41; failures of, 310; Guantánamo closure order, xvii; Guantánamo plan, 225–28; Guantánamo transfers, 309–10; on habeas rights, 217; kill policy of, 232–34; military commissions and, 225, 227; al-Qosi and, 254; Slahi and, 230; torture excuses of, 221–22; torture investigations under, 219–20; on torture policy, 17; on transparency, 219; whistleblowers and, 240

O'Connor, John, 28

Al Odah v. United States Government, 31–34, 37, 188

Oederline, Bridget, 79

Office of Homeland Security, 24

Office of Legal Counsel (OLC): Barr in, 70; Geneva Conventions and, 50–52; on legality of torture, 53–55; under Obama, 222; torture memos, 13–14, 89–91, 124, 149; Yoo at, 33–34

Office of Professional Responsibility (OPR), 238

Office of Special Plans, 69

OGA (other government agency), 160

Olshansky, Barbara, 24–25, 60, 108, 109–10, 117, 216–17

Olson, Ted, 41

Omar, Abu, 176

Open Society Foundation (OSF), 229

Operation Harriet Tubman, 28

OPR (Office of Professional Responsibility), 239

Organization of American States (OAS), 177

Ortiz v. Gramajo, 25–26

other government agency (OGA), 160

Padilla, Jose, 85

Paglen, Trevor, 81–82

El Pais, 237

Palestine Branch (Syria), 153

Palestinians, 3, 4, 121, 126

Panetta, Leon, xv, xvi, 219

Pappas, Thomas, 128, 162

Parella, Keith, 296

Parrish, Patrick, 205, 246, 250–53, 256, 258

Passaro, David, 238

Paust, Jordan, 49

Pearlstein, Deborah, 91, 119, 125

Pentagon: Abu Ghraib and, 84; ARB of, 101–2; Army Field Manual, 49, 131, 135, 145, 222, 229; CSRTs and, 94; ICRC and, 229; interrogation techniques and, 130–32; JTF-GTMO, 56, 74, 109, 265, 266; media and, 75, 249; Mora and, 57; neocons in, 73; under Obama, 244; Office of Special Plans, 69; al-Qahtani and, 112; SERE and, 56; Slahi and, 181; Swift on, 59–60; UCMJ, 46, 52, 66, 79, 130, 143–44; Unlawful Enemy Combatant Review Board of, 214; Yoo and, 89. *See also* JAGs (judge advocates general); military commissions; 9/11 case; Rumsfeld, Donald; "war on terror"

PEN USA, 230

Perkins, Abigail, 291–92

Perkins Coie (law firm), 141–42

persons under custody (PUCs), 75

PFLP (Popular Front for the Liberation of Palestine), 126

Philbin, Patrick, 50

Phoenix program, 2

Pillsbury Winthrop (law firm), 189

Pinochet, Augusto, 5–6, 168–69

Pinochet precedent, 170

plane spotters, 80, 81

plea bargains, 249, 255, 257–58, 264, 304–6

Plessy v. Ferguson, 46

Poems from Guantánamo (Falkoff), 105

Pohl, James: bin al-Shibh and, 280; on courtroom monitoring, 275–76; on discovery, 293–94; on protective order, 277; retirement of, 296; role of, 275; SSCI report and, 289; torture and, 281; USS Cole case and, 284

Poitras, Laura, 62

Poland investigations, 219–20

Polish government investigation, 313–14

Popular Front for the Liberation of Palestine (PFLP), 126

Porterfield, Kate, 248, 252

Posner, Eric, 166

post-traumatic stress disorder (PTSD), 114, 245, 252

Powell, Colin, 51, 72, 171
Pradhan, Alka, 292–93, 295
presidential power. *See* executive power
Priest, Dana, 10, 102–3
Prince, Prescott, 207
Princeton University, 91
"Professors Strangelove" (Ristroph),
    166–67
propaganda, 69, 73, 219
proportionality standard, 79
protective order, 95–96, 108–9, 276–77, 284
Protocols I and II, Geneva Conventions, 45
PTSD (post-traumatic stress disorder), 114,
    245, 252
public opinion, 102–3, 125–27, 173
PUCs (persons under custody), 75
Pul-e-Charkhi prison, 202

Qaddafi, Muammar, 71, 72
al-Qaeda: Iraq connection, 70–72, 74;
    relations with al-Bahlul, 196; relations
    with Khadr, O., 151, 154; Shura Council
    of, 180
al-Qahtani, Mohammed, 56, 57, 112, 131,
    207, 271, 310
Qatada, Abu, 99
al-Qosi, Ibrahim, 63, 254, 255, 268
Quirin, 45–46

Racketeer Influenced and Corrupt Organi-
    zations Act (RICO), 194
Radack, Jesselyn, 234–35
Rahim, Tahar, 231
Rahman, Gul, 293
Rahman, Omar Abdel, 286
Rasul, Shafiq, 30, 39, 103
Rasul v. Bush: aim of, 32; amicus strategy
    in, 37–39; arguments and dismissal,
    33–34; *Boumediene* in relation to, 189;
    consolidation of, 37; decision in, 41–42,
    92; effects of, 93; Graham and, 138–39;
    Habib merged with, 34; impact of, 20;
    JAGs and, 60; lawyers for, 32; *Al Odah*
    in relation to, 31, 188; oral arguments,
    40; origin of, 9–10, 25–30; playbook for,
    39–40; response to, 94, 103–4; ruling
    in, 14; Supreme Court and, 39–42

Ratner, Michael: Abu Ghraib victims and,
    171–72; accountability case of, 171–72;
    career of, 25–30; characteristics of, 125;
    on civil litigation, 149–50; on detainee
    list, 109; Four Key Principles of Being a
    Radical Lawyer, 26; at news conference,
    174; outside DC District Court, *35;*
    significance of, 9, 312; *The Trial of
    Donald Rumsfeld,* 173; universal juris-
    diction and, 169. *See also* Center for
    Constitutional Rights (CCR)
Al-Rawi, Bisher, 98–99, 104
Reagan, Ronald, 24
Reagan administration, 126
rectal prolapse, 282
Reed College, 308
Reglan, 266
Reid, Richard, 228
Rejali, Darius, 308, 309
Remes, David, 104, 106–8, 139, 264–65,
    267
rendition, detention, and interrogation
    (RDI) program: Bush on, 16; challenge
    to, 155, 156; documents on, 272–73;
    in Egypt, 70–71; hearing on, *158;*
    HRW on, 138; investigations into,
    80–82, 219; SSCI investigation of, 219;
    SSCI report on, 288–89; timeline of,
    292–93
repatriation of detainees: Afghan detain-
    ees, 202; *Arar,* 154; Darbi, 264, 309;
    Habib, 103; Hamdan, 195; Jawad, 201;
    Khadr, 263; Mohammed, N. U., 187,
    220, 264; Obama and, 228; al-Qahtani,
    310; al-Qosi, 255, 264; Slahi, 231; Tali-
    ban, 191; Tipton 3, 39
Republic of Ireland, 3
Ressam, Ahmed, 179
Rice, Condoleezza, 159–60
RICO (Racketeer Influenced and Corrupt
    Organizations Act), 194
Ridge, Tom, 150
Ristroph, Alice, 166–67
Rives, Jack, 58
The Road to Guantánamo (Winterbottom),
    103
Roberts, John, 66, 67, 190

Robertson, James, 66, 230
Robinson, Jeff, 208
Rockefeller, Nelson, 25
Romig, Thomas, 58
Rona, Gabor, 77–78, 83, 119, 125, 141
Roosevelt administration, 23–24, 45–46
Rosenberg, Carol, 183–84, 207, 245, 246, 248–49, 279, 306
Ross, Brian, 234–35
Royal Canadian Mounted Police (RCMP), 151, 153, 154–55
Royall, Kenneth, 46
Royce, Sylvia, 114
Ruiz, Walter, 244, 272, 282, 290, 298
Rumsfeld, Donald: on Abu Ghraib, 85; accountability of, 171–76; *Ali v. Rumsfeld*, 128–29, 162–65; authorization of torture by, 56–57, 58; Geneva Conventions and, 49; *Hamdan* in relation to, 15–16; on Iraq war, 73; "known unknown," 68; Mora on, 17; pursuit of, 171–76; *Rumsfeld v. Padilla*, 84–85; on "torture," 86–87. See also *Hamdan v. Rumsfeld*

Salloum, George, 153–54
Salt Pit, 81–82, 159
Saltzburgh, Stephen, 132, 133–34
Sanchez, Ricardo, 74–75, 83, 85, 128, 162
Sandkuhler, Kevin, 58
Sands, Bobby, 267
Sands, Philippe, 174–75, 220
Satterthwaite, Meg, 137
Scalia, Antonin, 40, 41–42, 135, 190
Scarry, Elaine, 91
Scheppele, Kim, 90–91
Schmidt, Randall, 130–31
Schmidt-Furlow Report, 130–32
Schmitz, Charles, 61, *65*, 192, 193
Schneider, Harry, 141–42
Schroeder, Jim, 37
Schwartz, Matthew, 255, 260
Schwartz, Michael, 274
secrets, state: busting of, 84–92; classified information, 286–88, 293–94; investigations into, 80–82; lawyer-client relations and, 106; *El Masri* and, 161–

62; privilege to withhold, 155, 156; in "war on terror," 69; WMD and, 71; Zubaydah and, 313–17
security clearances, 116, 276–77, 284
Senate Armed Services Committee (SASC), 17, 130–35, 273
Senate Judiciary Committee, 66
Senate Select Committee on Intelligence (SSCI), 219, 285, 288–89, 308, 312
Sennels, Nicolai, 260
September 11, 2001, 1–2. *See also* 9/11 case; "war on terror"
Seton Hall University, 99, 115, 116
Shaffer, Sharon, 11, 15–16, 48, 63, 64, 254
Shamsi, Hina, 129, 137
Shapiro, Jonathan, 208
Sharon, Ariel, 170
Shearman & Sterling (law firm), 31
Shephard, Michelle, 203, 249, 258, 261
Shikaki, Muna, 255
Shin Bet, 3
shock the conscience doctrine, 118
Siems, Larry, 230
Sifton, John, 79, 80–82, 137
Singh, Amrit, 83, 89, 120–21
60 Minutes II, 12, 84
Slahi, Mohamedou Ould, 114–15, 178–82, 230, 231
Smithfield airport, 81
Snyder, Rebecca, 204
Sosbee, Gretchen, 207
Sotomayor, Sonia, 315–16
Soufan, Ali, 275
de Sousa, Sabrina, 176
Southern Center for Human Rights, 105
Sowards, Gary, 272, 295–96, *300*
Spanish investigation, 220, 236–39
Spath, Vance, 285
Speer, Christopher, 204, 241
Speer, Tabitha, 258, 260, 262
Spriggs and Hollingsworth (law firm), 98
Stafford Smith, Clive: clients of, 100; Hicks and, 30, 220–21; identifying detainees and, 39, 104; on the law, 232; Mohamed and, 183–84; public relations strategy of, 102; *Rasul v. Bush* and, 9–10
state secrets privilege, 155, 313–17

unitary executive thesis: Geneva Conventions in relation to, 50, 52; Gorsuch on, 316; in legalization of torture, 53–55; Muslim immigrants in relation to, 23–24; under Obama, 232–34; Obama and, 311; rejection of, 123

United States Constitution, 23, 27, 143, 164, 187, 190

United States v. Reynolds, 156, 316

universal jurisdiction, 168–71

University of Texas, Austin, 91

Unlawful Enemy Combatant Review Board, 215

unlawful enemy combatants, 8–9, 29, 47, 50, 242

unprivileged enemy belligerents, 242

UN Special Rapporteur on Torture, 236

Urbina, Ricardo, 224

USA PATRIOT Act, 24

US Army Counterintelligence, 235

USS Bataan, 70

USS Cole bombing, 208, 227, 284

USS Cole hearing, 285

Vandeveld, Darrel, 198, 200–201

Velasco, Eloy, 237, 238

Vice, 234–35

Vietnam War, 2

Vokey, Colby, 204

"W," Lieutenant Colonel, 256–57

al-Walid, Mahfouz Ould, 178–79. *See also* al-Mauritani, Abu Hafs

Walker, Edward, 70

walling, 299, 301, 302, 311

Wall Street Journal, 87, 89, 181

war council, 50, 56

War Crimes Act, 16, 51

Warner, John, 130, 131

Warner, Margaret, 87, 88

"war on terror": as an act of war, 8; capture and detention in, xvi; CIA role in, 52; as illegitimate, 242; investigations of, 79–80; launch of, 1–2; narrative about, 69; origin and purpose of, xvii, 69; targeted killing in, xvii; Yoo on, 87–88.

See also Bush administration; military commissions; new paradigm; rendition, detention, and interrogation (RDI) program

Washington Independent, 246

Washington Post: on black sites, 138, 160; on Cheney, 136; Crawford in, 207; Habib in, 102–3; Kurnaz in, 100; torture memos and, 89–90; on torture policy, 10

waterboarding, 14, 55–56, 223, 307–8

Watt, Steven, 29, 32–34, 121, 157, 162, 168

Waxman, Seth, 188, 189

Wazir, Haji, 216

weapons of mass destruction (WMD), 68

Weinglass, Leonard, 107

Weiss, Peter, 168, 169, 171

Welner, Michael, 252, 259–60, 261

whistleblowers, 234–35, 240

Whitecross, Mat, 103

Whitling, Nathan, 204

Wikileaks, 235

Williams, Brian, xvi

Wilner, Tom, 31–32, *35*, 100–101, 115–16, 188–89, 264

Wilson, Rick, 32–33, 113–14, 146–47

Winterbottom, Michael, 103

Wishnie, Michael, 217

Witness against Torture, 26

Wolfowitz, Paul, 69

Wood, Carolyn, 75

Wood, Jeffrey, 305

World War II, 23, 76–77

Worthington, Andy, 264

Worthy Fights (Panetta), 219

Wright, Jason, 283–84

writ of certiorari, 37–39

Xenakis, Stephen, 250, 252, 260

Yale Law Journal, 59

Yale Law School, 28, 217

Yoo, John: accountability case against, 172; accountability of, 236–39; Geneva Conventions and, 50–52; Guantánamo and, 33; on legality of torture, 53–55; Margolis on, 239; on the *News Hour*

Yoo, John *(continued)*
    with Jim Lehrer, 87–89; Spanish case
    against, 220; on torture, 125; torture
    memos of, 89–91

Zanetti, Gregory, 201
Zaragoza, Javier, 237
al-Zarqawi, Abu Musab, 74

Zero Dark 30, 278
Ziglar, James, 150
Zinck, Arlette, 261–62
Zubaydah, Abu: Bush on, 145; *The Forever
    Prisoner,* 313; Poland and, 220; *United
    States v. Husayn (Abu Zubaydah),*
    314–17; value of, 52–53; on waterboard-
    ing, 223; waterboarding of, 55–56

Founded in 1893,
UNIVERSITY OF CALIFORNIA PRESS
publishes bold, progressive books and journals
on topics in the arts, humanities, social sciences,
and natural sciences—with a focus on social
justice issues—that inspire thought and action
among readers worldwide.

The UC PRESS FOUNDATION
raises funds to uphold the press's vital role
as an independent, nonprofit publisher, and
receives philanthropic support from a wide
range of individuals and institutions—and from
committed readers like you. To learn more, visit
ucpress.edu/supportus.